Preparation for IELTS General Training
For the 2009 Updated Syllabus

IELTS Target 5.0

Leading to IELTS Academic

Course Book

Chris Gough

live
LANGUAGE
live-language.com

Garnet
EDUCATION

Published by
Garnet Publishing Ltd
8 Southern Court
South Street
Reading RG1 4QS, UK

This edition first published 2010.

ISBN 978 1 85964 557-4

British Library Cataloguing-in-Publication Data
A catalogue record for this book is available from
the British Library.

Production
Project manager: Simone Davies
Project consultants: Fiona McGarry, Rod Webb
Editorial: Vale Dominguez, Sarah Mellowes
Design and layout: Neil Collier, Mike Hinks
Illustration: Doug Nash
Photography: Getty Images, Corbis, Clipart, iStockphoto,
photo of Roald Amundsen on page 46, photographed by
Syahidah Osman Cawley, courtesy of the National Library of
Australia (nla.pic-an23814274).

Audio recorded and produced by Matinée Sound & Vision Ltd.

Garnet Publishing wishes to thank Doug Mackie, Synergy Total
Business Solutions and the staff of Saudi Development and Training
(SDT) for their assistance in the development of this project.

The author and publisher would like to thank the following
for permission to reproduce copyright material:
Article on pages 51 and 52 adapted from article '15 Successful
Entrepreneurs Who Didn't Need College' with kind permission
of Bytestart.co.uk.
Article on page 69 produced with kind permission of British
Mensa Limited. For more information on British Mensa the High
IQ Society, please visit their website http://www.mensa.org.uk
Article on page 116 adapted from article 'How to reduce office
waste and save money' with kind permission of Bytestart.co.uk
Dictionary extracts on page 150, copyright Longman Active
Study Dictionary © Addison Wesley Longman 1998.
Information in Reading 2, sections A1 and B2 on pages 154
and 155, copyright U.S. Geological Survey Department of the
Interior/USGS U.S. Geological Survey.
Article on page 180 adapted from article 'A Dozen Guidelines
for Using E-mail', http://www.businessknowhow.com
Article on page 191, 'Bullying and harassment at work: Guidance
for employees', reproduced under the terms of the Click-Use
Licence, with permission from ACAS, http://www.acas.org.uk
Article on page 220 reprinted with permission from go2 –
British Columbia Canada's tourism human resource association,
http://www.go2hr.ca
Permission to reproduce an adapted version of the article
'Why People Shop on the Web' from
http://www.useit.com/alertbox/990207.html on page 224
granted by Jakob Nielsen, Nielsen Norman Group.
Article on page 234, 'Higher World Tobacco Use Expected by
2010', adapted with permission of the Food and Agriculture
Organization of the United States.
Use of WV tobacco data on page 238 sourced from WV
statistics brief, West Virginia Health Statistics Center, Bureau
for Public Health © September 2000.
Article on pages 240 and 241, 'The Developing World's New
Burden: Obesity', adapted with permission of the Food and
Agriculture Organization of the United States.
Article on pages 243 and 244 sourced from article 'Waste
Disposal and Waste Management', http://ezinearticles.com
Article on pages 253 and 254 adapted from article
'Environmental Impact of Tourism', www.ecoholidaying.co.uk

Every effort has been made to trace the copyright holders and
we apologize in advance for any unintentional omissions. We
will be happy to insert the appropriate acknowledgements in
any subsequent editions.

Printed and bound
in Lebanon by International Press: interpress@int-press.com

Contents

Book map

General Training

Unit 1	Life
Speaking	personal information
Vocabulary	family / stages of life
Listening	listening for specific information
Reading	skimming
Writing	organizing / types of letter / beginnings and endings / a personal letter

Unit 2	Learning
Speaking	looking back / answering questions about the past
Vocabulary	subjects at school / expressing preferences
Listening	listening for numbers and dates
Reading	scanning / short answers
Writing	structuring a letter / stating your purpose / closing a letter

Unit 3	Work
Speaking	talking about work and jobs / introduction to exam task 2
Vocabulary	work / jobs / liking and disliking a job
Listening	listening for gist
Reading	scanning for paraphrased language
Writing	register / a letter of application

Unit 4	Achievements
Speaking	talking about success / answering exam task 3 type questions / two-way discussion
Vocabulary	success and achievements
Listening	predicting content / listening for paraphrased language
Reading	making sure that information is given in the text / recognizing distracters
Writing	understanding the task / deciding what to say / organizing your points

Unit 5	Thoughts
Speaking	how people think / expressing opinions / using the right expression
Vocabulary	ways of thinking
Listening	understanding and labelling diagrams
Reading	guessing unknown words and phrases / understanding new words and phrases from words you already know
Writing	understanding instructions / presenting a balanced argument

Unit 6	Place
Speaking	describing where you live / talking about towns and cities / comparing places
Vocabulary	places / describing places
Listening	maps and plans / noticing how information is repeated
Reading	paragraphs / topic sentences
Writing	paragraphs and topic sentences / supporting sentences

Unit 7	Movement
Speaking	saying how often you do something / answering questions about travel / expressing opinions
Vocabulary	methods of transport / ways of travelling
Listening	completing a summary / making sure answers fit
Reading	recognizing facts and opinions
Writing	linking words

Unit 8	Time
Speaking	talking about time / questions and answers / answering the question
Vocabulary	time or no time / time expressions
Listening	completing a table
Reading	completing a summary with a choice of words / making sure answers fit
Writing	making a request

Unit 9	Money
Speaking	talking about money / shopping habits and preferences / expressing opinions / follow-up comments
Vocabulary	comparing time and money / words with opposite meaning
Listening	identifying key words that you don't know
Reading	understanding references
Writing	elements of a good composition / introducing opinions

Unit 10	Feelings
Speaking	saying how you feel / disagreeing politely
Vocabulary	situations and feelings / extreme adjectives
Listening	classifying
Reading	using topic sentences to predict
Writing	complaining and requesting / linking words

Unit 11	Health
Speaking	lifestyle / talking about health problems / telling stories
Vocabulary	typical health problems / accidents
Listening	flow charts
Reading	sentence completion
Writing	writing a discursive composition / nouns that add cohesion

Unit 12	Nature
Speaking	talking about climate, weather and temperature / answering the question properly
Vocabulary	climate / weather conditions
Listening	recognizing register / understanding formal and informal language
Reading	recognizing different text types
Writing	deciding what to say / writing the main part of a composition

Unit 13	Construction
Speaking	talking about home and neighbourhood / contrasting ideas
Vocabulary	describing your home / neighbourhood
Listening	spelling answers correctly
Reading	coping with longer texts
Writing	a letter of complaint / spelling and punctuation

Unit 14	Technology
Speaking	talking about technology / giving examples
Vocabulary	machines, appliances, devices and gadgets / effect verbs
Listening	understanding different accents
Reading	timing yourself / improving your reading speed
Writing	having enough to say / making sure you write enough

Unit 15	Society
Speaking	discussing social issues / fitting a punishment to a crime / explaining what you mean when you can't remember a word
Vocabulary	social issues / crime and punishment
Listening	transferring answers to the answer sheet
Reading	checking your answers on the answer sheet
Writing	choosing what to say and how to say it

Book map

Academic section

Unit 1	Life	
Reading	applying your reading skills to an academic text	
Writing	interpreting and describing bar charts	
Unit 2	Learning	
Reading	reading for gist / reading for detail / dealing with unknown vocabulary	
Writing	interpreting and describing pie charts	
Unit 3	Work	
Reading	recognizing paraphrased language / dealing with statistics	
Writing	interpreting and describing line graphs / linking a description together	
Unit 4	Achievements	
Reading	understanding references and linking	
Writing	describing a flow chart / using the passive to describe a process / linking a description of a process together	
Unit 5	Thoughts	
Reading	timing yourself / checking answers	
Writing	composition content (difference between General Training and Academic writing task 2) / improving compositions for the Academic exam	

Introduction

How this course works

IELTS Target 5.0 is aimed at students who want to take the IELTS exam while studying at a pre-intermediate level. The aim is to prepare you for the General Training exam rather than the Academic exam, though some additional Academic exam practice is provided at the end of the course.

Scoring 5.0 in the General Training exam is more realistic than doing so in the Academic exam. The length and academic content of the reading passages in the Academic exam, together with the more challenging writing tasks, makes the Academic course far more demanding.

This book consists of 15 units (with an additional five units for the Academic section) and develops in terms of challenge, to take you from a strong elementary to intermediate level. The earlier units focus on basic skills and basic language, including sentence structure and spelling. The texts and recordings are short and simplified to guide you and give you confidence. By the end of the course, you will be tackling texts and working with language that is close to the level of what you will deal with in the exam.

Each unit consists of five modules, which are briefly summarized below.

Speaking and Vocabulary

The focus is on speaking exam practice and preparing you for the type of interaction you can expect with the examiner. There is frequent practice in understanding and answering appropriately the type of questions that the examiner is likely to ask. The vocabulary selected is the vocabulary that you are most likely to need during the speaking exam. You are also encouraged to record and revise vocabulary that is particular to your interests, and that you will need to remember in order to talk fluently about your life. There are frequent reflective tasks that allow you to assess your progress and talk about concerns you may have.

IELTS Target 5.0 doesn't have a grammar syllabus. Grammar is dealt with mainly as revision, as it is assumed that you will be studying grammar on a general English course at the same time you work through this course. Some major grammar points are dealt with a little more thoroughly, but generally the aim is to develop your ability to use the grammar to communicate or to recognize it when you are reading.

The grammar checks in each unit focus attention on key grammar points as they arise. If you feel that you need further practice with a particular grammar point, you should use an appropriate grammar resource in your own time or ask your teacher to help you in the lesson.

The speaking section in each unit focuses attention on a key pronunciation point. Sometimes this involves practising difficult individual phonemes, and sometimes it involves working with stress and intonation. These points are there to help improve your pronunciation in the Speaking Module of the exam.

Listening

The Listening Module is roughly divided into two parts. The first part aims to engage you in a topic, pre-teach key vocabulary and then focus on a key skill or particular IELTS exam technique. The second part aims to practise the skill or technique, and then encourage you to reflect and develop. Each unit focuses on a different skill or technique, but those skills and techniques are revised as the course progresses. All listening tasks are just like the ones you will tackle in the exam.

Reading

The Reading Module is designed like the Listening Module. Earlier units focus on a number of short texts and general reading skills, while later units deal with longer texts and provide practice with specific exam technique.

Both the Listening and Reading Modules end with a focus on key vocabulary in context. The aim here is to focus on the semi-formal vocabulary that you are likely to meet in the recordings and texts which make up the IELTS exam. Sometimes you are encouraged to select vocabulary from a text that you think will be particularly useful to you and that you should record and revise.

Writing

The Writing Module focuses equally on the two parts of the writing exam. Earlier units focus more on correspondence tasks – letter and e-mail writing – while later units focus on the more challenging discursive compositions. Each unit provides analysis of and practice with a particular writing skill or writing technique that is required for the exam. There is a focus on step-by-step guided writing, and there are model compositions for all of the writing tasks.

Consolidation and Exam Practice

This is divided into two parts. The first part revises the speaking focus and vocabulary presented in the first module. Occasionally, a speaking skill will be developed and there might be a new focus. The second part practises listening, reading or writing skills under something closer to exam conditions. The units in the first section of the book practise two skills with short tasks that students are able to manage. The units in the second two sections focus on one skill and provide fuller exam practice.

Exam tips and Question-type tips

These tips occur all the way through the course. They are there to help you know how to approach the various tasks that make up the exam, and to provide advice on how to go about getting the highest score possible in the exam. They also give advice that will help you to improve your all-round level of general English.

Reviews

There is a review at the end of each of the three sections. The aim is not simply to revise language that has been learnt, but to reflect on what has been achieved and what needs most work. There are tasks that encourage you to revise the vocabulary you have learnt independently and to reflect on which of it is most useful to you.

Mock tests

There are three mock tests provided as pamphlets in the book. The first two tests are designed to be slightly more challenging than the content of the course, but not quite as challenging as the actual exam. The third mock test is at the level you can expect from the exam. You should do the tests when you have completed the relevant section of the Course Book, i.e., test 1 when you have completed the first section and so on.

Workbook

There are Workbook tasks for each of the first four modules in the Course Book units. You might complete these tasks in class if your teacher feels that you need further practice with a point, or complete them for homework. In the Course Book Reading Modules, direct reference is made to these Workbook tasks, as the tasks specifically focus on the content of the Reading Module.

As you work through the course, you will learn more about the exam and what you have to do in each module. By the end of the course, you will know everything about every part of the exam and what is expected of you. When you have finished the General Training course, you will be ready to either sit the General Training exam or to take a short course that will prepare you for the Academic exam.

IELTS Target 5.0 Academic

Some students are studying at a pre-intermediate or intermediate level, but need to pass the Academic IELTS exam in order to enter university or apply for a job. At the end of IELTS Target 5.0 General Training, there is a short course that provides practice specifically for the Academic exam.

IELTS Target 5.0 Academic focuses on the reading and writing skills that you need to progress toward the Academic exam, and will prepare you to sit the exam within a few weeks. There is a longer introduction to IELTS Target 5.0 Academic and some introductory tasks for you to complete at the beginning of that section.

1 Life

Speaking 1: talking about personal information

A Match the pictures a–f with the questions 1–6.

1. Are you studying or are you working? __
2. Do you have brothers and sisters? __
3. Where are you living at the moment? __
4. What do you do in your free time? __
5. Do you enjoy travelling? __
6. What do you hope to do in the future? __

B Ask and answer questions 1–6 with a partner.

Grammar check

In American English, 'Do you have ...?' is frequently used.
In British English, 'Have you got ...?' is frequently used.
Answer these questions.

1. Which two questions are in *present continuous*?
2. Why is a continuous form used in the two questions?

Speaking 2: exchanging personal information

A Match the following questions 1–8 about people's lives with the answers a–h.

1. Where are you from?
2. What's your city like?
3. How old are you?
4. What do you do for a living?
5. Do you have a big family?
6. Are you married?
7. Do you have any children?
8. What are your hobbies and interests?

a. It's very big and very busy.
b. I read a lot and sometimes play chess.
c. No, I'm single.
d. From Riyadh. It's the capital city.
e. Yes, one son. His name's Sam.
f. Yes, I have five brothers and two sisters.
g. I'm an accountant.
h. I'm twenty-four.

B 🎧 Listen and check your answers.

C Ask and answer questions 1–8 in Exercise A with a partner.

Vocabulary 1: members of your family

A 🎧 Listen and write the words. Focus on your spelling.

1. _____ 2. _____ 3. _____ 4. _____ 5. _____
6. _____ 7. _____ 8. _____ 9. _____ 10. _____

Vocabulary 2: stages of life

A Label the pictures with the correct words.

| middle age   death   birth   childhood   retirement   adolescence |

_____ _____ _____

_____ _____ _____

B Cover Exercise A and write the stages in the order that they come in life.

1. *birth* 2. _____ 3. _____
4. _____ 5. _____ 6. _____

Vocabulary 3: using key words and phrases to speak

A Check the highlighted words and then answer the questions with a partner.

1. Were you born in the same place as your parents?
2. Do any of your other relatives live in the same place?
3. Are your grandparents retired?
4. Are any of your friends teenagers?
5. Do you know somebody who has more than five children?
6. When does somebody become an adult in your country?

Watch out!
typical errors

My brother has three childs. ✗
He is teenager. ✗
Where did you born? ✗

1

Listening 1: listening for specific information

A Read sentences 1–10 and look at the gaps. What kind of information is missing? Match each of the ideas a–j with a sentence.

1. I'm staying at the _Ocean_ Inn on Tenth Avenue. _g_
2. She died in _____, a year after her husband. ___
3. You can contact us on _____. ___
4. The best person to talk to is Tom _____. ___
5. The whole package costs $ _____. ___
6. The host family address is 56 _____ Lane. ___
7. He started playing the violin at just _____ years old. ___
8. Simon and Rebecca have known each other for _____. ___
9. The tour ends in _____ on the fifteenth of July. ___
10. The next meeting will be on _____. ___

a. the name of a city
b. a person's surname
c. somebody's age
d. a date
e. a phone number
f. a period of time
g. the name of a hotel
h. a year
i. the name of a street
j. the price of something

B In which answers do you need to use capital letters? In which answers can you write figures as the answer?

C 🎧 Now listen and check your ideas.

D 🎧 Listen again and fill in the missing information.

Listening 2: practising listening for specific information

Exam tip: In section 1 of the Listening Module, you often need to fill in missing information. In other parts of the exam, you also need to listen for information such as names and dates.

A 🎧 Listen and complete the notes about two people who work at Esco Engineering. Write <u>no more than three words or a number</u> for each answer.

ESCOEngineering — Staff Data

Name: Peter (1) _____

Address: (2) _____ Argyle Street,
Tunbridge Wells, Kent TN3 5RQ

Tel. no. 07984 645792

Age: (3) _____

Marital status: Married
(has (4) _____, two boys and a girl)

Date of joining company: 08 / (5) _____

ESCOEngineering — Staff Data

Name: Jane (6) _____

Address: 72 (7) _____ Road,
Crowborough, Kent CR3 5RQ

Tel. no. 07984 (8) _____

Age: (9) _____

Marital status: (10) _____

Date of joining company: 02 / 2005

B Check the key on page 266. How many questions did you answer correctly?

C Tick the sentences about the listening task that are true for you and think about how you can answer more questions correctly next time.

1. I read the instructions carefully.
2. I read the questions and predicted the type of answer I needed to write.
3. I used capital letters when necessary.
4. I understood all the words on the answer sheet.
5. I spelt all my answers correctly.

Question-type tip: In the Listening and Reading Modules, the instructions will often tell you to write <u>two</u> or <u>three</u> words as your answer.

Key vocabulary in context

Fill each space with one word from the staff data file.

1. Your _____ is where you live.
2. Your _____ is how old you are.
3. When you fill in a form, _____ _____ is more formal than saying 'Are you married?'

Reading 1: skimming

Exam tip: It is important to know the source of a text, for example if it comes from a newspaper, a magazine or a journal.

A Read the sources 1–6 below. Skim the texts a–f and match each with a source 1–6.

1. information from a box or packet _e_
2. an e-mail to a friend __
3. an advertisement __
4. a letter about a job interview __
5. part of an article from a science journal __
6. part of a letter written to a newspaper __

A

New Message

Send   Chat   Attach   Address   Fonts   Colors   Save As Draft

To: graham
Cc:
Subject:

Hi Graham,
Sorry, I won't be able to play golf on Saturday as planned. Some of my wife's relatives are coming for the weekend so I'll have to be here. I should be free one day next week – I'll call you.

Sorry again,
Dave

B

Do you want to lose weight fast?

It's easier than ever before!
Try our new product for a slimmer, happier future.

Phone Trixie on 01256 987742

C

Dear Sir,
I am writing to say how shocked I am by the behaviour of many teenagers in the city centre. They congregate in large groups, they are aggressive and they use very bad language. Young people don't seem to understand that older people like me ...

D

The birth of triplets is becoming more and more common. Technology which assists reproduction is the main cause. The use of fertility drugs and the placing of three or four embryos in the uterus can result in multiple births. Another cause may be the number of older women having children. Women over the age of thirty are more likely to have twins or triplets.

E

Care & Use

- Each cartridge will filter 150 litres of water and should be replaced every month.
- Fits most leading brands.
- Before first use, wash with hot soapy water and dry.

F

Dear Miss Sulaiman,

Thank you for your letter applying for a place on our part-time English for Work course. We would like to invite you for an interview on 12th March at 2 p.m.

Yours sincerely,

Mr J Sullivan
(Director of Studies)

B Talk with a partner. Discuss how you completed the task. Did pictures help? Did you identify key words? Did the design of each text help you to identify its source? Did you use any other techniques?

Exam tip: It is also important that you know the purpose or function of a text (why the text has been written).

C Skim the texts again and answer these questions. You might be able to answer some questions without reading again.

1. In which text does somebody complain? ___
2. Which text is an apology? ___
3. Which text makes an appointment? ___
4. Which text wants people to buy something? ___
5. Which text explains why something happens? ___
6. Which text tells you how to do something? ___

D Read this short text about reading skills. Circle the correct option from each pair.

Skimming is looking *slowly / quickly* through a text to get a *general / detailed* picture of what it is about. You might skim through a magazine to see which stories are interesting or skim the first few pages of a book to see if you want to read it. You often skim *before / after* you read a text more carefully. In the IELTS exam, you skim a text in order to identify which parts you need to read again more *quickly / slowly*.

Reading 2: practise skimming

Exam tip: In various parts of the Reading Module, you will need to skim read.

A Read the sources 1–6 below. Skim the texts A–F and match each with a source 1–6.

1. part of an e-mail to a friend ___
2. a formal invitation ___
3. an advertisement ___
4. an extract from a biography (a book about the life of a person) ___
5. part of a web page that gives advice ___
6. a story from a newspaper ___

A

PERSPECTIVES OF WORK AND JOB SATISFACTION

People often see work from one of three perspectives. All three perspectives are important for job satisfaction, but one is usually the most important.

B

To: [   ]

... and I must say that I'm really enjoying life here in New York. My job's great and my new apartment is just fantastic. So I hope you can come and visit me soon. I can't wait to show you all the sights ...

C

Mohandas Karamchand Gandhi

was born in Porbander, a coastal town in western India, on 2 October, 1869. His father, Karamchand Gandhi, was an important figure in the state of Porbander. His mother, Putlibai, was Karamchand's fourth wife, the first three wives having died in childbirth.

D

You are invited
to celebrate the wedding of
Susan Mary Bradshaw
and
Daniel Lee Marshall
At 2 p.m. on Saturday 17th March
St Anne's Church, Brighton
R.S.V.P.

E

Recently retired?

Enjoy later life with **Makethemost.com**.
This site is designed for people
over 60 who want to continue making
the most of later life and who want to
plan and enjoy retirement.

Check out Makethemost.com now!

F

Train Driver Loses Fight for Life

Terry James, the train driver who was injured in last week's tragic train crash in Luton, has lost his fight for life. He died early yesterday evening at King's Hospital.

B Check the key on page 266. How many questions did you answer correctly?

C Tick the sentences about the reading task that are true for you and think about how you can answer more questions correctly next time.

1. I read the instructions carefully.
2. I skimmed the text quickly to do the task.
3. I looked for key words and phrases to help me match.
4. I didn't worry about all the words that I don't know.
5. I'm pleased with how quickly I did the task.

Key vocabulary in context

Look at these sentences and then look again at the key word in the texts. Circle the correct option from each pair.

1. If something **improves**, it *gets better / is not so good*.
2. An **increase** means that something *goes up / goes down*.
3. Your **perspective** is *what you do at work / how you see things*.
4. An important **figure** is an important *person / building*.
5. When there is a **wedding**, somebody *dies / gets married*.
6. If you are **injured**, you *die / are hurt*.

WB For focus on reading skills, go to Workbook page 5.

Writing 1: organizing your writing

 Exam tip: To write well, you need to plan and organize. When you do the Writing Module, you won't spend all the time you have actually writing.

A Put these stages of the writing process into a logical order.

a. Quickly note down lots of ideas. ___
b. Read your work and check for errors. ___
c. Read the question and the instructions very carefully. ___
d. Write your letter or composition. ___
e. Decide which ideas you are going to include in the composition. ___
f. Make a rough plan with paragraph headings. ___

B Talk with a partner. You have 20 minutes to write a letter of about 150 words. How long should you spend on each of the stages in Exercise A?

Writing 2: types of letter / starting and ending letters

A These are the types of letter that you might need to write in the first section of the IELTS Writing Module. Match each type with one of the opening lines A–F.

1. a personal letter
2. a job application
3. a formal business letter
4. a letter requesting information
5. a letter of complaint
6. a formal letter of apology

A
Dear Sir/Madam,
I would like to know more about the Sports Science course that you run at your college.

B
Dear Sir/Madam,
I am writing to express my dissatisfaction at the service I received at one of your restaurants last weekend.

C
Dear Mr Jones,
I am writing to inform you that I will not be able to attend the conference in January.
I really am very sorry.

D
Hi Louis,
Thanks for the photos – I got them this morning. I love the picture of Greg with that snake!

E
Dear Mrs Cole,
I am a colleague of Martin White and I am writing as one of his referees to support his application for ...

F
Dear Mr Lucas,
I am writing to apply for the job advertised in yesterday's *Daily Argus*.

B Highlight the useful phrases that are used to open a letter. Then choose one of the opening lines, look at it for 30 seconds, close your book and write it in your notebook.

C Now decide which of these endings are appropriate for each letter A–F.

1. I look forward to hearing from you soon.
Yours faithfully,
Mark King

2. Once again, I would like to apologize.
Best wishes,
Lucy Hayes

3. Anyway – must get on now. See you at Jake's party next week. Love to Claire.
Best,
Tom

4. I look forward to receiving your reply.
Yours faithfully,
Graham Downs

5. I fully recommend him for the position.
Yours sincerely,
Simon Fox

D Talk with a partner. Answer these questions.

1. When do you close a letter with *Yours faithfully* and when with *Yours sincerely*?
2. When is it acceptable to use *Best wishes* or *Regards*?
3. What are some other ways of ending an informal personal letter?

Writing 3: organizing points in a personal letter

A You are going to stay with a family in Britain and you want to write a letter to introduce yourself. Which of the information in the box below would you include?

| your family   your appearance   why you're learning English   your age |
| your favourite music   your friends   where you live   your studies or job |
| your favourite food   your name   your hobbies and interests   your personality |

B Read the letter below and put the ideas in Exercise A into the order in which they appear. Does Bruno include the same points that you wanted to include?

_____ Mr and Mrs Gray,

I'm Bruno and I'm 22. I live in Valencia, which is a big city on the east coast of Spain.
I live with my mum and dad and my sister, Lola, but I hope to go to university in Barcelona next year and I want to get a flat with some friends. My dad is a lawyer and my mum works part-time at a nursery school. I've got a brother called Carlos.

In my free time I play football and tennis, and I sometimes go rock climbing. I really enjoy most sports and want to study sports psychology next year. I love going out to discos, too, and I especially love rap music.

People say I'm very friendly and outgoing, and I like to think I'm generous. I know I can be a bit stubborn sometimes – I like to do things my own way. I need to improve my English for my studies, but I also love travelling, and the best way to meet people is to speak good English.
I am looking forward to meeting you both very soon.

_____ ,

Bruno

C Start and end the letter in an appropriate way.

WB Go to Workbook page 6 for the writing task.

Speaking

A Talk with a partner. Answer these questions about the first part of the Speaking Module.

1. How long does the first part of the Speaking Module take?
2. Is it about a third or about half of the total Speaking Module?
3. What kind of questions will the examiner ask?

B Look at these possible questions. Tick them if you think they are easy to answer and cross them if they are difficult to answer. Then compare your thoughts with a partner.

1. What do you like doing in your free time? —
2. Which part of the world would you most like to visit? —
3. Why are you learning English? —
4. How long have you lived there? (your hometown) —
5. Who was your favourite teacher at school? —
6. Tell me about a famous person that you admire? —

C Walk around the class. Practise asking and answering the questions with other students.

Vocabulary

A Write one word to complete each sentence below.

1. Your mother and father are your _____.
2. Your father's father is your _____.
3. Your mother or father's brother is your _____.
4. Your mother or father's sister is your _____.
5. Your son's sister is your _____.
6. The children of your uncles and aunts are your _____.
7. All of the people in your family are your _____.

B Fill the gaps with a word made from the root words in the box.

1. What do you do for a ___living___?
2. One of my uncles has got ten _____.
3. I didn't have any brothers and sisters, but I had a very happy _____.
4. I want to be happily _____ before I'm thirty.
5. My father seems to be very happy in his _____.

| live |
| child |
| child |
| marry |
| retire |

C 🎧 Mark the main stress on these key words from the unit. Then listen and check. Practise saying the words.

1. interests 2. family 3. relatives 4. teenager 5. retirement 6. adolescence 7. improve

Errors

A There are errors in all of these sentences (sometimes more than one). Correct them.

1. He's from new york.
2. My father's engineer.
3. Have you brothers and sisters?
4. I have 22 years.
5. His name's alan murray.
6. I work for a company called friendly products.
7. Where was you born?
8. I write to apply for job in yesterday's newspaper.

Listening

A 🎧 **For questions 1–4, listen and complete the notes. Write <u>no more than three words or a number</u> for each answer.**

Name of guest: Charles (1) _____.

Number of nights: (2) _____.

Home address: 25 North Road,
                 (3) _____.
                 MA2 4CP

Room: (4) _____.

For questions 5–7, listen and choose the correct answer.

5. Why is the guest travelling?
   a. on holiday
   b. on business
   c. for a football match

6. What was the guest's meal on the plane like?
   a. big and very good
   b. small but very good
   c. small and not very good

7. Where is the guest going to eat?
   a. in the hotel restaurant
   b. in a restaurant outside the hotel
   c. in his room

For questions 8 and 9, label the map. Write the correct letter A–F next to the places below.

8. Mamma Mia's   ____
9. the bank   ____

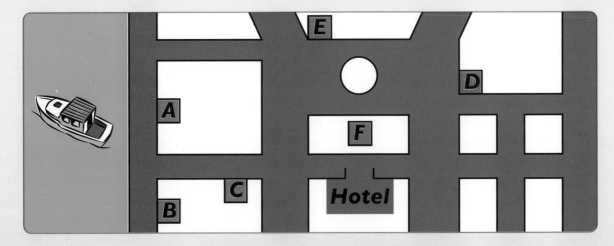

Question-type tip: In the Listening and Reading Modules, you often have to choose answers from options.

Reading

A Look at this extract from a web page for one minute and decide which subject 1, 2 or 3 it is about.

1. how to get a good job
2. why most people are unhappy at work
3. different ways of thinking about a job

Perspectives of work and job satisfaction

A. People often see work from one of three perspectives. All three perspectives are important for job satisfaction, but one is usually the most important.

B. **It's a job.** If you see work as a job and no more, you focus mainly on the financial rewards. In fact, you might have very little interest in the work you do. If a job with more pay comes along, you'll probably take it.

C. **It's a career.** If you see work as a career, you want to advance. You want to climb the career ladder as far as possible or be among the top professionals in your field. You're motivated by the status and power that go with the job.

D. **It's a calling.** If you see your job as a calling, you focus on the work itself. You work for the satisfaction and fulfilment the work brings rather than for financial gain or career advancement.

E. Do you recognize yourself? One perspective isn't necessarily better than the others. But it's helpful to think about why you work if you're unsatisfied with your job and it's making you unhappy. Think about why you took your current job in the first place and whether that is a factor in your lack of job satisfaction.

B The text has five parts, A–E. Skim the text again and match each part with one of these sentences.

1. Some people want to be important. ___
2. People see work in different ways. ___
3. People should think about why they do their job. ___
4. For some people, money is not important. ___
5. Some people work only for money. ___

Question-type tip: In the Reading Module, you often need to match sentences or questions with parts of a text.

2 Learning

Vocabulary 1: subjects at school

A Correct the spelling for the school subjects.

1. mathmatics _____
2. histery _____
3. geografy _____
4. siense _____
5. kemistry _____
6. fisics _____
7. biolagy _____
8. economiks _____

B Check that you understand the meaning of each subject. Tick the ones that you studied at school.

Speaking 1: looking back

A Match the pictures a–f with the sentences 1–6.

1. My favourite subject at school was Chemistry. ___
2. I really enjoyed sports at school. ___
3. I wasn't very good at Maths. ___
4. The teachers at school were very strict. ___
5. We had to wear a school uniform. ___
6. I had to do homework every night. ___

> **Pronunciation check**
> 🎧 Listen to the pronunciation of these subjects.
> Practise saying the ending /ɪks/, as in 'Physics', 'Mathematics', 'Economics'.

B Talk with a partner. Use the pictures to talk about what you remember about school.

Grammar check

We use the *past simple* to talk about finished time. Regular verbs end in ~*ed*, but there are some spelling rules that you need to remember.

Write the past form of these verbs into the sentences.

learn   stop   decide   study

1. I _____ to swim when I was five years old.
2. I _____ Medicine at university.
3. I _____ to leave university and find a job.
4. I _____ learning guitar because I was too busy.

Remember to use *did* in negative and question forms.

I didn't like school much.   *Where did you learn ...?*

There are a lot of irregular verbs, and some of them are used very frequently. You need to learn them.

Write the past form of these verbs.

1. know _____   2. read _____   3. think _____   4. teach _____   5. choose _____

There is no past form of *must*, so we use *had to*. *Had to* is followed by the base verb.

We had to wear a uniform to school.

Pronunciation check

🎧 Listen to the pronunciation of the regular verbs in the sentences. Note the difference between /t/ and /d/ and /id/ at the end of verbs.

1. I finished my homework late last night.
2. I played football after school.
3. I hated Physics at school.

Speaking 2: answering questions about the past

A   🎧 Look at these questions about being at school. Then listen to some students answering them. Tick the speaker who gives a better answer.

1. Did you enjoy being at school?   Speaker 1 ___   Speaker 2 ___
2. What was your favourite subject at school?   Speaker 1 ___   Speaker 2 ___
3. Who was your favourite teacher at school?   Speaker 1 ___   Speaker 2 ___

B   Walk around the classroom. Ask and answer questions 1–3 in Exercise A.

Vocabulary 2: likes and preferences

A   Look at how the highlighted words and phrases are used in these sentences. Write (P) if the speaker is positive or (N) if the speaker is negative.

1. I really liked learning Mathematics at school.   ____
2. I didn't like History very much.   ____
3. I liked Physics, but I preferred Chemistry.   ____
4. My favourite subject was Economics.   ____
5. I really hated learning History.   ____
6. I loved learning on computers.   ____
7. I always enjoyed my English classes.   ____
8. I was very keen on sports when I was at school.   ____
9. I thought Geography was really boring.   ____
10. The most interesting subject was Science.   ____

B   Talk with a partner. Talk about the subjects you studied at school using the words and phrases above. Say why you liked or didn't like some subjects.

2

Listening 1: listening for numbers and dates

A Work with a partner. Practise saying these numbers.

16   60   100   160   166   600   606   616   660   666

B Listen and check. Then practise saying the numbers again.

C Listen and write the numbers that you hear.

1. _____   2. _____   3. _____   4. _____
5. _____   6. _____   7. _____   8. _____

D Listen and practise saying these bigger numbers.

1,000   10,000   100,000   1,100   1,500   1,550   1,555

E Unjumble the letters to write the twelve months of the year in the spaces.

yanurja   arybruef   amrhc   prail   yam   neuj
January   _____   _____   _____   _____   _____
ujyl   austgu   bersetepm   oberoct   vemnoerb   mdeecerb
_____   _____   _____   _____   _____   _____

F Cover Exercise E and write the twelve months of the year in the spaces. Be careful with your spelling.

January   _____   _____   _____   _____   _____
_____   _____   _____   _____   _____   _____

G Listen to the pronunciation of the months. Then practise saying them.

H Write the ordinal numbers in the spaces below.

1. (1)_____   2. (2)_____   3. (3)_____   4. (4)_____   5. (5)_____
6. (6)_____   7. (7)_____   8. (8)_____   9. (9)_____   10. (10)_____
11. (12)_____   12. (15)_____   13. (20)_____   14. (25)_____   15. (30)_____

I Listen to the pronunciation of the ordinal numbers. Then practise saying them.

J Listen to someone saying the date below in two different ways.

December 15

K Practise saying these dates in two ways.

January 10   March 20   April 25   September 30

L Listen and write the dates that you hear.

1. _____   2. _____
3. _____   4. _____

M Talk with a partner. Answer these questions with a date.

1. What date is your birthday?
2. What date is your mother's birthday?
3. What date is your father's birthday?
4. What date is Christmas Day?
5. What date is New Year's Eve?
6. What date is American Independence Day?

Listening 2: practise listening for numbers and dates

Question-type tip: You will need to listen for numbers and dates in various parts of the Listening Module. The information will always be in the same order as the questions.

A 🎧 A man is telephoning his local college about a course. For questions 1 and 2, listen and choose the correct answer.

1. Graham wants to do a course in …
   a. Physics
   b. Geography
   c. Photography
   d. Philosophy

2. Graham wants to know about …
   a. the beginner's course
   b. the intermediate course
   c. the advanced course

For questions 3–8, complete the man's notes. Write <u>no more than three words or a number</u> for each answer.

Course starts – (3) _____.
There are (4) _____ lessons over thirteen weeks.
Course finishes (5) _____.
Course costs (6) £ _____ paid in advance. No refund.
Between (7) ____ and 10 students in the class. (8) ____ people on last course.

For questions 9–12, complete the booking form that the receptionist fills in.

Name: (9) _____.
Address: Flat (10) _____, (11) _____ Chelsea Court.
Age: (12) _____.

B Check the key on page 266. How many questions did you answer correctly?

C Tick the sentences about the listening task that are true for you and think about how you can answer more questions correctly next time.

1. I read the instructions carefully.
2. I read the questions and predicted the type of answer I needed to write.
3. I used capital letters when necessary.
4. I spelt all my answers correctly.
5. I know why I got some answers wrong.
6. I am pleased with how many questions I answered correctly.

Key vocabulary in context

Cross out any wrong words in these sentences.

1. My History *course / class / lesson* begins at 9.00 a.m.
2. The *course / class / lesson* lasts for 13 weeks.
3. It is a small *course / class / lesson*. There are only six students.

2

Reading 1: scanning

A These five extracts are from the same web page. Skim them quickly and say what they are all about.

In Britain, you have to be 17 before you can start learning to drive. You need a provisional driving licence, which costs £38. You can apply for the licence before your seventeenth birthday but must wait until you are 17 before you take any lessons. All learner drivers must display 'L' plates on the vehicle they are driving.

It is best to learn with an approved driving instructor. You can practise driving with another qualified driver, but that driver must be over 21 and must have had a full driving licence for at least three years.

Some people learn to drive more quickly than others, but on average it takes about 40 hours of lessons and about 20 hours of further practice. Most people have one two-hour driving lesson per week, but it is possible to do a more intensive course. You should only take your test when you feel that you are ready.

The main purpose of the practical driving test is to ensure that you can drive safely. The test lasts about 40 minutes and is designed to test a range of driving skills. More people fail the test than pass it.

More people fail their practical driving test than pass it, probably because not enough people are really prepared for the test when they take it. The most common fault during the driving test is not observing carefully before moving onto a main road from a smaller road.

B Talk with a partner and answer the questions.

1. Can you drive?
2. When did you get your licence?
3. How many driving lessons did you have?
4. Did you pass your test the first time you took it?

Exam tip: In the Reading Module, you will save a lot of time if you can find the answers to specific questions quickly without reading all of a text again.

C Scan the extracts and answer these questions as quickly as possible.

1. How long is the average driving lesson? _____
2. How old must you be before you can help somebody learn to drive? _____
3. How much does a provisional driving licence cost? _____
4. How long does the practical driving test last? _____
5. What must a learner driver have on his or her vehicle? _____

Question-type tip: In the Reading and Listening Modules, you sometimes need to write short answers to questions. The instructions will say how many words you can use.

D Scan again and decide if these statements are (T) true or (F) false.

1. You must be 17 before you can apply for a provisional driving licence. ___
2. You can help other people learn to drive as soon as you have your licence. ___
3. Most people pass their driving test the first time they take it. ___
4. A lot of people take their test before they are ready for it. ___

E Choose the correct definition below.

1. *Scanning* is reading a text quickly to get a general idea of what it's about.
2. *Scanning* is reading a text very carefully to understand every part of it.
3. *Scanning* is looking for specific information in a text.

Reading 2: practise scanning

Exam tip: In various parts of the Reading Module, you need to scan a text for specific information. You should practise scanning exercises and try to do them more quickly as your English improves.

A Read the web page about swimming lessons. Match each part of the page with a picture.

Swimming – safe and fun!

There is no special age at which children should learn to swim, but it is an advantage to learn early. Learning to swim can frighten small children, and getting a professional to do the teaching is usually the best option. However, parents can do a lot to make sure that learning to swim is safe and fun.

A Prepare well
> Ask family and friends if they know a good teacher.
> Find out if your local swimming pool has lessons.
> Make sure that the teacher is qualified and ask to see a teaching certificate.

B Have the right clothes and equipment
> Buy comfortable swimwear.
> Buy goggles to keep water out of your child's eyes.
> Buy a swim cap to keep long hair out of the way.
> Buy plastic sandals so that your child does not walk in dirty water with bare feet.

C Safety comes first
> Check how deep the water is before your child enters the pool.
> Remember that armbands will not always keep your child above the water.
> Stay with your child if he or she is in deep water.

Swimming is easier for some children than others, and your child needs support. Tell your child that he or she is doing well. Do not push your child to do anything before he or she is ready.

☐　　　　　☐　　　　　☐

B Answer these questions about learning to swim using <u>no more than three words</u>.

1. Who is the best person to teach your child to swim?

   _____

2. Who can help you to find a good teacher?

   _____

3. What should you ask the teacher to show you?

   _____

4. What can keep water out of your child's eyes?

   _____

5. What should your child wear on his or her feet?

   _____

6. What do all children need from their parents?

   _____

C Check the key on page 266. How many questions did you answer correctly?

Exam tip: Sometimes you can answer a short answer question by taking a word from the text even if you don't know it. Be careful, though – it isn't usually so easy!

D Tick the sentences about the reading task that are true for you and think about how you can answer more questions correctly next time.

1. I read the introduction and the title and looked at the pictures before I read the text.
2. I skimmed the text to complete task A.
3. I am pleased with how quickly I did task A.
4. I read more carefully to do task B.
5. I knew which part of the text to look at again to find each answer.
6. I knew what to write for each answer.
7. I was pleased with how many answers were correct for task B.

Key vocabulary in context

Look at these nouns from the text. Use them to complete the sentences below.

| safety   support   professional   advantage |

1. If you play basketball, being tall is a big _____.
2. When children do something difficult, they need _____ from people around them.
3. A _____ is a person who does something for money.
4. Most parents worry about the _____ of their children.

Cover the text and match the adjectives 1–4 with the nouns a–d. Then check your answers in the text.

1. comfortable   a. hair
2. deep / dirty   b. swimwear
3. long   c. feet
4. bare   d. water

WB For focus on reading skills, go to Workbook page 8.

Writing 1: structuring a letter

Exam tip: In the first part of the Writing Module, you have to write a letter. It might be a letter to a friend or to somebody that you do not know. Sometimes you will need to ask for information or apply for a position. Often you will need to explain a situation and say what you want somebody to do.

A You are writing a letter to somebody explaining a problem that you have. Put these stages of the letter into the correct order.

___ Explain the situation and how it affects you (in what way it is good or bad for you).

___ Say what you want the other person to do.

___ State the purpose of your letter.

B Answer these questions with a partner.

1. How many sentences should you write to say why you are writing?
2. How long should the main part of your letter be?
3. How many sentences should you write to close your letter?

Writing 2: stating your purpose

Exam tip: Each paragraph of your letter must have a purpose (it must be clear why you have written it). The first paragraph should state the purpose of the whole letter (why you are writing the letter).

A Look back at Writing 2 in the Writing section in Unit 1. Look at how the purpose of the letter is stated in each of the opening lines.

B Look at the advertisement and the notes that a student has made on it. What is the advertisement for and why is the student unhappy?

Two-week and four-week intensive courses in business English

Small groups *16 students in class!*

Highly qualified teachers *3 different teachers – and not very good!*

Free Course Book and Workbook *Got Course Book after 1 week – no Workbook*

Modern school in city centre *Old building – 5km from centre!*

C A student is writing to a language school about a business English course. Which opening line is best? What is wrong with the other three?

1. I am really angry with you because my business English course was so bad.
2. I am writing about a business English course I recently took at your school.
3. I am writing to tell you that my English has not improved at all because I learnt nothing on the course I did with you.
4. I want some money back from your school because I am not happy with the course I did at your school.

D Write the opening line for each of these situations.

1. You write to a tour operator to complain about a hotel that you stayed in.

   _____.

2. You write to tell a friend that you cannot go to his wedding.

   _____.

3. You write to a telephone company to say that your line is not working.

   _____.

Writing 3: organizing the main part of a letter

A Here is the main part of the letter to the language school. Put the lines 1–4 into the correct place at the beginning of each section.

1. During my stay, there were three different teachers.

2. Your advertisement promises that the Course Book and Workbook are provided,

3. You claim that your school is modern and in a central location.

4. Your advertisement says that the business English classes are small.

I studied on an intensive two-week course, but I learnt very little.

_____ I expected to study in a group of between six and eight students, but I was in a large class of 16. It was difficult for the teacher to give time to everyone.

_____ Nobody explained why, and none of the teachers seemed to have experience in teaching business.

_____, but this was not true. I received my Course Book on the Monday of the second week so could only use it for a week. I never got the Workbook.

_____ In fact, the building is old and the classrooms are not suitable. The technology is out of date. The building is 5km from the city centre, and I needed to catch a bus to get there from where I was staying.

B Read the completed letter on page 266.

Writing 4: closing a letter

A Talk with a partner. What do you think the student wants the language school to do?

B Here is the final part of the letter to the language school. Delete <u>five</u> unnecessary words. Then check on page 266.

I hope you to understand why I am unhappy with the service your school was provided. In total I paid the 1,200 euros for the course and I would like that you to refund 50% of that. I am look forward to hearing from you.

C Look at the exam practice section on page 33 for the writing task.

Speaking

A Complete each of these questions with the correct question word.

1. _____ was your favourite subject at school?
2. _____ was your best friend at primary school?
3. _____ did you get to school in the morning – did you walk or take a bus?
4. _____ did you go to college instead of staying at school?
5. Do you remember any school trips? _____ did you go?
6. In some countries, children learn languages from an early age. _____ did you start learning English?

B 🎧 Listen and check.

C 🎧 Listen again and notice how the second speaker answers each question.

D Write <u>five</u> questions about being at school or learning something. Then walk around the class and practise asking and answering the questions.

Vocabulary

A Write <u>eight</u> school subjects on the diagram without looking back. Focus on your spelling.

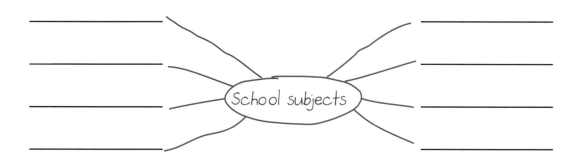

B Complete the sentences with the correct form of the verbs below.

| have fail pass apply do |

1. I _____ my homework before I went to bed.
2. You can _____ for a driving licence before your seventeenth birthday, but you can't _____ lessons until you are seventeen.
3. I _____ my driving the first time I took it. I was very pleased.
4. Many people _____ their driving test because they are not ready to take it.

Watch out!
typical errors
I made my homework. ✗
I made my driving test. ✗

C 🎧 Mark the main stress on these words. Then listen and check. Practise saying the words.

1. favourite   2. advantage   3. professional   4. safety   5. licence   6. certificate   7. support

Errors

A Correct the mistakes highlighted below.

1. Did you make your homework last night?
2. I didn't like school. I must do tests every week.
3. My father teached me to swim.
4. I didn't like very much Maths at school.
5. I was very keen in Geography.
6. I missed my driving test the first time I took it.

Exam Practice

Reading

Exam tip: In the Reading Module, there are three sections: social survival, training survival and general reading. Each section can have more than one passage, so there will be between four and six passages to read. There are 40 questions in total. You have one hour to read the passages and to write answers on a separate answer sheet. The passages gradually become more difficult. The text below is written at your level and there are 12 questions. You should try to complete the task in about 20 minutes.

A Read the passage and answer the questions that follow.

Are A Levels Just Too Easy?

Text A

Students all over Britain are getting very good A level* results. They should be happy and their parents should be proud. However, that is not so easy when everyone is telling you that the exam is too easy and that your results do not mean anything.

Text B

The number of passes has increased every year for 21 years, and now more than 20% of students are getting an A grade** in the exam. In the 1970s, only 10% got an A grade, while 20% failed the exam with an E grade. Now those percentages are reversed. Important people in education and business say that A level results have no value. They are worried that the exam does not show which students should be going to the top universities.

Text C

Other people say that the number of passes is increasing because students are improving and study-ing harder. They say that teaching has improved and that teachers know how to train students to pass the exam. Most students study five A level subjects but then only take the exam in the three subjects they are best at. Experts have studied exam questions and exam results, and they say that recent exams are not easier than the exams of twenty years ago.

Text D

It seems that the situation is like that in some sports events. Every year, a record is broken because athletes are becoming faster and stronger. In the long jump***, for example, the sandpit was made longer because athletes were jumping out the end of it. Some people in education believe that it is time to make questions in the A level exam more difficult so that questions really test the strongest students. This would provide better information to universities about who should get onto courses and better information to businesses about who should get the best jobs.

* A levels are advanced exams. Students stay on at school or go to college to study for A levels. Students take between two and five A levels, usually when they are 17 or 18 years old.

** An A grade is the highest grade you can get.

*** A sports event where athletes try to jump as far as possible.

Questions 1–7

The passage has four parts. In which part do you find the following information?
Write the letter in the space. Use some letters more than once.

1. Why people are worried about A levels becoming too easy. ___
2. What can be done about the problem. ___
3. How students should feel when they pass exams. ___
4. Some reasons why more students are getting better grades. ___
5. Numbers of students who pass or fail the exam. ___
6. Comparing exams with sport. ___
7. Both students and teachers are doing better. ___

Questions 8–12

Answer these questions using <u>no more than three words</u>.

8. What percentage of students got an A level A grade in 1970? _____
9. What percentage of students get an A level A grade now? _____
10. How many A level subjects do most students study? _____
11. How many A level exams do most students take? _____
12. Which sporting event are A level exams compared with? _____

Writing

A Talk with a partner. Decide if these sentences about the first part of the IELTS Writing Module are (T) true or (F) false.

1. The examiner will look at how your letter is organized. ___
2. You can use the same words and phrases in a formal and informal letter. ___
3. You need to write at least eight paragraphs. ___
4. You should start by saying why you are writing. ___
5. The examiner is not interested in the vocabulary that you use. ___
6. You should try to link ideas together into longer sentences if possible. ___
7. You can use as many words as you like in your letter. ___
8. It does not matter how you end your letter. ___

B You recently took six one-hour driving lessons at the Learn Fast Driving School. You are not happy for these reasons.

- You had three different instructors.
- The instructors were late and the lessons were under one hour.
- The instructors explained too much and didn't let you practise enough.
- The cars were older than you expected and not clean inside.

Write a letter to Learn Fast Driving School. Use at least 150 words.

Remember to …

- state the purpose.
- explain the situation.
- say what you want the driving school to do.

 Exam tip: Remember that you have 20 minutes, but you should spend some time thinking about what to include and then organizing your ideas. Leave about three minutes for checking for errors when you have finished.

3 Work

Speaking 1: talking about work

A Look at the four photos and think about the kind of work that the people are doing. Think for one minute about what you want to say about each photo.

B Work in pairs. Take turns to choose a photo and talk about it. Try to talk for about one minute about each. Use phrases from the box.

> This picture shows people ... ing.   These people work in / on / for ...
> This is a good job because ...   I would / wouldn't like to do this job because ...
> This job is easy / difficult / interesting / boring because ...

Vocabulary 1: jobs and saying what you do

A 🎧 Listen and write the job names. Be careful with your spelling.

1. accountant   2. _____   3. _____   4. _____
5. _____   6. _____   7. _____   8. _____

B 🎧 Listen again and mark the main stress on each word.

C Circle the correct preposition in each sentence.

1. I work for / (as) an architect.
2. I work for / as an oil company.
3. I work at / in the fashion industry.
4. I work in / on an office.
5. I work with / by computers.

D Talk about your job or the job you want to do using the structures in Exercise C.

 Exam tip: The examiner will probably ask you about work. Practise saying in different ways what you do or would like to do. Use a dictionary to find specialist words, but check with somebody that you are using the words properly.

E Check the highlighted words and mark each sentence (P) positive or (N) negative.

1. I think my job is very interesting. <u>P</u>
2. It's a very boring job. It's too easy and I don't meet anyone. ___
3. It's very rewarding. I can go home knowing I've really helped somebody. ___
4. My job is challenging. I have to think quickly sometimes. Not everyone could do it.
5. My job is a bit repetitive. Every day is the same as the day before. ___
6. It's too stressful. My doctor told me to find another job soon. ___

F Cover Exercise E and write the six adjectives in your notebook. Check your spelling.

Speaking 2: talking about jobs

A Answer these questions with a partner.

1. What jobs do the people in your family do?
2. Do any of your friends or family have a job you would really like?
3. Is there a job you would like to do more than any other?

Grammar check
We use *would* and *could* when a situation is not real.

What job would you most like?   (the person will not really have this job)
Do you think you could do his job?   (the person will not really try to do the job)

Pronunciation check
🎧 Listen and notice the pronunciation of *would you* /wʊdʒuː/ and *could you* /kʊdʒuː/. Practise saying the sentences.
1. What job would you most like?
2. Do you think you could do this job?

Exam tip: In the second part of the Speaking Module, you have to talk about a topic for about two minutes. The examiner will give you a card with the topic and some points to think about. You have a minute to prepare and write notes. You can ask the examiner about anything that you don't understand.

B Here are two typical cards for part 2 of the Speaking Module. Work with a partner – one of you is A, the other is B. Think about the topic for a minute and make notes.

A

> **Describe a job you think is really difficult.**
> **Say ...**
> • what the job is.
> • why it is difficult.
> • why some people do it.
> • why you wouldn't like to do it.

B

> **What is the best job in the world?**
> **Say ...**
> • what the job is.
> • why it is such a good job.
> • what type of person does it.
> • if you think you could do it.

C Take turns to speak about what's on your card for about two minutes.

3

Listening 1: listening for gist

A Look at the pictures. Talk to a partner about what is happening in each.

B 🎧 Listen to the four extracts and match them with the pictures. Write the number of the extract in the box.

C With a partner, discuss how you completed the task. Answer these questions.

1. Did you use the pictures to get ideas to listen for?
2. Did the speakers' voices (stress and intonation) help?
3. Did you hear any key words or phrases that helped?

D Read this short text about listening skills and fill the gaps with the words below.

> word   details   topic   skimming

When you listen for gist, you listen to understand the general (1) _____ of the dialogue or conversation (the situation and what the people are talking about).
You are not listening for specific (2) _____ and you don't need to understand every (3) _____. If you understand the gist of a conversation, it will be easier to understand the details if necessary. Listening for gist is similar to (4) _____ a text when you read.

Exam tip: When you listen for gist, predicting what you will hear is very important. In the exam, you will not have photos, but a map, a diagram or a table will help you predict. You can also predict by looking at the questions and noticing key words and phrases.

E Look at the four images below. You will hear a short extract for each. What can you predict about each extract?

 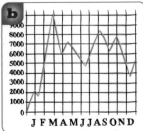  

F 🎧 Listen to the four extracts and match them with the images in Exercise E.

1. ___   2. ___   3. ___   4. ___

Listening 2: practise listening for gist

Exam tip: Sometimes you will need to listen for gist rather than for specific information. But remember – understanding gist will help you understand details, too.

A 🎧 Listen to the four extracts. For questions 1–4, match the extracts with the pictures. Write the number of the extract in the box.

Read through the questions. Then listen to the extracts again. For questions 5–12, choose the correct answer a, b or c.

Extract 1

5. Toby has come to the office ...
   a. for an interview.
   b. to start work.
   c. to prepare for a new job.

6. It is Toby's ...
   a. first visit.
   b. second visit.
   c. third or fourth visit.

7. Keith is ...
   a. Julie's boss.
   b. Julie's assistant.
   c. an important customer.

Extract 2

8. The man is talking about ...
   a. a new building.
   b. his garden.
   c. a design for a car.

9. The man speaking knows that ...
   a. everyone will drive to work.
   b. everyone will cycle to work.
   c. some people will drive and others cycle.

Extract 3

10. Debbie is phoning Robert to ...
    a. give him good news.
    b. tell him there is a problem.
    c. arrange a meeting.

Extract 4

11. The man is selling ...
    a. products for the home.
    b. books.
    c. new kitchens.

12. The woman ...
    a. is very interested.
    b. is not at all interested.
    c. doesn't understand what the man wants.

B Check the key on page 266. How many questions did you answer correctly?

C Tick the sentences about the listening task that are true for you and think about how you can answer more questions correctly next time.

1. The pictures helped me to make predictions about each topic.
2. It was quite easy to match the pictures to the extracts.
3. I didn't understand all the words in the questions.
4. Understanding the gist helped me to understand detail.
5. I am pleased with how many of questions 5–12 I answered correctly.

Key vocabulary in context

Match the words and phrases from listening task 1–4 with definitions a–d.

1. design
2. staff
3. customer
4. product

a. what a company makes to sell
b. a person who buys something
c. all the people who work for a company
d. a drawing that shows what something will look like

3

Reading 1: scanning for paraphrased language

 Exam tip: In the second part of the Reading Module, the texts will always be related to work. You might read a job application or a page of staff rules, for example.

A Look at the photos. Answer these questions with a partner.

1. What is each job?
2. What is good and not so good about each job?
3. Would you like to do any of the jobs?

B Use a dictionary to check these words and then match each with one of the photos.

a. farms ___   b. flights ___   c. pitch ___   d. tips ___

C Read the title of the passage on the next page. Will each person say good things or bad things about the job?

 Exam tip: Always read the heading or title of a passage. It will help you predict what it is about.

D Read the four short texts and circle the job in each as quickly as possible.

E Scan the four texts and use the highlighted parts to answer these questions. Write the letter of the text in the space. In which text does the writer say that ...

1. he or she was very tired?   ___
2. he or she got a lot of money from the job?   ___
3. he or she got no money for doing the job?   ___
4. he or she had free time to enjoy?   ___

 Exam tip: In some scanning exercises, you need to look quickly for parts of the text that mean the same as the words and phrases in the question. You will not find the exact words and phrases from the question in the text.

F Scan the text again to answer these questions in the same way. Highlight the parts of the text that provide the answer. In which text does the writer say that ...

1. he or she enjoyed working outside.   ___
2. he or she met famous people.   ___
3. he or she doesn't do the job now.   ___
4. people don't think the job is interesting.   ___

The Best Job I Ever Had

Text A

I had the best job in the world for three years and I didn't even get paid for it. From when I was 12 until when I was 15, I was a ball boy at Old Trafford. That's where Manchester United play their home matches. When the ball went off the pitch, I had to get it and give it back to one of the players as quickly as I could. I saw some great football matches and met footballers and football coaches from all round the world.

Text B

People think that being a waitress is boring and repetitive, but it's the best job I ever had. I worked in a very nice restaurant where all the customers had plenty of money. The restaurant didn't pay me very much, but I made a fortune from the huge tips that the customers gave me. I always did my job well because I knew that if the customers weren't happy, they wouldn't give me a tip.

Text C

The job I'm doing now pays very well, but it's quite boring and very stressful. I think I was happiest when I was picking fruit in France. My friends and I were students, and we travelled around France working on farms. We picked grapes and strawberries. We worked very long hours, and at the end of the day I was exhausted, but I was in the sunshine all day and I was working with the people I knew best.

Text D

These days, I stay at home and look after my two children, but for ten years I had the best job in the world. I was an air hostess working on international flights. I flew to Australia and South America. During the flights, I was very busy and the passengers were sometimes quite difficult, but I got three days off before the journey back. The airline put me in the best hotels and I had a great time. I saw some wonderful places in those ten years.

Reading 2: practise scanning for paraphrased language

A Look at the job titles in the advertisements on the next page and check that you understand them.

B Read the job advertisements and answer the questions. For questions 1–3, match each job advertisement with a description a–d. Write the letter of the description in the space. There is one description that you do not need.

1. advert A ___   2. advert B ___   3. advert C ___

a. You will deal with people who want to buy or who have already bought a product.
b. You will sell something.
c. You will design something.
d. You will work with money.

For questions 4–9, write the letter of the advertisement in the space.
Which advertisement says that ...

4. you must know how to use a computer. ___
5. you will work closely with someone in a high position. ___
6. you will learn how to do the job when you start. ___
7. people are happy with the service provided by the company. ___
8. you will often talk to people directly. ___
9. you need to apply before a certain date. ___

 Exam tip: When you are doing a reading exercise quickly, you might want to guess answers, and sometimes that's possible. However, you will feel more confident if you find the part of the text that provides the answer.

A

ACCOUNTS DIRECTOR / FINANCIAL MANAGER

Up to £70,000 a year + company car.

A position managing our financial services and working directly with the chief executive. You should be a qualified accountant with experience in management.

Closing date for application: 11 March 09
Interviews: April 09

B

Our market is growing and we are looking for a:

SALES EXECUTIVE

As part of our busy sales team, you will be ambitious. You will deal face-to-face with people regularly and must have excellent communication skills. You will be quick to understand new ideas and put them into practice.

You will receive full training and a good salary.
For more information, please call 01456 554796.

C

Customer Service Administrator

Lewes, East Sussex

Good salary + benefits

We have more than a million satisfied customers in the UK, and we provide the highest quality service. To continue our success, we are looking for a full-time customer service administrator.

The successful applicant must have previous experience and be computer-literate. He or she will need a friendly, professional telephone manner.

To apply, please send your CV to Sonya_Groves@Sureguard.co.uk

C Highlight the parts of the adverts that give the answers to questions 4–9. Then compare your ideas with a partner.

D Check the key on page 266. How many questions did you answer correctly?

E Tick the sentences about the reading task that are true for you and think about how you can answer more questions correctly next time.

1. I read the instructions for the questions carefully.
2. I skimmed the advertisements to answer questions 1–3.
3. I answered questions 1–3 quickly.
4. I read more carefully to answer questions 4–9.
5. It was quite easy to find the information I needed for questions 4–9.
6. I am happy with how many questions I answered correctly.

Key vocabulary in context

Circle the correct word from the three options. You can find the correct options in the job adverts.

1. A more formal word for job is *position / protection / preparation*.
2. If you do a job for a long time, you have *experiment / experience / expression*.
3. If you want to do well in a job, you are *ambitious / amazing / absent*.
4. Another way to say 'give' a service is *prove / produce / provide*.
5. If a company is doing well, it has *surprise / success / support*.

F Highlight words and phrases in the adverts that you think are useful.

Exam tip: It is not possible to learn all the new vocabulary from a text that you read, and usually it is not very helpful to try. Focus on words and phrases that are useful to you.

WB For more focus on reading skills, go to Workbook page 10.

Writing 1: register

A Discuss with a partner. Which definition of register is correct?

1. *Register* is planning and organizing your writing.
2. *Register* is spelling words correctly and using punctuation.
3. *Register* is making sure that what you write is grammatically correct.
4. *Register* is using the right words and phrases for the situation – using words and phrases that are formal or informal.

B Mark the following types of letter (VF) very formal, (QF) quite formal or (INF) informal.

1. an e-mail to a friend telling him about a party you are having ___
2. a letter to a tour operator complaining about a holiday ___
3. a letter to a family in Britain that you are going to stay with ___
4. a letter to a college asking for information about a course ___
5. a letter to your cousin thanking him for a present ___
6. a letter to a friend apologizing because you cannot go to his wedding ___
7. a letter that you send with your CV when applying for a job ___

 Exam tip: The letter that you write for the first part of the Writing Module will probably be formal. You might have to write a more personal letter, but it will not be very informal.

C Match the formal expressions 1–8 with the informal expressions A–H.

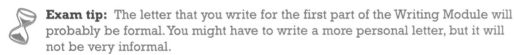

1 **Dear Sir / Madam**	A **Sorry for any trouble I caused.**
2 **I am writing to inform you that ...**	B **Let me have all the info a.s.a.p.**
3 **I will not be able to attend the ...**	C **Can't wait to hear all about it!**
4 **Could you send the information to my home address?**	D **Best wishes**
5 **I look forward to hearing from you.**	E **I wanted to tell you about ...**
6 **Thank you once again for your advice.**	F **Hi Phil, how's it going?**
7 **I apologize for the inconvenience.**	G **I can't make it to ...**
8 **Yours faithfully / sincerely**	H **... and thanks again for all your help.**

Exam tip: Almost anything can be expressed formally or informally. You need to learn the most common words and expressions that are used in certain types of composition.

Writing 2: a letter of application

A Talk to a partner. Look again at advert B on page 40.
What type of person is the company looking for?

B Read the cover letter that Ahmed sent with his CV.
Do you think he would be suitable for the position?

Dear Mr Lucas,

I am writing to <u>get</u> the position of sales
executive that I saw advertised in yesterday's *Daily Argus*. I <u>want a job</u>
in sales, and I am interested in working for your company.

I recently finished a Business Studies degree at York University. I <u>did very
well</u> in Economics and Marketing. Part of my degree course <u>was about</u>
designing and developing new ideas. I learn quickly and work well with
other people.

My father runs an import and export company, and from the age of 16
I have helped him in his office. I have learnt <u>a lot about business</u> and
communicated with clients both on the telephone and face-to-face.

I am outgoing and confident and I enjoy a challenge. I think I would be the
right person for a position in your company. I can attend an interview at any
time and <u>really want to hear</u> from you.

Yours sincerely,

Ahmed Khatani

C Below are some tips on how to organize an application letter. Write the number
of each tip in the boxes on the letter.

1. Say that you are qualified for the job – mention education and experience.
2. Say where you saw the job advertised.
3. Say something about your personal qualities.
4. State your purpose for writing.
5. Close the letter in a polite, positive way.

D Some words and phrases in the letter are underlined because they are too
informal. Replace them with the words and phrases below.

> look forward to hearing   apply for   involved   hope to work
> achieved very high grades   many useful business skills

E Read the complete model letter on page 267 and check your answers.
Does it sound better than Ahmed's first letter?

WB Go to Workbook page 11 for the writing task.

Speaking

A Work with a partner. Discuss this advice about the second part of the IELTS Speaking Module. Tick the correct advice A or B.

1. A The examiner will give you some pictures to talk about.
    B The examiner will give you a card to read.
2. A Don't worry if you don't understand words or phrases on the card.
    B You can ask the examiner about words and phrases that you don't know.
3. A You should try to talk about each of the points on the card.
    B You can talk about whatever you like.
4. A You should try to use a range of words and phrases.
    B You must use advanced vocabulary.
5. A The examiner will listen for grammatical mistakes.
    B It doesn't matter if you make grammatical mistakes.
6. A You will score a higher grade if your pronunciation is clear.
    B Your pronunciation must be perfect.

B Look at this card for part 2 of the Speaking Module. Are there any words you don't know?

C 🎧 Listen to a student doing the exam. Which words does he check? Highlight them on the card.

D 🎧 Look at the tapescript and listen again. Notice how the student asked questions and how the examiner answered.

E Practise answering the question. Try to talk for about a minute.

> **What is the best job in the world? Say ...**
> • what the job is.
> • what personal qualities you need.
> • what is so appealing about the job.

Vocabulary

A Match a word on the left with a word on the right to make six common two-part expressions.

past	applicant	1. ____ ____
computer	qualities	2. ____ ____
long	executive	3. ____ ____
personal	hours	4. ____ ____
successful	experience	5. ____ ____
chief	literate	6. ____ ____

B 🎧 Listen and write these words from the unit in your notebook. Check your spelling. Then mark the main stress on each word.

Errors

A There are errors in all of these sentences (sometimes there is more than one). Correct them.

1. I work at an engineer.
2. I work with the food industry.
3. I think I have a really good work.
4. I get good salary.
5. Do you like work in another country one day?
6. I will meet the other staffs tomorrow.
7. I saw advertisement in the evening star.
8. I might apply to this job. It looks interesting.

3

Listening

A You will hear three people talking about working from home. Before you listen, talk to a partner. What are some of the good things and bad things about working from home?

 Exam tip: In the Listening Module, you will not have a picture and you will not be able to talk about the situation before you listen. But you will have time to look at the questions and should predict as much as you can.

B 🎧 Look through the questions carefully. Then listen and answer the questions.

For questions 1 and 2, choose the correct answer a, b or c.

1. Simon started working from home because ...
   a. he wanted to.
   b. his company wanted him to.
   c. his family wanted him to.
2. Why are Simon's company happy for him to work from home?
   a. They can pay less money.
   b. Now they can move to a smaller office.
   c. The main office is too small.

🖐 **Question-type tip:** Sometimes you need to choose a number of answers from a larger number of options.

For questions 3–8, choose <u>six</u> answers from A–J. Which of these points do the speakers mention when they talk about working from home?

A   People in the office sometimes stop you working.
B   You always do more work when you are at home.
C   At home, you sometimes start work later than you planned.
D   It's easy to waste time watching TV.
E   Your family don't always let you do your work.
F   Most people wear a suit when they work from home.
G   You don't need to look smart when you work from home.
H   There are more technical problems with computers.
I   Not seeing other people all day can be difficult.
J   You get a lot of phone calls when you work from home.

3. ___   4. ___   5. ___   6. ___   7. ___   8. ___

Reading

A Read the passage and answer the questions. For questions 1–8, write the letter of the text in the space. In which text does the writer say that ...

1. it was very hot. ___
2. it was sometimes very cold. ___
3. he or she worked with somebody he or she didn't like. ___
4. he or she started work very early. ___
5. he or she did not get much money for doing the job. ___
6. he or she left the job suddenly. ___
7. time went very slowly. ___
8. some parts of the job were worse than others. ___

For questions 9–12, complete the notes with words from the passage.
Write <u>no more than two words or a number</u> for each answer.

Question-type tip: In the Reading and Listening Modules, you will sometimes need to complete notes with words from the text. The instructions will tell you how many words you can use.

9. In text A, the writer bought a bicycle with the money that he or she _____.
10. In text B, the writer spent all day looking forward to going _____.
11. In text C, the writer says that the restaurant _____ as the evening went on.
12. In text D, the writer says that if he or she _____, his or her boss complained.

The Worst Job I Ever Had

Text A
I think the worst job I ever had was when I was about 14. I had to deliver newspapers before I went to school. I had to be at the shop by about 6.30 a.m. and then, when the round was finished, I went home for breakfast. I remember icy winter mornings when all I wanted to do was stay in bed. At the beginning of the round, when the bag was full of newspapers, it was really heavy. I did it for about two years and I saved enough money to buy a bicycle.

Text B
When I was at school taking my A levels, I worked all day Saturday on the checkout at the local super-market. It was really boring and really repetitive, and when I think about it now, not very well paid at all. I remember looking at the clock on the wall and thinking that the hands weren't moving. The customers were mostly friendly, but all I wanted was to finish and go home.

Text C
When I was a student, I washed up in the kitchen of a big restaurant. The heat in the kitchen was terrible, and it was always so noisy. It was definitely the most horrible job I have ever done. At the beginning of the evening, it wasn't too bad, but as the restaurant became busier the work started to pile up. Washing plates and dishes was quite easy, but cleaning the pots and pans that were used to cook in was impossible.

Text D
I was really unhappy when I worked as a secretary for a company in Liverpool. The job itself wasn't so bad, but my boss was really unfriendly and he seemed to enjoy making life difficult for me. He complained if I was two or three minutes late, but always gave me something to do just before it was time to go home. One day, I decided that I had had enough, and I just walked out of the office and never went back.

4 Achievements

Speaking 1: talking about achievements

A Look at the photos and think about *achievement* and *success*. Think for one minute about what you want to say about each photo.

Sheikh Khalifa bin Zayed Al Nayhan

Tanni Grey-Thompson

Ainan Celeste Cawley

Norman Foster

Margaret Thatcher

Roald Amundsen

B Work in pairs. Take it in turns to choose a photo to talk about.

C 🎧 Listen to some people talking. Match each extract with one of the photos in Exercise A.

1. _____   2. _____   3. _____   4. _____   5. _____   6. _____

Vocabulary 1: achievement and success

A Look at these words and phrases. Then listen again and write the letter of the photo when you hear them.

1. powerful ___
2. mental and physical strength ___
3. child prodigy ___
4. courage ___
5. creating something ___
6. wealth ___
7. overcome a difficulty ___
8. had a big influence ___

B Look at the tapescript on page 283. Look at how the words and phrases in Exercise A are used.

Grammar check

We use the *present perfect* to talk about achievement if the person is still alive or still achieving.
He is only 30 but he has achieved a lot. / I haven't really achieved what I want yet.
We use the *past simple* if the person is dead or has stopped achieving.
Ghandi achieved great things in his life. / Pele achieved a great deal during his career.

Watch out!
typical errors

I don't achieve what I want yet. ✗
I don't have achieved what I want yet. ✗

Vocabulary 2: words that go together

A In each list of collocations, one option is wrong. Use a dictionary and cross it out.

1. have   an achievement / success / an influence on something / a few difficulties
2. achieve   an ambition / a lot in life / a great deal / a difficulty
3. overcome   a difficulty / an obstacle / an ambition / a disability

B There are nine possible expressions in Exercise A. Close the book and write <u>five</u> of them in your notebook. Think about sentences that use them.

> **Pronunciation check**
> 🎧 Listen to the contractions in these sentences.
> 1. I've achieved a lot this year.   2. He's overcome many difficulties.
> Now listen to how the negative forms *haven't* /hævnt/ and *hasn't* /həznt/ are pronounced in natural speech.
> 3. I haven't achieved what I wanted to.   4. She hasn't done everything yet.
> Now listen to how *have you* /hævjuː/, *has he* /hæz iː/ and *has she* /hæz ʃiː/ are pronounced in these questions.
> 5. Have you achieved all that you hoped?   6. Has he done what he wanted to do?
> 7. Has she been successful?
> Practise saying all the sentences.

Speaking 2: saying who you think is successful

A Look at the card for part 2 of the Speaking Module. You have a minute to think about what you want to say and make notes.

> **Who do you know who has achieved something special?**
> **Say ...**
> • who the person is.
> • what they have achieved.
> • why the achievement is special.
> • how the achievement has influenced other people.

B Walk around and talk with other students. Compare your answers to the question.

Speaking 3: having a two-way discussion

Exam tip: In the third part of the Speaking Module, the examiner will expand the topic in part 2. He or she will ask you to express your opinion on related topics. The topics will be more abstract – less personal than in part 2.

A Mark these questions (E) easy to answer or (D) difficult to answer.

1. Are people born to achieve or do they learn to achieve?   __
2. Why are some people better achievers than others?   __
3. Is it easier for people to achieve if they have a good education?   __
4. Do you have to make money to be successful?   __

B Talk with a partner. Answer the questions.

4

Listening 1: predicting content

A Look at the first line of some instructions for a listening task and answer the questions that follow.

Listen to somebody giving a talk about why some children achieve more at school than others.

1. Does it help you to listen to a talk if you are told what the talk is about first?
2. What sort of predictions can you make about the talk before you listen?

B Look at the instructions for the listening task in Exercise A again.

1. Predict some of the reasons that the speaker will give.
2. Predict some key words and phrases that you will hear.

Exam tip: In the second part of the Listening Module, you will hear a speaker giving a talk. Before you listen, you are told the topic of the talk. This should make the tasks easier, and you should try to make predictions about content and key vocabulary.

C Look at these first lines from a Listening Module.

1. Listen to somebody giving a talk about the life of a brilliant scientist.
2. Listen to somebody giving a talk about how to start your own business.
3. Listen to somebody giving a talk about how older people can continue to learn.

D Now look at this typical question from the Listening Module. Which topic above does it refer to?

The speaker says that you need to ...
a. find out about competition in the local area.
b. only provide a service that nobody else is providing.
c. charge less than other companies that provide a similar service.

E Can you guess which answer in Exercise D is correct without listening to anything?

Exam tip: It is sometimes possible to guess answers from what you know about a topic, but it is better if you actually hear the speaker provide the answer.

Listening 2: listening for paraphrased language

A Tick the advice below that is correct.

1. Multiple choice is easy. You look at the words in the questions and then listen for them.
2. Multiple choice is not so easy, because the words in the questions are not the same as the words that you hear.

Exam tip: In some parts of the Listening Module, you listen for specific information, like names and numbers, but in other parts you need to listen for clues. You need to hear words and phrases that mean the same as those in the question and understand when ideas are expressed in different words.

B 🎧 Listen to this extract that provides an answer to the question in Listening 1D. Choose a, b or c.

C 🎧 Listen again and identify the words and phrases that provide the answer and tell you that the other options are wrong. Then check the tapescript on page 284.

Listening 3: practise predicting and paraphrasing

A Look up 'set goals' in a dictionary and make sure you understand its meaning.

B 🎧 Listen to somebody giving a talk about how setting goals can help you achieve more.

For questions 1–4, choose the correct letter a, b or c.

1. The speaker says that achievement means ...
   a. making money.
   b. the same thing to everyone.
   c. getting what you want.
2. The speaker says that to achieve something, you must ...
   a. really want it.   b. believe that getting it is possible.   c. talk about it a lot.
3. The speaker says that setting goals will ...
   a. help you understand what is really important to you.
   b. stop you worrying about the future.
   c. help you to do well in business or to become an athlete.
4. The 'big picture' means ...
   a. setting short-term goals.   b. planning a long way ahead.
   c. one important area of your life.

For questions 5–9, choose **five** answers from A–H. When the speaker talks about different areas of life, which of these does he mention?

A the job you do   B money
C being very well-educated   D marrying the right person
E having a family   F playing different sports
G not doing things that are bad for your health   H leisure time

5. _____   6. _____   7. _____   8. _____   9. _____

For question 10, choose the correct letter a, b or c.

10. The speaker says that ...
    a. making other people happy is very important.
    b. you must forget about other people completely.
    c. you must think about yourself first.

C Check the key on page 267. How many questions did you answer correctly?

D Tick the sentences about the listening task that are true for you and think about how you can answer more questions correctly next time.

1. It helped to know the topic of the talk before I listened.
2. I looked through the questions and made predictions.
3. I guessed some answers correctly before I listened.
4. I listened for paraphrased language.
5. I am happy with how many questions I answered correctly.

4

Reading 1: making sure that information is given in the text

A Look at the picture of Ainan Celeste Cawley. You talked about him earlier in this unit. Answer these questions with a partner.

1. What do you remember about Ainan from the short listening extract?
2. What else would you like to know about him?

B Look at these sentences about Ainan and guess whether they are (T) true or (F) false.

1. He is a very unusual child.   __
2. His parents want him to go to university.   __
3. He is the cleverest child in Singapore.   __
4. He has already passed Chemistry A level.   __
5. Everyone thinks he is ready for university.   __
6. Even as a baby, he was very advanced.   __
7. He watches a lot of TV.   __
8. His father taught him all about Chemistry.   __

C Read the article below and check your answers. Then mark the sentences in Exercise B (T) true, (F) false or (NG) not given.

Prodigy Ready for University?

Seven-year-old Ainan Celeste Cawley is a child prodigy, and his parents are searching for a university that will take him at such a young age. His father says that a brilliant mind could be lost if he is not given a place.

Ainan's mother is from Singapore and his father from Britain. He has already passed his O level* Chemistry, and he is studying to take his A level**, but some experts believe that not having a normal childhood can do long-lasting damage and do not believe he should go to university just yet.

Ainan's father says that Ainan was always a special child. He could walk when he was only six months and talk in long sentences when he was one. As a very small child, he enjoyed reading science books and could understand difficult scientific texts. His parents think that he is like other children in many ways. He draws and paints and he loves watching Mr Bean on TV.

His father first realized that Ainan was very interested in chemistry when, at six years old, he picked up a Chemistry O level paper and answered all the questions. It was then discovered that he had learnt all about the subject by surfing the Internet.

* An exam that school students in some countries take when they are 16.

** An exam that school or college students in some countries take when they are 18.

Exam tip: You have already practised true/false questions in this book, but in the Reading Module the task is a little more difficult. You can also answer (NG), which stands for Not Given, so you have three options. When you do this kind of task, do not use your own knowledge of the topic or assume that an answer is obvious. You must find the answer in the text.

D Look at these comments that a student has made about the questions in Exercise B. Which questions does the student answer correctly?

1. 'The text says that Ainan is a *prodigy* and later that he is *special*, so the answer is true.'
2. 'His parents are *searching* for a university, so again the answer is true.'
3. 'He is only six and he is going to university, so nobody in Singapore is cleverer than him. The answer is true again.'
4. 'He has passed his O level, but he is studying now for his A level, so this one is false.'
5. 'The text only says what his mother and father think. It doesn't say what everyone thinks. The answer is not given.'
6. 'This is easy. He could walk when he was six months, so the answer is true.'
7. 'The text only mentions one programme, *Mr Bean*, so the answer is false.'
8. 'No, this one is false. The text says he *learnt by surfing the Internet*, so his father didn't teach him.'

E Check the real answers on page 267. Did you make any of the same mistakes?

Reading 2: recognizing distracters

Exam tip: The questions will sometimes try to trick you. For example, the question will include words from the text that make you think an answer is true when it is not.

A Look at this question from Reading 1B again. Why could you make a mistake if you read too quickly?

> 4. He has already passed Chemistry A level. __

Reading 3: practise finding the right information

A Look only at the four names in the text below. What is each person famous for?

B The text is about successful business people who don't have a degree. Read it and answer the questions.

For questions 1–4, match the headings below with the names. There is <u>one</u> more heading than you need. Write the letter into the space.

a. Not what others wanted
b. Changing a whole industry
c. Regrets about leaving university
d. So many different ideas
e. A difficult early life

1. Richard Branson __   2. Coco Chanel __   3. Henry Ford __   4. Bill Gates __

Who Needs a Degree to Succeed in Business?

Most people assume that working hard in high school and going to the right college or university is the best way to end up with a successful career. Parents and teachers spend much of their time emphasizing the need for a good education and warning the young about what will happen if they don't get the best grades.

But is a degree really so important? There are many graduates who never find the well-paid job they think they deserve. On the other hand, there are plenty of entrepreneurs and high-fliers who dropped out of school and became millionaires. Here are just a few.

Richard Branson is best known for his sense of adventure. He dropped out of school at the age of 16 and started his first successful business venture, a magazine called *Student*. He is the owner of the Virgin brand that has 360 companies, ranging from record labels and music stores to airlines, banking and Internet services.

When Coco Chanel was 12 years old, her mother died and her father ran away. She spent six years in an orphanage. At 18, she started work as an assistant to a tailor. Later she became one of the world's best-loved fashion designers. The perfume that carries her name, Chanel No. 5, ensures that she is still famous today.

At 16, Henry Ford left home to become an apprentice to a machinist. He soon became an engineer and later started the Ford Motor Company. His first major success, the Model T, allowed him to open a large factory and start the assembly-line production that revolutionized the way cars were manufactured.

Between 1995–2006, Bill Gates was the world's richest person but he was a college dropout. His parents hoped he would be a lawyer, but he left Harvard College in 1975 to set up his own computer software company and become a pioneer of technological advance.

Of course, just because these people are or were hugely successful doesn't mean that everyone can get to the top in business without a college or university degree. However, if you really do have an entrepreneurial spirit, a degree may just be an extra!

Related Articles: Inspiration at work

For questions 5–12, decide if the information given below agrees with the information given in the passage. Write (T) true, (F) false or (NG) not given.

5. Parents and teachers tell young people that they should study hard. ___
6. Most people who go to college don't get the job they really want. ___
7. All the most successful people in the world have been to university. ___
8. Richard Branson started producing a magazine while he was a student. ___
9. Coco Chanel liked making perfume more than designing clothes. ___
10. Henry Ford always wanted to make cars. ___
11. Bill Gates left college to go into business. ___
12. Most people can be successful without a good education. ___

C Highlight the parts of the text that provide the answers.

D Check the key on page 267. How many questions did you answer correctly?

E Tick the sentences about the reading task that are true for you and think about how you can answer more questions correctly next time.

1. I skimmed the passage to answer questions 1–4.
2. I was happy with the time it took to answer questions 1–4.
3. I read more slowly and carefully to answer questions 5–12.
4. I found the information that provided answers and I didn't need to guess.
5. I am happy with the time it took to answer questions 5–12.

Key vocabulary in context

Mark these words and phrases (L) if they are more related to learning and (W) if they are more related to work.

1. degree ___
2. career ___
3. education ___
4. best grades ___
5. graduates ___
6. entrepreneur ___
7. business venture ___
8. apprentice ___
9. college dropout ___

WB For focus on reading skills, go to Workbook page 13.

Writing 1: understanding the task

A Look at the photos and answer the questions below with a partner.

1. What do the images have in common?
2. What different ideas of success and achievement do the photos show?

B Look at the instructions for a typical writing task.

> In today's world, success and achievement are too often measured by wealth and the material possessions that a person has acquired.
>
> Do you agree with the statement?

C Now tick the comment in each pair below that is true for you.

1. a. I understand all the words in the statement.
   b. I don't know some words in the statement.
2. a. I understand the statement and I can answer the question.
   b. I don't understand the statement, so I can't answer the question.

D Look at the instructions again below and the notes that a student has made on them.

> things people have, like big houses and cars   how much money somebody has
>
> In today's world, success and achievement are too often measured by wealth and the material possessions that a person has acquired.
>
> managed to get   If you measure something, you say how big it is.
>
> Do you agree with the statement?

Writing 2: deciding what to say

A Make sure you understand the writing task above and tick the comments below that are true for you.

1. I don't know what to say about this topic. I could not write about it even in my own language.
2. I know what I want to say, but it's very difficult to say in English.
3. I can say what I want to say about this topic quite easily in English.

 Exam tip: In the second part of the Writing Module, you need to express your views on a topic like this one. You do not need to be an expert on the topic, but you must have something to say. Think about how you would answer the question in your own language first.

B Work in small groups. Brainstorm some points that you could make.

C 🎧 Two British students are brainstorming ideas before they do this writing task. Listen and note down the points they make.

D Now look at the composition that one of the students has written. Does it include all the points that he and his partner discussed?

There are different ways to measure success and achievement. Being best at a sport, discovering or inventing something, helping people and even saving a life are all important achievements. Just looking after your family and making them happy is an achievement. However, I think it is true that now too many people believe that success and achievement is about wealth and having things like a big house and a fast car.

People think wealth is so important because they see images on TV and in magazines. They want to be like a film star or famous footballer, and they think everyone else does too. Most people can name hundreds of actors or rock stars, but they do not know the names of doctors or scientists. People know teachers and nurses are important, but they do not think they are really successful. People who work in advertising make money, and so people consider them successful.

Of course, there are times when people recognize other kinds of achievement. During the Olympics, for example, athletes are very popular because they win medals, not because they are wealthy. However, people do not remember those athletes for long. They are more interested in footballers, and I think that is because footballers are so rich.

The world will be better if more people realize that real success and achievement means being happy and doing things because you want to. I think, though, that the more young people watch TV, read magazines and surf the Internet, the more they will measure success and achievement by wealth and by the material possessions that a person has acquired.

E 🎧 Listen to the students in Exercise C again. Highlight the points in the composition as you hear them.

F Choose <u>one</u> option below about the answer the student has given.

1. He has agreed with the statement and given evidence to say why.
2. He has disagreed with the statement and given examples of why he thinks it is not true.
3. He has balanced his arguments and has neither agreed nor disagreed with the statement.

Writing 3: organizing your points

A Put the stages into the order in which they appear in the composition.

___ Give plenty of evidence that shows why you agree with the statement.
___ Begin the summarizing paragraph with a strongly expressed opinion.
___ Repeat the main idea of the statement and say again that you agree with it.
___ Say that you agree with the statement.
___ Show that you understand the statement – define key words in the statement.
___ Give an example of why some people might not agree with the statement.

Exam tip: However you answer the question, you must organize points logically. The examiner must be able to read your composition easily.

B Look at the exam practice section on page 57 for the writing task.

Speaking

A In the third part of the Speaking Module, you need to express your opinions. Mark these sentences (T) true or (F) false.

1. If you don't know what to say, you can ask for another question. __
2. You must try to answer the questions that the examiner asks. __
3. You must show that you know a lot about the topic. __
4. You should think for a moment before you answer the questions. __
5. You can ask the examiner to explain a word that you don't understand. __
6. You must say something that the examiner will agree with. __
7. You should speak clearly and fairly slowly. __
8. Your language must always be grammatically correct. __

B Look again at this question from the unit. Can you remember how you answered it?

Are people born to achieve or do they learn to achieve?

C 🎧 Listen to some students answering the question. Mark each speaker (G) good answer or (NG) not a good answer.

Speaker 1 __   Speaker 2 __   Speaker 3 __   Speaker 4 __

D Which speaker in Exercise C ...

a. makes grammatical mistakes and uses simple vocabulary but gives a good answer. __
b. understands the question but doesn't give a full answer. __
c. doesn't understand the question and should ask to hear it again. __
d. uses grammatically correct language and a range of vocabulary to give a very full answer. __

E Answer these two questions with a partner.

1. Does being successful mean doing better than other people?
2. Can you only enjoy success if other people know about it?

Vocabulary

A Fill the gaps with a word made from the root words in the box.

1. I think Mustafa will have a very _____ career.
2. She had to overcome a number of early _____.
3. My brother works hard, but he isn't very _____.
4. You need great mental _____ to be a real achiever.
5. Martin's father is a very _____ man.
6. Most people think that a good _____ is very important.

success
difficult
ambition
strong
power
educate

B Which **one** phrase in the list does not collocate with *have*? Cross it out. Then write sentences using all the other words in the list in your notebook.

a. have ambition   b. have a dream   c. have an idea
d. have problems   e. have difficulties   f. have an effect
g. have an influence   h. have a failure   i. have success

Errors

A There are errors in all of these sentences (sometimes more than one). Correct them.

1. James has made a lot of success in business.
2. I don't have achieved what I want yet.
3. He was teached Chemistry at school.
4. My father had an influence in my decision.

4

Reading

A Read the advertisement on the opposite page for an exhibition in London.

For questions 1–3, match the pictures below to the appropriate section of the text. Write the letter in the space.

1. ___   2. ___   3. ___

For questions 4–7, identify which section contains the following information. Write the letter of the section in the space.

4. People have not seen some of the film ever before.   ___
5. Many different types of achievement are included in the exhibition.   ___
6. The exhibition uses both very old and very modern technology.   ___
7. People can see things from all over the world.   ___

For questions 8–14, decide if the information given below agrees with the information given in the advertisement. Write (T) true, (F) false or (NG) not given.

8. You can relive both positive and negative experiences.   ___
9. Some famous world leaders have been to the exhibition.   ___
10. You can experience walking on the Moon.   ___
11. The World Cup goals have all been filmed recently.   ___
12. You can beat a famous boxer and a famous tennis player.   ___
13. There is nothing for people who like painting and books.   ___
14. There is no need to pay for small children.   ___

July 29th – September 5th

London History Museum
Special exhibition
Human Achievement on Film

A **Human Achievement on Film** is an exhibition you cannot miss. See photographs and film of Man's greatest achievements. From the earliest film of the nineteenth century to the wonders of digital photography, satellite TV and virtual reality – you will be taken on a tour of the events that have changed our world. You can experience for yourself amazing and terrifying moments of success and failure. You will be part of history.

B **World leaders**
See thousands of the best-loved photographs of the people who have steered us through history. Relive the events that have put us where we are now. Watch previously unseen film of Queen Victoria, Martin Luther King and Lenin, and learn about the techniques that great speakers use to inspire us. Then step into a virtual world and make a speech to an audience of millions!

C **Science and invention**
Enjoy a journey through 120 years of scientific achievement. See photographic collections from Alaska to Australia! Enjoy some wonderful moments captured on film. Watch the earliest clips of Man's attempts to fly, and then experience failure for yourself as you crash one of the first gliders! Then take those first legendary steps on the Moon in your very own spacesuit!

D **Sport**
See the photographs and film that inspire every hopeful athlete. Wonder at the earliest Olympic images and celebrate the goals from the World Cups of yesterday. Experience the joy of winning and the heartbreak of losing. Climb into the ring and fight a round with Muhammed Ali or grab a racket and try to return a few of Roger Federer's serves!

E **And more**
Enjoy images and exhibits celebrating every area of human achievement. Exploration, discovery, architecture, engineering, medicine, art and literature and much more – it's all here.

'An unmissable experience!' *The Times*

'A unique journey' *The Daily Mail*

Museum open daily from 9 a.m. to 6 p.m.   Adults £6.50   Children £3.00   Under-fives free

Done

Writing

A Look carefully at the instructions for this writing task. Highlight the key words, check them in a dictionary and make sure you understand what you have to do.

> You cannot achieve great things with talent alone. You must work hard and have the support of people around you.
>
> Do you agree with the statement?

B Work with a partner. Brainstorm points that you could include in the composition. Make notes in your own language if you want to.

C Write the composition. Try to use about 200 words. Look again at the composition in the Writing section and follow the stages in Writing 3A.

5 Thoughts

Vocabulary 1: thought processes

A The pictures show people thinking in different ways. Complete the captions with a verb from below.

| predict | concentrate | imagine | consider | decide | calculate |

'This is very difficult to _____.'

'I _____ a fall in the price of oil.'

'Can you be quiet? I can't _____.'

'Can you _____ living somewhere like that?'

'Mm, I can't _____ which one I want.'

'I'll _____ your offer and call you in a few days.'

B 🎧 Listen and check your answers.

C Put the words below in the spaces to make common expressions.

| a decision | your brain | an idea | a thought | your imagination | a prediction |

1. have _____ / _____
2. make _____ / _____
3. use _____ / _____

Grammar check

Many of the verbs in this lesson are state verbs, and so they are not used in a continuous form.

I think his new film is very good. ✓
NOT I'm thinking his new film is very good. ✗

We say I don't think + affirmative verb clause.
NOT I think + negative verb clause.

I don't think he's listening. ✓
NOT I think he isn't listening. ✗

Watch out!
typical errors

I'm thinking it will rain. ✗

Sorry, I'm not understanding. ✗

I think Peter will not come to the party. ✗

Speaking 1: how people think

A Look at the pictures. With a partner, talk about how each person has to think.

doctor   clothes designer   surveyor   businessmen

Example: *'The businessmen have to calculate, consider options and make decisions.'*

B Answer these questions with a partner.

1. Are you good at making decisions?   2. Are you good at making predictions?
3. Are you good at calculating figures?   4. When do you find it difficult to concentrate?
5. Do you have a good imagination?

Speaking 2: expressing opinions

Exam tip: In the first part of the Speaking Module, the examiner will ask about your life. He or she will expect you to express an opinion.

A Look at these questions and think about how you could express an opinion in your answer.

1. So, are you going to university next year?
2. Tell me something about your job.
3. Do you work hard?
4. Tell me about your hometown.
5. What do you do in your free time?

B 🎧 Listen to some students answering the questions. For each question, tick the speaker who gives the better answer.

1. Speaker A __ 2. Speaker A __ 3. Speaker A __ 4. Speaker A __ 5. Speaker A __
   Speaker B __   Speaker B __   Speaker B __   Speaker B __   Speaker B __

C 🎧 Listen again and complete the phrases below.

1. I'm really looking _____ to it.
2. Yes, but I don't _____.
3. I really _____ living there.
4. I'm very _____ on basketball.

D Ask and answer the questions in Exercise A with a partner.

5

Listening 1: understanding diagrams

A Look at the diagrams below and answer the questions with a partner.

1. What does each diagram show?
2. What can you predict about what you will hear?

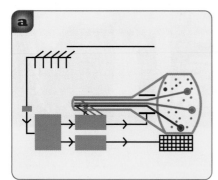

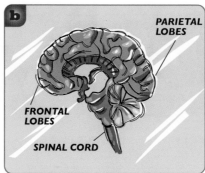

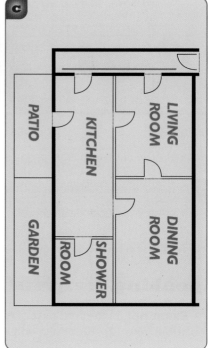

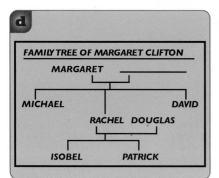

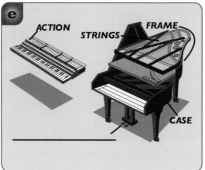

B 🎧 Listen to these extracts from five listening tasks. Match each with one of the diagrams in Exercise A.

1. _____   2. _____   3. _____   4. _____   5. _____

C 🎧 Listen again and fill in the missing information on each diagram. Use <u>no more than two words</u> for each.

D Mark these statements about completing diagrams (T) true or (F) false.

1. You can only complete the diagram if you know a lot about the topic. __
2. The labels that you have to complete are in the same order as the information that you hear. __
3. You should look at the diagram carefully before you listen. __
4. You don't need to look at the diagram while you are listening. __
5. The answers are always the exact words that you hear. __
6. You need to think about using an article (*a / an / the*) with your answers. __

 Exam tip: You might need to label a diagram for some questions in the Listening Module. The fourth part is often an academic lecture given by one speaker, and labelling diagrams is common. Sometimes you will need to write words onto a diagram and sometimes you will need to match labels to parts of a diagram.

Listening 2: practice with diagrams

A 🎧 Listen to the continuation of the lecture about the human brain. Look at the diagram before you listen. For questions 1–6, match the parts of the brain 1–6 with the parts a–f in the diagram. Write the letters in the space after each number.

1. spinal cord   __
2. cerebellum   __
3. pituitary gland __
4. brain stem   __
5. cerebrum   __
6. thalamus   __

a ———

                                                    c

                                                    d
b ———   e
                                                    f

For questions 7–14, complete the descriptions. Use <u>one word only</u> for each answer.

7. The cerebrum has _____ hemispheres.
8. The cerebrum controls voluntary _____.
9. The cerebellum helps us with balance and our understanding of _____.
    The thalamus processes information that our body senses.
10. The hypothalamus tells us when we are hungry or thirsty or when we need
    to _____.
11. The midbrain sends _____ from the brain to other parts of the nervous system.
12. The medulla oblongata regulates how quickly or slowly our _____ beats.
13. The spinal cord _____ the brain to the rest of our body.
14. Hormones from the pituitary gland regulate how quickly we _____ and how
    quickly we age.

B Check in the key on page 267. How many questions did you answer correctly?

C Tick the sentences about the listening task that are true for you and think about how you can answer more questions correctly next time.

1. Looking at the diagram and reading through the questions helped me to
    predict content.
2. The task was difficult because I didn't know anything about the topic.
3. The specialist vocabulary made the task more difficult.
4. I didn't worry about specialist vocabulary because I didn't use those words
    in the answers.
5. Most of my spelling was correct.
6. I am happy with how many questions I answered correctly.

Exam tip: Don't worry if you don't know a word you need to label a diagram. You will hear it explained on the recording. Sometimes you need to copy them onto your answer sheet, but usually you will only need to match them with a letter.

Key vocabulary in context

Use the correct form of these verbs from the listening extract to complete these sentences.

function	control	balance	process

1. The liver _____ the food and liquid that goes through our system.
2. An engine doesn't _____ without petrol.
3. This switch _____ the temperature in the room.
4. It is difficult to _____ on one leg if you close your eyes.

5

Reading 1: guessing unknown words and phrases in context

A Look only at the highlighted word and phrase in the extract below. Do you know either of them?

Having a good memory is certainly an advantage. My brother seems to have a brain with a huge capacity for new information. He remembers everything he sees or hears and has a very successful career. My brain seems to work differently – in fact, I have a memory like a sieve. Information goes straight in and straight back out.

B Read the whole extract and then talk with a partner. Try to explain the highlighted words.

C Answer the questions about the highlighted word and phrase.

1. Tick the correct definition for capacity.
   a. how long something is ___   b. how much something can hold ___
   c. how fast something travels ___

2. Tick the correct picture of a sieve.

Exam tip: When you are reading, you don't want to worry about the meaning of every word. However, some words are vital to understand the text or to answer a question correctly. You will not have a dictionary in the exam, so it is important that you learn to guess the meanings of words in context – from the other words around the word that you don't know.

D Look only at the highlighted words in these extracts. Then read the extracts and tick the correct definition of the highlighted word that follows.

1. It is difficult to understand even the gist of a conversation or talk if you have no idea of the topic before you listen. Knowing what the topic is helps you to tune in. You can then listen for key words and make more sense of the information you hear.
   Tune in means ...
   a. start to understand.   b. be an expert on a subject.
   c. do something better than other people.

2. As people grow older, they need to exercise both their bodies and their minds. Jogging or playing golf can keep people physically healthy, while reading and playing games can help them to stay alert.
   Alert means ...
   a. quick and ready to react.   b. slower than usual.   c. big and strong.

3. It was very late and I had been driving for several hours. The fact that I was so tired affected my judgement. I didn't slow down and hit the back of another car that was waiting at the traffic lights.

Judgement is ...

a. the need to drive carefully.   b. a lot of cars in the same place.

c. the ability to understand a situation.

Reading 2: understanding new words and phrases

Exam tip: You will read more quickly if you can guess new words from words that you already know. The word you know can be part of a new word or part of a new phrase or expression.

A Look at these words and phrases and guess what they mean. Compare with a partner.

| brainy | brainless | daydream | over my head | in two minds |

B Now look at the highlighted words and phrases in context and circle the correct option in the definition that follows.

1. James is the brainy one in the class. If you need help with a question, ask him.
   Brainy means **not busy / very clever**.

2. When I went on holiday last year, I left the bathroom window open. Somebody climbed in and stole my TV and DVD recorder. I can't believe I did something so brainless.
   Brainless means very **stupid / unkind**.

3. I was daydreaming and I walked right past my office. I had to turn round and walk back.
   Daydreaming means **not concentrating / thinking about important things**.

4. Tariq was sick and missed a few lectures. When his friends were talking and comparing notes, it all went over Tariq's head.
   If something goes over your head, you **listen very carefully / don't understand it at all**.

5. I'm in two minds about taking this job. It's very well paid, but it's very challenging. I'd have lots of money, but I'd have to work around sixty hours a week.
   If you are in two minds about something, **you can't make a decision / really want it**.

C Complete these sentences so that they are true for you. Then compare with a partner.

1. _____ is the brainy one in my family.

2. I was in two minds about _____.

3. Once I was daydreaming and I _____.

4. _____ is the one in my family with a memory like sieve.

Reading 3: practice with unknown words and phrases

A Look at the highlighted words and phrases on the next page but do not check them in a dictionary. You will need to guess their meanings to answer the questions.

B Read this advertisement for a course that improves your memory. For questions 1–6, decide if the information given below agrees with the information given in the advertisement. Write (T) true, (F) false or (NG) not given.

1. The course will show you new ways to remember names and faces.   __

2. Most successful people have met a world leader.   __

3. People who are very successful in business have a good memory.   __

4. None of the Memory Enhancer techniques have been tested.   __

5. Doing the course will make you more like other people.   __

6. Claire and David did the course in order to get better jobs.   __

For questions 7–12, complete the sentences below with words taken from the passage. Write no more than three words for each answer.

7. The Memory Enhancer course consists of _____ lessons.
8. You can achieve a number of _____ by registering for the course.
9. Even if people _____ you, you will remember them.
10. Phone numbers and addresses will be stored in your memory and you will be able to easily _____ them.
11. You will be able to concentrate more clearly and _____ for longer.
12. _____, you can learn how to give long talks and become more confident.

Memory Enhancer A course you'll never forget!

Learn the techniques that will help you memorize names, faces and so much more.

Successful people have very good memories! If you don't believe us, ask anyone who's met a world leader or a business tycoon. The people who really make things happen don't forget. Now you, too, can recall names and numbers in seconds – using scientifically proven techniques, Memory Enhancer is a course that will put you ahead of the rest.

'Memory Enhancer changed my life!' Claire Brown

'I've said goodbye to my diary!' David Stone

These are just two of the satisfied customers who signed up for Memory Enhancer and, in ten easy lessons, improved their lives forever.

Here are just a few of the gains you can achieve when you register right now:

- Memorize the names and faces of everyone you meet and never forget them. Impress people you've recently met by remembering them when they've forgotten you.
- Easily retrieve essential data. Have phone numbers, addresses, pin numbers and other bank details stored in your memory.
- Store dates and figures for tests and exams. Never fail another test in your life.
- Develop clearer concentration and extend the time you can focus on detail.
- Be more alert when you drive or operate machines.
- Memorize long speeches and presentations in minutes. Feel your confidence grow.
- Achieve more at work, make more money and be happier!

Enter your name and e-mail address here to register now – free of charge

Name: [   ]   E-mail: [   ]   **Register Now >>>**

C Check the key on pages 267 and 268. How many questions did you answer correctly?

D Tick the sentences about the reading task that are true for you and think about how you can answer more questions correctly next time.

1. I could guess the meaning of most highlighted words in context.
2. Guessing unknown words and phrases helped me to answer the questions.
3. I was happy with how quickly I found the information that I needed.
4. I am happy with how many questions I answered correctly.

Key vocabulary in context

Complete the sentences below.

| remember | recall | memorize |

1. I met an interesting man at the meeting, but I can't _____ / _____ his name.
2. Now, you must _____ to lock the door when you leave.
3. The best way to learn irregular verbs is to write them down and _____ them.

WB For focus on reading skills, go to Workbook page 15.

5

Writing 1: understanding instructions

A Look at the pictures and answer the questions below with a partner.

1. What do the photos have in common?
2. What is the difference between the two types of lesson?
3. What are the advantages of learning a language in a group?
4. What are the advantages of having a one-to-one lesson?

B Look at the instructions for a typical writing task. Answer the question that follows with a partner.

> As part of a class assignment, you have been asked to write about the following topic:
> Do you think it is better to learn a language in a group with other students, or is it better to have private one-to-one lessons?
> Give reasons for your answer and include any relevant examples from your experience. Write at least 250 words.

1. Do you understand what you have to do, or are there words in the instructions that you don't know?

C Look at the notes a student has made on the instructions. Is the task clearer now?

something you write for your teacher

As part of a class assignment, you have been asked to write about the following topic:
Do you think it is better to learn a language in a group with other students, or is it better to have private one-to-one lessons?
Give reasons for your answer and include any relevant examples from your experience.
Write at least 250 words. *mention things that I know from what* *'Relevant' means say only things connected*
I must say why I think something. *has happened in my life* *with the topic.*

Exam tip: In the second part of the Writing Module, the instructions will be like this or very similar. Make sure you know what the highlighted words and phrases mean.

Writing 2: presenting a balanced argument

A Look at this page from a student's notebook. Notice how he has organized points to help him plan his composition.

group lesson +	group lesson –	one-to-one +	one-to-one –
you can practise with other students	there is a lot of noise	teacher can give all his/her attention to you	it is very intensive

B Copy the table into your notebook. Then add these points to the correct column.

1. The teacher can deal immediately with any difficulties you have.
2. You have to listen to other students making a lot of mistakes.
3. You only have one other person's opinion in a discussion.
4. You meet new people and make new friends – sometimes from other cultures.
5. One-to-one lessons are very expensive.
6. If you talk in pairs, the teacher can't always hear what you are saying.
7. The teacher can go through your written work with you and explain the things you don't understand.
8. You feel nervous because the teacher watches you when you read or do an exercise.

Exam tip: If you do not have a strong opinion about a topic or you see both sides of an argument, you should write a balanced composition. Brainstorm points that support both sides of an argument and then organize them.

C Look at these two compositions. Which one do you prefer?

A

People want to learn one-to-one because the teacher can give them all his attention. In a group, the teacher must give his attention to all the students, and it takes too long. If you have a one-to-one lesson, you can tell the teacher what you want to study, but if you study in a group, you must do what other students choose to do. In a group, you must also listen to mistakes other students make, and in a one-to-one, you don't have to. If you have a one-to-one class, the teacher can listen to everything you say and correct your pronunciation and the mistakes you make. In a bigger class, the teacher cannot listen to everything that everyone says and so does not hear mistakes. If you study in a group, you can meet lots of people and make new friends, but in a one-to-one you will not meet anyone but the teacher. In a bigger class, you can play games and lessons are more fun, but in a one-to-one class, lessons are boring and intensive. Learning in a group is better for some students and learning in a one-to-one class is better for others.

B

These days, it is a big advantage to speak another language, and English is probably the most useful. Students at university are learning English, and children are learning English earlier at school. Companies want people who work for them to speak good English.

Most students learn English in a group. There is one teacher and anything from ten to thirty students. However, some people think you learn more quickly and make better progress if you have a one-to-one class and the teacher gives you all of his or her attention.

Of course, if there is only you and the teacher, you will get all the attention, and the teacher can deal with your difficulties immediately. The teacher can listen to everything you say and correct the mistakes you make. He or she can look at your written work with you and explain what you do not understand. Most importantly, you can tell the teacher what you want to learn in the lesson and ask to revise something. You don't have to do what other students choose, and you don't have to listen to their mistakes.

On the other hand, learning one-to-one is intensive, and in a discussion you only have the opinion of one other person. In a group, there are more people to share ideas with. You can play games and have fun in class. When I was studying in London, I met interesting people from many other countries. I learnt about other cultures and made new friends.

If you have plenty of time to learn a language, it might be more enjoyable in a group. If, however, you need to learn quickly, one-to-one lessons might be best. Remember, though, that one-to-one lessons are very expensive!

D Discuss with a partner what you like and don't like about the two compositions. Then look at the examiner's comments on page 268.

WB Go to Workbook page 15 for the writing task.

Speaking

A Look at this advice about the IELTS Speaking Module. Tick the advice that you think is best.

1. You must use advanced vocabulary to impress the examiner.
2. You shouldn't try to use vocabulary that you don't know properly, but you should try to use the right words and phrases for the situation.
3. The examiner doesn't listen to the vocabulary you use, so you can say whatever you like.

B Look at these questions and think about how you could answer them.

1. Is your job ever challenging?
2. Do you have to think creatively in your work or studies?
3. Do you have any hobbies that involve a lot of thinking?

C Look at the answers that some students give to the questions in Exercise B. For each, tick the answer that you think is better.

1. Is your job ever challenging?
   Student A: Yes, I must think very much about what to do. ___
   Student B: Yes, I have to make important decisions every day. ___
2. Do you have to think creatively in your work or studies?
   Student A: Yes, I must think hard to make things in my mind. ___
   Student B: Yes, I have to use my imagination all the time. ___
3. Do you have any hobbies that involve a lot of thinking?
   Student A: Well, I play golf, and to play well you really have to concentrate. ___
   Student B: Well, I play golf, and I must think very hard all the time. ___

D Ask and answer the questions in Exercise C with a partner. Choose your vocabulary carefully.

Vocabulary

A Correct the spelling mistakes in these words.

1. concider _____
2. pridiction _____
3. immagination _____
4. consentrate _____
5. disision _____
6. memary _____

B 🎧 Listen and mark the main stress on the words in Exercise A above.

C Fill the gaps with a word made from the root words in the box.

1. All this noise is affecting my _____.
2. Come on – use your _____.
3. I don't really know enough to make a _____.
4. I need to be very _____ in my job.
5. Mind-mapping helps you to think _____.

concentrate
imagine
judge
create
create

Errors

A There are errors in all of these sentences (sometimes more than one). Correct them.

1. I'm sorry. I haven't done a decision yet.
2. Sorry, I'm not remembering your name.
3. I think I won't pass this test.
4. Are you sure you recalled to close all the windows?
5. I'm looking forward at the weekend.

5

Listening

A 🎧 You will hear someone giving a talk about how mind-mapping can help you think more clearly.

For questions 1–6, listen and complete the notes. Write <u>no more than three words or a number</u> for each answer.

1. You can think _____ if you use mind maps.
2. Mind-mapping helps you to solve _____ in a creative way.
3. Drawing a mind map will help you see how parts of a topic or subject _____.
4. Mind-mapping is quite different from conventional _____.
5. By seeing the 'shape' of a topic, you will know which individual points within it are _____.
6. Mind maps are compact, so it is easier to _____ what you have written down.

For questions 7–14, label the time management mind map below. Write <u>no more than three words or a number</u> for each answer.

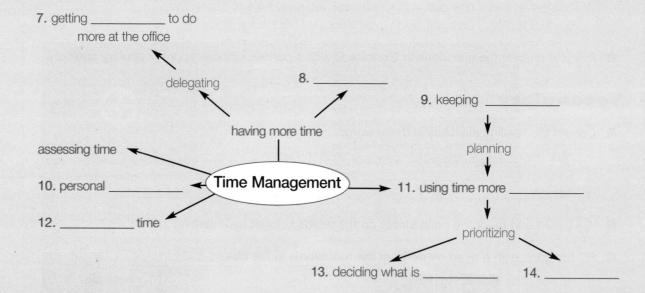

7. getting _____ to do more at the office

delegating

8. _____

9. keeping _____

having more time

planning

assessing time

10. personal _____

Time Management

11. using time more _____

12. _____ time

prioritizing

13. deciding what is _____

14. _____

Reading

 Exam tip: In this exam practice task, the text is authentic (real and not made easier for students) and so quite challenging. The questions, however, are a little easier. You should identify the key words and phrases that provide answers and guess their meanings from the context.

A Read this information page about an organization called Mensa.

For questions 1 and 2, choose the correct letter a, b or c.

1. You can only be a member of Mensa if you are ...
    a. a scientist or a doctor.   b. very intelligent.   c. very tall.

2. Mensa ...
    a. is a political organization.   b. only accepts people from some countries and religions.
    c. is not concerned with where its members are from or what they believe.

For questions 3–5, choose <u>three</u> letters a–f.

What are Mensa's objectives?
    a. to know who is very intelligent and to help those people use their intelligence well
    b. for people with high intelligence to get better jobs
    c. for people to understand more about intelligence
    d. to help people who are not intelligent to learn
    e. to make the world a safer place for people to live
    f. for members to enjoy being part of the organization

3. ___   4. ___   5. ___

For questions 6–10, decide if the information given below agrees with the information given on the information page. Write (T) true, (F) false or (NG) not given, if you think the answer is not in the text.

6. Most members of Mensa know each other. ___
7. Members of Mensa all work in similar professions. ___
8. Mensa has some very young and some very old members. ___
9. Intelligent people enjoy communicating with other intelligent people. ___
10. Mensa is a very serious organization for very serious people. ___

What is Mensa?

Mensa was founded in England in 1946 by Roland Berrill, a barrister, and Dr Lance Ware, a scientist and lawyer. They had the idea of forming a society for bright people, the only qualification for membership of which was a high IQ. The original aims were, as they are today, to create a society that is non-political and free from all racial or religious distinctions.

The society's official objectives are:

- to identify and foster human intelligence for the benefit of humanity
- to encourage research in the nature, characteristics and uses of intelligence
- to provide a stimulating intellectual and social environment for its members

The society welcomes people from every walk of life whose IQ is in the top two per cent of the population, with the objective of enjoying each other's company and participating in a wide range of social and cultural activities.

Mensa members come from all walks of life and almost every job and profession. Every age group is represented, from pre-school children to members in their eighties, nineties and beyond!

What almost all Mensans have in common is the desire to make contact with other lively minds – in person, in print or online – and enjoy being both entertained and informed.

The essence of Mensa membership is fun and stimulation for the individual. Mensa members read voraciously and enjoy the widest range of interests, leisure pursuits and hobbies.

The atmosphere at all Mensa meetings is welcoming and convivial. Most Mensans are friendly and sensitive people who welcome the chance to make new friends and expand their horizons.

Click here to view our Frequently Asked Questions.

Review 1

Speaking and Vocabulary

A Talk with a partner. Answer these questions about the Speaking Module of the IELTS exam.

1. How many parts are there in the Speaking Module?
2. How long does each part last?
3. What happens in each part? How are the parts different from one another?

B Look at some comments made by students who are studying for the IELTS exam. Tick the ones that you most agree with.

☐ 'I think the first part of the speaking exam, when the examiner asks about your life, is quite easy. It's more difficult to think about what to say when you have to read a card.'

☐ 'I prefer the second part of the speaking because reading the card gives you ideas and you have time to plan what to say.'

☐ 'I don't like the third part of the speaking exam. You have to think quickly and you don't always have the words to express your opinion.'

☐ 'The third part of the Speaking Module is the most challenging but the most interesting. I can tell the examiner what I think – not just give him facts.'

☐ 'I try to learn as much vocabulary as I can – especially very common expressions. I think having the words is more important than being perfectly accurate in the speaking exam.'

☐ 'When I learn new words, I make sure I can pronounce them correctly. If the examiner can't understand what I say, he will get bored and give me a low grade.'

☐ 'It's important that you keep it simple. You should only say what you know you can say. If you don't know how to use the present perfect continuous, you shouldn't try to.'

C Write two comments of your own. Then compare with a partner.

D Write important words and phrases that you have learnt so far under each heading.

family and friends

_____
_____
_____
_____

stages of life

_____
_____
_____
_____

learning

_____
_____
_____
_____

expressing a preference

_____
_____
_____
_____

my words and phrases

work and jobs

_____
_____
_____
_____

achievement and success

_____
_____
_____

thinking

_____
_____
_____

Listening

A Answer these questions with a partner.

1. How many parts are there in the Listening Module of the IELTS exam?
2. How many questions do you think there are in total?
3. How are the various parts of the Listening Module different from one another?
4. Does the Listening Module gradually become more challenging?
5. What type of tasks have you practised so far?

B Tick the statement about listening in each pair that is true for you.

1. A I often understand the gist of a talk or conversation but not the details.
   B I can often hear details, but don't really understand what the people are talking about.
2. A It's easier to listen to just one person giving a talk.
   B I prefer listening to a conversation between two or more people. The context is clearer.
3. A I don't like writing when I'm trying to listen. I prefer it when I need to circle a letter or tick a box.
   B I don't mind writing when I'm listening if it's just a number or a name that is spelt for me.
4. A It's difficult to catch the words when I have to listen and complete notes.
   B I can usually catch the words I need, but then I don't have time to write them.
5. A I don't like looking at maps or diagrams when I'm trying to listen.
   B I like tasks with a map or diagram because the context is clearer.
6. A My listening has improved, and now I answer more questions correctly.
   B My listening is not really improving. I still answer a lot of questions incorrectly.

Reading

A Answer these questions with a partner.

1. How many sections are there in the Reading Module?
2. How many passages will you have to read?
3. How many questions are there in total?
4. How long do you have to answer all the questions?
5. How are the texts in the Reading Module different from one another?
6. Do the texts gradually become more challenging?

B Answer these questions with the same partner.

1. What is the difference between **skimming** and **scanning**? Give an example of each.
2. What is the **source** of a text? Give an example.
3. What is the **function** of a text? Give an example.
4. What is **paraphrasing**? How could you paraphrase *this question isn't so easy*?
5. What do we mean when we say *understand a new word or phrase **in context***?

C Give yourself a score out of five for the progress you are making with each of these reading skills.

skimming / reading for gist   ___
scanning / reading for specific information   ___
general reading speed   ___
understanding new words and phrases in context   ___
recognizing paraphrased language   ___

D Tick the statement below that is true for you.

A I am happy that my reading has improved since I started this course.
B I don't think my reading has improved since I started this course.

Task-type tip: There are some listening and reading tasks that you haven't practised yet.

Writing

A Circle the correct option in these statements about the Writing Module of the IELTS exam.

1. You will have to write *one / two / three* compositions.
2. You have *30 minutes / one hour / two hours* to write the compositions.
3. In the first part of the Writing Module, you will have to *describe charts and graphs / write a story / write a letter*.
4. For the first part of the Writing Module, you must write *100 / 150 / 200* words.
5. In the second part of the Writing Module, you will have to *present an argument or express an opinion / describe a person or place / write a report*.
6. For the second part of the Writing Module, you must write *150 / 200 / 250* words.

B When you write, you must consider all of the points below. For now, which <u>two</u> points are most important? Tick them.

1. You must answer the question and make points that are relevant to the question.
2. You must make sure that what you write is grammatically correct.
3. You must use a range of vocabulary and choose the right words and phrases.
4. You must organize your composition so that the examiner can read it easily and understand what you want to say.
5. You must use the right number of paragraphs and the right linking words and phrases.
6. You must use the right register – your writing must be appropriately formal or informal.
7. You must make sure that all your spelling is correct.
8. You must make sure that all your punctuation is correct.

C Answer these questions with a partner.

1. Which of the two compositions is easier for you to write?
2. How long will you spend writing the first composition?
3. How long will you spend writing the second composition?
4. Do you write too much or not enough for the first composition? Why?
5. Do you write too much or not enough for the second composition? Why?
6. Is your writing improving? Tick the aspects of your writing that have improved recently.

☐ understanding the question and knowing what to write
☐ planning and noting down ideas
☐ organizing ideas
☐ using paragraphs
☐ linking ideas together
☐ using the right register
☐ using a wider range of vocabulary
☐ spelling
☐ punctuation

What next?

You've only completed a third of the course, so don't worry if you haven't improved all aspects of your English. There is plenty of time to learn more and practise the skills and tasks that you find difficult. Here are some things that you should do now. Decide which ones you'd like to do first. Number them.

☐ Find as many opportunities to speak English as you can. If you have friends or relatives who speak good English, practise with them once or twice a week. Practise with other students in your class when you have a break or after the lesson. Practise talking about the topics that you will have to talk about in the exam.

☐ If listening is difficult, ask to borrow CDs and listen at home or on the bus or train. Listen to English that is at your level to give you confidence, and listen to English that is a little more challenging so that you know what to expect in the exam. Listen to extracts which have a tapescript so that, after you listen, you can read and check what you didn't understand and why you didn't understand it.

☐ Read as much as you can. Borrow books from a library and read articles in magazines and newspapers. Try to read any letters or documents in English that are related to your job. Read texts that are at your level to give you confidence, and read texts that are a little more challenging so that you know what to expect in the exam. When you read, notice how the text is organized. Look at how paragraphs and topic sentences are used and how words and phrases are used to introduce ideas. Practise reading without a dictionary so that you can guess the meaning of new words and phrases in context.

☐ Note down new vocabulary and make sure you revise it. Note down words and phrases that will help you talk about what is important to you. Note down words and phrases that will help you in the reading and listening modules and words and phrases that you can use when you write. Check the word and phrase list for each of the units you have studied in the Course Book.

☐ Practise writing sentences and short paragraphs to improve your grammatical accuracy, spelling and punctuation. Write complete compositions to practise organizing and linking. Do the writing tasks in the Course Book and Workbook, and ask your teacher to give you more writing tasks if you need more practice. Look at model answers to exam questions and notice how students answer questions. When you learn important new words and phrases, make sure you remember how to spell them.

Go on to the next section of the Course Book. Make sure you practise all aspects of your English, but focus on what you are having problems with. Don't worry if you don't make progress in all areas at the same time. It is much easier to learn English if you enjoy it!

6 Place

Vocabulary 1: places

A Look at the map and the photos and answer these questions with a partner.

1. Do you know any of the places shown?
2. What do you think each person will say about where he or she lives?

B Check the following words and phrases and predict which person will use them.

| huge city | tiny village | large port | small town | tourist destination |
| island | seaside resort | rural | capital | economic centre | fishing village |

C 🎧 Listen and tick the words and phrases as you hear them.

> **Grammar check**
>
> Remember, the *present perfect* is used to talk about your life until now. Here are four ways to say the same thing. Complete each with a word from below.
>
> | whole | since | always | all |
>
> 1. I've lived in Cairo _____ my life. 2. I've lived in Cairo my _____ life.
> 3. I've _____ lived in Cairo. 4. I've lived in Cairo _____ I was born.
>
> Practise saying the sentences.

Speaking 1: describing where you live

Exam tip: In the first part of the Speaking Module, the examiner might ask you about where you live. You should describe it and express an opinion.

A Think about words and phrases you would use to describe the place where you live. Talk with a partner about where you live.

Vocabulary 2: describing places

A Match the adjectives 1–5 with their opposites a–e.

1.	big	a.	modern
2.	busy	b.	boring
3.	old	c.	small
4.	beautiful	d.	quiet
5.	exciting	e.	ugly

B Match the adjectives 1–5 with their meanings a–e.

1.	It's a very **impressive** sight.	a.	too dirty
2.	The centre is very **crowded**.	b.	very nice to look at
3.	The city centre is quite **historic**.	c.	too many people
4.	The city centre is so **congested**.	d.	very old
5.	The air in the city centre is **polluted**.	e.	too much traffic

Grammar check

We use *superlative adjectives* to compare one thing with all the other things of its type. *The biggest city in the world.*

What are the rules for forming *superlative adjectives*?

Write the superlative form of these adjectives.

1. old _____   2. hot _____   3. ugly _____
4. modern _____   5. exciting _____

We use *very* before an adjective to make it more extreme. *It's a very nice city.*

We use *too* when we don't like something or there is a problem. *It's too dirty.*

We use *much* before an uncountable noun. *There's too much traffic.*
We use *many* before a countable noun. *There are too many people.*

Watch out!
typical errors

It is the most big city in my country. ✗
It is the bigger city in my country. ✗
It is biggest city in my country. ✗
My city is too beautiful. ✗
There are too much people. ✗

Pronunciation check

The ~*est* at the end of superlatives is pronounced /ɪst/. The /t/ is not pronounced clearly in fast natural speech, especially when the following noun begins with a consonant.

🎧 Listen and practise these phrases.
1. the biggest city   2. the tallest building   3. the busiest street

The /t/ at the end of *most* is not pronounced clearly in fast natural speech, especially when the following adjective begins with a consonant.

🎧 Listen and practise these phrases.
1. most beautiful   2. most congested

Speaking 2: talking about towns and cities

A Here are two typical cards for part 2 of the Speaking Module. Work with a partner – one of you is A, the other is B. You have a minute to think about it and make notes.

A

> **Describe a town or city that you really like.**
> **Say ...**
> - which town or city it is.
> - where it is.
> - when you went there.
> - why you like it so much.

B

> **Describe a town or city that you don't like.**
> **Say ...**
> - which town or city it is.
> - where it is.
> - when you went there.
> - what you don't like about it.

B Take it in turns to speak about what's on your card for about two minutes.

6

Listening 1: maps and plans

A 🎧 Listen and match the extracts with the maps.

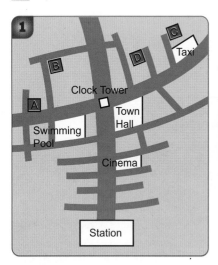

B 🎧 Listen to the first extract and match the letters on the map with the places below.

1. Hastings   __   2. Isle of Wight   __   3. Brighton   __
4. Bournemouth __   5. Tunbridge Wells __   6. Eastbourne   __

C 🎧 Listen to the second extract and complete each space with <u>one</u> word.

1. The Alhambra _____ is in the city of Granada.
2. The town of Ronda has a famous _____ bridge.
3. The Sierra Nevada is a _____ range and popular ski resort.
4. Much of the north of Andalusia is a National Park and _____.
   There are some large _____ in the area.

D 🎧 Listen to the third extract and circle Leo's apartment on the map.

Listening 2: listening for specific information

 Exam tip: When you are listening for specific information, the speaker will often repeat information you need to answer a question. If you don't catch something, listen carefully to see if the speaker repeats the word or phrase you need.

A 🎧 Listen again. Notice examples of a speaker repeating information.

B Look at the tapescript on page 289 and highlight examples of a speaker repeating information.

Listening 3: listening for specific information

A 🎧 Listen to a man talking to a group of people at a weekend work conference in a hotel.

For questions 1–4, choose <u>four</u> correct statements from A–H.

In the hotel…

|A| there are three bars. |B| there is a roof terrace.
|C| the main restaurant is for guests only. |D| guests can have coffee and snacks on the third floor.

|E| there are nice views from all the rooms. |F| there is a 24-hour gym and health club.
|G| there is a swimming pool. |H| guests must pay to use the sauna.

1. __   2. __   3. __   4. __

For questions 5–10, match the places with the letters on the map. You do not need to use all the letters on the map.

5. swimming pool __   6. boating lake __
7. cinema __   8. The White Orchid – Chinese restaurant __
9. Leonardo's – Spanish and Mexican restaurant __   10. The Pink Coconut – jazz bar __

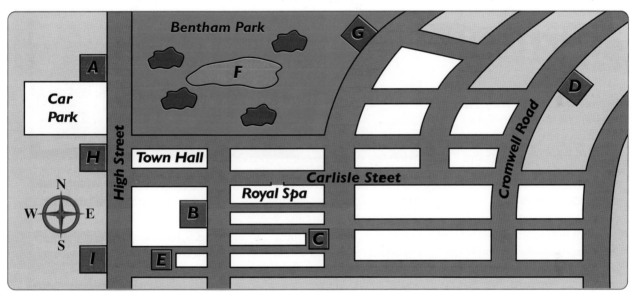

B Check the key on page 268. How many questions did you answer correctly?

C Tick the sentences about the listening task that are true for you and think about how you can answer more questions correctly next time.

1. Looking at the map and reading through the questions helped me to predict content.
2. I looked at the map while I was listening to questions 5–10.
3. I heard the speaker repeat some of the information I needed.
4. I am happy with how many questions I answered correctly.

Key vocabulary in context

Fill each space with the correct preposition.

1. ____ the north / south / east / west 2. a town ____ the coast
3. an island ____ the coast of … 4. the first ____ the right / left
5. next ____ the car park 6. ____ the corner
7. ____ the middle of the park / the high street 8. ____ the end / the top / the bottom of the street

> **Watch out!**
> **typical errors**
> It's opposite to / of / from the park. ✗
> *Opposite* is a preposition so there's no need for another one!

6

Reading 1: understanding the function of paragraphs

A Have you visited any of these European cities? What do you know about them?

Barcelona   Paris   London   Prague   Venice   Rome   Athens   Istanbul

B Which of the cities in Exercise A would you most like to visit? Why?

C You will read a text about Barcelona. What do you think the text will mention?

D Read this text and check.

BARCELONA

Barcelona is the second largest city in Spain and the country's main industrial centre. The city is the capital of Catalonia, a large region in the north-east which borders with France. It is an important Mediterranean port.

At 100 sq km, Barcelona is quite small, but the industrial area around the city adds another 500 sq km to the metropolitan area. The city is divided into two parts. The Old City faces the sea and is where the historical buildings, such as the cathedral, are located. A modern area, *the Eixample*, surrounds the Old City. Located here are more famous buildings, such as the church of *La Sagrada Familia*.

Barcelona is one of the most important cultural centres in Europe. There are six universities and a number of other colleges. There are several museums, including the *El Museu Picasso* (The Picasso Museum), and Spain's most important theatre, *El Gran Teatre del Liceu*. Barcelona is also the home of one of the world's most famous football teams.

Today, Barcelona is one of the most visited cities in the world. Tourists come to see the architecture and enjoy the city's busy lifestyle. The people of Catalonia hope that Barcelona will continue to be successful into the 21st century.

E Answer these questions with a partner.

  1. How many paragraphs does the text have?
  2. Why do writers use paragraphs to break up a text?

F Circle the correct option in these statements about using paragraphs.

  1. People write in paragraphs to *make a text look nice / give a text logical structure*.
  2. Paragraphs break a long text into chunks so that it is *easier / more difficult* to read.
  3. Each paragraph should deal with *one subject / three or four subjects*.
  4. You should start a new paragraph when you *change the subject or make a new point / think the paragraph you are writing is too long*.
  5. Paragraphs in a text must all be *the same length / can be different lengths*.
  6. The first sentence of a paragraph is usually *not very important / the most important*.

G Read the text about Barcelona again. Look at how the paragraphs give the text structure.

Reading 2: understanding topic sentences

A Read the text and decide where the first line of each paragraph fits.

1. Modern Venice is trying to overcome many problems.
2. Venice is a city and large port in the north east of Italy.
3. There are no cars or trucks on the islands of Venice.
4. Tourism is very important to the economy of Venice.
5. Around 400 bridges connect the islands that make up Venice.

Venice – Queen of the Adriatic

__ It is the capital of the province, also called Venice. Venice is built on over 100 islands created by around 150 canals in the lagoon at the top of Adriatic Sea.

_5_ A single road and rail link connects the city to the mainland. This link is protected from the sea by man-made sandbanks. One large canal, the Grand Canal, runs from north-west to south-east and divides the city into two halves.

__ The bridges are for pedestrians only. For hundreds of years, the most common method of transport was the gondola, a traditional boat that is controlled by a single oar. Today, these boats are mainly for tourists. Small motor boats transport local people and produce.

__ The city is considered one of the most beautiful in the world, and tourists come in their millions to see the canals, the squares, the architecture and the art museums. There is a popular film festival every year. The islands of Murano and Burano are famous for glass products and Venetian lace.

__ Because the ground is soft, the city is sinking and buildings need to be made stronger. The area has flooded a number of times, and the sea has caused huge damage. The population is slowly leaving the city as jobs become more difficult to find. Some people are afraid that Venice will be a city where nobody lives – a place only for tourists to come and photograph.

B Look at the first sentence of each paragraph again. Tick the statement below that is true.

1. The first sentence of a paragraph should tell the reader what the rest of the paragraph will be about.
2. The first sentence of a paragraph does not need to be related to what is in the rest of the paragraph.

Exam tip: The first sentence of a paragraph is usually the topic sentence. This means that it tells the reader what the rest of the paragraph will be about. Sentences in the rest of the paragraph should support the topic sentence. If a sentence is not related to the topic sentence, the writer should start a new paragraph.

Reading 3: practice with paragraphs and topic sentences

Exam tip: Reading and understanding the topic sentence will help you to read more quickly. When you read for gist, you can sometimes skip the rest of the paragraph if the topic sentence is clear. When you are doing the Reading Module, understanding the topic sentence will help you to know where to look back to find answers.

A Read only the topic sentence of each paragraph in the text on the next page, and get an idea of what the text is about.

B Read questions 1–5 and guess which paragraph the information will be found in.

C Read the text and answer all the questions.

For questions 1–5, say in which paragraph the following information is found.
Write the letter in the space.

1. A lot of people come to buy things. __   2. People go to Dubai for different reasons. __
3. There are some very nice things to look at. __   4. Dubai has grown in size. __
5. There are a lot of interesting things to do. __

There's Something for Everyone in Dubai

A Dubai is the second largest of the emirates which make up the United Arab Emirates. In the 1950s, it was a tiny coastal village. Now it is a huge modern city with a population of over 700,000. It offers an excellent modern lifestyle and is known around the world as a top tourist destination.

B Dubai has something for everyone. Holidaymakers can enjoy a relaxing break, and people looking for adventure can find something new and exciting. The excellent hotels and facilities make it a popular place for business conferences and exhibitions.

C Dubai offers many unusual holiday experiences. Visitors can go on a desert safari or drive in the sand dunes in a four-wheel-drive. They can try sand skiing, watch camel racing or learn how to hunt with falcons. More relaxing is a cruise in a wooden dhow in the Gulf or a visit to the old city markets.

D There are many opportunities to take photographs. The traditional architecture is amazing, and there are many magnificent palaces and mosques. Visitors can visit a Bedouin village and see camels and herds of goats. There are beautiful desert oases and the best sunsets in the world.

E Many people come to Dubai for the shopping. Visitors enjoy everything from modern malls to traditional markets. Low customs duties mean that many products are less expensive than products bought in other countries. While Dubai's official language is Arabic, many shopkeepers speak English. *Bur Juman Centre* and *Al Ghurair Centre* are places that every shopper should try.

For questions 6–11, complete the sentences below with words taken from the passage. Write <u>no more than three words or a number</u> for each answer.

6. More than _____ people now live in Dubai.
7. Some visitors come to Dubai to relax, while others come for _____.
8. International companies arrange their _____ in Dubai because it has such good facilities.
9. Cruising in a wooden dhow is _____ than activities like sand skiing.
10. Visitors like to _____ of the many beautiful sights during their trip.
11. Many products are less expensive in Dubai because of the _____.

D Check the key on page 268. How many questions did you answer correctly?

E Tick the sentences about the reading task that are true for you and think about how you can answer more questions correctly next time.

1. Reading the topic sentence at the start of each paragraph helped me to read more quickly.
2. Reading the topic sentences helped me to guess where information would be.
3. I was happy with how quickly I answered questions 1–5.
4. I knew where to find the information to answer questions 6–11.

WB For focus on reading skills, go to Workbook page 18.

Writing 1: preparing for the task

A Look at the pictures. What do they say about city life and country life?

B In the first column, mark the comments (CL) if the person is talking about city life and (CO) if they are talking about country life. Look up any new words.

1. 'There are museums and galleries and more choice of bars and restaurants.' ____ ____
2. 'It's so nice to see trees and fields instead of concrete.' ____ ____
3. 'Travelling around on public transport can be very stressful.' ____ ____
4. 'It's much too quiet. There's nothing to do.' ____ ____
5. 'There are more jobs and they are better paid.' ____ ____
6. 'The air is much fresher.' ____ ____
7. 'I don't always feel safe walking around, especially at night.' ____ ____
8. 'You always see the same people. You don't meet anyone new.' ____ ____

C In the second column, mark each comment (P) if it is positive and (N) if it is negative.

D Which of the comments in Exercise B can you use to talk about your life? Compare with a partner.

E Look at the instructions for a typical writing task. Then answer the questions with a partner.

> Do you think life is more enjoyable if you live in a big city, or is country life the better option? Give reasons for your answer and include any relevant examples from your experience. Write at least 250 words.

1. Is it an easy topic to write about? Do you have something to say about it?
2. Would it be better to express a strong opinion or write a balanced argument?

Writing 2: paragraphs and topic sentences

A You have decided to write a balanced argument. Here are some ideas for what should go in each paragraph. Put them into a logical order. There is not one correct order.

__ Say what is bad about living in the country.
__ Say what is bad about living in a big city.
__ Say what is good about living in a big city.
__ Express your own opinion and say which option you prefer.
__ Show that you understand the question and say that different people like different lifestyles.
__ Say what is good about living in the country.

B Read a student's composition. Is the order the same as yours?

In today's world, more and more people are living in cities. Most people move to cities to find work or to do a job that is better paid. Some people really enjoy city life, but many people would prefer to live in the country if they could.

_____ There are museums and galleries and more places to enjoy your leisure time and do sports. There is more choice of bars and restaurants and generally more nightlife. Most people prefer shopping in a city.

_____ Travelling on public transport is difficult and the roads are usually very busy. Because of the traffic, the air is polluted and the streets are not so clean. In my experience, city centres are not always safe, and people feel nervous walking around at night.

_____ because there are trees and fields and they don't have to look at concrete buildings all the time. Life is generally slower and there is more time to relax. The air is much fresher and people feel that their lifestyle is healthier.

On the other hand, _____ People get bored of seeing the same people every day and not meeting any new people. As I said, it is difficult to find a well paid job and most people do not want to travel to and from a city every day.

Personally, _____ There is more to do and I can meet more interesting people. I can have a better job and make more money. When I am older and have children, I might want to live in the country and enjoy a quieter life.

C Write the topic sentences in the correct spaces.

1. People like living in the country
2. Everyone would agree that there is more to do in a big city.
3. In today's world, more and more people are living in cities.
4. while I am young, I want to live in a big city.
5. However, city life is stressful.
6. country life can be too quiet, and sometimes there is nothing to do.

Exam tip: Notice that a topic sentence doesn't have to be a complete sentence and that short phrases can introduce a topic sentence. You will learn more about introducing your opinions later.

The sentences that come after the topic sentence in a paragraph are supporting sentences. They should explain the topic sentence or give examples.

D Look at the supporting sentences in the composition above.

WB Go to Workbook page 19 for the writing task.

Speaking

A Look again at Speaking 2 from this unit. Remember how you answered the question on your card.

B Now look at these follow-up questions. Mark them (E) easy to answer or (D) difficult to answer.

1. Which city in the world would you most like to visit? ___
2. Why do so many people live in cities? ___
3. Are some cities becoming too big? ___
4. Do you enjoy city life or would you like to live somewhere quieter? ___

C 🎧 Listen to some students giving good answers to the questions.

D 🎧 Read the answers below. Then listen again and fill in the missing words.

1. I'd really like to go to Beijing and see the Forbidden City. I _____ China is a very exciting place to visit.
2. I think they have to live in cities because of their job. In Thailand, people _____ and come to Bangkok because it is the _____ to find work.
3. Yes, I think so. I don't know the biggest city, but Mexico City and Shanghai are huge. There are a lot of _____ and pollution is a problem. The capital of my country is Istanbul. It is very crowded, and it is very expensive to _____ an apartment.
4. I really enjoy living in Tehran. The university is the best in Iran, and I meet people from all over the country. There is much more to do in Tehran than there is in _____.

E Ask and answer the questions in Exercise B with a partner.

Vocabulary

A Answer these questions with words from the unit. Focus on your spelling.

1. What is the most important city of a country called?   the _____
2. What is smaller, a town or a village?   a _____
3. What do we call a country or part of a country that is surrounded by water? an _____
4. What do we call a town or village that a lot of people visit for a holiday?   a _____
5. What is the opposite of pretty or beautiful?   _____
6. Which verb means to go under water?   _____

B Fill the gaps with a word made from the root words in the box.

1. The old city centre is very _____.
2. _____ is a problem in most big cities these days.
3. There are some _____ buildings in the city centre.
4. More and more _____ are coming to Dubai.
5. _____ is important to the economy of many countries.

| history |
| pollute |
| impress |
| tour |
| tour |

Errors

A There are errors in all of these sentences. Correct them.

1. I live in this city all my life.
2. London is the more big city in England.
3. Venice is most beautiful city in Italy.
4. There is too much people in most cities.
5. There is too many traffic in my city.
6. The college is opposite to the park.

6

Listening

A 🎧 You will hear an estate agent (a person who sells houses) showing a man and woman a house.

For questions 1–5, listen and complete the notes in the estate agent's diary.

Name(s) of client(s):   Mr and Mrs (1) _____

Time of appointment: (2) _____

Property address: (3) _____ Park Avenue
(4) _____ Havelock Road
(5) _____ Whitely Road

For questions 6–8, write the letter of the three houses the estate agent shows the couple. The first house is number 6, the second one is number 7 and the third one is number 8.

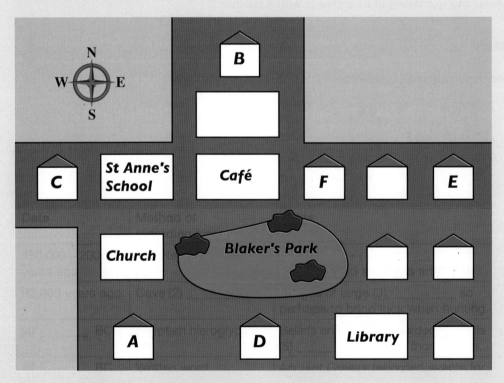

6. ____   7. ____   8. ____

For questions 9–12, write the rooms into the spaces below.

9. _____
10. downstairs _____
11. _____
12. _____

```
┌─────────────────────────────┐
│   ┌─────────────────────┐    │
│   │      GARDEN         │    │
│   ├─────────────────────┤    │
│   │      PATIO          │    │
│   │        ┌─┐    ┌──┐  │    │
│   │  12    │ │    11     │    │
│   │        │ │    ┌──────│    │
│   │        └─┘    10     │    │
│   │                      │    │
│   │  HALL         9      │    │
│   └─────────────────────┘    │
└─────────────────────────────┘
```

B 🎧 **Listen to a lecturer talking to a group of students about what makes a good city. For questions 13–20, choose the correct answer a, b or c.**

13. The speaker says that when people arrive in a city for the first time, they ...
    a. want to see big buildings.
    b. expect to see mountains and rivers.
    c. soon know what they like and do not like.

14. The speaker says that people in cities ...
    a. want different options when they move around.
    b. want to move around the city by car.
    c. think that public transport is slow.

15. The speaker says that a lot of people ...
    a. like their job.
    b. live in nice houses.
    c. become richer because they own a house.

16. The speaker says that people choose to live ...
    a. in a place they really like.
    b. somewhere that is not too expensive for them.
    c. where there are a lot of other people.

17. The speaker says that people are not happy if ...
    a. they feel unsafe in their homes.
    b. the area they live in is unsafe.
    c. they spend too much time at home.

18. The speaker says that ...
    a. people want different things from the place they live.
    b. everyone wants to know their neighbours.
    c. everyone wants to meet new people.

19. The speaker ...
    a. says that Zurich is the best place to live because it is small.
    b. says that Zurich is the best place to live because people are rich.
    c. does not say why Zurich is the best place to live.

20. The speaker ...
    a. says that everyone would like to live in Switzerland.
    b. thinks that what works in Switzerland can work in other parts of the world.
    c. suggests that it will be difficult to make very big cities nice places to live.

7 Movement

Vocabulary 1: methods of transport

A Label the pictures with the correct phrases.

| drive | travel by bus | travel by train | take a taxi | ride a bicycle | travel by boat | fly |

Speaking 1: saying how frequently you do something

A Match the expressions 1–6 with the explanations a–f.

1. I **always** drive to work.
2. I **usually** go to work by bus.
3. I **(very) often** travel by train.
4. I **occasionally** take a taxi.
5. I **rarely / don't very often** travel by boat.
6. I **never** ride a bike.

a. I do not do this at all.
b. I do this a lot.
c. I sometimes do this but not a lot.
d. I do it this way more than any other way.
e. I do not do this any other way.
f. I do not do this a lot.

B Match these phrases with some of the phrases 1–6 in Exercise A. There is more than one correct answer.

| three times a week | once a month | every day | twice a year |

> **Grammar check**
> *Adverbs of frequency* come before the main verb.
> *I sometimes walk to work. / I never travel by boat.*
>
> *Time expressions* like *every day / once a week / twice a month* usually come at the end of the sentence.
> *I go to the gym twice a week.*
>
> When we use *always* and *usually*, we have to give more information for it to have meaning.
> *I always / usually play football on Tuesday.* ✓
> NOT *I always / usually play football.* ✗

C Talk to a partner about how often you travel by the methods of transport in Vocabulary 1A.

D Do you ever use any methods of transport that have not been mentioned?

Vocabulary 2: ways of travelling

A Use a dictionary and match these words and phrases with the pictures on the previous page. Some of them can go with more than one picture.

| journey   wait in a queue   motorway   get seasick   take off   land   economical |

Speaking 2: answering questions

A Look at these questions and think about how you would answer them.

1. Do you enjoy driving? —
2. Do you like flying? —
3. Do you often use public transport? —
4. Do many people in your country ride bicycles? —
5. Have you ever made a long journey by boat? —

Watch out!
typical errors
Do you enjoy to drive? ✗

B 🎧 Listen to some students answering the questions. Match each speaker with a question.

C Ask and answer the questions in Exercise A with a partner.

Speaking 3: expressing opinions

A Look at these questions that an examiner might ask during the third part of the speaking exam. In the first column, mark each one (E) easy to answer or (D) difficult to answer.

1. Is there a good public transport system in your country? __ __
2. How can we make people use cars less? __ __
3. Is it a good idea to ban cars from city centres? __ __
4. Are too many people flying these days? __ __
5. How will people travel around in the future? __ __

B 🎧 Listen to some students answering the questions. In the second column, match each speaker with a question.

Exam tip: The examiner doesn't expect you to say something really clever to answer a question. He doesn't expect you to have a solution to a problem. You can use quite simple language and still give a good answer.

C Look at the tapescript on page 292. Notice how each speaker expresses an opinion using quite simple language.

D Walk around the class. Ask and answer the questions in Exercise A.

7

Listening 1: completing a summary

A Talk with a partner. Answer the questions.

1. Do you drive your own car?
2. Add up how much it costs to keep a car on the road. Check the meaning of these words and phrases.

| insurance | road tax | annual service | repairs | fall in value |

B Look at the picture and guess the answers to the questions with a partner.

1. What is special about the car?
2. Who uses the car?
3. Why do people choose to use a car like this?

C 🎧 Listen to the first part of a talk about belonging to a car club. Answer the questions in Exercise B.

Question-type tip: You have practised completing sentences or notes as you listen. Sometimes you will complete a summary of a talk or part of a talk.

D 🎧 Listen again and complete the summary of the talk below. Use <u>no more than three words or a number</u> in each space.

If you live in a city, belonging to a car club is very economical. Using a club car costs much less each year than running your (1) _____. It costs a lot of money to keep a car on the road, but you may only use it at (2) _____. Insurance, road tax, servicing and repairs are all expensive, and many people have to pay for (3) _____ on top. The average car is worth (4) _____ less at the end of each year. Anyone can join a car club and use a car whenever they like. They can collect a car from close to where they live and, at the end of their journey, leave it in (5) _____.

Exam tip: As you know, you will not always hear the exact words and phrases that you see in the summary. You need to look at the words before and after the space to make sure that the words you write fit logically and grammatically.

Listening 2: making sure answers fit

A Look at the correct answers to Listening 1D on page 269 and read the tapescript on page 293.

B Now answer these questions about the changes that you needed to make.

1. The speaker uses the words you need but what changes?
2. Why is the correct answer *the weekend* and not *once a week*?
3. How does the preposition before the space help you predict the answer?
4. Which words are used in the summary that are not used in the talk? Was this a difficult space to fill?
5. How does the word *end* change in the summary?

Exam tip: There are tasks which ask you to fill spaces in notes and summaries in both the Listening and Reading Modules of the exam. These tasks test your ability to listen and read but also test your spelling and grammar.

Listening 3: practise completing a summary

A 🎧 With a partner, write three questions about belonging to a car club. Then listen to the rest of the speech and check if your questions are answered.

B Read the summary below. Think about the type of word or phrase that goes into each space.

C 🎧 Listen again and complete the summary. Remember, you may not hear the exact words that appear in the summary. Use <u>no more than three words</u> for each answer.

It is very easy to use a club car. You can borrow a car for an hour if you only need to make a (1) _____, or much longer if you want to. The minimum time you can borrow a car from large car hire companies is (2) _____, which is longer than most people need. There are several cars in each area, all parked in private spaces, which other drivers are (3) _____ to use.

It is very easy to (4) _____ a car. This can be done online or by telephone. If somebody else (5) _____ the car you want, there will be another one. You can make a booking just before you use a car or make a booking a long way (6) _____. If you decide that you need a car (7) _____, you can change the booking time from inside the car. You use your membership card to (8) _____ the car and then key in your ID number.

The annual (9) _____ fee is £60 and there is an hourly rate for car use. (10) _____ costs 15p a mile. You receive a monthly bill which explains all charges.

D Check the key on page 269. How many questions did you answer correctly?

E Tick the sentences about the listening task that are true for you and think about how you can answer more questions correctly next time.

1. I read through the summary carefully before I listened.
2. I could predict the type of word or phrase that I needed for most spaces.
3. I understood the speaker and knew which words to write in the spaces.
4. I spelt most of my answers correctly and used capital letters when necessary.
5. I am pleased with how many questions I answered correctly.

 Exam tip: If you understand what the speaker says but don't know how to make your answer fit the space, write what you hear. Always write something in a space.

7

Reading 1: recognizing facts and opinions

A Answer these questions with a partner.

1. Do many people travel by train in your country?
2. Is the railway system good in your country?
3. How often do you travel by train?
4. What do you like / not like about travelling by train?

B Look at the picture of a train. Check the words below and then use them to talk about the picture and predict what is in the newspaper story below.

| speed | motors | locomotive engine | carriage | passengers | airlines |

C Read the text to check your ideas.

AGV Is the Future of Trains, *The Scientist*, 2008

A new high-speed train will soon be operating in Europe. The AGV (Automotrice Grande Vitesse) can travel at 360 km per hour. It will travel 1,000 km in just three hours. The previous highest speed for a European train was 320 km per hour.

The huge French engineering company, Alstom, has built the train. Motors are located under each carriage so there is no need for a locomotive engine to drive the train. This means the train will be able to carry more passengers.

Alstom's chief executive says that the new train is the equal of any German or Japanese train and that railway companies will now be able to compete with airlines. He compares the AGV to the world's largest passenger plane, the Airbus A380. A spokesman for Air France admits that airlines are concerned about the number of passengers who might switch to using trains for journeys within France.

An engineer who was part of the team that built the AGV says that the day the train was tested was the most exciting day of his life. He thinks that almost every engineer in the world would like to be in his shoes at the moment.

The French president says that it is great news for France. He recognizes that Alstom have invested money in research and development, and he believes the company has shown courage in developing such a futuristic train.

Exam tip: Texts often contain both facts (statements that are certainly true) and opinions (what somebody believes). You will find a text easier to read if you can recognize what is fact and what is opinion.

D Mark these ideas from the story about the AGV (F) fact or (O) opinion.

1. A new high-speed train will soon be operating in Europe. ___
2. Motors are located under each carriage. ___
3. The new train is the equal of any German or Japanese train. ___
4. Railway companies will now be able to compete with airlines. ___
5. It is great news for France. ___
6. Alstom has invested money in research and development. ___

Question-type tip: Sometimes you need to match a person mentioned in the text with something he or she says. Often this will be an opinion. The words and phrases in the task will not be exactly the same as those in the text.

E Mark each of the opinions below with one of the following abbreviations.

ACE   Alstom's chief executive
SAF   a spokesman for Air France
E   an engineer who helped to build the train
FP   The French president

1. It is very brave of Alstom to build a train like this.   _____
2. The AGV is like a huge aeroplane.   _____
3. Other people would like to be doing what I am doing.   _____
4. More people will probably want to use trains now.   _____

F Highlight the lines in the text that provide the answers. Then compare with a partner.

Reading 2: practise identifying facts and opinions

A Talk with a partner. What is and where is Heathrow?

B Look at these three headings. Check any words you don't know and decide what each story could be about. Compare with a partner.

| Heathrow to Grow | Everyone Wants Third Runway | Jobs Lost at Heathrow |

C Now skim-read the text about Heathrow Airport on the next page and choose the correct heading. Write it in the space at the top of the text.

D Read the text more carefully and answer the questions.

For questions 1–6, mark each of the opinions below with one of the following abbreviations.

TS   transport secretary
SAG   spokesman for the action group
BAAE   BAA executive
STS   shadow transport secretary

1. Newer planes do not make so much noise.   _____
2. An expansion of Heathrow will bring money into Britain.   _____
3. It would be better to get more people travelling by train.   _____
4. The government will pull down buildings to expand the airport.   _____
5. Heathrow will become less important if it does not grow.   _____
6. Heathrow has been too busy for a long time.   _____

For questions 7–10, decide if the information given below agrees with the information given in the passage. Write (T) true, (F) false or (NG) not given.

7. The transport secretary says that some people could be out of work.   __
8. The transport secretary and the spokesman for NoTRAG agree about noise levels.   __
9. The BAA executive says that Heathrow has been the busiest airport in the world for 15 years.   __
10. The spokesman for NoTRAG says that flying is not the only way to travel.   __

There has been a strong reaction to plans to expand Heathrow, already one of the biggest and busiest airports in the world. The plans mean building a third runway and a sixth terminal building, and people are very unhappy.

The government would like the third runway to be operating by 2020. The transport secretary* says that Britain depends on Heathrow as a link to the world economy. She believes that Heathrow will lose some of its reputation as a world airport if it is not expanded, and she warns that some of the 170,000 jobs at the airport could be lost.

People opposed to the expansion have set up an action group and called it NoTRAG (No Third Runway Action Group). A spokesman says that noise from planes on a new runway will affect more than fifty towns. He adds that building a sixth terminal will mean destroying around 700 homes, including one whole village. However, the transport secretary says that modern planes are becoming cleaner and less noisy and that the problem would not be so great.

The company that runs Heathrow Airport is BAA. Their chief executive says that the airport has been running at full capacity for more than 15 years and that it must expand. He believes that a third runway could be worth around £10 billion a year to the economy.

The spokesman for NoTRAG says that a third runway would mean around 900 flights more each day, and that other methods of transport should be developed instead. The shadow transport secretary** agrees. She believes that a third runway will mean more noise and pollution and feels that high-speed rail links are a much better option.

* Transport secretary – the person in the government who is responsible for transport.
** Shadow transport secretary – the person in the opposition party (the party not in power) who is responsible for transport.

E Check the key on page 269. How many questions did you answer correctly?

F Tick the sentences about the reading task that are true for you and think about how you can answer more questions correctly next time.

1. Skimming the text first helped to get an idea of what it was about.
2. I tried to read the topic sentences and then skim the rest of each paragraph.
3. I knew what was a fact and what was an opinion.
4. I was happy with how quickly I answered the questions.
5. I am getting better at guessing the meaning of new words and phrases in context.
6. I am happy with the number of questions I answered correctly.

Key vocabulary in context

Use words from the text to complete these sentences. The paragraph in which you can find the word is given.

1. I'm going to tell my boss that I'm leaving my job. I don't know what his _____ will be. (1)
2. We had no electricity for an hour, but the machines are _____ again now. (2)
3. The restaurant is expensive, but it has a very good _____. (2)
4. Of course, most smokers are _____ to a smoking ban. (3)
5. The fire destroyed the _____ building. There was nothing left. (3)
6. I'm afraid the room's _____ is 45 people. I can't let anybody else in. (4)

WB For focus on reading skills, go to Workbook page 20.

Writing 1: linking words

A Look at the picture. What is the problem?
Have you ever been in this situation?

B A woman is writing to an airline to complain about a delayed flight.
Look at the notes she made before she wrote the letter.

> Flight to Greece – delayed 9 hours
> Flight due to leave 12.45 – left 21.45
> spoke to one manager – very unhelpful
> Long wait very difficult – with two small children
> Very long delay – only sandwiches and one drink
> arrived in Greece – too late to catch bus – take taxi –
> very expensive
> arrived hotel 2 a.m. – could not unpack bags
> not in bed until 2.45 a.m.

Talk with a partner. How could you use the words below to link some of the notes together?

and	but	which	when	because	so	who	although

Example: *a flight to Greece which was delayed for nine hours.*

C Read the letter and delete the wrong option in each pair of linking words.

I am writing about a flight to Greece (1) *which / when* was delayed for nine hours. It was Flight FK254. It was due to leave Gatwick at 12.45 p.m. (2) *but / and* finally left at 21.52.

We asked the staff at the airport why there was such a long delay, (3) *so / but* they could not tell us anything. I spoke to the senior check-in manager, (4) *who / which* was very unhelpful. He clearly did not have time to answer my questions.

Having to wait for so long was especially difficult (5) *because / so* I was with my two small children. They were very tired (6) *and / but* did not understand why there was a problem. (7) *Because / Although* it was such a long delay, your airline provided only sandwiches and one drink for each person.

(8) *When / So* we arrived in Greece, it was too late to catch the bus to our hotel (9) *but / so* we had to pay for a taxi, (10) *and / which* was very expensive. We did not arrive at our hotel until 2 a.m. (11) *When / Although* the hotel staff were very friendly, it made us feel uncomfortable. We finally got to bed at 2.45 a.m. (12) *and / but* could not unpack our bags until the next morning.

I hope you understand why I am dissatisfied with the service your airline provided. I would like you to pay for the cost of the taxi, which was 75 euros, and compensation for the delay. I look forward to hearing from you.

D Check the answers. Is it clear how all the linking words are used?

Grammar check

In *relative clauses*, we use *which* for things.
a flight which was delayed

We use *who* for people.
a manager, who was very unhelpful

We use *when* for time.
When we arrived in Greece, it was ...

We do not need to use a comma when we define something.
I am writing about a flight which was delayed. ✓ (We are defining the flight.)
NOT *I am writing about a flight.* ✗

We can use *that* instead of *which*.
a flight that was delayed

We use a comma when we add more information.
We had to pay for a taxi, which was very expensive.
We had to pay for a taxi, and that was very expensive.

So is a linking word, but it can also be an adverb.
We had to wait for so long.
Such is also an adverb.
It was such a long delay.

When do we use *so* and when do we use *such*?

Complete these sentences with *so* or *such*.

1. The queue was _____ long that I decided to go back later.
2. It was _____ nice weather that we decided to go to the beach.
3. There was _____ much noise. I couldn't sleep.
4. I didn't know you lived in _____ a big house.

Writing 2: practice with linking words

A Write each of the following as one sentence. Use the linking words in brackets and use a comma when necessary.

1. I was late. There was a delay at the airport. (because)

   _____.

2. It was raining. We decided not to play football. (so)

   _____.

3. It was raining. We played football. (although)

   _____.

4. There's the man. He works in the local shop. (who)

   _____.

5. I worked until 9 p.m. It made me very tired. (which)

   _____.

6. I arrived at the airport. All the taxis had gone. (when)

   _____.

WB ▶ Go to Workbook page 21 for the writing task.

Speaking

A Complete each sentence about your free-time activities.

1. I always _____ before I go to bed.
2. I usually _____ at the weekend.
3. I very often _____.
4. I occasionally _____.
5. I don't very often _____.
6. I rarely _____.
7. I never _____.
8. I _____ three or four times a week.
9. I _____ once a month.
10. I _____ every day.

B Here are two typical cards for part 2 of the Speaking Module. Work with a partner – one of you is A, the other is B. You have a minute to think and make notes.

A

> **Describe the method of transport that you use most often.**
> **Say ...**
> • what the method of transport is.
> • what you use it for and how often.
> • why it is better than other methods of transport.
> • what the disadvantages are.

B

> **Describe a method of transport that you do not like using.**
> **Say ...**
> • what the method of transport is.
> • what you use it for and how often.
> • what you don't like about it.
> • how it could improve.

C Take turns to speak about what's on your card for about two minutes.

Vocabulary

A Fill the gaps with a word made from the root words in the box.

1. People often ride a bicycle because it is _____.
2. If you are a young driver, _____ will cost more.
3. The _____ of Heathrow is not popular with everyone.
4. There is a _____ charge of £300.
5. I was quite surprised by Paul's _____.
6. A lot of our profit goes into research and _____.

economy
insure
expand
year
react
develop

Errors

A Correct the spelling mistakes.

1. ocasionaly _____
2. usally _____
3. jurney _____
4. kue _____
5. pasingers _____
6. engin _____

B There are errors in all of these sentences. Correct them.

1. I ride often my bicycle.
2. I go every week to the gym.
3. Have you ever done a long journey by boat?
4. I didn't know that Manchester was so big city.
5. That's the man which told me.
6. There was a delay on the train which made me late.
7. Who's going to pay the tickets?
8. Do you belong for any clubs?

Reading

Exam tip: This is a checklist for this reading practice task.

✓ Use the instructions and the pictures to help you predict what the text is about.
✓ Skim the text to get a general idea of what it is about.
✓ Notice how paragraphs give the text structure and how topic sentences tell you what a paragraph is going to be about.
✓ Understand what is fact and what is an opinion.
✓ Scan to find the information you need to answer questions.
✓ Recognize language that is paraphrased in the questions.
✓ Check that your answers are grammatically correct and spelt correctly.

A Read a web page which gives advice about how to travel around in India. Match the paragraphs A–E with the pictures 1–5.

How to get around India

India is a huge country, and there are lots of different ways to travel around. However, we should warn you that although travelling in India is exciting, it is not always easy. Airlines cancel flights and trains are delayed. Buses often do not arrive at all. You must always allow plenty of time and assume that you will arrive late!

A. Because India is so big, flying is often the best option. Prices have fallen recently, even to remote mountain regions and islands. Although flying is now more popular, airports cannot always deal with the amount of air traffic. Most airports have only one runway and a few boarding gates. The queues to check in are very long and move very slowly. Not all airports have air conditioning.

B. The railway system in India is the biggest in the world. Trains are not always on time, but the system works. Travellers can choose from a number of classes, ranging from regular to luxury. It is the best way to see the real India and to enjoy its natural beauty. Local travellers are usually happy to talk with tourists, so you will make friends, too. There are also three tourist trains which operate in the most popular parts of the country and visit the best-loved sights. They are really moving five-star hotels and, if you can afford it, travelling on one is an amazing experience.

C. Taking a bus is the most popular way of making a short journey, and the only cheap way to get to villages that are not on the railway system. Each area has its own bus service, which usually has a number of classes. Ordinary class buses are cheap but very crowded, and you will not usually get a seat. Express buses are more comfortable and have air conditioning, but you will be lucky if you find one with a toilet. Whatever class the bus, a journey by road can be slow and uncomfortable.

D. You can drive in India with an international licence, but it is not an enjoyable experience. Most city streets are narrow and in a very bad condition. The highways that link cities are better, but traffic either moves very slowly or very fast. Drivers do not follow rules and there are often accidents. We advise hiring a car with a local driver. Salaries in India are low, and hiring a driver adds little to the cost of hiring the car. Hiring a driver is safer, and he will probably know something about the local area.

E. Travelling by motorbike is popular among travellers in India. You will not experience the same delays as you will if you drive a car, and it is an exciting option. You must still be aware of how dangerous driving in India can be. We advise travellers to buy a second-hand bike rather than a new one. Small bikes with engines from 100cc to 150cc can be bought very cheaply.

Question-type tip: For some matching tasks, you must read the instructions very carefully. There may be numbers or letters that you do not need to use.

B For questions 1–5, match the methods of transport (1–5 below) with the statements A–G. There are two statements that you do not need to use. Write the correct letter in the spaces 1–5 below.

1. flying
2. travelling by train
3. travelling by bus
4. travelling by car
5. travelling by motorbike

A It's a good way of meeting people as you travel.
B You can either do this yourself or pay for somebody to do it for you.
C Tourists can only travel first class.
D You will probably have to stand during your journey.
E It is quicker and more enjoyable than driving a car.
F More people are doing it, and the cost is now less than it was.
G This method of transport only exists in India.

1. __   2. __   3. __   4. __   5. __

For questions 6–10, decide if the information given below agrees with the opinions expressed in the passage. Write (T) true, (F) false or (NG) not given.

6. If you fly, you will have to wait a long time and will probably get hot.   __
7. Tourist trains are expensive but very good quality.   __
8. You have to pay to use a toilet on most buses.   __
9. Hiring a driver to drive you around is an expensive option.   __
10. You should not buy a motorbike that somebody else has used.   __

For questions 11–15, complete the summary below with words from the text. Use <u>no more than two words</u> in each space.

Travelling in India is always interesting, but there are often problems and, wherever you go, you will probably be (11) _____. Flying is a popular option, but airports are small and it takes a long time to (12) _____. If you travel by train, you will see the (13) _____ of India and meet people. Buses are not very comfortable, but they are cheap and you can (14) _____ to places that trains do not run to. Roads are not very good in India and drivers do not follow rules. Travelling by car or motorbike can be (15) _____ and you must be careful.

8 Time

Speaking 1: time

A Talk with a partner. Look at the people in the two pictures. How do they see time differently?

Vocabulary 1: time or no time

A Check the highlighted words and phrases in these questions about the two pictures. Then answer them with a partner.

1. Who has plenty of time?
2. Who is short of time?
3. Who is always in a hurry?
4. Who likes to take time to do things?
5. Who doesn't want to waste time?

Vocabulary 2: time expressions

A Complete the sentences with the correct form of the verbs below.

spend	pass	save	have	waste	take

1. Sorry, I don't _____ time to help you now. I'll try to do it later.
2. If you _____ your time to do it, you'll do a much better job.
3. At the weekend, I like to _____ time with my family.
4. I think every minute is important. I don't like to _____ time.
5. When I'm on the train, I often play computer games on my laptop to _____ the time.
6. Booking flight tickets online instead of going to a travel agent really _____ time.

B Match the words and phrases 1–5 with the words and phrases a–e that have the same meaning.

1. in the future   a. for ages
2. for a long time   b. straightaway
3. immediately   c. ages ago
4. a long time ago   d. from now on
5. at first   e. to begin with

C Use the pairs of phrases in Exercise B to complete these sentences.

1. James is my oldest friend. I met him _____ / _____.
2. I've known Peter _____ / _____. We went to the same university.
3. I didn't really like Lucy _____ / _____, but now she's a good friend.
4. I want you to deal with the problem _____ / _____. Not tomorrow or next week.
5. You were lucky there wasn't an Accident. You must be more careful _____ / _____.

Speaking 2: questions and answers

A Talk with a partner. Answer these questions.

1. How long have you known your best friend?
2. How long does it take to get from your hometown to the capital of your country?
3. How long does it take you to get ready in the morning?
4. How long did you spend at college or university?

B Ask and answer these questions with the same partner.

1. Do you have much free time? How do you like to spend it?
2. Are you usually in a hurry or do you like to take your time?
3. How do you pass the time during a long flight or train journey?
4. Do you ever feel that you are wasting time?

Speaking 3: answering the question

A Look at these questions from the third part of the Speaking Module. Think about how you would answer them.

1. Does modern technology really save us time, or is it just one more thing to worry about?   —
2. Does modern technology mean that some people have *too much* free time?   —
3. Do people spend too long thinking about the future instead of enjoying now?   —
4. What is more important – time or money?   —

Exam tip: You must answer the questions that the examiner asks. You can't just say something that you have practised. If you don't understand the question, ask the examiner to repeat it or explain what he or she means.

B 🎧 Listen to some students answering the questions in Exercise A. Mark each sentence (Y) if the student answers the question and (N) if the student doesn't.

C 🎧 Listen again as you read the tapescript. Notice that answers do not have to be grammatically perfect to be good answers.

D Walk around the class. Ask and answer the questions in Exercise A with different classmates.

Listening 1: completing a table

A You will hear a talk to a class of students. Look at the pictures. What do you think the topic of the talk will be?

Question-type tip: In both the Listening and Reading Modules of the exam, you will sometimes need to complete information in a table.

B Look at the table below. Answer these questions with a partner.

1. How does a table help you predict what you will listen to?
2. How does the table help you know what you need to listen for?
3. Match parts of the table to the pictures in Exercise A.

Exam tip: A table helps you because you can predict how a talk will be organized and divided into parts. You know when the speaker is going to go from one topic to another because you can follow the squares on the table.

C Listen to the first part of the talk and complete the table. Write <u>no more than two words or a number</u> for each answer.

Date	Method of recording history	Notes
150,000 – 200,000 years ago	Storytelling	Not reliable – (1) _____ forgotten and elements added.
32,000 years ago	Cave (2) _____	Images of large (3) _____ so perhaps to bring luck when hunting.
(4) _____ BC	Egyptian hieroglyphics	Beliefs and events recorded on walls (5) _____ and on monuments.
(6) _____ BC	Written word	Ancient Greeks recorded events for (7) _____ generations. First (8) _____ lived in Greece.

D Compare answers with a partner. Did the table format make the task easier?

Listening 2: practise completing a table

A 🎧 Listen to the second part of the talk and answer the questions.

For questions 1–12, complete the table. Write <u>no more than two words or a number</u> for each answer.

Date	Method of recording history	Notes
8th century AD	Paper and woodblock (1) _____	More books – so more people learnt (2) _____.
(3) _____ century AD	Printing press	(4) _____ produced more quickly.
1605	First (5) _____	People knew about events more quickly.
Mid-19th century	(6) _____	People saw reality of war. People wanted to know the (7) _____.
End of nineteenth century	Motion picture camera	First (8) _____ images.
1930s	Television	History brought into people's (9) _____.
Today	(10) _____ TV / Internet	Every (11) _____ is recorded. People watch as it happens.
	Video camera / mobile phone	People can record (12) _____ history.

B Check the key on page 269. How many questions did you answer correctly?

C Tick the sentences about the listening task that are true for you and think about how you can answer more questions correctly next time.

1. I looked at the table carefully before I listened.
2. The table helped me predict the type of word or phrase that I needed for most spaces.
3. I understood the speaker and knew which words to write in the spaces.
4. I spelt most of my answers correctly and used capital letters when necessary.
5. I am pleased with how many questions I answered correctly.

Key vocabulary in context

Circle the correct option in these sentences.

1. A **century** is *a hundred / a thousand years*.
2. A **generation** of people is a group of people who live *in the same place / at the same time*.
3. A **tradition** is something that people have *done for a long time / just started doing*.
4. **Historians** are people who *study the past / can look into the future*.

Pronunciation check
Century is pronounced /'sentʃəri/.
🎧 Listen to these phrases and then practise saying them.
1. eighteenth century   2. nineteenth century   3. twentieth century

8

Reading 1: understanding the general idea

A Talk in small groups. Look at the picture and answer the questions.

1. Do you know the movie?
2. Who are the two characters in the picture?
3. What are they trying to do?
4. What happens in the rest of the movie?
5. Do you believe that time travel is possible?

B Read the text and put these key words into the correct space.

physics	stories	moments	scientists

Time Travel – Fantasy or Reality?

Time travel is the idea of moving between different (1) _____ in time in the same way that it is now possible to move between different points in space. Time travel would involve sending objects backwards in time to a moment before the present, or forwards from the present to the future, without the need to experience the period in between.

Based on theories of time dilation, gravity and relativity, one-way time travel into the future might be possible, but it seems that the laws of (2) _____ would not allow time travel backwards into the past. People argue that if you travelled back in time, you could change events.

Changing events would probably lead to a chain of other events that would mean that you would not be born and so would not exist.

Some (3) _____, however, believe that travelling back in time might take the traveller to a parallel universe. This means that the moment the traveller arrived in the past, his history would begin to change from the history he has already experienced.

Many books and films have told (4) _____ of time travel, but the well-known scientist, Stephen Hawking, suggests that time travel is not possible because nobody from the future has visited Earth. He believes that if generations from the future could travel in time, they would be visiting us.

Reading 2: completing a summary

A Complete this summary of the first two paragraphs of the text using words from the box. You do not need to use all the words.

moments	time	past	people	points
existence	history	objects	possibility	space

Time travel would mean moving between points in time in the same way that we now move between points in (1) _____. That means travelling backwards into the (2) _____ or forwards into the future without living through the (3) _____ in between. It seems that forward travel is a (4) _____ but that travelling back in time is probably not. If a person could travel back in time, they might change something in a way that would threaten their (5) _____. Stories about time travel are very popular, but if time travel is possible, why are (6) _____ from the future not visiting us?

B Compare your answers with a partner. Why do some words not fit in some spaces?

Question-type tip: Sometimes when you complete a summary, you will choose words from the text. Sometimes you will choose words from a box.

C Talk with a partner. Mark these statements about the task you have just done (T) true or (F) false.

1. The words in the box will always be words from the text. —
2. Choosing words from a box is easier than choosing words from the text. —
3. It is clear which words in the box I should use and which I should not. —
4. When I use a word, I should cross it out so that I don't use it again. —

Exam tip: Choosing words from the box is not easier than choosing words from the text. The words in the box are not always the same as the words in the text. The words in the box that you don't need are usually similar in meaning to the words that you need. Once you have used a word from the box, cross it out.

D Complete the summary below with words from this box.

different	living	future	believe	visiting	unlikely
coming back	future	change	popular	similar	history

Time travel would mean travelling between points in time in a way that is (1) _____ to how we now move between points in space. That means travelling backwards into the past or forwards into the (2) _____ without (3) _____ through the time in between. It seems that forward travel is a possibility, but that being able to travel back in time is (4) _____. If a person could travel back in time, they might (5) _____ something in a way that would threaten their existence. Books and movies tell stories of time travel, but if time travel is possible, why are people from the future not (6) _____ to visit us?

E Check your answers and then answer these questions with a partner.

1. How is the second summary task different from the first?
2. How do the two task types test different aspects of your English?

Exam tip: Sometimes the words in the box are all the same part of speech (usually nouns) and the task checks overall comprehension. Sometimes the words in the box are different parts of speech and the task tests your grammar, too. Always read the summary carefully and look at what comes before and after a space so you know what part of speech to use.

The summary will not always be a summary of the whole text. Often it will summarize part of the text and you will need to first identify which part.

Reading 3: practising completing a summary

A Do you remember the highlighted words in these questions? Check and answer the questions with a partner.

1. At what age do people retire in your country?
2. How do most people spend their retirement?

B Read the web page, which gives advice about different ways of spending retirement.

For questions 1–4, match the headings a–e with the sections. Write the letters in the spaces. There is one heading that you do not need to use.

a. Carry on working   b. Go back to school   c. Travel the world
d. Give somebody a hand   e. Get out more

Retirement Opportunities

Retiring might mean having more time to do the things you have always wanted to. Or it might mean looking for new ideas to do things you never thought you would enjoy. Either way, there is a whole range of opportunities that you can enjoy in retirement.

1 __
Learning can be fun and a great way to relax and meet people. It doesn't need to be formal study, and you don't need to study for a qualification. It's easy to find free courses and, if you're learning for fun, you can choose anything you find interesting – whether it's something new or a subject you already know about. Look at our education and learning section for more advice and links to local colleges.

2 __
When you retire, you'll probably have more time to enjoy your favourite leisure activities, and you will probably be keen to take up a new interest or activity to fill your spare time. Our sports, leisure and tourism section has information about what you can do in and around the local area.

3 __
Doing voluntary work allows you to work in a way that suits your timetable. It's a very good way to put into use your skills and experience to help others, and at the same time learn something new. There are all sorts of organizations that need volunteers. Think about what you can offer and what you want to get from it.

4 __
Reaching the age that you are entitled to a pension doesn't mean that you have to stop working. You can either continue to work and claim your pension entitlement, or delay your claim and get paid more later.

Related Information: Further and Higher Education   Over 60s   Reduced costs of travel

Done

For questions 5–12, complete the summary below with words from the box. You do not need to use all the words.

voluntary work	fun	retirement	study	different	wait
work	stop	leisure	first time	hobby	experience

When you retire, you will have time and there are many (5) _____ ways to enjoy it. You can do what you have always wanted to do or try new things for the (6) _____. A lot of people go back to college and learn something. They have (7) _____ and meet people. Other people want to enjoy their favourite leisure activities, and many begin a new (8) _____. Helping others by doing (9) _____ is a popular way of using skills and experience. You should remember, though, that being of (10) _____ age doesn't mean that you can't (11) _____. Many retired people claim a pension and have a job, or (12) _____ until later to start claiming.

C Check the key on page 269. How many questions did you answer correctly?

D Tick the sentences about the reading task that are true for you and think about how you can answer more questions correctly next time.

1. I read the summary and looked at the words in the box carefully before I started the second task.
2. I found it challenging to read the text and the summary at the same time.
3. I thought about both the meaning of words and if they fitted grammatically into the summary.
4. I was happy with how quickly I answered the questions and the number I answered correctly.

WB For focus on reading skills, go to Workbook page 23.

Writing: making a request

9.00 AM	study
10.00 AM	
11.00 AM	meeting supervisor
12.00 AM	
13.00 AM	LUNCH
14.00 AM	write report
15.00 AM	history class
16.00 AM	review for test
17.00 AM	
18.00 AM	

A Answer these questions with a partner.

1. Do you have enough time to do everything you need to do?
2. Do you ever feel that you have too much to do in too little time?
3. Do you sometimes need to delay things you have to do because you don't have time?

B Look at the instructions for a writing task below. Highlight the key words and check that you understand what you have to do.

You chose to study four subjects at college, but you also need to do a part-time job to support yourself. You are finding it impossible to do everything properly.

Write a letter to your college explaining why you need to give up one of your courses. Ask if it is possible to have a refund.

Write at least 150 words. You should spend about 20 minutes on this task.

C Answer these questions with a partner.

1. Is it an easy or difficult letter to write?
2. Do you know what to say?
3. Should the letter be formal or informal?
4. Write the opening line, stating why you are writing.

D The letter should be formal. Tick the option in each pair below that is right for the letter.

1. A I'm writing because I can't do one of my courses anymore.
   B I am writing to ask if it is possible for me to give up one of the courses I am studying.

2. A Now I do four subjects and I've got a part-time job.
   B I am currently studying four subjects and doing a part-time job.

3. A There's too much work and it's all too much for me.
   B I am finding it impossible to cope with so much work.

4. A When the academic year began, I was confident that I had the time.
   B At the start, I thought I could do everything.

5. A I now realize that that is not possible.
   B I was wrong!

6. A I do not want to give up History of Art, but I am afraid I have no other option.
   B I don't want to give up History of Art but I have to.

7. A I want my money back.
   B I would like to know if it is possible to claim a refund.

8. A I apologize for any inconvenience that I will cause.
    B Sorry if I've made some problems for you.

9. A Thanks for everything.
    B Thank you for your kind consideration.

E Read the model letter and check your answers in Exercise C.

Dear Professor Cameron,

I am writing to ask if it is possible for me to give up one of the courses I am studying. The course I want to give up is History of Art, which is on Tuesday and Thursday mornings. I am currently studying four subjects and doing a part-time job. I am finding it impossible to cope with so much work.

When the academic year began, I was confident that I had the time to study four subjects and continue to work. I now realize that that is not possible. I enjoy History of Art and I do not want to give it up, but I am afraid I have no other option. I must continue working while I study in order to support myself.

I would like to know if it is possible to claim a refund for the History of Art course as I have only been to two of the lessons. I apologize for any inconvenience that I will cause. I am sure that with the extra time I have, I can focus better on my studies. Thank you for your kind consideration.

Yours sincerely,

Brian Howard

Exam tip: Try to learn some typical fixed expressions for each type of letter. Even if your vocabulary is limited and you make grammatical mistakes, you will gain marks if you use the right expressions in the right place.

F Highlight expressions that you want to remember and use when you write a request letter.

G Cover the letter. Seven words are spelt incorrectly in these typical expressions. Correct them.

1. I am writing to ask if it is posible for me to ...
2. I am curantly studying ...
3. I am finding it inpossible to cope with ...
4. I do not want to ... but I am afraid I have no other opsion.
5. I apolagize for any inconviniance ...
6. Thank you for your kind considarasion.

H Look at the exam practice section on page 108 for the writing task.

Speaking

A Complete these sentences so that they are true for you.

1. I like to **take my time** when I _____.
2. I'm often **in a hurry** when I _____.
3. If _____, I think it's best to _____ straightaway / immediately.
4. I would like to **have more time** to _____.
5. I **spend too much of my time** _____.

> **Grammar check**
> If the phrase **spend time** is followed by a verb, the verb is in the *~ing* form.
> *I spend a lot of my time travelling to meetings.*

B Look again at the questions from the third part of the Speaking Module on page 99.

C 🎧 Listen to some students answering the questions. How do they give themselves time to think?

D 🎧 Listen again and fill the gaps below.

1. Mm, that's _____ question.
2. _____?
3. Mm, I haven't really _____ before.
4. I don't know if _____ that in only a minute. It's _____ question.

Exam tip: If the examiner asks you a difficult question and you need time to think, there are several expressions you can use before you give an answer.

E Work with a partner. Ask difficult questions and practise giving yourself time to think.

Vocabulary

A Fill the gaps in these sentences with key words from the unit. Some letters are given to help you.

1. People don't want more lies. They want the t _ _ _ h.
2. I apologize if my decision has caused any inc _ _ v _ _ _ _ _ _ _.
3. Do you believe that life ex _ _ _ _ on other planets?
4. America was discovered in the fifteenth c _ _ _ _ _ _.
5. I'm finding it difficult to c _ _ _ with so much work and so little time.
6. It is very unl _ _ _ _ y that people will be able to travel in time soon.
7. I hope the next gen _ _ _ _ _ _ _ will look after the planet better than we do.
8. Do you know where the tr _ _ _ _ _ _ n of shaking hands started?

Errors

A There are errors in all of these sentences. Correct them.

1. How much time have you been to Europe?
2. How long time will you stay in Paris?
3. How long do you know your best friend?
4. It's not good to waste the time.
5. In future I hope to study in the USA.
6. First I didn't like Tony, but now I think he's really nice.
7. I spend a lot of my free time to play golf.
8. I passed two weeks in Greece last year.

8

Writing

A Look carefully at the instructions for this writing task. Highlight the key words and make sure you understand what you have to do.

> You are currently studying on a full-time course at a university. Something has happened and you need to take two weeks off.
>
> Write a letter to the principal of the university requesting the time off and explaining why you need it.
>
> Write at least 150 words.

 Exam tip: Sometimes you will need to invent some of the information that you write in your letter – what course you are studying, when you need to take time off and why you need to take time off, for example.

B Look at these pictures and answer the questions with a partner.

1. Why does the student want to take time off from his studies in each case?
2. Do you think they are all good reasons for taking time off from a course you are studying?

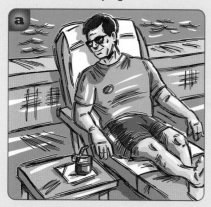  

C Answer these questions with a partner. You will need to invent answers.

1. What course are you studying?
2. When do you need the time off?
3. What has happened? Why do you need the time off?
4. Are you going to apologize?
5. Are you going to request that your lecturers tell you in advance what they will do in the lectures that you miss?
6. Are you going to request that your lecturers give copies of any materials to one of your classmates?
7. How are you going to close your letter?

D Write the letter. For now, you should take 30–40 minutes to write your letter, but remember that in the exam that will mean less time for the more difficult second composition.

_____

_____

_____

_____

_____

_____

_____

_____

_____

_____

_____

_____

_____

_____

_____

_____

_____

_____

_____

_____

_____

_____

_____

_____

_____

_____

9 Money

Vocabulary 1: time and money

A Look at this expression. Do you say the same thing in your language? What does it mean?

> Time is money

B Look at these phrases from the last unit. If it is possible to say *money* in place of *time*, write *money*. If not, put a cross.

1. He's got plenty of time / _____.
2. How do you like to spend your time / _____?
3. I like to take my time / _____ to do things well.
4. I'm a bit short of time / _____.
5. It'll save time / _____.
6. It's a good way to pass the time / _____.
7. It's a waste of time / _____.

Speaking 1: talking about money

A Walk around the class. Ask and answer these questions.

1. Do you know somebody who has plenty of money?
2. Do you have any friends who are a bit short of money?
3. Do you enjoy spending money or do you prefer to save money?
4. What do you think is a waste of money?

Speaking 2: shopping habits and preferences

A Look at the pictures and talk about how each type of shopping is different.

B Circle the option in each statement about shopping that is true for you.

1. I *quite like / don't mind / really hate* shopping in supermarkets.
2. I *rarely / sometimes / often* shop in small local shops.
3. I *rarely / sometimes / quite* often go shopping at a market.
4. I *don't like / quite like / love* shopping for clothes.
5. I *don't like / quite like / love* shopping for books, CDs and DVDs.

C Compare your ideas in small groups.

D Check the highlighted words and tick the sentences below that are true for you.

1. I still pay for most things in cash.
2. I use my debit card to pay for most things now.
3. I use my credit card to pay for expensive things.
4. I pay my bills online.
5. I never pay anything by cheque these days.

E Compare your answers with a partner.

Grammar check
Notice the different ways that *pay* is used.
pay + direct object or amount   *pay a bill / pay $20*
pay for + what it is you buy   *pay for a meal*
pay by + how you pay   *pay by cheque / pay by debit card* BUT *pay in cash*

Pronunciation check
🎧 Listen to how *of* /əv/ and *for* /fə/ are pronounced weakly in these phrases.
1. plenty of money   2. short of time   3. pay for the meal   4. save for the future
Practise saying the phrases.

Vocabulary 2: opposites

A Use these opposite word pairs to complete the sentences.

wealth / poverty   cheap / expensive   overpaid / underpaid   borrow / lend

1. Personally, I think designer clothes and accessories are much too _____.
   A pair of sunglasses just can't be worth $500. People I know buy _____
   clothes at the market.
2. I think it's wrong that a small number of people have huge _____ while people
   all over the developing world live in _____. Many people can't afford food and
   clothes for their children.
3. The banks _____ people too much money. People _____ more than they
   should and get into debt. They end up losing everything.
4. I think film stars and footballers are _____. They earn crazy amounts of money while
   other people earn very little. Nurses and school teachers are _____ in my opinion.

B 🎧 Listen and check your answers.

C Cover Exercise A and write the opposite pairs in your notebook.

Speaking 3: expressing opinions

A Here are two typical cards for part 2 of the Speaking Module. Work with a
partner – one of you is A, the other is B. Talk about your card.

A
**Describe a job that you think is overpaid.
Say ...**
• what the job is.
• why you think it is underpaid.
• who does a more important job.

B
**Describe a job you think is underpaid.
Say ...**
• what the job is.
• why you think it is underpaid.
• what a fairer salary would be.

9

Listening 1: practise identifying key words that you don't know

A Work with a partner. Say what you think is happening in each of these pictures.

B 🎧 Listen to four short extracts. Match each with a picture from Exercise A.

1. ___ 2. ___ 3. ___ 4. ___

 Exam tip: When you are listening, there will sometimes be one key word that you don't know. Sometimes, you will need to guess the meaning in context so that you can answer a question.

C 🎧 Listen again and mark these statements (T) true or (F) false.

Extract 1: The woman is happy with the price she paid for the jeans.   ___
Extract 2: The customer knows the name of the money used in Russia.   ___
Extract 3: The school has enough computers for all the children.   ___
Extract 4: Somebody stole money from the woman.   ___

D What was the key word in each extract? Compare with a partner. Pronounce it.

Exam tip: In the Listening Module, the words you need to write as answers will usually be quite simple words. Sometimes, you might need to write a word that you don't know as an answer. You will need to listen carefully and guess the spelling.

E 🎧 Listen again and write the words you hear into the spaces. You will need to guess the spelling.

1. I think I got a _____, don't you?
2. I don't know what the _____ in Russia is.
3. We're trying to _____ money to buy computers ...
4. Somebody's just taken my _____. I was taking it out of my handbag ...

Listening 2: practise identifying key words

A 🎧 Some students are conducting a survey about people's spending habits. Look at the questions on the survey.

Listen and match each extract to a question on the survey. Write the question number in the space. You will not hear all the questions on the survey answered.

Extract 1: question ___   Extract 2: question ___
Extract 3: question ___   Extract 4: question ___

Class 5C   Spending Habits Survey 10/09/2008   Person 1: man about 40

1 Which income band are you in?   Low   Average   High
2 How much money do you feel you have to spend?
   Less than you need   Enough to live on   More than you need
3 What do you spend most of your money on?
4 How do you usually pay for what you buy?
5 What do you think is good value for money?
6 What do you think is a waste of money?
7 Do you ever buy things that you can't really afford?
8 Are you a spender or a saver?

B 🎧 Listen to the whole survey in the correct order and answer the questions.

For questions 1–4, choose the correct letter a, b or c.

1. Which income band is the man in?
   a. low   b. average   c. high
2. The man feels that he has ...
   a. less money than he needs.   b. enough money to live on.   c. more than he needs.
3. The man spends most of his money on ...
   a. things he really likes.   b. what he has to.   c. eating out in restaurants.
4. The man uses cash to pay ...
   a. for most things.   b. his bills.   c. for things which are not planned.

For questions 5–9, complete the notes. Use <u>no more than two words</u> for each answer.

5. The man's telephone and Internet broadband _____ is good value for money.
6. £22 a month for the man's telephone and Internet is a good _____.
7. When you drive a new car out of the _____, it is immediately worth less money.
8. The man says that he likes to _____ himself occasionally.
9. The man thinks that it is important to save for a _____.

C Check the key on pages 269 and 270. How many questions did you answer correctly?

D Tick the sentences about the listening task that are true for you and think about how you can answer more questions correctly next time.

1. Reading the questions on the survey helped me to predict content.
2. I identified key words that I didn't know.
3. I could answer questions 1–4 by guessing the meaning of the new words in context.
4. I could guess the meaning of some new words and phrases from words
   I already I knew.
5. I spelt most of the words correctly to answer questions 5–9.
6. I am happy with how many questions I answered correctly.

Key vocabulary in context

Complete these sentences with words from this module.

1. Some organizations _____ money to help feed the poorest people.
2. If you _____ yourself, you buy something nice for yourself.
3. A bargain and a good _____ mean more or less the same thing.
4. The _____ in Japan is yen.
5. Men usually keep money in a wallet, while women carry a _____.

9

Reading 1: understanding references

A Answer these questions with a partner.

1. When do people normally open their first bank account?
2. How many different accounts do people normally have?
3. What's the difference between a debit and a credit card?
4. How are people paid their salaries in different countries?

B Match the four texts to the sources below.

1. an e-mail to an online advice service
2. a formal letter to a bank
3. an e-mail to a friend
4. information on a web page

A ... and I really want a car, but I just can't afford one at the moment. I'm sure my dad would lend me the money if I asked him, but I don't want to do that. You know my dad – I'd have to tell him exactly what I want it for and then answer hundreds of questions.

B Different banks have different rules about allowing customers credit facilities. Some banks like to know that customers can manage their account correctly before they offer them an account with credit facilities. They might say that the customer should open a 'basic bank account' first. This is an account which allows the customer to have his or her salary paid into it and to set up direct debits so that he or she can pay bills directly.

C I'm going to live in the USA for a year, and I want to know if I can open a bank account before I get there. People have told me that opening an account without an address can be difficult, and that some banks won't even discuss it if they don't meet the customer face-to-face. Can you help?

D ... while I was conducting business at your ATM located in Norfolk Road, my debit card was not returned from the machine. Because the bank was closed at the time, I could not report this and nobody could help me. Please ensure that my card is returned to me at once or that a new one is issued immediately.

C Read the texts again. Write what each highlighted word refers to.

Text A	one	a car
	him	
	that	
	it	
Text B	This	
	his or her / he or she	
Text C	there	
	it	
	they	
Text D	this	
	one	

Exam tip: When you read, it is important to understand how words and phrases relate to each other. You will understand how a text is organized and read more quickly if you can see how one word or phrase refers back or forwards to another.

D Delete the wrong option in each pair of reference words.

A There are three main types of bank account: a basic account, a current account and a savings account. Customers might choose any of **their / these** at different times in **their / they** life.

B These days, most parents like to open a bank account for their children. **They / Them** try to pay money into **that / it** regularly so that when the child is older, he or she will have some savings. I opened an account for my daughter when she was six years old and **it / one** for my son when he was only four.

C Temples and palaces were used like banks thousands of years ago before there was money. People left valuable possessions **their / there** because they knew **they / them** would be safe.

D ATMs started to appear in the late 1960s and you now see **they / them** everywhere. The first mechanical cash dispenser was actually in operation in New York in 1939. It was not popular **that / then**, however, and it was soon removed from the bank where it was located.

> **Watch out!**
> **typical errors**
>
> My brother wants a dog but I don't like they. ✗
>
> I'm going to buy an ice cream. Do you want it? ✗

Reading 2: practise understanding references

A Skim the web page on the next page and tick the sentence below that summarizes it.

1. Most managers know how to save money.
2. Most businesses could do more to save money.

B Read the web page again and highlight any reference words. Is it clear what each refers to?

C Read the web page carefully and answer the questions.

For questions 1–5 decide if the information given below agrees with the information given in the text. Write (T) true, (F) false or (NG) not given.

1. Most businesses lose money because of the waste they produce.   __
2. Many managers frequently change the way they run their office.   __
3. People usually read the marketing mail they receive in the post.   __
4. Office workers don't care about wasting paper.   __
5. Staff throw things away because it is the easy option.   __

For questions 6–11, complete the summary with words from the text. Use <u>no more than three words</u> for each answer.

Most managers do not realize that the amount of waste their business creates means they are making less (6) _____ than they could be. It is not difficult (7) _____ the amount that is thrown away and to make savings. Computers can be used effectively to cut costs, but they should not be (8) _____ overnight. Savings can also be made by using (9) _____ that use less energy and last longer, and by wasting far less paper. Thinner, recycled paper is cheaper and (10) _____ of a sheet should be printed on. Printing (11) _____ wastes money if a document is not going to be seen by customers.

How to Save Money in the Workplace

Businesses everywhere create an enormous amount of unnecessary waste. This not only has an impact on the environment, it also has a hugely damaging effect on the profit that companies make. By making a few changes to the way the office is run, managers can reduce waste and make considerable savings to their business.

Technology Use modern technology to your advantage. Why send out promotion material in the post when it can be done more effectively by e-mail? Your marketing mail is more likely to reach the person you want it to instead of the waste-paper basket, and you will also save money on paper, envelopes and postage.

Energy Ensure that everyone switches off their computers at night. Computers left on standby use 50% of the electricity they use when they are actually in operation.

Use energy-efficient light bulbs – they are more expensive than ordinary ones but last eight times longer, use a quarter of the energy and give the same brightness. This could save around 100€ during the bulb's lifetime.

Paper Paper is probably the biggest source of waste in any office, with the average office worker using up to 50 sheets of A4 every day.

Set printers and photocopiers to print on both sides of the paper. This can reduce the amount of paper used in your office by 50% immediately.

Use recycled paper. Producing recycled paper uses between 28–70% less energy and it is cheaper to buy.

Use 80g paper sheets instead of thicker paper. Thicker paper is more expensive and the thicker the paper you use, the more paper you waste.

Printing Ask whether it is really necessary to print in colour for internal documents, as it is nearly 50% cheaper to print a document in black and white.

Think about how you are going to dispose of the print cartridge. It might be more convenient to put it in the bin but it is far more resource efficient to recycle.

There are all sorts of other ways savings can be made. Remember – saving the environment can mean saving yourself money, too.

D Now check the key on page 270. How many questions did you answer correctly?

E Tick the sentences about the reading task that are true for you and think about how you can answer more questions correctly next time.

1. I could quickly see what reference words referred to.
2. Understanding references helped me to answer some questions.
3. I find T/F/NG tasks easier than I did a few weeks ago.
4. I find summary completion tasks easier than I did a few weeks ago.
5. I was happy with the number of questions I answered correctly.

Key vocabulary in context

Circle the correct option in each sentence.

1. **Waste** is what you want to *keep / throw away*.
2. **Profit** is money *made / lost*.
3. If you **reduce** something, you make it *more / less*.
4. If something is **efficient**, it *works well / doesn't work well*.
5. The **source** of something is where it *comes from / ends up*.

WB For focus on reading skills, go to Workbook page 25.

9

Writing 1: elements of a good composition

A Look at the instructions for a typical writing task. Is it a topic you want to write about?

> It is not right that film stars, singers and footballers are paid more money than they can spend while people all over the world do not have enough money to feed their children.
>
> Do you agree with this statement?
>
> Give reasons for your answer and include any relevant examples from your experience. Write at least 250 words.

B Read the composition a student wrote and make notes about what you like and don't like. Then compare with a partner.

It's absolutely terrible that some people like film stars and footballers are paid so much money when there are millions of very poor people in the world. They can't afford to feed their children and don't even have clean water to drink.

People say that films stars and footballers entertain us and create jobs for other people but that's rubbish. It's disgusting that they can make more money in one day or one evening than most people can make in a year. Some people don't even make that much money in a lifetime.

People should be paid according to how useful their job is - not how much money they make for other people. If there wasn't any teachers or nurses, society couldn't continue and so they should make as much as a rock star.

Film stars, singers and footballers do an important job and we need to have them in the world, but it is completely crazy that they can be so rich so quickly.

C A teacher has read the composition and made some comments. Mark <u>five</u> comments below (Y) yes, this is true and <u>five</u> comments (N) no, this is not true.

1. The composition is difficult to read. I don't know what you are trying to say. ___
2. The composition is too short. You need an introduction and a longer conclusion. ___
3. You don't answer the question. A lot of what you say is not relevant. ___
4. The composition is badly organized and there are no paragraphs. ___
5. You express your opinions too strongly using very informal expressions. ___
6. There should be more linking words and phrases to introduce ideas and opinions. ___
7. There are a lot of spelling mistakes – sometimes with very simple words. ___
8. There are a lot of basic grammatical mistakes. ___
9. Sometimes it is not clear what reference words refer to. ___
10. You shouldn't use contractions in a composition like this. ___

D Find at least <u>one</u> example of each true comment in the composition. Compare with a partner.

Writing 2: introducing opinions

A Read the student's second composition. Highlight parts that make it better than the first.

Famous people like film stars, singers and footballers are paid huge amounts of money. It seems that every year they can demand more and more money for what they do. They are paid so much, in fact, that they probably do not know what to spend it on.

<u>In my opinion</u>, it is wrong that these people have so much money to spend when many people in developing countries all over the world cannot afford to feed their children. In these countries, some people do not even have clean water to drink or a proper place to live. <u>Of course</u>, film stars and footballers entertain people, generate money and create jobs for other people, but <u>I do not believe</u> that they should earn more in one day or in one evening than most people can earn in a year or perhaps even in a lifetime.

<u>I think that</u> people should be paid according to how useful their job is rather than how much money they can generate. If teachers and nurses stopped doing their jobs, society could not function properly. These key workers should be paid properly for the jobs they do.

<u>To sum up</u>, I would say that although entertainers have an important role to play in society, it is unfair that they are paid so much compared with so many other people in the world.

<u>Perhaps</u> there could be a limit on how much people can earn, or perhaps people who earn huge amounts of money should pay more tax.

B Which phrase below can replace each <u>underlined</u> word or phrase in the composition? Use one of the phrases below twice.

Clearly	I think it is wrong	In conclusion	I wonder if	To my mind

1. In my opinion   _____
2. Of course   _____
3. I do not believe that _____
4. I think that   _____
5. To sum up   _____
6. Perhaps   _____

Exam tip: You will need to express your opinion in the second composition in the Writing Module, but you shouldn't express it too aggressively. Introduce opinions and try to make them softer.

WB Go to Workbook page 25 for the writing task.

Speaking

A Match each statement 1–5 with a follow-up comment a–e.

1. I don't mind shopping in supermarkets. ___
2. I prefer shopping in small local shops. ___
3. I don't really like shopping for clothes. ___
4. I really enjoy shopping for DVDs. ___
5. I don't enjoy shopping in markets. ___

a. I always want a pair of shoes or a jacket that I can't afford.
b. It's not much fun, but everyone has to do it.
c. I usually find something I want to see.
d. They're too busy, and a lot of what they sell there isn't very good.
e. The shopkeepers are so much more friendly.

B Listen and check your answers.

C Practise saying the complete sentences as you heard them on the recording.

D Talk about each situation so that it's true for you.

Example: *I don't like shopping in supermarkets. I usually let my mother do it.*

Vocabulary

A Look at this vocabulary web. Add the words below to the correct column.

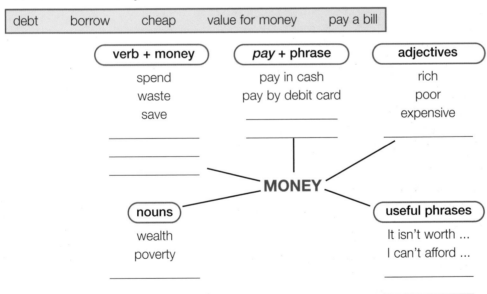

| debt | borrow | cheap | value for money | pay a bill |

verb + money
spend
waste
save
_____
_____
_____

***pay* + phrase**
pay in cash
pay by debit card
_____

adjectives
rich
poor
expensive
_____

MONEY

nouns
wealth
poverty
_____
_____

useful phrases
It isn't worth ...
I can't afford ...
_____
_____

B Work with a partner. Look back at the unit and add more words and phrases to each column.

Errors

A There are errors in all of these sentences. Correct them.

1. Who's going to pay for the bill?
2. I spend a lot of money in clothes.
3. My brother borrowed me some money.
4. Can I lend your dictionary a minute?
5. I'm interested in the USA but I've never been that.
6. My parents have never travelled in his life.
7. My sister wants a new bicycle but my dad won't buy her it.
8. To my opinion, people should try to save money.

9

Listening

A 🎧 **You will hear a man giving a talk to some Economics students about managing money.**

For questions 1–6, choose the correct letter a, b or c.

1. The speaker ...
   a. thinks that the students are too young to worry about money.
   b. thinks that the students should start thinking about money now.
   c. is surprised that the students do not have any money.

2. The speaker thinks that most people ...
   a. do not have time to manage their money.
   b. start thinking about money too early in life.
   c. do not have as much money as they need.

3. The speaker says that anyone who wants to manage their money well ...
   a. must decide what they want from life and when they want it.
   b. needs a lot of money to be happy.
   c. must take risks with their money.

4. The speaker says that most people ...
   a. have more than one house.
   b. will not buy anything that costs as much as a house.
   c. spend too much on the house they buy.

5. The speaker says that ...
   a. people who have expensive holidays do not manage money well.
   b. travelling round the world is a waste of money.
   c. money spent on a holiday is money that cannot be spent on something else.

6. The speaker says that ...
   a. most of the students will retire when they are 50.
   b. people have to plan carefully if they want to retire early.
   c. people can only retire early if they are very rich.

For questions 7–13, complete this summary of the final part of the talk. Use no more than two words in each space.

Too many people think that the (7) _____ they have is what is left after they pay all their expenses. People should think more about their assets and what they are (8) _____. They should also remember that they might have more surplus cash if they reduce their (9) _____.

Somebody might decide that selling their house and buying a (10) _____ one makes financial sense or that running (11) _____ is unnecessary. People must then decide how to invest their money and whether they want to take the (12) _____ of losing it. Not everyone knows the best way to invest money, and it is a good idea to (13) _____ from somebody who does.

B 🎧 You will hear the owner of a taxi firm talking to his accountant.

For questions 14–19, complete the information in the table. Use <u>no more than two words or a number</u> for each answer.

	Now	Before
Number of taxis operating at airport	(14) ___	10
Number of taxis operating in city centre	16	(15) ___
Reasons for reduction of drivers at airport	15% fewer (16) _____ arriving at airport. Fewer evening arrivals so more people use the (17) _____.	
Reasons for increase of city-centre drivers	More people to use taxis in the central (18) _____. More people to book taxis (19) _____.	

For questions 20–23, complete the notes. Use <u>no more than two words or a number</u> for each answer.

20. James thinks that Mehmet made a decision without thinking _____ enough.
21. Mehmet looked at the _____ and not at the separate sides of his business.
22. James thinks that Mehmet now has too many _____ working for him.
23. Mehmet says that people could find a job _____ and might not come back to him.

10 Feelings

Speaking 1: your feelings

A Answer these questions with a partner.

1. Are you an emotional person?
2. Do you show your feelings or do you hide your feelings?

Vocabulary 1: situations and feelings

A Talk with a partner. Use these adjectives to talk about how the people in the pictures are feeling.

> happy   sad   angry   disappointed   bored   nervous   excited   upset   proud
> frightened   relaxed   confused   worried   surprised   annoyed   scared

B 🎧 Listen to some students and check the pronunciation. Then practise saying the words.

C How do you feel right now? Ask your partner how he or she is feeling.

> **Grammar check**
>
> When we talk about how we feel at a particular moment, we can use *be* + adjective.
> *I'm sad. / He's nervous. / She was very disappointed.*
>
> We use *adjectives* when we talk about how things make us feel.
> **Subject + *get* + adjective**
> *I get angry when ... / He gets upset if ...*
> **Subject + verb + object**
> *It worries me. / It frightens me. You're confusing me. / She really annoyed me.*
> **Subject + *make* + object + adjective**
> *It makes me happy / sad / nervous. It made me so angry. / He made her very proud.*
>
> Remember that the ~ed adjective describes how the person feels.
> The ~ing adjective describes the thing.
> *I'm bored today. / This book is really boring.*
> *I was disappointed with the movie. / The movie was disappointing.*

Speaking 2: saying how you feel about things

A Look at these questions and think about how you would answer them.

1. What makes you happy?
2. When were you last excited about something?
3. What makes you really angry?
4. What do you worry about?
5. When did you last get nervous about something?
6. What do you do to relax?

B 🎧 Listen to some students answering the questions. Make notes.

C Walk around the class. Ask and answer each question in Exercise A with a different classmate. Then ask some similar questions with more of the adjectives from Vocabulary 1A.

Vocabulary 2: extreme adjectives

A Match the adjectives 1–6 with the more extreme adjectives a–f.

1. good ___
2. bad ___
3. happy ___
4. surprised ___
5. angry ___
6. frightened ___

a. furious
b. terrified
c. fantastic
d. amazed
e. terrible
f. delighted

B 🎧 Listen to some students using extreme adjectives to answer questions.

C 🎧 Listen again and complete these sentences.

1. I get absolutely furious when people are _____.
2. I _____ last year. I was absolutely terrified before I _____, but then when I _____, it was absolutely fantastic.
3. When _____, I was absolutely delighted.

Watch out!
typical errors

I'm very furious. ✗
I'm absolutely happy. ✗
I was amazing to see her again. ✗

 Exam tip: If you're telling the examiner how you feel about something, try to use vocabulary and stress and intonation that makes the examiner want to listen.

D Here are two typical cards for part 2 of the Speaking Module. Work with a partner – one of you is A, the other is B. You have a minute to think about it and make notes.

A

Describe something exciting that happened to you recently.
Say ...
- what happened.
- where you were.
- who you were with.
- how you felt.

B

Describe a surprise that you have had recently.
Say ...
- what happened.
- where it happened.
- who you were with or if you were alone.
- why you were so surprised.

E Take it in turns to speak about what's on your card for about two minutes.

10

Listening 1: preparing to listen

A Look at these questions about phobias. How many can you answer?

1. What is a phobia?
2. How many people have phobias?
3. What examples of phobias are given?
4. What may cause phobias?

B 🎧 Listen to the introduction to a radio programme about phobias. Answer the questions in Exercise A.

C Look at the pictures. What phobia does each show?

D 🎧 Listen to the rest of the programme. In what order does the speaker mention the phobias in Exercise C?

Listening 2: classifying

A 🎧 Read the questions carefully. Then listen again and answer them.

What does the speaker say about each of the phobias 1–5?

Write:
  P   if the person with the phobia does not like being with other people
  H   if the person with the phobia stays away from parts of his or her house
  T   if thinking about it can make it worse
  C   if it can be cured easily

1. arachnophobia   ___
2. social phobia   ___
3. aerophobia   ___
4. agoraphobia   ___
5. claustrophobia   ___

B Read these statements about the task you have just done. Mark them (T) true or (F) false.

1. There was quite a lot to read in the instructions.   ___
2. It was easy to know what you had to do.   ___
3. You needed to read and listen at the same time.   ___
4. The speaker made the points P, H, T and C in that order.   ___
5. You needed to use some letters more than once.   ___

Question-type tip: Some listening and reading tasks ask you to classify. There are usually more instructions to read, and you need to be sure about what you have to do. The speaker will answer the questions in the correct order but, of course, he or she won't mention each point in the same order. You need to read carefully before you listen and continue to read as you listen.

Listening 3: practise classifying

A 🎧 Listen to the same speaker talking about three more phobias. Match the pictures with the extracts. There are two pictures that you do not need.

Question-type tip: In this task, the extracts are in the correct order but the statements that you have to listen for are not. You must read the statements carefully first so that you know what to listen for.

B 🎧 Listen again and answer the questions.
For questions 1–6, write:

A If the statement refers to the first extract.
B If the statement refers to the second extract.
C If the statement refers to the third extract.

1. This phobia affects people at a particular time of the year.   —
2. People with this phobia will not go to some public places.   —
3. This phobia may cause people to hurt themselves.   —
4. This phobia mostly affects very young people.   —
5. People might think this phobia is a normal condition.   —
6. People with this phobia will not watch something on the television. —

C Check the key on page 270. How many questions did you answer correctly?

D Tick the sentences about the listening task that are true for you and think about how you can answer more questions correctly next time.

1. I understood the overall gist and matched the pictures easily.
2. I understood the instructions for the classifying task quite easily.
3. I needed time to read all the points before I was ready to listen.
4. I am happy with how many questions I answered correctly.
5. I would find this task more difficult if I only heard the recording once.

Key vocabulary in context

Circle the correct option in each sentence.

1. If you **suffer from** something, *you enjoy it / it is a problem for you*.
2. If you **panic**, you *behave normally / do things without thinking*.
3. If you **avoid** something, you *don't go near it / try to find it whenever you can*.
4. If something is **approaching**, it is *coming towards you / going away from you*.

Reading 1: preparing to read

A Tick the correct definition of stress below.

  A Stress is a feeling of worry because of problems in your life.

  B Stress is a feeling of excitement because something good is going to happen.

  C Stress is a feeling of happiness because everything in your life is as you planned it.

B Talk in small groups. What are the most common causes of stress?

Reading 2: using topic sentences to predict

A What do you remember about topic sentences? Complete each statement with <u>one word only</u>.

1. The topic sentence should tell the reader what the rest of the _____ is about.
2. Other information in the paragraph should _____ the topic sentence.
3. If information is not related to the topic sentence, the writer should start a _____ paragraph.

B Here are the topic sentences from seven paragraphs in a text about stress. Read them and then answer the questions that follow with a partner.

Paragraph 1: Stress is worry and anxiety in your life.

Paragraph 2: The most common cause of stress is having financial problems.

Paragraph 3: Pressure and worry at work is another cause of stress.

Paragraph 4: There is lot of stress in people's personal relationships.

Paragraph 5: Many people suffer stress because of their health.

Paragraph 6: People become very anxious about the little problems they face every day.

Paragraph 7: People have found ways to deal with stress.

1. Do you get a clear idea of what the text will be about from reading only the topic sentences?
2. Can you see how the text will be organized from looking only at the topic sentences?
3. Can you predict what supporting information will be in each paragraph?
4. In which of the paragraphs will each of these supporting ideas be?

    • the car breaking down __

    • between 50 and 60 possible causes of stress __

    • an elderly relative moving into the family home __

    • the cost of living is rising __

    • yoga or other forms of relaxation exercise __

    • their boss does not understand them __

    • losing eyesight or hearing __

C Now read the text and check your answers.

Life Can Be Stressful

Stress is worry and anxiety in your life. Stress stops you relaxing, it is the most common cause of heart disease and it can lead to cancer. Stress can cause poor concentration, can affect judgement and can result in accidents. Stress can be the cause of family break-ups, violence and even suicide. So what are the main causes of stress in a typical modern lifestyle? A study has identified between 50 and 60 possible causes of stress, and here are the five most frequent.

The most common cause of stress is having financial problems. People cannot do the things they want to do because they lack money. Debts are growing because mortgage repayments are increasing and credit card bills need to be paid. The cost of living is rising, and it all adds up to worry.

Pressure and worry at work is another cause of stress. People worry that there is change and people worry when there is no change. They may feel that their boss does not understand them or that he makes life difficult for them. If people think that they are doing their job badly or that they are about to lose their job, it is a huge cause of anxiety.

There is lot of stress in people's personal relationships. Disagreements with a husband or wife, arguments with children and difficulties with relatives can all cause anxiety. An elderly relative moving into the family home or an older child leaving are both causes of tension. The death or the serious illness of a family member or close friend is a major cause of stress.

Many people suffer stress because of their health. Common illnesses, like heart disease and high blood pressure, are a common worry. As people grow older, they become anxious about losing their eyesight or hearing. People worry about gaining weight and losing weight and about not having the time to lead a healthy lifestyle.

People become very anxious about the little problems they face every day. Difficulties getting to work on the train or the car breaking down are common causes of worry, and people spend time thinking about machines and devices around the house that have gone wrong. People have lists of tasks that are never completed, and they worry that they will never have time to relax.

People have found ways to deal with stress. Some do yoga or other forms of relaxation exercise to prevent them from becoming over-anxious, while others claim that taking part in hard physical activity helps them to work off stress. Everyone should make sure that they spend some time every day doing what makes them happy. Stress is a killer.

D Did reading the topic sentences first make the text easier to read?

Exam tip: Remember that when you are doing the Reading Module, understanding the topic sentence will help you to know where to look back to find answers.

Reading 3: practise predicting from topic sentences

A Read only the topic sentence highlighted in each paragraph in the text on the next page, and think about ...

- what the whole text is about.
- how the text will be organized.
- what supporting information will be in each paragraph.

B Read questions 1–6 and guess which paragraph the information will be found in.

C Read the text and answer all the questions.

For questions 1–6, say in which paragraph the following information is found.
Write the letter in the space.

1. People like to see results. ___
2. People need change. ___
3. People will stay in the same job. ___
4. People like to decide some things for themselves. ___
5. People need to talk. ___
6. Managers should tell workers that they are pleased. ___

Happy People Do More Work!

A These days, people who run a business know that it is important to look after the people who work for them. Recent research shows that if employees feel good about their work, they are not only happier, but they are more likely to work harder and perform better. They will take less time off sick and are less likely to leave the company. So what exactly makes people happy at work? We asked 100 people employed by large and small businesses, and these are the five most important factors.

B People need to achieve something. They want to see that the decisions they make and the work they do have an end result. People enjoy solving problems and doing things that help other people. Bosses should realize that workers are happy when they are working hard, not when they are doing nothing.

C People want to be appreciated. They don't necessarily want somebody to keep telling them that they are doing a great job, but they do want somebody to recognize what they have achieved. It doesn't take much for a boss to say 'well done' occasionally, but many bosses just don't think of it.

D People want to work with people they like. Being part of a team is very important for most employees, and enjoying the company of colleagues makes people want to go to work in the morning. They don't expect colleagues to be their best friends, but they want to have a conversation and share a joke. Most people don't enjoy working alone for too long.

E People need a degree of freedom. They want to control their own time and make their own decisions. Employees want their bosses to trust them and respect them. Nobody likes working in an environment where somebody is constantly telling them what to do or watching to check that they are busy.

F People enjoy learning something new. They either want to learn how to do something for the first time or how to do something better. Most people like to feel that they are creating something and don't feel they are doing this if they are repeating a routine day after day.

For questions 7–14, complete the summary with words and phrases from the box.

benefit	succeed	better	achieve	decide	appreciate
creative	colleagues	friends	control	tell	improve	same

If employees feel happy at work, both they and the companies they work for
(7) _____. Workers generally do a (8) _____ job if they are happy. It is important
for employees to feel that they (9) _____ something and that the people they work
for (10) _____ it. Most people enjoy their job more if they work with (11) _____
who they can communicate with. Employees do not like having a boss who wants to
(12) _____ everything they do, and nobody likes being watched. People like to feel
that they can learn something new or (13) _____ something they are already
doing. Nobody enjoys doing the (14) _____ thing day after day.

D Check the key on page 270. How many questions did you answer correctly?

E Tick the sentences about the reading task that are true for you and think about how you can answer more questions correctly next time.

1. I understand better how the topic sentence makes a paragraph easier to read.
2. I predicted what would be in each paragraph from reading the topic sentences.
3. I'm reading texts more quickly than I was.
4. I am happy with how many of the questions I answered correctly.

Key vocabulary in context

Complete the sentences with these verbs.

appreciate   deal with   respect   trust

1. Very small children don't really _____ how much their parents do for them.
2. Children should _____ people older than them, like teachers.
3. My children are young, but I _____ them to cross the road safely.
4. Some parents don't know how to _____ difficult children.

WB For focus on reading skills, go to Workbook page 28.

Writing 1: preparing to write

A Answer these questions with a partner. Check the highlighted words.

1. Are you generally a sociable person?
2. Do you enjoy other people's company or do you prefer spending time alone?
3. Do you get on with most people or do you have disagreements easily?

B Check the highlighted words and then complete each sentence so that it is true for you.

1. It is really annoying when people _____.
2. It really irritates me if people _____
   when I'm trying to _____.
3. It annoys me if somebody _____
   without asking first.
4. It is very irritating if somebody _____
   when I want to sleep.
5. It makes me furious if people _____.

C Compare your ideas with a partner.

D Talk with a partner. Have you ever shared a room with somebody? Did you get on or did you have problems?

Writing 2: linking words

A Look at these instructions for a typical IELTS writing task.

You are living in a college residence where all the students are in shared rooms. You are not happy with the student you are sharing with because he/she is very inconsiderate. You are finding it difficult to study and sometimes to sleep.

Write a letter to the manager of the college residence and say that you want a new roommate or to move to a new room. Explain why.

Write at least 150 words. You should spend 20 minutes on this task.

B Answer these questions with a partner.

1. Is it an easy or difficult letter to write?
2. Do you need to invent everything, or do you have experience of a situation like this?
3. Can you think of some examples of your roommate's inconsiderate behaviour?
4. Are you going to write in a formal or informal register?

C Read the letter that a student wrote. Write three sentences about what you like.

Example: *It is well organized and easy to follow.*

Dear Mr Grant,

I am writing to inform you that I would like to either move to a new room or have a new roommate. I know that normally students do not change rooms in the middle of the term. _____, the student who I am sharing with at the moment is very inconsiderate and I am finding things very difficult.

_____, he is very noisy. He listens to loud music a lot or plays his guitar. I have asked him to wear headphones but he refuses. _____, he comes back to the room very late two or three times a week. Sometimes he makes calls on his mobile in the middle of the night.

He _____ frequently invites his friends to the room without asking me first. On two occasions, his friends from outside the residence have slept on the floor. _____, he sometimes borrows my things without asking. He took my electronic dictionary to a lecture last week.

_____ of all this, I am very unhappy. I am not able to study in my room and I am losing sleep. _____, I think that moving to a new room is the best solution, and I would appreciate it if you could arrange this as soon as possible.

Yours sincerely,

Javier Moreno

D Use each linking word below once to complete the letter. Use a capital letter if necessary.

| finally | what's more | also | however | therefore | as a result | firstly |

E Write each linking word from Exercise D in a space below.

This introduces the first point I want to make about a situation. _____
These introduce more points about the same situation. _____ / _____
This introduces the last point I want to make about the situation. _____
This introduces a viewpoint that is different from what was said before. _____
These introduce the result or consequence of something that was mentioned before. They are similar to 'so'. _____ / _____

Exam tip: Linking words and phrases help to organize a composition, but only use them if you are confident that you know how to use them properly. A lot of students try to use linking words because they think they should, but they use them in the wrong way.

WB Go to Workbook page 28 for the writing task.

Speaking

A Look at these exchanges between an examiner and some students. Then listen. What do you think about the students' answers?

1. Examiner: So, were you disappointed when you didn't get into university?
    Student: No, I didn't care.
2. Examiner: So, working in advertising must be very exciting.
    Student: No, it's very boring most of the time.
3. Examiner: Are you nervous about the exams that you're taking next month?
    Student: No, I'm not nervous. I like exams.
4. Examiner: What did you think of London? Did you get confused travelling around on the tube?
    Student: No, it was easy.

B Listen to these students answering the same questions. How are their answers better?

Exam tip: You don't have to agree with the examiner, but if you disagree or want to correct a comment he makes, you should do it politely. Introduce your comment with a phrase that tells the examiner you are going to disagree with him.

C Look at the tapescript and listen again. Highlight expressions you want to use.

D Practise the exchanges with a partner.

Vocabulary

A Correct the spelling mistakes in these words.

1. emosional _____
2. disapointed _____
3. anoying _____
4. fritened _____
5. fewrious _____
6. anksious _____
7. angsiety _____
8. preshure _____
9. soshiable _____
10. apresiate _____

B Listen and mark the main stress on the words in Exercise A above. Then practise saying them.

C Fill the gaps with a word made from the root words in the box.

1. It was all very _____. I didn't know what to do.
2. I was absolutely _____ when the plane took off.
3. I don't think many people find true _____ in life.
4. There was great _____ when the circus started.
5. Being a politician must be very _____.
6. Yoga is a very popular form of _____.

| confuse |
| terrify |
| happy |
| excite |
| stress |
| relax |

Errors

A There are errors in all these sentences. Correct them.

1. This film is really bored.
2. I'm feeling very exhausted today.
3. She's absolutely disappointed about it.
4. It really puts me angry when people say that.
5. Most people are afraid about spiders.
6. It's a difficult problem to deal for.

10

Reading

A Read these topic sentences from the five paragraphs of a text about getting angry and match them with the pictures below. Write a number in the white box in each picture.

1. People who get angry easily are not being kind to their heart.
2. Anger causes the body to react in the same way that it does when it is attacked.
3. People who get angry easily are also more likely to have an unhealthy lifestyle.
4. People can change the way they react to stress, though.
5. Doctors suggest several techniques that help angry people to remain calm and not lose control.

An Angry Heart

People who get angry easily are not being kind to their heart. People who lose control because they have to wait in a queue, because the driver of another car upsets them or because they have a small disagreement with their husband or wife are more likely to have a heart attack than those who remain calm. In fact, men who become angry when they feel stressed are three times more likely to suffer from heart disease later in life than those who do not.

Anger causes the body to react in the same way that it does when it is attacked. The nervous system prepares itself for fight or flight. That means staying where you are and dealing with the situation or running away from the situation as quickly as possible. When the nervous system is on alert, the heart produces adrenaline, and that makes it more sensitive.

People who get angry easily are also more likely to have an unhealthy lifestyle. Because they are less able to deal with stress, they may do other things as a result. They are more likely to smoke and drink a lot of alcohol, and they may have a very poor diet. Their anger may also mean that they have poor

relationships at home or at work, and that adds to the problem.

People can change the way they react to stress, though. They need to accept that they cannot change the situation they are in but can change the way they react to it. They need to ask themselves if it really matters that they are stuck in traffic and will arrive home fifteen minutes later than they planned. And they need to think more about how their reactions affect other people and if it is worth losing the respect of other people for no reason.

Doctors suggest several techniques that help angry people to remain calm and not lose control. Doing exercise is an excellent way to relieve stress and generally puts people in a good mood. Taking a deep breath and counting to ten helps people to calm down and gives them time to think clearly about the situation they are in and how they should react to it. Some doctors say that writing down your feelings on a piece of paper when you are very angry is a good idea. It is a way of getting the anger out and is much better than losing control and shouting at people.

B Answer the questions.

For questions 1–6, decide if the information given below agrees with the opinions expressed in the passage. Write (T) true, (F) false or (NG) not given.

1. A lot of people have a heart attack when they are driving.   —
2. Remaining calm will help you to live longer.   —
3. Most people run away from a dangerous situation.   —
4. Producing a lot of adrenaline is always good for your heart.   —
5. People smoke and drink alcohol because they think it helps to deal with stress.   —
6. Angry people feel calm when they are at home.   —

For questions 7–12, complete the notes with words from the passage. Write <u>no more than two words or a number</u> for each answer.

7. Angry people need to learn how to _____ differently when they feel stress.
8. They need to think about how much a certain problem really _____.
9. They need to think more about how _____ are affected when they lose control.
10. If people exercise or do yoga, they suffer less from _____.
11. People should _____ before they react, and counting to ten helps them to do that.
12. Expressing _____ in writing is better than expressing them physically.

Review 2

Speaking and Vocabulary

A Answer these questions with a partner.

1. Do you feel that your speaking is generally improving?
2. Do you know what kind of questions the examiner will ask you in each part of the exam?
3. Do you feel more confident about answering those questions?

B The questions below practise the topics that you learnt in Units 6–10. Work in pairs. One of you is student A, the other is B. Ask and answer with your partner.

Student A
1. What do you like about the town or city you live in?
2. Do you prefer a city lifestyle or a more rural lifestyle?
3. How do you usually travel around your town or city?
4. Do you usually have enough time to do all the things you want to do each day?
5. Do you like shopping?
6. What makes you happy?

Student B
1. What is the most beautiful city you have visited?
2. Does your town or city have good facilities for entertainment and leisure activities?
3. How often do you fly? Do you enjoy flying?
4. How do you usually spend your free time?
5. When it comes to money, are you a saver or a spender?
6. What annoys you or makes you really angry?

C Write important words and phrases that you have learnt in Units 6–10 under each heading.

places	city and country life	travel and transport
_____	_____	_____
_____	_____	_____
_____	_____	_____
_____	_____	_____

feelings	**my words and phrases**	time expressions
_____		_____
_____		_____
_____		_____
_____		_____

money	say how often you do something
_____	_____
_____	_____
_____	_____
_____	_____

Listening and Reading

The thoughts below are from the 'exam tips' in the reading and listening sections of Units 6–10.

A Complete each sentence about listening, using <u>one word only</u>.

1. When I am listening for specific information, like writing names of places on a map, the speaker will often _____ information that I need to answer a question.

2. Sometimes I will have to complete a short _____ of what I heard on the tape. I need to spell words correctly and make sure they _____ grammatically. However, if I'm not sure how to fill a space, I should write what I think I hear.

3. Having a table will help when I listen, because I can predict how the talk will be organized and _____ into parts. I will know that the speaker is going to move to a new topic within the talk.

4. I will sometimes need to understand the meaning of a key word I don't know from the context. I might have to _____ the spelling of a new word if it is part of an answer.

5. If a task asks me to classify, I will need to read the _____ carefully so that I know exactly what to do. I will need to look at points as I listen because they will not be in the same _____ as I hear them.

B Complete each sentence about reading using <u>one word only</u>.

1. In the IELTS Reading Module, passages which are advertisements, leaflets or information pages will be clearly divided into sections. Texts will be clearly divided into _____.

2. Reading the _____ sentence, which is usually the first sentence, of each paragraph will help me to read more quickly. I will often be able to predict quite a lot about a text just by reading the _____ sentence.

3. I will understand a text better if I can quickly see what is _____ and what is opinion.

4. When you complete a summary, you will either need to use words from the text or choose words from a _____. If the words come from a _____, they will not always be words from the text. I should always look at what comes before and after a space in a summary so I can check that answers _____ grammatically.

5. I will read more quickly and understand texts better if I see how one word or phrase _____ back or forwards to another. I need to understand how _____ words, like 'it', 'this', 'there' and 'one', are used.

C Answer the questions (Y) yes or (N) no.

1. Has your listening and reading improved since the last review section?   __
2. Do you feel more confident about doing well in the tasks?   __
3. Are you dealing better with words and phrases that you don't know?   __
4. Are you happy with the number of correct answers you are achieving in the tasks? __

 Exam tip: Don't worry if your scores for some tasks are the same as they were earlier in the course. The tapescripts are getting longer. Vocabulary and grammatical structures are more challenging!

Writing

You will hear an interview with an IELTS examiner. He talks about marking compositions.

A 🎧 Look at the interviewer's first question and then listen to the first part of the interview. Mark these statements (T) true, (F) false or (NG) not given.

What is the difference between the Academic exam and the General Training exam in terms of the Writing Module?

1. The General Training writing exam is easier than the Academic writing exam. __
2. In the General Training writing exam, students need to write about graphs and charts. __
3. Not many students do well in the second part of the Academic writing exam. __
4. For General Training students, writing a letter is usually the easier of two tasks. __

B 🎧 Look at the interviewer's second question and then listen to the second part of the interview. Put the points into the order in which you hear them.

What do you look for when you mark an IELTS composition?

__ A letter or composition should have paragraphs.
__ The student should use the appropriate register.
__ The student must use the right number of words.
__ Points or ideas need to be linked with both reference words or linking words.
__ The composition must be easy to read.
__ Each paragraph should start with a topic sentence.
_1_ The student must answer the question.
__ Points must be organized into a logical order.

C 🎧 Look at the interviewer's third question and then listen to the third part of the interview. Complete the summary below. Use <u>no more than two words</u> for each answer.

What about vocabulary, spelling and accurate grammar?

If students are aiming for a lower score in the IELTS exam, they do not need to use very (1) _____ vocabulary. They should try to use the (2) _____ or phrase if they know it, but it is important to keep things simple. They should only use words and phrases that they know how to use (3) _____. For students aiming for a lower score, it is more important to use (4) _____ grammatical structures accurately than to try to use complicated structures that they do not really know how to use.

D Read the tapescript on pages 302 and 303.

E Give yourself a mark out of ten for how much your writing has improved.

0 —————————— 5 —————————— 10

My writing has not
really improved at all.

My writing is much better
than it was at the beginning
of the course.

What next?

You've now completed two-thirds of the course. You've heard most of the different types of talk or conversation that you will hear in the Listening Module, and you've read most of the different types of text that you will have to read in the Reading Module. You've practised almost all of the task types for each Module. You should feel more confident about taking the exam now, but don't worry if there are still parts that you find difficult. There is plenty of time to practise those parts and to deal with any problems you are having. Here are some things that you should do now. Decide which ones you'd like to do first. Number them.

☐ Continue to speak English every time you get the opportunity. Now you know what sort of things the examiner will ask you in the spoken exam, practise talking about those things. If you have friends or relatives who speak good English, try to have short conversations with them that practise what you have been learning and try to use new vocabulary that you have learnt.

☐ There are lots of websites that have short clips with people speaking English. Even if you don't understand everything people say, you will pick out some words and phrases and become more familiar with the pronunciation patterns of the language. Watch a movie in English from time to time if you can. Continue to borrow CDs to listen to if you need extra practice with the Listening Module of the exam.

☐ Continue to read as much as you can. You should be able to follow more challenging texts now, so look at English newspapers and magazines more frequently. There are thousands of websites in English, and you can always find something that you are especially interested in. Continue to think about the organization of a text and note down new vocabulary that you think will be useful to remember. Try to use the vocabulary when you speak or write.

☐ As your English improves, you may feel that you want to learn and remember more vocabulary than is realistic. Make sure you learn and revise vocabulary that is useful and that you can use to communicate. As well as single new words, you should learn words that you already know used in new ways. You should learn how words go together to form common phrases and expressions.

☐ If you are still having difficulty with basic writing skills, continue to practise writing sentences and short paragraphs. Practise your spelling and punctuation. If you feel that your writing has improved, practise writing more compositions. Continue to look at as many model answers to exam questions as you can. This will help you know what to write and how to write it in the exam.

Go on to the next section of the Course Book. Make sure you practise all aspects of your English, but focus on what you are having problems with. Don't worry if you don't make progress in all areas at the same time.

11 Health

Vocabulary 1: healthy or unhealthy?

A Check the highlighted words and phrases and mark each of these sentences (H) healthy or (U) unhealthy in the first column.

1. I do regular exercise and like to stay fit.   __ __
2. I'm a bit overweight.   __ __
3. I walk or ride a bicycle and like to get fresh air. __ __
4. I eat lots of fresh fruit and salad.   __ __
5. I eat lots of fried food and frozen food.   __ __
6. I drink plenty of water during the day.   __ __
7. I drink a lot of fizzy drinks.   __ __
8. I really like sweets, chocolate and cakes.   __ __
9. My job gives me a lot of stress.   __ __
10. I smoke.   __ __

Speaking 1: lifestyle

A Look again at Vocabulary 1A. In the second column, write (T) true for you or (N) not true for you. Then talk with a partner about your lifestyle.

Vocabulary 2: typical health problems

A Complete each sentence with a health problem below.

headaches	cough	hay fever	poor eyesight	flu	allergic to

1. People often say they have _____, but usually it's just a bad cold.
2. A lot of people are _____ something. It could be a type of food, or animals like cats or dogs.
3. A lot of people suffer from _____ in spring. They get sore eyes and a runny nose.
4. People who smoke are more likely to get a _____ than people who don't smoke.
5. Some people get bad _____ if they concentrate for too long. It can make life difficult.
6. If people have _____, they need to wear glasses.

B Use a dictionary to find any words and phrases that you need to talk about any health problem you have or somebody you know well has. Then compare with a partner.

> **Pronunciation check**
> The *ough* at the end of words is sometimes pronounced in different ways. Sometimes it is pronounced /ɒ/, sometimes /ʌ/ and sometimes /əʊ/. It is difficult to know which way is correct if you see a new word.
> Decide how these words are pronounced.
> 1. cough   2. enough   3. though   4. rough
> 🎧 Listen and check your answers.

Speaking 2: talking about health problems

A Walk around the classroom. Find at least one person who ...

1. has had a bad cold/flu recently.   2. is allergic to something.   3. has a bad cough at the moment.
4. suffers from hay fever.   5. often gets bad headaches.   6. has poor eyesight.

B Talk with a partner. What should a person with each of the problems above do?

Example: *If you've got poor eyesight, you should wear glasses or contact lenses.*

Vocabulary 3: accidents

A Match the phrases below with the pictures.

1. break a bone   2. get an electric shock   3. burn yourself   4. need stitches   5. be stung   6. be bitten

Speaking 3: telling stories

A Talk with a partner. Ask and answer these questions.

1. Have you ever needed stitches in a bad cut?   2. Have you ever had an electric shock?
3. Have you ever broken a bone?   4. Have you ever burnt yourself?
5. Have you ever been stung by a bee / a scorpion?   6. Have you ever been bitten by a dog / a snake?

Grammar check

We use the *passive voice* when we want to focus on what happened to somebody rather than who or what did the action. Sometimes who or what did the action is also important, so we put it at the end of the sentence and use *by*.

Have you ever been stung by a bee? ✓
NOT *Has a bee ever stung you?* ✗
The second question is not wrong, but it isn't very natural.

Make these two sentences passive.
1. Has an animal ever attacked you? _____
2. Yes, a neighbour's dog attacked me when I was little. _____

We ask *What were you doing?* if we want to know about before an accident.
What were you doing when you got an electric shock? → *I was working in the house.*
We ask *What did you do?* if we want to know about after an accident.
What did you do when you got the electric shock? → *I went to lie down.*

B Talk with a partner. Ask and answer the questions in Exercise A again. Say ...

where you were   what you were doing   what you did

Listening 1: flow charts

A Look at part of a flow chart below and then answer these questions with a partner.

1. What is a flow chart?
2. What does this flow chart show?
3. What do these words mean?
   symptoms   diagnosis   treatment

Cold and flu

Follow the chart so that you know how to treat the symptoms of a cold or the flu and whether or not you need to see a doctor. Other conditions can have the same symptoms as a cold or the flu.

SYMPTOMS		DIAGNOSIS		TREATMENT
↓ BEGIN HERE				
① Do you have a fever?	→ NO	You may have a cold.	→	Get plenty of rest and drink lots of water.
↓ YES				
② Do you have a sore throat and headache but not a runny nose?	→ YES	You may have strep throat – a bacterial infection.	→	Get plenty of rest and drink lots of water. See a doctor if the fever lasts more than 48 hours. He may give you antibiotics.
↓ NO				
③ Did your symptoms start suddenly? Do your muscles ache? Do you have a sore throat and a runny nose?	→ YES	You may have the flu.	→	Get plenty of rest and drink lots of water. Medicine that you can buy at a chemist will relieve some of the symptoms.
↓ NO				

Grammar check
First conditional type sentences can be used to talk about possibility and give advice.
If you have a sore throat and a runny nose, you may have the flu.
If you have the flu, you should get plenty of rest.

B 🎧 Look at the next part of the flow chart. Listen and complete the notes using <u>no more than two words</u> for each answer.

④ Do you have a bad cough and is it difficult to (1) _____?	→ YES	You may have bronchitis.	→	Get plenty of rest and drink lots of water. If you (2) _____, stop completely for a while. Medicine that you can buy at a chemist will relieve the (3) _____. If symptoms get worse, contact (4) _____.
↓ NO				
⑤ Do you have a runny nose and sore eyes?	→ YES	You may be (5) _____ something.	→	Try medicine that you can buy at a chemist or ask your doctor for advice.

Question-type tip: A flow chart shows a series of events or actions and their possible results. In the Listening Module of the exam, you will sometimes need to complete notes on a flow chart. Having a chart like this helps you, because you can predict how the talk will be organized and divided into parts. You know when the speaker is going to go from one topic to another.

Listening 2: practice with flow charts

A 🎧 Look at the first part of a flow chart that shows you what to do if you have a headache. Listen and complete the notes using <u>no more than two words</u> for each answer.

Headaches

There are different reasons why you may have a headache. You may also have other symptoms. Follow the chart so that you know what to do if you have a headache.

SYMPTOMS   **DIAGNOSIS**   **TREATMENT**

↓ BEGIN HERE

① Do you have a fever or other symptoms of a cold? Have you been sick? → **YES**   You may have a bad cold or (1) _____ . →   Get plenty of rest and drink lots of water. (2) _____ that you can buy at a chemist will relieve some of the symptoms.

↓ NO

② Do you have a very bad headache and a stiff (3) _____ ? Does normal light hurt (4) _____ ? → **YES**   You may have meningitis – a serious condition that can affect your (5) _____ . →   You MUST see your doctor or go to a (6) _____ immediately.

↓ NO

③ Have you hit (7) _____ recently? → **YES**   You may have concussion – a serious condition caused by (8) _____ pushing against your brain. →   You MUST get immediate treatment.

B Check the key on page 270. How many questions did you answer correctly?

C Tick the sentences about the listening task that are true for you and think about how you can answer more questions correctly next time.

1. Looking at the flow chart helped me make predictions about what I would hear.
2. I understood the speaker and knew which words to write in the spaces.
3. I spelt most of my answers correctly.
4. I am pleased with how many questions I answered correctly.

Key vocabulary in context

Match the words 1–4 with the words a–d to make common noun phrases from the text.

1. runny   a. muscles
2. sore   b. nose
3. aching   c. neck
4. stiff   d. throat / eyes

11

Reading 1: preparing to read

A Answer these questions with a partner.

1. What is the most common way of trying to lose weight in your country?
2. Do men and women try to lose weight in different ways?
3. Do many people go on a diet?
4. Do many people join a fitness club or a group for people who want to lose weight?

B Read the extract from a web page that gives advice about finding a fitness club.

Fitness club

More and more people want to lose weight and stay in shape. Being overweight is not good for your confidence, and it can lead to other health problems. Most people need a little help and motivation when it comes to exercise, so joining a fitness club may be the best solution. However, finding a local fitness club that suits your needs might not be so easy.

There are fitness clubs all round the country, and each has its own atmosphere. Fitness clubs offer a wide range of facilities and activities, so it is just about finding the right one for you.

Whether you want to lift weights and work out on machines, play tennis, swim or join a yoga class, a good fitness club will usually have the answer. There are so many different clubs that it's important to choose one that you are comfortable with so that you want to keep going.

Membership for fitness clubs can be expensive, so you want to be happy with the club you choose and you want to go along as often as possible. If you only go once a month, or stop going completely, you will waste a lot of money. There are usually some great offers available at fitness clubs, so you should shop around.

You can use our pages to find the right club in your area, but then it's up to you to get yourself there and to start getting in shape!

Reading 2: sentence completion

A Using the extract above, complete each sentence with the correct ending A–G from the box. Not all of the endings need to be used.

1. Finding the right fitness club for you ... ___
2. Being comfortable with your fitness club ... ___
3. Not going to your fitness club regularly ... ___
4. Shopping around ... ___

A is a waste of money.
B is usually quite cheap.
C can be difficult.
D will stop you losing weight.
E will often mean that you get a good deal.
F might make you unhappy.
G means that you will keep going to it.

B Choose the correct option in each pair of sentences about Exercise A.

1. A You can match beginnings and endings logically without looking at the text.
   B You must read the text carefully to check that it says the same as what the sentence says.
2. A Matching the beginnings and endings is easy. You just have to find the ending that fits grammatically with the beginning.
   B Matching is not so easy because all the endings fit grammatically with all the beginnings.
3. A The sentence endings have a wide range of grammatical structures.
   B The sentence endings begin with the same part of speech.

Task-type tip: You may have to do a task where you match sentence beginnings with sentence endings. There will always be more endings than beginnings, so you don't have to use all the endings.

Exam tip: All the endings will start with the same part of speech, so you can't just match grammatically. Don't guess answers that seem to make sense – look carefully to find answers in the text.

Reading 3: practice with sentence completion

A Look at this advertisement for a chain of clubs that helps people to lose weight. Scan the text and answer these questions.

1. What is the chain called?
2. Who is the woman in the picture?
3. How can you find your nearest club?

B Skim the text for one minute only. Then cover the text and talk with a partner. Find three things that you both remember.

C Read the text again and answer the questions.

Do you want to lose weight, feel great and enjoy life?

Well, act now – come along and meet your local **FEELGOOD** coach.

The first meeting is free for all!

Joining one of our FEELGOOD clubs has many benefits.
- Meet new people in a motivating but friendly environment.
- We will measure your weight each week to help you assess your progress and keep you motivated.
- We will give you individual advice that will ensure you achieve your goals, and we will help you to set yourself new goals.
- Each week, we will provide new products that you can try out and purchase if you are satisfied.
- We will help you change the shape of your body and show you why simply eating less doesn't necessarily equal weight loss.
- We will introduce you to people who we have already helped and show you videos that tell the story of their progress. **'If I can do it, anyone can do it!'**
- We will charge you only £5 for each weekly meeting and only £15 for a whole month of meetings. There are no penalties for missed classes!
- We will give you a whole month of free meetings if you introduce a friend to **FEELGOOD!**

We have clubs all over the south-west.
Call 01564 698 140 to find out where your nearest FEELGOOD club is.

For questions 1–8, complete each sentence with the correct ending A–J from the box. Not all of the endings need to be used.

1. Nobody has to ... ___
2. People who join a FEELGOOD club can ... ___
3. Getting individual advice will help members ... ___
4. Members can try out new products and ... ___
5. People do not always lose weight just because they ... ___
6. Members who have previously been successful can ... ___
7. People who miss a class do not have to ... ___
8. Members whose friends join a FEELGOOD club do not have to ... ___

```
A   buy them if they are happy.
B   eat less.
C   be seen on film.
D   pay less to attend meetings.
E   pay for the first meeting.
F   do as well as possible.
G   pay for a month.
H   join another club.
I   enjoy various benefits.
J   pay for it.
```

D Check the key on pages 270 and 271. How many questions did you answer correctly?

E Tick the sentences about the reading task that are true for you and think about how you can answer more questions correctly next time.

1. I skimmed the text to get a general idea.
2. I read the sentences in the task carefully before I read the text again more carefully.
3. I knew what to look for when I read the text again.
4. It was quite difficult to choose the correct ending because there are a lot of options.
5. I am happy with how many of the questions I answered correctly.

 Exam tip: If it is difficult to find the correct ending for a beginning, cross off the endings that you know are definitely wrong. It is easier to make a decision if you have fewer options.

Key vocabulary in context

Check the key word in the text and then circle the correct option in each sentence.

1. If something is **motivating**, it makes you want to *do well / stop doing something*.
2. If you **assess** something, you *think about it and make a judgement / say that you don't like it*.
3. **Purchase** is *more / less* formal than 'buy'.
4. You receive a **penalty** if you do something *well / wrong*.

WB For focus on reading skills, go to Workbook page 31.

Writing 1: preparing to write

A Talk with a partner. Look at the pictures and answer the questions.

1. How do the pictures show changing attitudes to smoking?
2. Have attitudes changed in your country? Can people smoke in public places?
3. Do you think it is right to ban smoking in public places?
4. Do you think smoking will ever be banned completely?

B Look at the instructions for a writing task below. Highlight the key words and check you understand what you have to do.

In many countries, smoking has been banned in all public places.
Do you think this is the right thing to do?

Give reasons for your answer and include any relevant examples from your experience. Write about 250 words.

C Answer these questions with a partner.

1. Is it an easy or difficult composition to write?
2. Do you have plenty to say about the topic?
3. Can you give any examples from your own experience?
4. Is it best to write a balanced argument or express a strong opinion?

Writing 2: nouns that help link a text

A Read a student's composition. Does he say what you would say?

Smoking is banned in public places in many countries. It is certainly banned in my country and in countries I have visited. Not long ago, it was normal to see people smoking in bars, on trains and buses and in their offices. I even remember people smoking as they walked round the supermarket when I was little. Now that idea would seem very strange and completely wrong.

People who support a ban say it is unfair for smokers to affect the health of non-smokers, and I tend to agree. If people smoke in crowded places, other people have to breathe in their smoke. Passive smoking kills. Hundreds of thousands of smokers need hospital treatment because of smoke-related illnesses, especially lung cancer. The money spent on that problem could be spent on other things.

The ban on smoking is not popular with everyone, though. Most smokers and even some non-smokers think that the decision is unfair and against human rights. They say that tobacco is sold in shops and do not understand why an activity that is legal should not be allowed in some places. They also argue that governments make money from the tax on tobacco and that many people are employed in the tobacco industry.

Personally, I think it is right that smoking is banned in public places. My father is a smoker and, although he is not happy about standing in the street outside his office to have a cigarette, he understands why the ban is necessary. He admits that, since the ban, he smokes less and that it might make him give up the habit completely.

B Discuss with a partner. What do you like about the composition? What is the purpose of each paragraph?

C Look at the highlighted words in the composition. What does each refer to?

1. **idea** refers to _people smoking as they walk round the supermarket_
2. **problem** refers to _____
3. **decision** refers to _____
4. **activity** refers to _____
5. **habit** refers to _____

Exam tip: We very often use general nouns like these to refer back or forwards in a text and to avoid repeating the same words. If you learn some of them, it will help you to read more quickly. If you use them when you write, they will help to organize and link ideas in your compositions.

D Read these short extracts and circle the correct option in each pair.

1. The World Cup is very important in terms of both sport and politics. It is an **incident / event** that brings people from all over the world together for over a month.
2. Police want information about an **incident / event** in Bournemouth town centre. Two men attacked another man outside a nightclub just before midnight on Friday.
3. The increasing number of older people who need hospital treatment is now one of society's most important **issues / situations**.
4. A lot of people in their fifties lose their job and have no other skills. They find themselves in a very difficult **issue / situation**.
5. Most people do not want to get involved if they see a fight in the street. They think it is a **matter / case** for the police to deal with.
6. Teachers and parents usually get together to deal with bad behaviour at school, but in some **matters / cases** the police need to get involved.

WB Go to Workbook page 31 for the writing task.

Speaking

A Look at this typical card for part 2 of the Speaking Module.
Is it easy to talk about it?

> **Describe a time that you hurt yourself.**
> **Say ...**
> • where you were.
> • what you were doing when you hurt
>   yourself.
> • what happened.
> • what you did when you hurt yourself.

B 🎧 Listen to a student talking and answer the questions.

1. Where was he?
2. What was he doing when he hurt himself?
3. What happened?
4. What did he do when he hurt himself?

C Did the student do well in the speaking task? How could he have done better?

D 🎧 Listen to the same student trying again. What does he do better the second time?

 Exam tip: If you need to tell the examiner about something that happened, use words that you heard on the recording to introduce ideas. They make your story more interesting to listen to.

E Work with a partner. Take it in turns to talk about what's on the card in Exercise A.

Vocabulary

A Complete each highlighted phrase with the correct preposition.

1. I like to stay _____ shape.
2. I like to get plenty _____ fresh air.
3. I'm allergic _____ the chemicals in some food.
4. I suffer _____ bad headaches.

B Correct the spelling mistakes in these words.

1. choclite _____
2. headache _____
3. gim _____
4. simtoms _____
5. asess _____
6. attitude _____

C Fill the gaps with a word made from the root words in the box.

1. Most people go on a diet to lose _____.
2. As people get older, they worry more about their _____.
3. Quite a lot of people are _____ to cat hair.
4. If you have concussion, you must get _____ immediately.
5. Yoga is an _____ that many people enjoy.

weigh
fit
allergy
treat
act

Errors

A There are errors in all these sentences. Correct them.

1. I cooked when I burnt my hand.
2. I bitten by a friend's dog once.
3. I was cut myself with a knife.
4. Have you ever stung by a bee?
5. I discovered that my arm was breaked.
6. I need to lose the weight.

Writing

A Look at the pictures and the first line of some writing task instructions below.

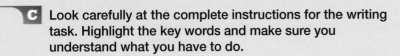

All over the world, life expectancy is increasing.

B Answer these questions with a partner.

1. What is good about more people living to an old age?
2. What are some of the problems of people living to an old age?
3. In your country, who usually cares for people when they are too old to look after themselves?

C Look carefully at the complete instructions for the writing task. Highlight the key words and make sure you understand what you have to do.

All over the world, life expectancy is increasing. Governments are finding it difficult to provide money for health care, and some people think that everyone should arrange private insurance to pay for health care.

Should health care be free for everyone, or should people pay for the care they need?

Give reasons for your answer and include any relevant examples from your experience.
Write about 250 words.

D Discuss these points with a partner.

1. Are you going to express a strong opinion or present a balanced argument?
2. Which of these points will you include in your composition?
   • Governments cannot afford to provide free health care for everyone.
   • Everyone should have free education and free health care.
   • Wealthy people should pay for health care.
   • Poorer people should have free health care.
   • How rich you are should not affect the quality of the health care you receive.
   • People who pay for health care should have the best doctors and hospitals.
   • Everyone should have free health care until they are 18.
   • People who smoke or drink a lot of alcohol should pay for their health care.
3. Are there any other important points you want to make?

Exam tip: When you do the second writing task, you may feel that it is difficult to find enough to say and that you can't write 250 words. The introduction is often the easier part to write, so make sure you write a solid introduction. The introduction to the composition in the Writing Module of this unit is 70 words.

E Look at this introduction to the composition that a student has written. Put the sentences into the most logical order. Do you like the introduction?

__ In the future, most people might live to be a hundred or more.

__ Of course, this is good if people can remain healthy, but most old people need more health care and governments are finding it difficult to provide the money that is needed.

__ People are living longer.

__ In some parts of the world, the number of young people is staying the same, while the number of old people is growing all the time.

F Write the composition. You can use the introduction above or you can write your own. Remember – you don't need to include all the points you discussed. Try to write around 250 words, but don't worry if your composition is a little shorter.

_____

_____

_____

_____

_____

_____

_____

_____

_____

_____

_____

_____

_____

_____

_____

_____

_____

_____

_____

_____

_____

12 Nature

Vocabulary 1: climate

A Look at the three dictionary extracts. Which is for *weather*, which is for *climate* and which is for *season*? Write the words in the spaces.

_____ *n* **1** [singular, U] the conditions at a particular place and time, such as sun, rain, wind and temperature.

_____ *n* **1** [C] the typical weather conditions in a particular area.

_____ *n* [C] **1** any of the four main periods in the year: winter, spring, summer or autumn.

B Write the seasons below.

1. grinps _____ 2. mumres _____ 3. nutmua _____ 4. newrit _____

C Check the highlighted words and phrases in these sentences and tick the sentences that are true for you. Then compare with a partner.

1. In my country there are four seasons.
2. In my country there is a dry season and a rainy season.
3. The weather in my country is very changeable. It can be sunny one day and cold and wet the next.
4. The winters in my country are mild. It is never really cold.
5. We often have extreme weather in my country. Sometimes it is very hot and sometimes it rains for four or five days.

Vocabulary 2: weather conditions

A Check the highlighted words and match the sentences with the pictures. Some pictures match with more than one sentence.

1. It's very hot and sunny. _____
2. It's very windy. _____
3. It's freezing cold. _____
4. There's a storm. / It's stormy. _____
5. There's a clear blue sky. _____
6. There's a lot of snow. / It's snowing. _____
7. It's very foggy. / There's a lot of fog. _____
8. It's a bit cloudy. / There's quite a lot of cloud. _____
9. It's raining heavily. / There's a lot of rain. _____
10. There's thunder and lightning. _____

B Mark these adjectives (G) good weather or (B) bad weather.

1. nice _____
2. lovely _____
3. horrible _____
4. miserable _____
5. beautiful _____
6. awful _____

Speaking 1: talking about climate and weather

A Talk with a partner about the photos on the opposite page like this.

It's really horrible weather. There's a storm and it's raining heavily.

B Now talk about the weather in any countries that you have visited.

Speaking 2: answering the question properly

A 🎧 Think about how you could answer these questions from the first part of the speaking exam. Then listen to some students and tick the speaker who gives a better answer.

1. What sort of climate does the area you live in have?   speaker 1 _____   speaker 2 _____
2. Tell me about the weather in your country.   speaker 1 _____   speaker 2 _____
3. Is there one season that you especially like?   speaker 1 _____   speaker 2 _____
4. Do you do the same things in summer as in winter?   speaker 1 _____   speaker 2 _____

Exam tip: When people ask a yes/no question, they usually expect more than just a yes/no answer. If the examiner asks you a yes/no question, he is inviting you to speak.

B Answer the questions in Exercise A with a partner.

Speaking 3: talking about temperature

A Check the highlighted words and complete these sentences so that they are true for you. Cross out the extra words.

1. The temperature on a hot summer day can reach _____°.
2. At night in winter, the temperature can fall to _____° / minus _____° / _____° below zero.
3. The highest temperature I have ever experienced was _____°.
4. The lowest temperature I have ever experienced was _____°.

Listening 1: a weather forecast

Today's weather

London

6°C

Brighton

A Look at the picture and answer the questions with a partner.

1. Who is the woman and what is she doing?
2. What are the symbols you can see on the map?
3. What do you think the woman will say about the weather?

B 🎧 Listen to the weather forecast and check your predictions.

C 🎧 Listen again and complete the notes. Use <u>no more than two words</u> for each answer.

1. People in the south-east can _____ very bad weather.
2. In the morning, there will be _____.
3. There may be _____ along the coast.
4. The weather should _____ a little as the day goes on.
5. _____ will be low for the time of year.

Listening 2: an everyday conversation

A Look at the picture and answer the questions with a partner.

1. Who are the people in the picture?
2. What do you think they are talking about?

B 🎧 Listen to the conversation and check your predictions.

C 🎧 Listen again and complete the lines. Use <u>no more than two words</u> for each answer.

1. Raining? It's absolutely _____ down.
2. It's really _____ out there too.
3. Never mind. They say it's going to _____ later on.

Listening 3: recognizing register

A Talk with a partner. How is the language used in the conversation different from the language used in the weather forecast?

Exam tip: The Listening Module has four sections. The speaker(s) will sometimes use formal language – a talk or a lecture. The speaker(s) will sometimes use informal language – a conversation or a talk to classmates. You will understand more if you recognize the register that the speaker is using.

B Look at the tapescript on pages 304 and 305. Highlight words and phrases that are formal or informal.

Listening 4: practise recognizing register

A 🎧 Listen to the four extracts and match them with the descriptions below.

1. an informal conversation between two speakers   Extract ___
2. a formal talk given by one speaker   Extract ___
3. an informal talk given by one speaker   Extract ___
4. a formal conversation between two speakers   Extract ___

B 🎧 Listen again to each extract and complete the tasks below.

Extract 1: For questions 1–3, complete the sentences. Use <u>no more than two words</u> for each answer.

1. People in Libya know about sandstorms because they live close to the _____.
2. Sandstorms occur when sand is carried by a _____.
3. A sandstorm looks like a big wall or _____ of sand coming towards you.

Extract 2: For questions 4–6, choose the correct answer a, b or c.

4. The first speaker thinks that Egypt will …
   a. not be hot enough.   b. be quite hot.   c. be too hot.
5. During the hottest part of the day, the second speaker plans to …
   a. go sightseeing.   b. relax at her hotel.   c. go to sleep.
6. The first speaker …
   a. thinks she went somewhere at the wrong time of year.
   b. does not want to go back to Morocco.
   c. only travels in spring or autumn.

Extract 3: For questions 7–9, label the diagram. Use <u>no more than two words</u> for each answer.

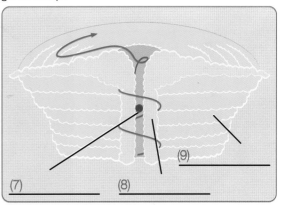

(7) _____   (8) _____   (9) _____

Extract 4: For questions 10–12, complete the notes a student has made. Use <u>one word</u> for each answer.

Floods caused by rising water level.

Can be (10) _____ – happening suddenly or creeping – happening slowly.

Floods caused by heavy rainfall or by (11) _____ melting.

Floods usually cause damage but can be good for soil – (12) _____ grow better after flood water.

C Check the key on page 271. How many questions did you answer correctly?

D Tick the sentences about the listening task that are true for you and think about how you can answer more questions correctly next time.

1. I recognized formal and informal language quite easily.
2. Recognizing the register helped me understand and complete the tasks.
3. I am pleased with how many questions I answered correctly.

Key vocabulary in context

Mark each sentence below (F) formal or (I) informal.

1. Conditions should improve later in the day. ___
2. Floods occur when there is a large amount of rainfall. ___
3. Most parts of the country can expect a cold night. ___
4. They say things will get better later on. ___
5. So, what happens when there's lots of rain? Does it flood? ___
6. They say it's going to be a bit chilly tonight. ___

12

Reading 1: preparing to read

A Look at the picture and talk to a partner. What has happened?

B In which parts of the world do earthquakes occur? Why do they occur?

C Look at these three images. Match each to one of the text headings below.

1. What to do when there's an earthquake ___
2. My earthquake terror ___
3. The science of earthquakes ___

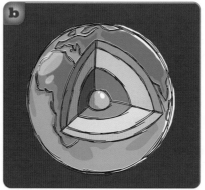

D Check these words and phrases. Which of the headings and images do they relate to? Compare your ideas with a partner.

grab	fault lines	stay calm	release energy	scramble
take cover	avoid being injured		tectonic plates	rush

Reading 2: different types of text

A Skim each extract below and match it with the correct heading and image.

1. As soon as I realized the ground was shaking, I rushed into the bathroom, where my little boy was in the bath. I knew that he was in a place that was very unsafe – under a window with a huge piece of glass right above his head. We had practised what to do in case of a quake and we knew where we would be safest. Unfortunately, there were no safe places inside the house and we had to try to get out to the garage as quickly as we could. ___

2. The Earth has four layers. The two top layers make up the thin outer surface of our planet. This outer surface consists of many pieces, tectonic plates, which move around slowly over thousands of years. Sometimes, when these plates collide, they push rock upwards to form mountains. At other times, the edges of the plates, the plate boundaries, become locked when they collide and they release a huge amount of energy that results in an earthquake. Almost all earthquakes occur along these plate boundaries, which are known as faults or fault lines. ___

3. If you are indoors, drop down to the floor. Take cover under a strong table or other suitable piece of furniture. Hold on to it tightly and move with it if necessary. Remain in the same position until the ground stops shaking and it is safe to move. Stay clear of windows, fireplaces and heavy furniture or appliances that may fall over. Stay inside to avoid being injured by falling glass or bricks. If you are in a crowded area, take cover where you are. Stay calm and encourage others to do the same. ___

B Now skim the second extract from each text and match them to the extracts in Exercise A.

1. If you are driving, stop if it is safe, but stay inside your vehicle. Stay away from bridges and tunnels. Move your car as far away from other traffic as possible. Avoid stopping under trees, lamp posts, power lines, signs or anything else that may fall down onto your vehicle. ___

2. I grabbed Daniel in my arms and scrambled through the house towards the back door. Before we could make it, a bigger shock hit us and threw us to the floor. I tried to protect my son the best I could as plates and glasses flew around and pictures crashed down from the walls. ___

3. An earthquake has three stages. Firstly, there are small earthquakes, called foreshocks, which occur in the same place as the larger earthquake that follows. Scientists do not know that an earthquake is a foreshock until the larger earthquake occurs. Then there is the main part of the earthquake, which is called the main shock. Finally, the main shock is always followed by aftershocks. These smaller earthquakes occur in the same place as the main shock. Depending on the size of the main shock, aftershocks can continue for weeks, months and even years after the main shock. ___

C Answer these questions about the three texts with a partner.

1. Which text has a lot of technical words?
2. Which text has examples of past tenses?
3. Which text has a lot of imperatives (verb forms that tell you to do something)?
4. Which text has more informal words and phrases, especially dramatic verbs?
5. Which text uses only the present simple?
6. Which text has examples of conditional structures?

Exam tip: In the Reading Module, you will need to read different types of text, and you need to be able to recognize them quickly. Notice the different styles of text and the type of language that is. The design of a text and pictures and diagrams help you to quickly recognize the type of text you are reading.

Reading 3: practice with different types of text

A Read 'The science of earthquakes' again carefully and answer these questions.

For questions 1–3, decide which of these statements about earthquakes are true. Choose <u>three</u> answers from A–F.

A When tectonic plates move, there are always earthquakes.
B Mountains are formed when there is an earthquake.
C Earthquakes are likely to occur in the same place.
D Foreshocks occur before there is a main shock.
E People always know that a main shock will follow a foreshock.
F Aftershocks go on for longer if the earthquake has been very big.

1. ___   2. ___   3. ___

B Read 'What to do when there's an earthquake' again carefully and answer these questions.

For questions 4–9, complete the summary with words and phrases from the box.

leave	quick	indoors	people	under	run away
traffic	place	table	floor	calm	outside

The best place to be when there is an earthquake is on the (4) _____. You will be safer if you can find a suitable piece of strong furniture to hide under. Do not try to go (5) _____ as you could be hit by falling bricks and flying glass. If there are a lot of (6) _____ around, do not try to run away. Make sure everyone is as (7) _____ as possible. If you are driving, you should stop, but do not (8) _____ your vehicle. Do not stop in any (9) _____ where something could fall and crush your vehicle.

C Read 'My earthquake terror' again carefully and answer these questions.

For questions 10–13, decide if the information given below agrees with the information given in the text. Write (T) true, (F) false or (NG) not given.

10. There was a window above the bath in the woman's house. ___
11. The woman knew her family would be safer in the garage. ___
12. The woman carried her son through the house. ___
13. The woman and her son were hit by flying glass. ___

D Check the key on page 271. How many questions did you answer correctly?

E Tick the sentences about the reading task that are true for you and think about how you can answer more questions correctly next time.

1. I find it quite easy to recognize different types of text.
2. Recognizing the different text types helped me to answer questions.
3. I find some types of text easier to read than others.
4. I am happy with how many of the questions I answered correctly.

Key vocabulary in context

Match these dramatic verbs with their definitions.

1. rush	a. move with difficulty
2. scramble	b. fall and make a noise
3. grab	c. move as fast as possible
4. crash	d. take quickly

Do the same with these more formal verbs and definitions.

1. consist of	a. allow to be free
2. collide	b. move towards each other and hit each other
3. release	c. stay in the same place
4. remain	d. to be formed from certain things

WB For focus on reading skills, go to Workbook page 34.

Writing 1: preparing to write

A Look at the two pictures and answer the questions with a partner.

1. What animals can you see in the two pictures?
2. Where are the animals in the two pictures? How are their lives different?
3. Do you think the animals are happier in either of the two environments?

B Talk with the same partner. Answer these questions.

1. Do you have a zoo in your town or city? If not, where is the nearest zoo to your hometown?
2. Which animals can you see there?
3. Do you go there often? Do you enjoy going to zoos generally?

C Look at the instructions for a writing task below. Highlight the key words and make sure you understand what you have to do.

As part of a class assignment, you have been asked to write about the following topic:

Some people think that zoos are cruel and that animals should be left in their natural environment. Others say that zoos are important because they are the only place that most children will ever see real wild animals.

What is your opinion on this issue?

Give reasons for your answer and include any relevant examples from your experience. Write about 250 words.

Writing 2: deciding what to say

A Discuss in small groups. Brainstorm some points that you could make in the composition. Organize your points in the columns below.

Zoos +	Zoos −	Natural environment +	Natural environment −
only place that children can see real wild animals			

B Look at these points that students made when discussing the issue. Which one of each pair of options do you think you will hear?

1. People see animals that they will probably never see in **the jungle / the wild**, like tigers and elephants.
2. Safaris are really **expensive / dangerous** and you don't see all the animals you want to see.
3. It's better to see an animal on TV in its natural **environment / place** than see it in a **little cage / big field** at the zoo looking miserable.
4. Animals don't **grow as big / live as long** in a zoo as they do in the wild.
5. Children shout and even throw things. Animals **suffer from stress / attack them**.
6. These days, animals are in big cages and they can climb and **run around / hunt**.
7. In big wildlife parks, lions are **forced / free** to walk around.
8. Some species of animal would **multiply / become extinct** if there were no zoos. Zoos help them to **develop / survive** and keep them safe.
9. One day, zoos may be the only place that many types of animal **exist / are happy**.

C 🎧 Listen to the discussion and circle the option you hear.

Writing 3: practise writing the main part of a composition

A Read the introduction and concluding paragraph of this composition.

There are zoos in most big cities all round the world, and thousands of people visit them. Nearly everybody goes to a zoo as a child, and it is probably the only time that they see real wild animals. Although most people like going to zoos, they understand that the animals are not in their natural environment and may not be happy. Some people even think that zoos are cruel and should be closed.

In my opinion, there is a need for zoos so that children can see real animals and not just read about them in books. However, the zoos should be modern and the animals well cared for. Their cages should be big enough that they can run around. The best solution would be to have more big wildlife parks where animals are in an environment like their natural one.

B Think about which points you want to make in the two main paragraphs. Make sure each paragraph has a purpose.

C Write the two paragraphs. You should spend about 25 minutes on this.

D Compare your composition with other students.

WB Go to Workbook page 35 for the writing task.

Speaking

A Look at these possible questions from the third part of the Speaking Module. Check any words that you don't know.

1. Do you believe the world climate is changing? ___
2. Is the climate changing in your country? ___
3. Do you think that global warming is a serious threat to our planet? ___
4. Do you think people are to blame for destroying the world's natural environment? ___
5. Should people do more to protect animals that are in danger of becoming extinct? ___

B Mark each question (E) easy to answer or (D) difficult to answer. Then compare with a partner.

C 🎧 Listen to some students and match the answers they give to the questions in Exercise B.

Speaker 1 ___   Speaker 2 ___   Speaker 3 ___   Speaker 4 ___   Speaker 5 ___

Exam tip: Remember – you can give simple answers to complex questions. The examiner does not expect you to be a scientist or politician! He/she is interested only in your English.

D Practise asking and answering the questions in Exercise A with a partner.

Vocabulary

A Answer these questions with words from the unit. Write the answers in your notebook if you need to practise spelling.

1. Which season is usually the coldest?
2. How do we describe weather that is not too hot and not too cold?
3. What is the noise that you hear during a storm?
4. What is the flash of electricity that you see during a storm?
5. How do we describe the weather when we can't see properly?
6. Which word describes animals that do not exist anymore?

B Complete these sentences with words from the unit. Some letters are given to help you.

1. When the water level rises, there may be a f __ __ __ __.
2. A hu __ __ __ __ __ __ __ __ or an e __ __ __ __ __ q __ __ __ __ can destroy a whole city.
3. Another way to say a minus temperature is b __ __ __ __ __   z __ __ __ __.
4. An informal word for very cold is f __ __ __ __ __ __ __ and an informal word for very hot is b __ __ __ __ __ __ __.
5. Animals are usually happier in their n __ __ __ __ __ __   en __ __ __ __ __ __ __ __ __ __.

C Correct the spelling mistakes in the words below.

1. wether _____
2. autum _____
3. tempriture _____
4. occer _____
5. damidge _____
6. priviously _____
7. releese _____
8. rimain _____
9. servive _____

Errors

A There are errors in all of these sentences. Correct them.

1. It was a big storm last night.
2. Do you think a weather will be nice?
3. It's raining very heavy outside.
4. At night, the temperature can fall under ten degrees.
5. It's absolutely hot today.
6. Floods usually make a lot of damage.

12

Listening

A 🎧 You will hear someone talking to some students about how to stay safe when there is lightning. Look at the notes below carefully before you listen.

For questions 1–10, complete this student's notes. Use <u>no more than three words or a number</u> for each answer.

Don't go outside or stand by the window.

Lightning can strike (1) _____ from storm centre.

Try counting seconds between thunder and lightning – more than (2) _____ is safe.

Cancel planned outdoor activities, like (3) _____ or golf, and stay away from

(4) _____ – it conducts electricity!

If outside in storm

Find a (5) _____ or shelter in your car.

Trees, bus stops, etc., do not give enough (6) _____.

No umbrellas in open spaces and definitely no (7) _____!

If doing s/th in water, get to dry land.

If at home

Don't take a bath or shower – lightning passes quickly through (8) _____.

Unplug electrical appliances.

If light goes out, use a torch. Don't light (9) _____ inside house.

Try to stay inside or under cover for (10) _____ after the storm passes.

B 🎧 You will hear an English family talking about their holiday options. Read the statements carefully before you listen.

For questions 11–16, mark each of the statements on the following page with one of the following abbreviations.

M mother
F father
J Justin – the son
E Ellie – the daughter

11. He/she doesn't want to go somewhere hot. ___
12. He/she doesn't want to visit a place where there are a lot of people. ___
13. He/she doesn't want to go somewhere cold. ___
14. He/she wants to see a big city. ___
15. He/she doesn't want to go somewhere where it's raining. ___
16. He/she doesn't want to spend a lot of time travelling. ___

C 🎧 You will hear a lecturer talking about avalanches. Look carefully at the questions and at the diagram and box of words.

For questions 17–19, complete the notes. Use <u>no more than two words</u> for each answer.

17. Loose, wet snow is dangerous because it is _____.
18. The person who starts the avalanche usually becomes _____ of it.
19. Avalanches are not started by _____.

For questions 20–24, match some of the words A–H in the box with the numbers on the diagram. Write the letters in the spaces.

```
A  track
B  debris toe
C  start zone
D  end zone
E  top point
F  trigger
G  avalanche bed
H  flanks
```

20. ___   21. ___   22. ___   23. ___   24. ___

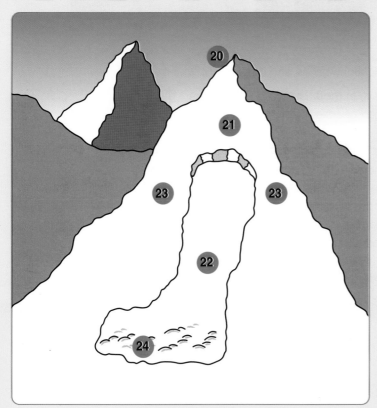

 Exam tip: Look at the tapescript for each of the extracts. Notice the different register that is used in each.

13 Construction

Vocabulary 1: describing your home

A Match the words and phrases with the pictures.

| apartment/flat | detached house | terraced house | cottage | bungalow | beach house |

B Check the highlighted words in the questions below and think about your answers.

1. Is the house or apartment/flat you live in **modern** or old? When was it **built**?
2. If you live in an apartment/flat, is it part of a big house or in an **apartment block**/a **block of flats**?
3. If you live in an apartment/flat, what **floor** is it on? (**ground floor/first floor**)
4. Do you (or your parents) **own** your house or apartment/flat or do you/they **rent** it?
5. How many **rooms** are there in your house or apartment/flat?
6. How big is your **bedroom/living room/bathroom**?
7. Do you have a **separate dining room** or do you eat in the **kitchen**?
8. Do you have a room that you use as a **study**?
9. Do you have a **spare bedroom** or a **guest room**?
10. Do you have a **garden** or a **roof terrace**?
11. Do any of the windows have a **balcony**?
12. Are there **good views** from the **windows/balconies/roof terrace**?

Speaking 1: talking about homes

A Talk with a partner. Say what type of home you have and then answer the questions in Exercise B above.

> **Grammar check**
> You can say *There are six bedrooms in my house* or *My house has six bedrooms.*
> *Is there a study?* or *Do you have a study?*

Exam tip: You have practised talking about towns and cities and now talking about homes. In the first part of the Speaking Module, the examiner may ask you about both. Make sure you learn the words and phrases that help you to talk about your life.

Vocabulary 2: your neighbourhood

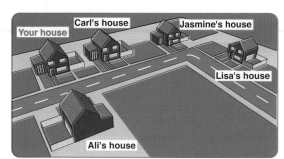

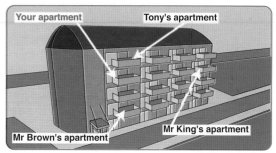

A Look at the street plan and notice where your house is. Check the highlighted phrases in the questions and then answer them with a partner.

1. Who lives in the house next door? _____
2. Who lives in the house opposite / across the road? _____
3. Who lives just down the road? _____
4. Who lives just round the corner? _____

B Look at the apartment block and notice where your apartment is. Check the highlighted words and phrases in the questions and then answer them with a partner.

1. Who lives in the flat upstairs / above yours?
2. Who lives in the flat downstairs / below yours?
3. Who lives on the same floor as you?

C Talk with a partner about your neighbourhood. Who lives near you?

Speaking 2: contrasting ideas

A 🎧 Listen to some students describing their homes. Which statement below is true?

1. They all like everything about their home.
2. None of them likes anything about their home.
3. They all have mixed feelings about their homes.

B 🎧 Listen again and fill each space with <u>one word</u>. Notice the incomplete highlighted phrases.

1. On the other _____, it's very close to where I work.
2. My room is small but I _____ it's cheap.
3. _____, our neighbours are not very friendly.
4. On the _____ side, it's very central.

> **Pronunciation check**
> 🎧 Listen again to sentences 1, 3 and 4 in Exercise B. Notice how the speaker pauses when a linking device introduces a contrast.
> Practise saying the sentences.

C Talk with a partner about your house or apartment and your neighbourhood. Say what you like and don't like. Contrast your opinions with the phrases from Exercise B above.

Listening 1: preparing to listen

A Here are two typical cards for part 2 of the Speaking Module. Work with a partner – one of you is A, the other is B. You have a minute to think about it and make notes.

A

> Describe a building you think is beautiful.
> Say ...
> • where the building is.
> • why it was built / what it's used for.
> • when it was built, if you know.
> • what you like about it.

B

> Describe a building you think is ugly.
> Say ...
> • where the building is.
> • why it was built / what it's used for.
> • when it was built, if you know.
> • what you don't like about it.

B Take it in turns to speak about what's on your card for about two minutes.

C Look at the picture. Answer the questions with a partner.

1. What is the building?
2. Where is it?
3. When was it built?
4. Why was it built?
5. Why do people think it is so beautiful?

Listening 2: spelling answers correctly

A You will hear a tour guide talking to some tourists about the Taj Mahal. Read the notes below and predict any answers you can.

B 🎧 Listen and complete the notes that one of the tourists made. Use <u>one word only</u> for each answer.

The (1) _____ have a sense of symmetry – same on both sides of building.
A large (2) _____ reflects the building – popular place for photos.
On top of the building is the (3) _____. People wonder at how the building can
support its (4) _____. There are four minarets – one in each corner.
Story of the Taj Mahal is very (5) _____. 1629 – Shah Jahan's (6) _____ wife
died. He was so sad that his (7) _____ turned white.
He decided to build a beautiful (8) _____ to remember her by. Work started in 1632.

C Mark each of the words 1–8 in the task like this:

A I know this word and it's easy to spell.
B I know this word but it's difficult to spell.
C I don't know this word but I can guess how to spell it quite easily.
D I don't know this word and I have no idea how to spell it.

1. __
2. __
3. __
4. __
5. __
6. __
7. __
8. __

Listening 3: practise spelling answers correctly

A The building in this picture is the Millennium Dome in London. Some people say it's the ugliest building in the world. Why don't they like it?

B 🎧 Listen to part of a lecture that an architect is giving about the Millennium Dome. Read the summary below before you listen.

For questions 1–8, complete the summary with words that you hear. Use <u>no more than two words</u> for each answer.

The speaker says that there are many ugly buildings, like (1) _____ blocks, but that the Millennium Dome is different. It was built to (2) _____ the beginning of a new century. It took a long time to plan and construct and it cost nearly (3) _____ pounds. He thinks it is the building's ugliness that makes it (4) _____.

The speaker mentions two buildings in the US that he thinks are also ugly – the public (5) _____ in Chicago and a museum in Seattle. However, he thinks the Dome is a (6) _____ example of design. The speaker agrees that the Dome has an (7) _____ design and impressive engineering, but he is disappointed with it.

The speaker says that the Dome will now be used to stage (8) _____ events.

C Check the key on page 272. How many questions did you answer correctly?

D Answer these questions about the listening task with a partner and think about how you can answer more questions correctly next time.

1. Which answers did you hear but spell wrongly?
2. Which answers did you hear and spell correctly?
3. Which words did you already know how to spell?
4. Which words did you have to guess the spelling of?
5. Are you happy with how many questions you answered and spelt correctly?

Key vocabulary in context

These verbs from the two extracts have been used in the wrong sentences. Correct the exercise.

1. The building was **reflected** by an American architect.
2. It will take at least five years to **celebrate** the new stadium.
3. When the new shopping centre opens, there will be a party to **support**.
4. In hot countries, houses are white so that they **design** sunlight back.
5. That bridge doesn't look strong enough to **construct** so much traffic.

13

Reading 1: preparing to read

A Look at the map and the picture and answer the questions with a partner.

1. What do you call a construction like this?
2. What is its purpose?
3. Where is this construction?
4. When was it built?
5. Why was it built here?
6. How has it changed the lives of people in the country?

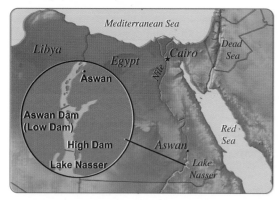

B Check the meaning of these. How are they related to the topic?

| flooding | agriculture | reservoir | overflow | concrete | electricity |

Reading 2: coping with longer texts

A Look at the text on the next page but do not read it yet. Tick the statements that are true for you.

1. I don't usually read texts this long in English. ___
2. It takes me a long time to read a long text like this. ___
3. I think it is more difficult to understand a long text than a short text. ___
4. There is usually more difficult vocabulary in a longer text. ___
5. I think it will be more difficult to find the information I need if the text is long. ___
6. By the time I get to the end, I have forgotten the beginning. ___

 Exam tip: The third part of the Reading Module is the most difficult and the text will be longer. It will be an article from a newspaper, magazine or journal or an extract from a book. There will probably be more than one task to do.

B Here is some advice about coping with longer texts. Complete each sentence with <u>one word</u>.

1. Read the _____ of the text and look at any pictures or diagrams with it.
2. Skim the text quickly for gist. A good idea is to read the _____ sentence at the beginning of each paragraph and the final line of the text. Notice any key words that are repeated in the text.
3. Read the _____ for the tasks carefully before reading the text again so that you have a purpose for reading and you know what to look for. Think about which parts of the text you will need to look at again for each task.

4. As you read again, don't worry about the meaning of every _____ and phrase. This will slow you down and is not necessary to answer questions.

5. Once you know which part of the text provides an _____, read it very carefully. If you don't know the meaning of a key word or phrase, guess it from the _____.

 Exam tip: Try not to be afraid of a text because it is long. You probably won't have to read every part, and you won't have to understand every word. Don't try to read the whole text before you know what you are looking for. You will not remember enough to answer questions.

Reading 3: practise reading longer texts

A Look again at the questions in Reading 1A and 1B and remember your answers. Then skim the text to check your ideas.

B Look carefully at the instructions and then read the passage to answer questions 1–17.

The Aswan High Dam

A The River Nile is the longest river in the world and it has always brought life to Egypt. Around 95% of the population of Egypt lives within 20 kilometres of this great source of water. When the Aswan High Dam was completed in 1970, it affected every person in the country. The dam prevented flooding that had previously destroyed homes and crops, it generated electricity and it provided water for a much greater programme of agriculture.

B There is a long history of attempting to control the Nile. Over 1,000 years ago, the Egyptian rulers first understood the importance of controlling the river and employed engineers to plan a dam of some sort. At that time, engineering and technological limitations meant that completing a successful project was impossible. Over the years, several architects were put in prison for not finding a solution.

C The beginning of the last century saw the first real attempt to build a dam on the Nile and there are, in fact, still two dams at Aswan. The first dam, the low dam, was constructed between 1889 and 1902 but never achieved what it was supposed to. It was soon discovered that the dam was not high enough and it was raised. Major work was carried out between 1907 and 1912 and then again between 1929 and 1933.

In 1946, the dam very nearly overflowed again, and this time it was decided that a second dam was the solution. It was to be built six kilometres upriver from the first dam.

D Planning for this second dam began in 1954, and construction began six years later. The dam was made of rock and covered with concrete. When construction was complete, the dam was 111 metres high and 1,000 metres wide. The dam's volume was over 44 million cubic metres. That is like building the Great Pyramid at Giza seventeen times. The reservoir created by the dam became the world's third largest reservoir and was called Lake Nasser. The lake is now 90 metres deep and covers an area 500 kilometres long and, at its widest point, 35 kilometres wide. 11,000 square metres of water can pass through the dam every second.

E The High Dam has brought many benefits. Land that was previously desert is now provided with water and is used for farming. The floods that hit the farmland along the river once a year no longer destroy the crops. Far more food is produced, and there is less need to import products from other countries. The dam powers 12 generators and produces half of Egypt's electricity production. When the dam was first built, many villages had electricity for the first time. A new fishing industry has developed around Lake Nasser and thousands of jobs have been created.

F As with any project of this size, there have been problems, too. The annual floods, though destructive, brought nutrients to the soil. There is now more farmland, but it is not as fertile as it once was. When Lake Nasser was first formed, flooding displaced around 90,000 people and new homes had to be provided for them. Several important archaeological sites were in danger from the new lake, and archaeologists had to move monuments to safer locations or give them to other countries. Fishing in the Mediterranean was badly affected as nutrients that flowed down the Nile and into the sea were trapped behind the dam. Water below the dam now moves more slowly, and many more people suffer from resulting diseases.

G Despite these problems, the construction of the Aswan High Dam and the creation of Lake Nasser has been a huge success and a great engineering achievement. Ask any Egyptian and he will tell you that the project has greatly improved the lives of most people. The project has shown how similar problems can be overcome in other countries and has had a huge influence on similar projects that aim to irrigate land that was once desert.

The reading passage has seven paragraphs, labelled A–G.

For questions 1–7, choose the most suitable heading for each paragraph from the list A–J in the box below. You do not need all the headings.

A Not all good news	B A terrible accident
C Others can learn from the project	D Most Egyptians live on the Nile
E A number of improvements	F The world's biggest dam
G A very old problem	H Everyone's a fisherman now
I Not quite right – try again	J A huge project

1. paragraph A ___ 2. paragraph B ___ 3. paragraph C ___ 4. paragraph D ___
5. paragraph E ___ 6. paragraph F ___ 7. paragraph G ___

Question-type tip: A common task for a longer text is matching headings with paragraphs. The instructions can be quite complicated – you may have letters, numbers and Roman numerals to look at. Read the instructions carefully and make sure you know what you have to write in the spaces.

For questions 8–12, complete the diagram with information from the text.

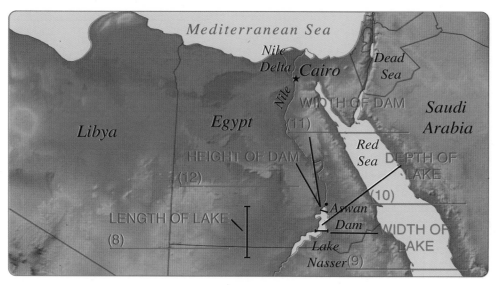

For questions 13–17, choose five answers from A–H.

Which of the following benefits and problems are mentioned?

A homes destroyed	B electricity in more homes
C work for people near Lake Nasser	D bigger catches of fish in the seas around Egypt
E people becoming sick	F more Egyptian exports
G changes to historic sites	H better soil

13. ___   14. ___   15. ___   16. ___   17. ___

C Check the key on page 272. How many questions did you answer correctly?

D Tick the sentences about the reading task that are true for you and think about how you can answer more questions correctly next time.

1. The length of the text didn't worry me.
2. Skimming the text first helped me get a general idea of what it is about.
3. I looked at the questions carefully, so I knew what to look for when I read more carefully.
4. I am happy with how many of the questions I answered correctly.

WB For focus on reading skills and key vocabulary in context, go to Workbook page 37.

Writing 1: preparing to write

A Answer these questions with a partner.

1. In your country, do most people own a house or apartment or do they rent one?
2. Where do people live when they leave their parents' house?
3. Do students rent an apartment if they leave their hometown to study?

B Check the highlighted words and answer the questions with the same partner.

1. What or who is a tenant?
2. What is a letting agency?
3. What is a landlord or landlady?
4. What is a deposit?

C In small groups, make a list of the possible problems that tenants can have when they rent a house or apartment.

> Perhaps the cooker or fridge doesn't work properly.

D 🎧 Listen to some people talking about problems they had when they rented an apartment. Did you mention any of the same things?

Writing 2: planning the composition

A Look at the instructions for a writing task below. Highlight the key words and check that you understand what you have to do.

You have just rented an apartment from a letting agency. You paid a deposit and a month's rent in advance. You now realize that the apartment is not in very good condition. It is summer, but the air conditioning does not work. The furniture is old and some of it is broken, and the apartment was not cleaned well before you moved in.

Write a letter to the agency explaining the problem and telling them what you want them to do. Write at least 150 words. You should spend about 20 minutes on this task.

B Talk with a partner and answer these questions about the writing task.

1. Is this a situation you can relate to? If it is not, can you use your imagination?
2. Do you know how to start and finish the letter?
3. Do you have ideas for what to include in the main part of the letter?
4. Are you going to use formal or informal language?

C Look at a student's letter on the next page. Is it similar to the letter that you planned to write? Do you like it?

D Look at these teacher's comments about the letter. Tick the one that is true.

1. There is a problem with content. You don't explain the problem or say what you want done.
2. It is not well organized. The points are not made in a logical order.
3. There is a problem with spelling and punctuation.

Dear Sir/Madam

I am writing to complane about an apartment that I am renting through your letting agency it is flat 3 at 74 belle view gardens I moved in a week ago and payed a deposit of £600 and a months rent in advans which was £750 I now realize that the apartment is not in a good condition and I am not at all happy

firstly the air conditioning is not working properly so the apartment is very hot all the time I have found it very dificult to sleep until late at night in this hot wether

secondly most of the ferniture is very old and some of it is broken the leg of the coffee table in the living room is broken and some cuboard doors do not close properly finally you told me that the apartment would be cleaned before I moved in however when I arived it was very dirty and I spent all day cleaning it myself

I am very disapointed and would like you to resolve the problem as soon as possible please arange for the air conditioning to be repared immediately then please contact the landlord about replasing the broken ferniture finally please refund a percentage of the advance I have paid for not cleaning the apartment properly I think £100 would be fair

I look forward to hearing from you

Your faithfully

Marco Bendetti

Writing 3: spelling and punctuation

A Look again at only the first paragraph of the composition. Complete the following tasks. Then check your answers on page 272.

1. There should be four sentences. Put in four full stops, including one at the end of the paragraph. Begin all new sentences with a capital letter.
2. There should be one comma. Put it in the right place.
3. One word should have an apostrophe before an 's'. Put it in.
4. Make sure that any names begin with a capital letter. There are three examples.
5. Three words are spelled wrongly. Correct them here.

_____   _____   _____

B Look at the second paragraph and complete the tasks.

1. There should be two sentences. Put in two full stops, including one at the end of the paragraph. Begin all new sentences with a capital letter.
2. There should be one comma. Put it in the right place.
3. Two words are spelt wrongly. Correct them here. _____   _____

C Look at the third paragraph and complete the tasks.

1. There should be four sentences. Put in four full stops, including one at the end of the paragraph. Make sure any words that start a new sentence begin with a capital letter.
2. There should be three commas. Put them in.
3. Three words are spelt wrongly. Correct them here.

_____   _____   _____

D Look at the final paragraph and the closing phrases. Correct any errors of punctuation and spelling. Then check your answers to all the tasks on page 272.

WB ▶ Go to Workbook page 37 for the writing task.

Speaking

A Here are four typical cards for part 2 of the Speaking Module. Work with a partner. Choose a card. You have a minute to think about it and make notes.

A

> **Talk about your neighbourhood.**
> **Say ...**
> - what type of houses there are.
> - what sort of people live there.
> - what you like about it.
> - what you would like to change.

B

> **Describe the home of a friend or family member.**
> **Say ...**
> - what type of building it is.
> - how many rooms it has.
> - when it was built.
> - what you like about it.

C

> **Describe a city that has a lot of interesting old buildings.**
> **Say ...**
> - which city it is.
> - which buildings are interesting.
> - when some of the buildings were built.
> - which building is your favourite and why.

D

> **Describe a city that has a lot of interesting modern buildings.**
> **Say ...**
> - which city it is.
> - what is interesting about the buildings.
> - what some of the buildings are used for.
> - which building is your favourite and why.

B Take it in turns to speak about what's on your card for about two minutes.

Vocabulary

A Match each word 1–6 with a word a–f to make common phrases.

1. apartment   a. house
2. spare   b. terrace
3. beach   c. room
4. ground   d. block
5. roof   e. door
6. next   f. floor

B Delete the wrong suffix in each of these words made from the root words in the box.

1. The new library is not my favourite build *er / ing*.
2. There is a lot of construct *ment / ion* along the coast.
3. A mirror shows your reflect *ment / ion*.
4. We live in a very nice neighbour *hood / ation*.
5. We had a big celebrat *ing / ion* at the end of the school year.

> build
> construct
> reflect
> neighbour
> celebrate

C Correct the spelling mistakes in these words.

1. agrakulture _____   2. atempt _____
3. concrite _____   4. cottidge _____
5. elictrisity _____   6. gest room _____
7. oposit _____   8. seperate _____

Errors

A There are errors in all of these sentences. Correct them.

1. There have five bedrooms my house.   2. My apartment is in the second floor.
3. I live in a house opposite to the park. 4. We live in the ground floor.
5. I live in the same street than my cousin. 6. When was built the Taj Mahal?

13

Reading

A Look again at the advice about reading longer texts in the reading section of this unit.

B Read the passage and answer questions 1–16.

The Oldest Building in the World?

A So what is the oldest man-made structure in the world? In the last ten years, archaeologists in Japan say they have answered that question – twice! However, the second discovery, made by one of Japan's leading archaeologists, was shown to be a case of fraud*.

B In 2000, the remains of an ancient building were discovered on a hillside in Chichibu, a small town to the north of Tokyo. Soon afterwards, at Kamitakamori, 600 miles to the north, a second discovery was made. In a layer of earth, archaeologists found large holes which they believed had held posts that had supported a primitive building, and several stone tools that had been used to construct it.

C The Chichibu discovery was one of the most important for many years, and both archaeologists and historians were very excited. Ten holes in the shape of two pentagons were discovered. These holes were made for posts that would have supported some kind of structure, like a hut. Thirty tools were also found. The site was dated to half a million years ago. Before the discovery, the oldest remains of a human structure were in France and dated back to around 300,000 years ago.

D Experts do not know whether the huts were used as permanent accommodation, or if they had a temporary function as a shelter or as a lookout for hunters. It is thought that primitive people at that time lived in caves and did not build houses of any kind. The discovery was important because it showed that 500,000 years ago Man had the ability to use technology in ways that we previously did not think were possible.

E Later in 2000, at the Kamitakamori site, archaelogists said that they had made a discovery that was 100,000 years older than the one at Chichibu. They found a number of deep holes and predicted that they had the same function as those at Chichibu. They believed that two round buildings had existed at the site. Several tools were discovered in a hole at the centre of the site.

F However, in 2003, the truth came out. A senior archaeologist had planted the tools so that he could take credit for such an important discovery. He buried stone tools that he had previously found at another site and covered them in soil. Unfortunately for him, his actions were caught on camera, and a national newspaper then told the whole story. The archaeologist explained that he had committed his crime because of the pressure on him to keep making important discoveries.

G The same archaeologist had worked on a number of very important archaeological projects before the Kamitakamori incident. He admitted that he had planted artefacts on other occasions. Some experts believe that there is now a question mark over some of Japan's historical records, and they want further investigation. It seems that we cannot be sure about what or where the world's oldest building really is.

* The crime of pretending something to be true when it is not (usually in order to get money).

For questions 1–4, use <u>no more than two words</u> from the passage for
each answer.

1. Before the Chichibu discovery, in which country had the oldest building been found?

   _____

2. What type of simple building do archaeologists believe once existed at the
   Chichibu site?

   _____

3. What shape were the buildings that were said to have once existed at the
   Kamitakamori site?

   _____

4. What did the senior archaeologist bury at the Kamitakamori site?

   _____

The passage has seven paragraphs, lettered A–G. For questions 5–9, say in
which paragraph you find the following information. Write the letter in the space.

5. why somebody was dishonest   ___
6. that primitive buildings may not have been houses   ___
7. the result of somebody's dishonest actions   ___
8. where the archaeological sites are exactly   ___
9. how experts felt about the discovery at Chichibu   ___

For questions 10–16, complete the summary with words from the box. You do not
need to use all the words.

Use capital letters if necessary.

earlier	similar	new	posts	round	later	tools
	structures	soil	different	half	real	

In 2000, an important archaeological discovery was made at Chichibu in Japan. The
remains of a building, dating back (10) _____ a million years, were found. There
were ten holes that experts believed had been used to hold (11) _____. These
posts had been used to support a structure of some kind. (12) _____ used to
construct the building were also found at the site. Then, a second discovery was
made. Some very (13) _____ holes were discovered at another site, and these
were said to date back to an even (14) _____ time. In 2003, the world learnt
that the second discovery was not (15) _____. A senior archaeologist had
planted the artefacts. He said that archaeologists were under pressure to keep making
(16) _____ discoveries.

Exam tip: This is the summary of the whole text. However, you will
sometimes have a summary that summarizes only part of a text,
and you will first have to identify which part it summarizes.

14 Technology

Vocabulary 1: machines, appliances, devices and gadgets

A Look at this list. Match the pictures with the words. Then mark each of the boxes (H) for 'this has changed home life', (W) for 'this has changed working life' or (B) for 'this has changed both'.

☐ computer / laptop ___   ☐ mobile phone ___   ☐ dishwasher ___
☐ microwave ___   ☐ video camera / camcorder ___   ☐ the Internet / e-mail ___
☐ satellite TV ___   ☐ fridge / freezer ___   ☐ digital camera ___
☐ DVD player / recorder ___   ☐ CD player ___   ☐ air conditioning ___
☐ central heating ___

Speaking 1: talking about technology

A Check the highlighted words and answer these questions about Exercise A above with a partner.

1. Compare how you have marked the boxes.
2. Which of the machines and appliances do you have in your home?
3. Which do you use frequently at work?
4. Which do you think are necessities? Which are luxuries?

B Discuss in groups of three and try to agree. Which <u>two</u> of these could you live without?

a car	an electric shower	a mobile phone
a television	a fridge	air conditioning	a computer

Grammar check

You can explain the purpose or function of something in different ways.

a *that* clause   *It's an appliance that keeps food cold.*
for + ~ing verb   *It's a device for making holes in paper.*
use + infinitive   *It is used to record music onto a disc. / You use it to heat up cold food or drinks.*

Pronunciation check

When the form of a word changes, the stress usually falls on a different part of the word.
The noun is *tech<u>no</u>logy*. The adjective is *techno<u>lo</u>gical*.
🎧 Listen and mark where the stress falls in these related words.
1. photograph   2. photography   3. photographic

Vocabulary 2: how technology affects you

A Complete each sentence with the correct verb form below.

saves	does	means	allows	makes

1. It _____ life much easier.
2. It _____ everything / the job so much more quickly.
3. It _____ a lot of time.
4. It _____ you to get on with other things.
5. It _____ you don't have to …

B Talk with a partner about how the technology you have at home and at work affects your daily life. Use the expressions from Exercise A above.

Speaking 2: giving examples

A Look at these possible questions from the third part of the speaking exam. Think about how you would answer them.

1. How has technology changed your life in the last five / ten years?
2. In what ways has technology changed the way people work?
3. Do people rely on technology too much these days?
4. What technological advances will there be in the next twenty years?

B 🎧 Listen to some students. Match each answer with a question above.

Speaker 1 ___   Speaker 2 ___   Speaker 3 ___   Speaker 4 ___

C 🎧 Listen again and complete the sentences. Use <u>one or two words</u> in each space.

Speaker 1: In factories, _____, machines have replaced people completely …
Speaker 2: … people who have money will want something faster, _____ a small helicopter or …
Speaker 3: … I see other campers with lots of machines and gadgets, _____ computer games and portable TVs.
Speaker 4: … life at work has changed the most, _____ the way I communicate with people.

D Walk around the class and ask and answer the questions in Exercise A with different classmates. Use the phrases in Exercise C to give examples.

Listening 1: understanding different accents

A Talk with a partner. Make a list of countries in which English is the first language.

B Check the highlighted words and answer these questions with the same partner.

1. Do people in different parts of your country have different accents?
2. In which part of your country do people have a very strong accent?
3. When you listen to English, can you recognize the difference between a British and an American accent?
4. Do you know any words or phrases that are different in British and American English?
5. Are there any other 'English' accents that you think you can recognize?
6. Are there any 'English' accents that you find difficult to understand?

C Match the four inventions in the pictures with the countries below.

| a. the United States | b. India | c. Australia | d. Scotland |

clay oven ___   television ___   space shuttle ___   boomerang ___

D 🎧 Listen to four people talking about the inventions and check your ideas.

Speaker 1 is from _____ and talks about _____.
Speaker 2 is from _____ and talks about _____.
Speaker 3 is from _____ and talks about _____.
Speaker 4 is from _____ and talks about _____.

E 🎧 Listen again. Can you hear different accents? Who do you think has the strongest accent?

Listening 2: practice with different accents

A 🎧 Listen to each speaker say more about each invention and complete the tasks.

For questions 1–5, choose <u>five</u> answers from A–H. Which of these statements about boomerangs does the speaker make?

A They were mainly used as toys.	B They were the first heavy man-made object to fly.
C They had different functions.	D They have been found around the world.
E They are different sizes.	F All of them return to the thrower.
G Perhaps people did not plan to invent one that came back to the thrower.	H Throwing one is easy.

1. ___   2. ___   3. ___   4. ___   5. ___

For questions 6–11, listen and complete the flow chart. Use <u>one word only</u> for each answer.

1925 – first (6) _____ demonstration at department store in
(7) _____
(silhouette images moved on (8) _____)

↓

1926 – demonstration at his laboratory to Royal Institute and Times Newspaper
(9) _____
(Improved (10) _____ – first real demonstration of television system)

↓

1928 – first (11) _____ transmission

For questions 12–16, complete the notes. Use <u>no more than three words or a number</u> for each answer.

Space race between US and Russia continued for (12) _____.
First man to walk (13) _____ – from USA.
Reusable space shuttle – first successful in (14) _____.
Space shuttle used as a laboratory to transport equipment or to collect or repair satellites.
Between (15) _____ people can travel on shuttle.
In the earth's (16) _____, then the shuttle glides to landing.

For questions 17–19, complete the short summary. Use <u>no more than two words</u> for each answer.

Remains of ovens have been found in many parts of the world. They were used mainly to (17) _____. In most places, it appears that village people (18) _____ an oven. In India, however, (19) _____ had one.

For question 20, tick the correct diagram of a 5,000-year-old oven.

B Check the key on page 272. How many questions did you answer correctly?

C Tick the sentences about the listening task that are true for you and think about how you can answer more questions correctly next time.

1. I could hear different accents, but it didn't make the tasks more difficult.
2. The strong accents made hearing some answers more difficult.
3. I am pleased with how many questions I answered correctly.

14

Reading 1: timing yourself

A Answer these questions about the IELTS Reading Module with a partner.

1. How many parts are there to the Reading Module?
2. How many texts are there likely to be in each part?

B Match each part of the Reading Module 1–3 with the possible text type a–c.

1. Part 1 – social survival
2. Part 2 – training survival
3. Part 3 – general reading

a. page of information about college or university
b. page of information related to work
c. article from newspaper, journal or magazine

C Answer these questions with a partner.

1. Which texts are likely to be the shortest or longest?
2. Which texts are likely to be easier or more difficult to read?
3. Should you spend an equal amount of time (20 minutes) on each part?
4. Should you spend an equal amount of time on each text?

Exam tip: The first part of the Reading Module will consist of two or three texts. These may be information leaflets or advertisements. They will be short, but they will contain a lot of information. The second part will consist of two texts. They will be information pages that relate to work and will come from leaflets, handbooks or websites. The texts will be a little longer than those in the first part. The third part will consist of one longer text, which will be an article of some kind.

It is not easy to decide how long to spend on each part. Most students plan to spend an equal amount of time (20 minutes) on each part. In the first part, there are more texts, but the questions are easier, while in the third part, there is only one text, but it is more difficult to read and the questions are more challenging.

Reading 2: improving your reading speed

A You are doing the first part of the Reading Module. Look at this information but not the text yet.

1. There are two texts, and you want to spend ten minutes on each.
2. The first text is a set of safety instructions for a dishwasher.
3. There are eight questions to answer about the first text.
4. The first four questions ask you to match pictures with parts of the text.
5. The last four questions ask you to write short answers.

B Talk with a partner. How long do you want to spend on each stage? Fill in the times.

1. Read the heading and look at the pictures. ___ minutes
2. Skim the text to get a general idea of what it's about. ___ minutes
3. Read the instructions and questions carefully and think about where in the text you will find answers. ___ minutes
4. Read the text again to match the pictures with the parts of the text. ___ minutes

5. Read the text more carefully to find the answers to the short questions. ___ minutes

6. Check your answers are spelt correctly and that you are
happy with them.   ___ minutes

Reading 3: practise improving your reading speed

A Read the text and answer the questions. Apply the timing for each stage that
you decided in Exercise B above.

AEJ Dishwasher – Important Safety Information

A Installation
This appliance is heavy. Care should be taken when moving it.
Make sure the appliance does not stand on the electricity
supply cable.
Any electrical work required to install this appliance should
be carried out by a qualified electrician.
Any plumbing work required to install this appliance should
be carried out by a qualified plumber.

B Child safety
This appliance is designed to be operated by adults.
Children should not be allowed to touch the controls.
Keep the packaging in which the appliance arrived away
from children.
Keep detergents in a safe place where children cannot
reach them.

C During use
Items that are contaminated by petrol, paint or acid must
not be washed in this appliance.
Never run the appliance with the door open. Always turn
the appliance off before opening the door.
Knives with long blades are potentially dangerous if
stored in this appliance.

Do not sit or stand on the door when it is open.
Unplug the appliance and disconnect the water supply if
you are away from your home for an extended period.

D Maintenance and repair
Take care when cleaning the bottom of the door and hinges
where there are sharp metal edges.
The appliance should be serviced only by a qualified engineer.
Under no circumstances should you attempt to repair the
appliance yourself. Repairs performed by inexperienced
persons can result in injury or serious damage to the appliance.

E Conservation
Help protect the environment. Materials marked with this
symbol * can be recycled. Check with your local council to
find out where there are local facilities for recycling this
appliance. Use only authorized sites to dispose of unwanted
electrical appliances. When this appliance is to be
discarded, cut off the electricity supply cable. Make the door
impossible to close so that a young child could not be
trapped inside.

For questions 1–4, match the pictures below with the correct section of the
instructions. Write the correct letter A–E in the space.

1. ___   2. ___   3. ___   4. ___

For questions 5–8, answer these questions using <u>no more than three words</u> for
each answer.

5. What should not be under the appliance when it is installed?

   _____

6. What could a small child drink if not kept somewhere safe?

   _____

7. Who should deal with any problems that may occur with the appliance?

   _____

8. Which organization can tell you what to do with an unwanted appliance?

   _____

B This text is one of two texts from the second part of the Reading Module. Read it and answer the questions. You have ten minutes. Time each stage of the reading process.

Staff Guidelines   4.3   E-mailing   November 2009

E-mail is now the most common form of communication both internally between staff in different departments and externally with our clients and business associates. It is essential that all staff e-mail appropriately and we advise you to read the following guidelines.

Remember that e-mail is not confidential. Even if you delete e-mails once you have sent them, they may be kept by the recipient and they will be stored on the computer hard-drive. Do not send anything in an e-mail that you would not write down and send on a piece of paper.

Make sure you send e-mails only to the intended recipient. If you are e-mailing frequently, it is easy to send information or an inappropriate comment to somebody who should not see it. Check names just before you hit the SEND button.

The language you use should be suitably formal. Of course, if you are in contact with people regularly, you can use a more informal style and say something more briefly than you might do in a letter. However, remember that you are representing the company

and you try to spell correctly, use acceptable grammar and avoid slang. Never use foul or offensive language in your e-mails.

Start and finish e-mails appropriately as you would in a letter. If you are contacting clients, you should generally start with 'Dear' and end the message with 'Regards' or 'Best wishes'.

Remember that people cannot see your face or hear the tone in your voice when you send an e-mail so they may not understand when you are trying to be humorous. Something written in print often comes across very differently from something said.

Be very careful about criticizing or reprimanding people in e-mails. Written remarks generally come across as far harsher than something said. Certainly do not use e-mail as an opportunity to say anything you would not say to somebody directly.

Finally, remember that not everyone will respond to your e-mails in five minutes just because some clients and associates do. People are busy and are not always in the office. Be patient.

For questions 1–7, decide if the information given below agrees with the information given in the text. Write (T) true, (F) false or (NG) not given.

1. Staff use e-mail more often than they use the telephone.   ___
2. Most people keep the e-mails they are sent for some time.   ___
3. People get angry if they receive e-mails that are meant for somebody else.   ___
4. Language used in e-mails should be the same as language used in letters.   ___
5. Staff should be careful about trying to be funny when e-mailing.   ___
6. E-mailing is a good way of telling somebody you are not happy
   about something.   ___
7. A lot of clients do not answer the e-mails they are sent.   ___

C Check the key on pages 272 and 273. How many questions did you answer correctly?

D Tick the sentences about the two reading tasks that are true for you and think about how you can answer more questions correctly next time.

1. I timed each stage of the reading process.
2. I read the text and answered the questions within ten minutes.
3. I am happy with how many questions I answered correctly.

Key vocabulary in context

Circle the correct dependent preposition in each phrase.

1. can **result** *by* / *in* injury
2. **dispose** *for* / *of* an unwanted appliance
3. **communication** *to* / *with* clients
4. be *in* / *at* **contact** *for* / *with* people
5. **respond** *at* / *to* an email
6. written *in* / *by* print

WB For focus on reading skills, go to Workbook page 40.

Writing 1: having enough to say

A Answer these questions with a partner.

1. What is the minimum number of words you can write for the first IELTS writing task?
2. What is the minimum number of words you can write for the second IELTS writing task?
3. Do you sometimes feel that you don't have enough to say for the first task?
4. Do you sometimes feel that you don't have enough to say for the second task?

B Look at the instructions for a writing task below. Highlight the key words and check you understand what you have to do.

> Some people think children use computers too much these days and that it is harming their development.
>
> Do you agree with that opinion?
>
> Give reasons for your answer and include any relevant examples from your experience. Write about 250 words.

C Talk with a partner. Brainstorm points you could make that agree and disagree with the opinion.

Children can use the Internet to learn about every part of the world.

D Now answer these questions with the same partner.

1. Do you have enough ideas to write 250 words?
2. Will you need to write a long introduction and conclusion in order to achieve the word limit?
3. Are you confident that you can write this composition well?

Children spend their time e-mailing instead of seeing friends face-to-face.

E Look at this composition. What is the problem?

Recently, the use of computers has increased dramatically. These days, most families have a computer at home and there are usually computers in a typical classroom at school. Clearly, children are using computers far more than they did in the past.

Personally, I think this is a good thing and that there are more advantages than disadvantages.

Everyone needs to know how to use a computer, so learning when you are young is good. The Internet has made it possible to find information about any subject and to learn about every part of the world.

However, I can understand why some people are concerned about children using computers too much. Some of the sites on the Internet are not appropriate for children, and they can visit chat rooms that might put them in danger. Some people think that if children work on computers, they will not read books or learn to write, but I disagree.

To sum up, I would say that computers are beneficial for children, but that an adult should regulate how much time they use one. Parents must make sure that children do not spend all their time e-mailing instead of going out with friends.

Writing 2: making sure you write enough

A Answer these questions with a partner.

Where in the composition from the previous page could the student ...
1. give an example to explain something more clearly?
2. add another point to make an opinion clearer or an argument stronger?
3. give an example from his own experience?

B Decide where in the composition each of these lines could be added.

1. When I was at school, I really enjoyed doing projects that involved looking for information online.
2. It is easier to learn how to use new technology when you are young than it is when you are older.
3. ... and that they are safe when they are online.
4. Most schools also have a computer lab where children learn IT skills.
5. I used computers at school, but it didn't stop me wanting to read books, too.
6. It is not always easy for parents to check what children are looking at.

C In this version of the composition put each of the lines in Exercise B where there is a letter. Then check your answers on pages 272 and 273.

Recently, the use of computers has increased dramatically. These days, most families have a computer at home and there are usually computers in a typical classroom at school.
(a) _____ Clearly, children are using computers far more than they did in the past.
Personally, I think this is a good thing and that there are more advantages than disadvantages. Everyone needs to know how to use a computer, so learning when you are young is good.
(b) _____ The Internet has made it possible to find information about any subject and to learn about every part of the world.
(c) _____
However, I can understand why some people are concerned about children using computers too much. Some of the sites on the Internet are not appropriate for children, and they can visit chat rooms that might put them in danger. (d) _____ Some people think that if children work on computers, they will not read books or learn to write, but I disagree.
(e) _____ To sum up, I would say that computers are beneficial for children, but that an adult should regulate how much time they use one. Parents must make sure that children do not spend all their time e-mailing instead of going out with friends
(f) _____

Exam tip: If your composition is too short, you may not need to make a whole new point. Sometimes you can just add examples and explanations that support a point you have already made.

D The following paragraph is from a composition which answers the question *How has modern technology changed our lives at work and at home?* Add a sentence that gives an example from your own experience.

Technology has changed home life enormously. People, especially women, used to spend all day sweeping floors, washing clothes and cooking. Now they have vacuum cleaners, washing machines and microwaves that can do the job in a quarter of the time.

_____

E Look at the exam practice section on page 184 for the writing task.

Speaking

A Complete each sentence with your own ideas. Plan what you want to say.

1. Most people in my country have modern appliances. In their kitchens, for example ...
2. Most people in my country have gadgets, like ... and ...
3. Technology has changed the way I live, especially ...
4. In my country, the price of electrical appliances, such as ... and ..., has fallen considerably.

B Compare your ideas with other people in the class.

C Here are two typical cards for part 2 of the Speaking Module. Work with a partner. One of you is A, the other is B. You have a minute to think about it and make notes.

A

Describe a machine or device you have bought recently.
Say ...
- what it is and what it does.
- where you bought it.
- how it has affected your life.
- if you are happy with it.

B

Talk about a machine or device that you have had a problem with.
Say ...
- what it is or was.
- where you bought it.
- what was wrong with it.
- what you did about the problem.

D Take it in turns to speak about what's on your card for about two minutes.

Vocabulary

A Correct spelling mistakes in each of these answers.

1. Do you think money should be spent on space _explarasion_? _____
2. The salesman gave us a _demmonstrasion_. _____
3. Some things in life are _nesesities_ and others are luxuries. _____
4. So many _technologicle_ advances have been made in this century. _____
5. I can't tell the _differense_ between a British and an American accent. _____
6. The use of computers has increased _dramatikly_. _____

B Answer these questions with a partner. Write the answers in your notebook if you want to.

1. What appliance do you use to heat up cold food?
2. What system keeps a building cool in hot weather?
3. What system keeps a building warm in cold weather?
4. What do we call a small portable computer?
5. What type of TV is transmitted from space?
6. What is another word for a small, clever device?
7. In which part of the fridge can you keep food for several months?
8. In which part of a cooker do you bake or roast food?

Errors

A There are errors in all of these sentences. Correct them.

1. It's a machine for dry your hair.
2. It's a machine what washes plates.
3. It makes the job really quickly.
4. I think people rely in technology too much.
5. James is good at communicating to people.
6. Nobody has responded for my e-mail yet.

14

Writing

A Answer these questions with a partner.

1. How many hours of television do you watch in a week?
2. Do you watch at least one thing on television every day?
3. Do you watch television selectively (choosing what you watch before you sit down to watch), or do you sometimes just watch what's on?
4. Do you ever feel that you have wasted time after you have been watching television?

B Look at the three photos. What do they say about how children spend their time?

C Look carefully at the instructions for this writing task. Highlight the key words and make sure you understand what you have to do.

Children spend too much time watching television instead of participating in activities with other children and playing sports.

To what extent do you agree or disagree with this statement?

Give reasons for your answer and include any relevant examples from your experience. Write about 250 words.

D Answer this question with a partner.

Are you going to agree or disagree, or would you prefer to write a balanced argument?

E Walk around the class and talk to classmates about the issue. Note down the points they make.

F Decide which of the points you want to include in your composition and then write it. Remember – you don't need to include all the points you discussed. Make sure you write 250 words.

_____

_____

_____

15 Society

Vocabulary 1: social issues

A Check the meaning of *social issue* in a dictionary. Then talk to a partner and make a list of social issues that exist in your country.

B Match the social issues with the extracts from newspapers. Highlight the words and phrases that help you decide.

1. crime __   2. racism __   3. drug abuse __
4. homelessness __   5. unemployment __   6. animal rights __

a   In big cities around the world, it is common to see people sleeping in the streets. Many of these people are young and have other problems, such as mental illness and drug addiction.

b   Many teenagers are taking heroin or crack cocaine. Police believe that half of the crime committed in the area is drug-related.

c   The economic problems that the country faces are likely to result in job losses. Six per cent of people could be out of work by this time next year.

d   Government statistics show that serious offences, including murder and rape, are decreasing, while less serious offences, including burglary and shoplifting, are on the increase.

e   The Football Association is concerned about the increase in the amount of abuse that black players are receiving from fans.

f   Several people have been arrested outside a laboratory where scientists are testing cosmetic products on rats and mice.

Speaking 1: discussing social issues

A Discuss in groups. Answer these questions.

1. Are any of the social issues above a problem in your country / in your city or town?
2. In which parts of the world are the social issues above a common problem?
3. Which of the issues are you most concerned about?
4. Are there any other social issues that you think are a problem in your country?

Vocabulary 2: crime and punishment

A Match the crimes 1–8 with the definitions a–h.

1. murder   a. entering somebody's home when they are not there and stealing
2. robbery   b. taking a person and asking for money to return them safely
3. theft   c. taking another person's life
4. burglary   d. stealing something with force (using violence – a gun / knife, etc.)
5. shoplifting   e. beating, hitting or kicking somebody during a disagreement
6. smuggling   f. stealing from shops
7. kidnapping   g. taking something illegal (drugs / guns) from one country into another
8. assault   h. a general word for stealing something without using force

B Cover Exercise A and write the words in your notebook. Focus on your spelling.

C Check the meaning of *punish* and *punishment* in your dictionary. Then complete each sentence 1–3 with an ending a–c.

1. If you park your car illegally, you will ... ___
2. If you murder somebody, you will ... ___
3. If you assault somebody, you may ... ___

a. *receive a fine / be fined.*
b. *receive a fine / be fined* or you may *go to prison / be sent to prison.*
c. *receive a life sentence / be given a life sentence / be sent to prison for life* or, in some countries, *face a death penalty / be sentenced to death.*

> **Grammar check**
> Notice how the same ideas can be expressed using an *active or passive form*.
> *You will receive a fine. / You will be fined.*
> The future passive form is: *will + be + past participle.*

> **Pronunciation check**
> When one word ends in a consonant and the next begins with a vowel, you hear the consonant sound at the beginning of the second word rather than at the end of the first.
> 🎧 Listen to these examples from the unit.
> 1. social issues   2. drug abuse
> 3. serious offences   4. have been arrested
> Practise saying the phrases.

Speaking 2: fitting a punishment to a crime

A Walk around the class and ask classmates what they think is the right punishment for each of the crimes in Vocabulary 2A.

> *If you take a person's life, you should go to prison for all of your life.*

Speaking 3: explaining what you mean when you can't remember a word

A Look at these possible questions from the third part of the Speaking Module. Think about how you would answer them.

1. Are there any crimes that are particularly common in your country?
2. Do you feel that London is a safe city to stay in? Is it as safe as Switzerland?

B 🎧 Listen and answer these questions.

1. How does the first speaker explain the word she can't remember?
2. Which word does the second student not know?

C Talk with a partner about crime or social problems that you don't know the correct word for. Explain what you mean.

> *A problem in my country is when the children at school do or say horrible things to another child.*

15

Listening 1: preparing to listen

A Look at the picture. Answer these questions with a partner.

1. What exactly does *homeless* mean?
2. Why do you think people become homeless?
3. Apart from not having a home, what problems do homeless people have?

B 🎧 Listen to somebody giving a talk about homelessness and check your ideas.

Listening 2: transferring answers to the answer sheet

A Answer these questions with a partner.

1. Which listening tasks do not involve writing words or phrases as answers?
2. Which tasks do involve writing words and phrases as answers?
3. During the listening exam, where do you write your answers as you listen?
4. At the end of the listening exam, where do you write your final answers?
5. How long do you have to transfer your answers to the answer sheet?
6. What problems can you have when you transfer your answers to the answer sheet?

B 🎧 Listen to the first part of the talk about homelessness again and answer these questions.

For questions 1 and 2, choose the correct answer a, b or c.

1. At the beginning of the talk, the speaker says that ...
   a. homelessness is not a big problem.   b. the people at the talk are selfish.
   c. he understands why people are worried.
2. The speaker says that most homeless people ...
   a. sleep outside.   b. do not sleep outside.   c. look for a safe place to sleep.

For questions 3–7, complete the notes. Use <u>no more than three words</u> for each answer.

People are homeless if ...
sleeping on (3) _____ at home of friend, staying in a (4) _____,
sleeping in any type of motor (5) _____,
poor condition of place they live in affects their (6) _____,
afraid of (7) _____ or physical abuse.

C Check this student's answer sheet. Which answers are correct? Which are not? What mistakes has the student made?

1. c
2. b
3. the floor or sofa
4. hotel or shelter
5. vikle
6. helth
7. violense

Exam tip: More than half of the tasks that can occur in the Listening Module involve writing words and phrases as answers. You MUST spell your answer correctly and you MUST NOT use more than the stated number of words. Use the ten minutes you have to transfer answers to the answer sheet properly. Transfer answers slowly and carefully and check all your answers two or three times.

Listening 3: practise transferring answers to the answer sheet

A 🎧 Listen to the rest of the talk about homelessness again. Answer the questions.

For questions 1–8, complete the summary below with words from the text. Use <u>no more than two words</u> for each answer.

People become homeless when there is no other (1) _____. Homeless people are poor and cannot (2) _____ rent or mortgage repayments. Most homeless people do not have (3) _____. There are usually other issues that homeless people must deal with. They might take (4) _____ or they might suffer from (5) _____ problems. Many homeless people have been in (6) _____ and so cannot find work or a place to live. Some people become homeless because they lose a home they have rented for a long time. Young people and women might leave home because of a (7) _____ family member. In many places, the value of (8) _____ has increased, and so renting or buying a home is impossible for the poorest people.

For questions 9 and 10, choose <u>two</u> answers from A–D.

Which of these ideas does the speaker mention in the final part of the talk that you hear?
 A Homeless people getting money from the government.
 B Permanent accommodation for homeless people.
 C Places where homeless people can eat.
 D What is happening to homeless people in other countries.

   9. ___   10. ___

B Transfer your answers to the answer sheet below.

1		6	
2		7	
3		8	
4		9	
5		10	

C Check the key on page 273. How many questions did you answer correctly?

D Answer these questions about the listening task with a partner and think about how you can answer more questions correctly next time.

 1. Which answers were easy to transfer?
 2. Which answers were more difficult to transfer?
 3. Did you get any answers wrong because they were not spelt correctly or transferred wrongly?
 4. Did you use the correct number of words for each answer?
 5. Are you happy with the number of questions you answered correctly?

15

Reading 1: preparing to read

A Look at the picture and answer the questions with a partner.

1. Who is the man on the left?
2. Who is the man on the right?
3. Is the man on the right behaving in an acceptable way?
4. Do you think this is something that happens a lot in workplaces in your country?

B Check *bully* in your dictionary. Now check the following words and phrases. How is each related to bullying?

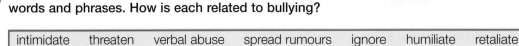

| intimidate | threaten | verbal abuse | spread rumours | ignore | humiliate | retaliate |

Reading 2: checking your answers

A Answer these questions with a partner.

1. Which of the reading tasks you have practised do not involve writing words or phrases as answers?
2. Which tasks do involve writing words and phrases as answers?
3. During the reading exam, where do you write your answers as you read?
4. Do you have to transfer answers to an answer sheet as you do in the listening exam?
5. Why is spelling not such a big problem with the reading exam?
6. What mistakes can you make when writing your final answers?

B Read this short extract about bullying and answer the questions.

Dan Olweus, a researcher from Norway, has defined bullying as when 'a person is exposed to negative actions over a period of time on the part of one person or a number of people, through physical contact, through words or in other ways.' Bullying can occur anywhere that humans interact with each other. This can be at school, in the workplace, in a neighbourhood or at home. Bullying can exist between different groups in society and even between countries. Bullying may cause individuals or groups of people to migrate from one part of a country to another or even to a new country.

For questions 1 and 2, answer the questions with words from the extract. Use no more than two words for each answer.

1. Where is Dan Olweus from? _____
2. What might people do if they are bullied? _____

For questions 3 and 4, decide if the information given below agrees with the information given in the extract. Write (T) true, (F) false or (NG) not given.

3. Most incidents of bullying only occur once. ___
4. Most people experience bullying at some time. ___

For question 5, complete this sentence with one word from the text.

5. Bullying is when somebody does something to you or says something about you that is _____.

C Check this student's answer sheet. What mistakes has the student made?

1. norway
2. migrate to a new place
3. ~~NG~~   F
4. ~~F~~   NG
5. negitive

Exam tip: In the Reading Module, you do not have extra time to transfer answers. You write answers directly onto the answer sheet as you read. Nearly half of the tasks that can occur in the Reading Module involve writing words and phrases as answers. You MUST spell your answer correctly – the words that you need to use occur in the text or the summary box, so make sure you copy them correctly. You MUST NOT use more than the stated number of words. If you change an answer, rub it out or cross it out completely. Your final answer must be clear.

Reading 3: practise checking your answers

A Read this information page about bullying in the workplace and answer the questions.

Workplace bullies – Don't let them get away with it

Bullying in the workplace is far more common than most people imagine. This type of bullying may be related to your race, your gender, your age, your religion, a disability or simply happen because somebody doesn't like your tastes or views on life. You may experience one isolated case or a persistent campaign over a period of time. You could be bullied by colleagues or by somebody in a position of authority who uses his or her power to hurt or upset you. If you are being bullied in your workplace, you don't have to accept it.

What exactly do bullies do?
Bullying at work can mean different things. These are some ways that people have described bullying:

- being intimidated or threatened
- being shouted at or verbally abused
- being treated unfairly
- being constantly criticized
- being laughed at or joked about
- having rumours spread about you
- being ignored or deliberately left out of conversations

Many people who are bullied think it's their fault. It isn't. No one has the right to bully.

Bullying is not always face-to-face
In these modern times, bullying is not necessarily face-to-face and not limited to the time that you are actually at work. You may receive threatening or abusive telephone calls, e-mails or text messages at any time of the day.

How do people feel when they are bullied?
Bullying humiliates people and makes them anxious. People suffer from stress and lose self-confidence. Bullying can lead to job insecurity, illness and absence from work. Some people may even resign as a result of being bullied at work. Frequent bullying has a negative effect on the atmosphere generally in any workplace.

Protect yourself
The best way to protect yourself is to tell your managers. If you are being bullied by someone in a management position, go to someone higher. Don't try to retaliate. If you do, you might make the situation worse or get into trouble yourself.

Here are some ways that you can deal with bullying in the workplace:

- don't ignore it – it won't stop bullies doing what they enjoy doing
- tell somebody who can do something about it immediately
- keep a record of any notes, e-mails or text messages that you have received
- check your company's staff handbook. It will tell you what your company should do about your situation

Don't become a bully yourself
You have a choice about whether to bully or not. It can be difficult not to join in if everyone else is bullying someone. It takes courage to step back, but bullying causes a lot of unhappiness and pain. If you find yourself bullying someone or know that someone you work with is being bullied, do something.

If you are being bullied or are worried about anything to do with bullying, you can call us and we can help.

For questions 1–6, complete each sentence with the correct ending A–H from the box. Write the letters onto the answer sheet below.

1. Bullying at work
2. Telling a manager
3. Face-to-face bullying
4. Retaliating
5. Ignoring bullying
6. Not being a bully when others are

A is brave.
B can mean you will be punished.
C is the best thing you can do.
D is a manager's job.
E makes no difference.
F has many different forms.
G will always stop bullying.
H is not always the approach.

For questions 7–12, complete the summary with words from the text. Use no more than two words for each answer.

People do not realize that bullying in the workplace is such a (7) … problem. People are bullied for a number of reasons. They may be bullied in an (8) … incident or a number of times over weeks or months. A person might be bullied by the people they work alongside or by a person who has (9) … . Bullies operate in various ways. They might do all sorts of things to upset people or simply ignore them and not invite them to join in (10) … . Bullying can cause stress and insecurity. In the end, it might cause somebody (11) … from a job. Generally speaking, (12) … in any workplace where bullying occurs is not good.

1		7	
2		8	
3		9	
4		10	
5		11	
6		12	

B Check the key on page 273. How many questions did you answer correctly?

C Answer these questions about the reading task with a partner and think about how you can answer more questions correctly next time.

1. Are you happy with the number of questions you answered correctly?
2. Did you make any mistakes?

Key vocabulary in context

Highlight five words or phrases in the information page that you want to remember. Then compare with a partner and test each other.

Grammar check
Notice how **passive ~ing forms** are used in the text.
Active: *If somebody is bullying you* …
Passive: *If you are being bullied, …*

WB For focus on reading skills, go to Workbook page 43.

Writing 1: preparing and planning to write

A Match each of these words and phrases with a picture.

a. antisocial behaviour ___   b. vandalism ___   c. begging ___   d. graffiti ___

B Answer these questions with a partner.

1. Why do you think each of these social issues exist?
2. Do you have any of the issues in your hometown or city?

C Look at the instructions for a writing task below. Highlight the key words and check that you understand what you have to do.

A friend of a friend has written to you asking for advice about staying in Bradlow, a town that you stayed in last year. You liked your host family and your language school, but you thought that the town was not ideal. There were a number of social problems and you did not always feel safe.

Write a letter to your friend explaining why he should think about studying in another town. Write at least 150 words. You should spend about 20 minutes on this task.

D Answer these questions with a partner.

1. You are writing to a friend of a friend, so will it be a formal or an informal letter, or will it be something in between?
2. Think of three or four points that you could advise your friend's friend about.

Writing 2: practise writing a letter

A Work in pairs.

Student A: Write the opening paragraph. State your purpose for writing and introduce the main point you want to make.
Student B: Write the concluding paragraph. Sum up the main point you have made and say that you hope your friend's friend enjoys his visit to Bradlow.

B Compare what you have written with your partner.

C Work together to write the main part of the letter. Tell your friend's friend all about Bradlow.

Writing 3: choosing what to say and how to say it

A Below are possible lines from a letter to your friend's friend. Look at these points.

- Some lines are relevant and others are not.
- Some lines are appropriately expressed and some are not.
- Some lines are grammatically correct and some are not.
- Some lines have spelling mistakes and some do not.

B Choose the ten lines that you think make up the complete letter and put them in order. Write the letters in the spaces below each paragraph.

Dear Samuel,

ⓐ Bradlow is horrible. You must not go there.

ⓑ I understand you're thinking of staying there soon. Personally, I would consider going somewhere else.

ⓒ I am writing to tell you about Bradlow. Leon did ask me to.

ⓓ I hear that you want to stay in Bradlow but is not good place.

ⓔ Leon asked me to write to you and tell you all about Bradlow where I stayed last year.

1. ___   2. ___

ⓕ My host family were such nice people and my school so good.

ⓖ However, Bradlow itself is not such a nice place to stay, in my opinion.

ⓗ But Bradlow is very small and quiet and I was bored most of the time.

ⓘ I was happy with my host family and the school where I studied was excellent.

ⓙ But Bradlow it was not a good place to feel comfortable.

3. ___   4. ___

ⓚ There are quite a lot of homeless people and sometimes they beg for money in the street.

ⓛ In the town centre, there are a lot of bars and discos and young people can be quite loud. I didn't feel very safe walking around in the evening.

ⓜ Nobody there has got a job and people are always asking for money.

ⓝ There are a lot of closed down shops and there is graffiti on buildings.

ⓞ I don't like dancing so I didn't like so many discos. I studied in my room most evenings.

ⓟ It is quite a poor town and there is a lot of unemployment. Teenagers get together in the shopping centre because there is nowhere else for them to go.

ⓠ The worst is the town centre. It is really dirty and a horrible place.

5. ___   6. ___   7. ___   8. ___

ⓡ So, have a fantastic time in Bradlow. I'm sure you will.

ⓢ Anyway, I hope you have a really good time, wherever you decide to stay.

ⓣ There is much more nice place to stay than Bradlow. Harkeley would be best for you I think.

ⓤ It depends what you want but I think there are nicer places to stay. I went to see some friends in Harkeley and it is very nice there.

ⓥ So, like I say, don't go to Bradlow. It's terrible. But have a good time if you go another place.

9. ___   10. ___

Best wishes,
Vicente

C Look at the model letter on page 273 and check your answers. Is the letter similar to the one you wrote with your partner?

D Look at the exam practice section on page 198 for the writing task.

Speaking

A Work in pairs. One of you is A, the other is B. Use a dictionary to look up the words in your box. Then explain them to your partner.

A	hijack	arson	discrimination	petition

B	cell	inmates	protest	ethnic minority

B Here are two typical cards for part 2 of the Speaking Module. Work with a partner. One of you is A, the other is B. You have a minute to think about it and make notes.

A

> **Talk about a social issue that affects your town or city.**
> **Say ...**
> - what it is.
> - why you think it exists.
> - how it affects people.
> - what could be done about it.

B

> **What type of antisocial behaviour upsets you most?**
> **Say ...**
> - what it is.
> - where and when it happens.
> - how it makes you feel.
> - what could be done about it.

C Take it in turns to speak about what's on your card for about two minutes.

Vocabulary

A Find ten crime-related words in the word grid. The words can go across or down.

K	V	R	O	B	B	E	R	D	K
U	A	M	K	G	U	T	N	I	I
T	N	U	I	T	H	E	F	T	L
S	D	D	D	I	I	R	N	I	L
N	A	A	N	T	I	R	E	P	E
R	L	L	A	F	I	N	E	R	G
Y	I	B	P	R	U	M	M	I	A
E	S	M	U	G	G	L	E	S	L
O	M	U	R	D	E	R	I	O	N
P	U	N	I	S	H	A	C	N	R

B Correct the spelling mistakes in these words.

1. rasism _____
2. unemploiment _____
3. berglery _____
4. asault _____
5. releese _____
6. temparary _____
7. perminant _____
8. threten _____

Errors

A There are errors in all of these sentences. Correct them.

1. If you murder, you will given a life sentence.
2. If you rob a bank, you will be send to prison.
3. Homeless people may be separated of their family.
4. If you are been bullied, you must tell somebody.
5. He is staying with friends temporary.
6. I am writing for tell you about Bradlow.

15

Listening

A 🎧 You will hear two people telephoning their local council to complain. Answer the questions.
For questions 1–5, choose the correct answer a, b or c.

1. The woman ...
   a. has called the council before. b. is calling for the first time. c. called the council yesterday.
2. The woman ...
   a. lives in the city centre. b. does not like football. c. is surprised by something.
3. The woman didn't call the police because ...
   a. she didn't want to call early in the morning. b. it was too late for them to do anything.
   c. she was too angry to stay calm.
4. The council telephonist says that ...
   a. everyone wants more cameras. b. it is right that homeowners must clean up graffiti.
   c. the council is very busy.
5. The council telephonist ...
   a. promises that telephone boxes will be cleaned soon.
   b. admits that the council must repair some public property.
   c. thinks that parents should stop their children spraying graffiti.

For questions 6–10, choose <u>five</u> answers from A–I. Which of the following is the man unhappy about?

A Rubbish is not collected regularly.	B Friday is not a good day for a rubbish collection.
C Birds make a problem worse.	D He was not told about a change.
E He has to clean the street himself.	F He has a difficult job.
G People put rubbish out on the wrong day.	H He does not like his neighbours.
I Rubbish collectors could do a better job.	

6. ___   7. ___   8. ___   9. ___   10. ___

B Transfer your answers to the answer sheet below. You have two and a half minutes.

1		6	
2		7	
3		8	
4		9	
5		10	

Reading

A Read the passage and answer questions 1–10.

A. The answer to this question depends on what, in your opinion, is the purpose of sending people to prison. Most people consider the impact that imprisonment has on criminals and how it affects their behaviour in the future. Some people will have different views about why we have prisons; politicians, policemen and the victims of crime, for example. Putting people behind bars appears to work for a number of reasons.

B. Most people regard a prison sentence as a fair punishment for certain serious offences or a number of less serious offences. The criminal does something wrong and society pays him back. He gets what he deserves. There are other forms of punishment, such as fines or community service, but imprisonment is what people expect when the crime cannot be ignored.

C. Violent criminals and those who offend again and again need to be locked up so that people are not in danger. A recent survey of offenders sent to prison showed that the typical offender admitted to committing 150 offences in the year before he was caught. On average, therefore, for each 1,000 criminals sent to prison for a year, there would be 150,000 fewer offences.

D. Many people believe that the fear of going to prison deters people from committing crime. People who might do wrong think again if they know that the punishment will mean being locked up. Some statistics suggest that in countries where punishment for certain crimes is very severe, the rate for that crime has fallen. Other people argue that people commit crime because they are desperate and that desperate people have no fear of punishment, whether it is prison or something else.

E. Prison is supposed to rehabilitate criminals. In prison, an offender has time to reflect on the crime he has committed and on the pain he has caused to his victim. Prisons have programmes for educating inmates and for teaching them new skills that they can use when they are released. Some people might argue, however, that in prison, offenders simply meet and mix with other criminals and come out knowing more about crime.

F. Finally, prison is an important institution. Every democratic country has prisons, and people believe that there are wrongdoers who should be inside them. If prisons did not exist or if softer punishments were given to serious criminals, people would not trust the justice system. It is possible that, in that situation, more people would take the law into their own hands and deal with criminals themselves.

For questions 1–6, match the section headings i–x with the sections in the text. You do not need to use all the headings. Write the numeral for each answer.

i. Prison life is too easy	ii. What sort of person goes to prison?
iii. Public confidence	iv. Fines might be the solution
v. Changing for better or worse	vi. Afraid of losing freedom
vii. Does prison work?	viii. An eye for an eye
ix. Most criminals are not caught	x. Protecting the public

1. Section A   ___
2. Section B   ___
3. Section C   ___
4. Section D   ___
5. Section E   ___
6. Section F   ___

For questions 7–10, answer each of these questions with words from the text. Use <u>no more than two words</u> for each answer.

7. Apart from imprisonment and fines, what form of punishment does the text mention?
8. How many crimes does the typical offender commit before he is caught?
9. Which word is the opposite of 'soft' when describing a punishment?
10. What are some inmates supposed to learn while they are in prison?

1		6	
2		7	
3		8	
4		9	
5		10	

Writing

A Look carefully at the instructions for this writing task. Highlight the key words and make sure you understand what you have to do.

> Prison is the only suitable way of dealing with the majority of offenders.
>
> To what extent do you agree or disagree with this statement?
>
> Give reasons for your answer and include any relevant examples from your experience. Write at least 250 words.

B Look back at the passage above. Highlight points that you could use in your composition.

C Walk around the class and talk to classmates about the issue. Note down the points they make.

D Decide which of the points you want to include in your composition and then write it.

_____

_____

_____

_____

Review 3

Speaking and Vocabulary

A Mark each of the following topics like this:

> (++)   I can talk about this topic easily and have plenty to say.
> (+)   I can talk about this topic quite well and have some things to say.
> (–)   I don't enjoy talking about this topic and don't know what to say.

1. keeping fit and doing exercise   ___
2. your diet   ___
3. the natural beauty of your country   ___
4. the climate and weather in your country   ___
5. your home   ___
6. your neighbourhood   ___
7. buildings in your country   ___
8. technology   ___
9. social issues   ___
10. crime   ___

B Discuss your answers with a partner.

C Work in pairs. Take it in turns to ask and answer questions about the topics in Exercise A.

D Write important words and phrases that you have learnt in Units 11–15 under each heading.

staying healthy
_____
_____
_____
_____

accidents and injuries
_____
_____
_____
_____

climate and weather
_____
_____
_____
_____

homes, houses and neighbourhoods
_____
_____
_____
_____

my words and phrases

technology
_____
_____
_____
_____

crime
_____
_____
_____
_____

social issues
_____
_____
_____
_____

Listening and Reading

A Work in pairs. Take it in turns to ask and answer the following questions about listening. The student asking the questions can look back at the unit and check the exam or question-type tips.

1. What type of information will you hear in the different parts of the listening exam?
2. Why is it sometimes easier to complete a flow chart or a table?
3. Will the speakers on the tape use formal or informal language?
4. Why might one speaker be more difficult to understand than another?
5. What do you need to do at the end of the listening exam?
6. How long do you have to transfer answers to the answer sheet?
7. What mistakes can you make when you are transferring answers?

B Work with the same partner. Ask and answer these questions about reading.

1. What do you remember about matching beginnings and endings of sentences? How can you make it easier to choose from a number of options?
2. How many different types of text can you remember? How can you know quickly what type of text you are reading?
3. Which passage is the longest passage? What type of text will it be?
4. What can you do to cope with a longer text more successfully?
5. Why is it important to time yourself when you read a text?
6. What is usually a waste of time when you are reading?
7. Why is it easier to write answers onto the question sheet during the reading exam than it is during the listening exam?

C Mark each of these statements (T) true or (F) false.

1. My listening has improved since I started the course. ___
2. I know what to listen for in order to answer questions. ___
3. I am happy writing answers as I continue to listen. ___
4. I am good at identifying key words even if I don't know them. ___
5. I feel confident about transferring answers in ten minutes. ___
6. My reading speed has improved since I began this course. ___
7. I feel confident reading any type of text now. ___
8. I understand the main idea of almost any text I read now. ___
9. I know what to look for in order to answer exam questions. ___
10. I don't worry about words and phrases I don't know anymore. ___

D Look at these comments that students have made about taking exams. Tick the ones that you most agree with.

'I get very nervous in exams. I can't concentrate on the tasks.' ___

'Some people are good at doing exams and some people are not.' ___

'If other students in the exam are writing a lot and seem to be doing well, it makes me anxious. I think I am not as good as they are.' ___

'My mind goes blank as soon as I sit down in an exam hall.' ___

'I worry too much about getting the answers right and not enough about whether I understand.' ___

'I can't sleep the night before an exam, so I'm always really tired during the exam.'

'Revising for exams is really boring.' ___

'Revising just before an exam is a waste of time. You either know it or you don't.' ___

Writing

A Look at the instructions for a writing task below. Highlight the key words and check that you understand what you have to do.

> Write to a friend telling him/her that you are taking the IELTS exam. Say why you are taking the exam and how you feel about it. Tell your friend that he/she should do the exam and why.
>
> Write at least 150 words. You should spend about 20 minutes on this task.

B Look at this student's attempt to write the composition. Talk to a partner about what you like and don't like about the composition.

> Hi Henri I'm Sorry that I didn't can come at your brothers weding last week I am very bisy resently. I'm taking an examination in english It called IELTS. I need it for go university next year. I just finish a course that help me prepare for this examination It dificult but I enjoy it too much. My speaking english is much better than before but I don't can write so good like can you see. Ha ha! The examination it is next friday and I am too nervos about it. There is a speaking part a lisening part a reading part and a writing part. The reading and writing parts is which I am nervos about. I think you should to take this IELTS examination too. Your good in english and so you can get high score I think it is good have this examination for find a work. ok goodby now William.

C Work in pairs. One of you is A, the other is B.

Student A: Highlight errors in the letter related to organization and grammar.
Student B: Highlight errors in the letter related to spelling and punctuation.

D Compare your ideas with a partner.

E Look at the version of the letter on page 274. The errors are highlighted. Then read the model letter below it.

F Write a similar letter to a friend of yours. Make sure you cover all the points in the instructions.

What next?

Congratulations! You've finished the course. You've heard the different types of talks or conversations that you will hear in the Listening Module and you've read the different types of text that you will have to read in the Reading Module. You've practised every task type for each module. Hopefully, you feel much more confident about taking the exam now. Here are some tips to prepare you for the exam.

✓ Revision doesn't have to be boring. It is boring if you do it for too long or try to do it all at once. It will make you feel anxious if you try to revise too much. Remember that revision means looking back at what you have learnt – not trying to learn things that you haven't learnt yet.

✓ Practise the Speaking Module with other students who are taking the exam. Revise the typical vocabulary that you need to talk about the most common topics of conversation. Make sure you know the words and phrases you need to talk about your own life.

✓ Revise for the Listening Module by borrowing tapes that practise IELTS listening tasks. Remember, though, that the important thing is to improve your all-round listening skills, so continue to follow the advice from the previous review sections.

✓ Revise for the Reading Module by doing reading sections from past IELTS papers and by doing the IELTS mock exams in this book. Look back at the Reading Modules from earlier units in this book. Look at how the texts have become more challenging and how your reading skills have improved.

✓ Revise when you would otherwise be wasting time. Revise at the bus stop or on the bus. Don't wait until the night before the exam to do all your revision. Remember that the important thing is to improve your all-round reading skills, so continue to follow the advice from the previous review sections.

✓ Practise writing compositions and ask your teacher or someone who reads English very well to check them. Continue to look at as many model answers to exam questions as you can.

✓ Try to get a good night's sleep the night before the exam. You don't want to feel tired. Make sure you arrive at the exam centre some time before the exam starts. You want to feel relaxed and confident – not in a terrible rush.

✓ Try not to be nervous. Remember that the important thing is to understand what you hear and what you read. If you can, you will answer questions correctly. Don't worry about how other people are doing – you are not in competition with them.

Key exam vocabulary

General Training reading and writing

The key vocabulary is a list of words that occur in IELTS Target 5.0 and that you should learn to improve your performance in the Reading and Writing Modules of the IELTS exam. It is a list of words and phrases that frequently occur in the type of texts that you will read in the IELTS General Training exam and which you will need to write effectively, especially in the second writing task. These words will also help you to understand certain topics in the Listening Module better.

Some very common words and phrases are not included in the list because you will already know what they mean and how to use them. Vocabulary that you will need for the speaking exam is not included in the list as this vocabulary is more personal to you. Look back at the first module of each unit to check particular words and phrases that you need to improve your speaking.

Spend some time checking all the words and phrases in the list and check anything you are not sure about in a good dictionary.

A
achieve (v)
achievement (n)
acquire (v)
activity (n)
advantage (n)
(can / cannot) afford
    (v phrase)
ambition (n)
ambitious (adj)
annual (adj)
apology (n)
applicant (n)
appliance (n)
application (n)
apply (for) (v)
appointment (n)
appreciate (v)
approach (v/n)
arrange (v)
assess (v)
atmosphere (n)
attempt (n/v)
attitude (n)
authority (n)
avoid (v)

B
ban (v/n)
behave (v)
behaviour (n)
belong to (v phrase)

C
calculate (v)
cancel (v)
capacity (n)
career (n)
case (n)
cause (v/n)
century (n)
challenge (n)
climate (n)
communication (with)
    (n/n phrase)
complain (v)
complaint (n)
concentrate (v)
congested (adj)
congestion (n)
consist of (v phrase)
construct (v)
construction (n)
(be in) contact (with)
    (n/v phrase)
control (v/n)
cope with (v phrase)
courage (n)
course (n)
create (v)
creation (n)
crime (n)
criminal (n)
currently (adv)

D
(cause) damage
    (n/v phrase)
danger (n)
dangerous (adj)
deal with (v phrase)
decide (v)
(make a) decision
    (n/v phrase)
degree (n)
delay (n)
(be) delayed (v phrase)
difficulty (n)
demonstrate (v)
demonstration (n)
design (n)
develop (v)
development (n)
device (n)
diagram (n)
disagreement (n)
discover (v)
discovery (n)
discuss (v)
discussion (n)
dispose of (v phrase)

E
economic (adj)
(the) economy (of a
    country) (n/n phrase)

educate (v)
education (n)
efficient (adj)
energy (n)
environment (n)
equipment (n)
exhibition (n)
exist (v)
existence (n)
expansion (n)
expand (v)
experience (n)
exploration (n)
explore (v)
export (v/n)
extend (v)
extinct (adj)
extreme (adj)
event (n)

F
facilities (n)
fail (v)
failure (n)
fear (n)
finally (adv)
finance (n)
financial (adj)
financial support
    (n phrase)
firstly (adv)
freedom (n)

frequently (adv)
function (v/n)

G
gain (n)
generation (n)
graduate (n)

H
habit (n)
historic (adj)
history (n)
however (conj)
(have an) idea (v phrase)

I
ignore (v)
illegal (adj)
(have an / use your)
   imagination
   (n/v phrase)
image (n)
imagine (v)
immediately (adv)
import (v/n)
impressive (adj)
improve (v)
improvement (n)
incident (n)
inconvenience (n)
inconvenient (adj)
increase (v/n)
industrial (adj)
industry (n)
influence (v/n)
(have an) influence (on)
   (n/v phrase)
information (n)
intelligent (adj)
invest (in) (v)
invitation (n)
involve (v)
issue (n)

J
judge (v)
(make a) judgement
   (n/v phrase)

L
limit (v/n)
luxury / luxuries (n)

M
magnificent (adj)
matter (n)
measure (v)
memorize (v)
memory (n)
modern (adj)

N
natural environment
   (n phrase)
necessity / necessities (n)

O
obstacle (n)
occasionally (adv)
offence (n)
offend (v)
operate (v)
operation (n)
(be) opposed to
   (v phrase)
overcome (v)
own (v)

P
penalty (n)
permanent (adj)
permanently (adv)
personal qualities
   (n phrase)
plenty (of) (n/adj phrase)
polluted (adj)
pollution (n)
position (n)
possibility (n)
poverty (n)
power (n)
powerful (adj)
predict (v)
(make a) prediction
   (n/v phrase)
prefer (v)
pressure (n)
prevent (v)
prevention (n)
process (n/v)
produce (v)
product (n)
profession (n)
professional (adj)
profit (n)
progress (n)

project (n)
property (n)
provide (v)
punish (v)
punishment (n)
purchase (v/n)

R
raise (money) (v phrase)
rarely (adv)
reach (v)
react (to) (v)
reaction (n)
recall (v)
receive (v)
record (v)
reduce (v)
reflect (v)
reflection (n)
release (v)
(be) released (from)
   (v phrase)
relevant (adj)
rely (on) (v)
remain (v)
(have a) reputation
   (n/v phrase)
respect (v/n)
respond (to) (v)
(as a) result (of)
   (n/prep phrase)
result (in) (v)
revise (v)
rise (v/n)
risk (n)
rural (adj)

S
safety (n)
separate (adj)
(be) separated (from)
   (v phrase)
situation (n)
social issue (n phrase)
solution (n)
solve (v)
source (n)
speed (n)
strength (n)
structure (n)
succeed (v)
success (n)
successful (adj)

suffer (from) (v)
support (n)
survive (v)
symptom (n)

T
technique (n)
technological (adj)
technology (n)
temporarily (adv)
temporary (adj)
therefore (adv)
(have a) thought
   (n/v phrase)
tourism (n)
tradition (n)
traffic (n)
transfer (v/n)
transport (n/v)
treat (v)
treatment (n)
trust (v/n)
truth (n)

U
unlikely (adj)

V
value (n)
victim (n)
violence (n)
violent (adj)
volume (n)

W
waste (v/n)
wealth (n)
whole (adj)
(be) worth (v phrase)

Work-related vocabulary

Check these words and phrases to help you with the second part of the Reading Module (training survival). Some are included in the general vocabulary and some are not.

A
accountant (n)
achieve (v)
achievement (n)
ambition (n)
ambitious (adj)
application (n)
apply (for) (v)
apprentice (n)
assistant (n)

B
boss (n)

C
career (n)
challenge (n)
challenging (adj)
client (n)
colleague (n)
communicate (with) (v)
communication (n)
company (n)
customer (n)

D
deal with (v phrase)

E
efficient (adj)
employ (v)
employee (n)
employer (n)
employment (n)
entrepreneur (n)
executive (n)

F
factory (n)
firm (n)

I
(the) ... industry (n phrase)
interview (v/n)

M
manage (v)
manager (n)
management (n)

O
office (n)
out of work (adj phrase)

P
past experience
    (n phrase)
pay (n)
pension (n)
position (n)
previous experience
    (n phrase)
produce (v)
product (n)
production (n)
profession (n)
professional (adj)
profit (n)

Q
qualified (adj)

R
repetitive (adj)
retire (v)
retirement (n)
rewarding (adj)

S
salary (n)
set up (a business)
    (v phrase)

staff (n)
stress (n)
stressful (adj)
succeed (v)
success (n)
successful (adj)

T
training (n)

U
unemployed (adj)
unemployment (n)

V
(business) venture
    (n/n phrase)

W
well paid (adj)
work (as / for / in / with) +
    noun (v phrase)
workplace (n)

Introduction

How the Academic course works

IELTS Target 5.0 Academic is for students who have studied IELTS Target 5.0 General Training but want to sit the Academic exam. Scoring 5.0 in the General Training exam is more realistic than doing so in the Academic exam, but some students need the Academic exam for entrance to university or to apply for certain jobs. If you need to sit the Academic exam, but are concerned that your general level of English isn't high enough, this supplement will prepare you to deal with the academic content of the reading passages and the more challenging writing tasks.

Since both the Listening and Speaking Modules of the Academic exam are the same as those in the General Training exam, this supplement practises only reading and writing. The course consists of five units and develops in terms of challenge, so that by the time you sit the exam, you will feel much more prepared and confident.

Since you will have no experience of the writing tasks that you have to tackle in the first part of the IELTS Writing Module, the Writing Modules in this book take a simple step-by-step approach, and gradually introduce you to possible task types.

As in the General Training course, the Reading Module is roughly divided into two parts. The first part aims to engage you in a topic, pre-teach key vocabulary and then focus on a key skill or particular IELTS exam technique. The second part aims to practise the skill or technique, and then encourage you to reflect and develop. The module ends with a focus on key vocabulary in context. The aim here is to focus on the semi-formal vocabulary that you are likely to meet in the texts which make up the IELTS exam.

The Writing Module focuses mainly on the first writing tasks, as you practised writing tasks that are very similar to those in the second part of the Academic Writing Module in the General Training course. Each unit focuses on how information can be presented in different types of figures, and on writing technique required for the exam. There is a focus on guided writing, and there are model compositions for all writing tasks. The final unit demonstrates how the discursive composition in the Academic exam is more challenging than that in the General Training exam.

Consolidation and exam practice at the end of each unit focuses on various elements of the two modules.

As in the General Training course, there are exam tips and question-type tips. They are there to help you know how to approach the various tasks that make up the exam, and to provide advice on how to achieve the highest score possible.

In the Workbook, there are tasks for each of the two modules in the Course Book units. You can study these in class or as homework tasks. Reference is made to these Workbook tasks in the Course Book Reading Modules, as the tasks specifically focus on the content of the Reading Module.

As you work through the course, you will learn more about the exam and what you have to do in each module. By the end of the course, you will know everything about every part of the exam and what is expected of you.

IELTS Academic exam – an introduction to students

Reading

A Discuss this question with a partner.

How is the Academic exam Reading Module different from the General Training exam Reading Module?

B Mark each of these statements about the Academic Reading Module (T) true or (F) false.

1. There are more passages to read than there are in the General Training exam. ___
2. The passages are longer than those in the General Training exam. ___
3. You will read the same type of texts as in the General Training exam. ___
4. You have to answer the same number of questions as in the General Training exam. ___
5. You will have to deal with more vocabulary that you don't know. ___
6. Grammatical structures will be simpler and easier to understand. ___
7. You will be able to use reading skills you learnt in the General Training course. ___

Exam tip: In the Academic Reading Module there are three sections, as in the General Training exam, and there are 40 questions to answer in total. However, there is only one passage in each section and those passages are longer. The texts come from books, journals and magazines, and are generally more academic in style than in the General Training – there are no advertisements, leaflets or information pages. You will need to deal with more vocabulary that you don't know and you will meet more grammatically complex structures. The Academic exam is more difficult, but you will be able to apply the reading skills you learnt when you were studying the General Training course.

C Look at these extracts from different types of text. Tick the two that are more academic in style. These are the types of text you will read in the Academic Reading Module.

1. If there is a careers advisor at your school, get some advice. He or she will know about the opportunities that exist in your area.

2. The successful applicant must be responsible and honest and willing to work hard. Previous experience is an advantage but not essential, as training will be given.

3. The South East (excluding London) has the UK's highest percentage of people working from home. Nearly a quarter of a million workers – 7% of the working population – are based at or usually work from home.

4. Jenny was falling behind at work. Every morning she woke up anxious about the day ahead of her. After work each day, she went home worrying about all the jobs she hadn't managed to get done.

5. Many women face the difficulty of how to find a balance between pursuing an ambitious career and being a responsible and caring mother.

Writing

A How is the Writing Module in the Academic exam different from the Writing Module in the General Training exam? Discuss with a partner.

B Highlight the option that is true in each of these statements about the Academic Writing Module.

1. There *are fewer / is the same number of / are more* writing tasks than in the General Training exam.
2. You have *less / the same amount of / more* time to complete the writing tasks.
3. You have to write *the same number of / more* words for each task.
4. For task 1, you have to write *a letter / a formal report based on data that you are given*.
5. For task 2, you have to write *a story / a discursive composition*.
6. Task 2 is generally *easier than / the same as / more difficult than* task 1 in the General Training exam.

Exam tip: The Academic Writing Module is different from the General Training Writing Module. For the first task, you have to write a report, usually for a university lecturer, based on data that you are given. You must write 150 words. The second task is a discursive composition like that in the General Training. However, the topic of the task will be more academic and a little more challenging than some of those you saw in the General Training course. You must write 250 words.

C Match these types of visual data with the figures below.

table	bar chart	flow chart	line graph	pie chart

1

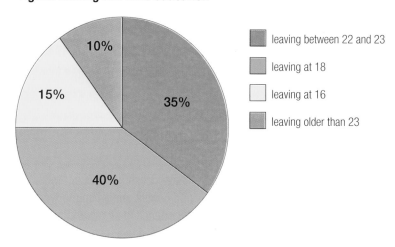

Age of leaving full-time education

- leaving between 22 and 23
- leaving at 18
- leaving at 16
- leaving older than 23

2

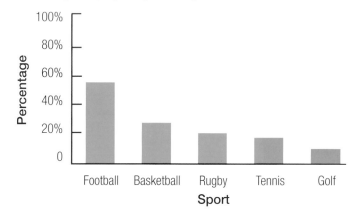

Sports played by 18–25-year-old males

3

Favourite pets of students in the school

	dogs	cats	rabbits	hamsters	fish	birds	tortoise
boys	136	112	58	61	60	19	7
girls	127	122	76	44	57	12	6

4

Ownership of home computer

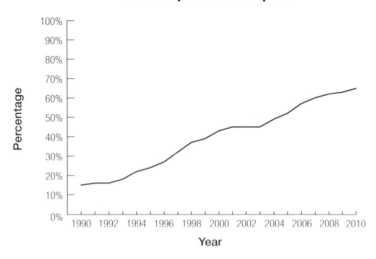

5

Advertising

 Exam tip: The data that you have to interpret in the first writing task is usually presented in the form of a graph, chart or table like those above. You may also have to describe a picture, such as a flow chart or diagram, of a process. In this book, you will practise interpreting and describing data from all these sources.

1 Work

Reading 1: reading skills

A Answer this question with a partner.

1. Which of the reading skills that you learnt when you studied for the General Training exam will be most useful when you read texts for the Academic exam?

B Look at the list of advice below and then do these two tasks.

1. In the first column, tick the advice that you think is most helpful for reading longer, more challenging texts.
2. In the second column, give yourself a mark from 1–5.

   1 = I am not so good at this and still need practice.

   5 = I am very good at doing this now.

   a. Use the instructions and any visual information to help you predict what the text is about.   —   —

   b. Skim the text quickly to get a general idea of what it is about.   —   —

   c. Notice how topic sentences tell you what a paragraph is going to be about.   —   —

   d. Read through the questions and decide which parts of the text you need to read again more carefully.   —   —

   e. As you read again, don't worry about the meaning of every word and phrase. Guess the meaning of new words and phrases in context. —   —

   f. Try to understand what is fact and what is opinion.   —   —

   g. Learn to recognize language that is paraphrased in the questions.   —   —

C Compare your list with a partner.

Reading 2: preparing to read

A Look at the pictures and discuss these questions with a partner.

1. What are the advantages and disadvantages of working from home?
2. What sort of jobs can people easily do from home?

B Check these words and phrases if you need to. Then talk to a partner. Why will each of them be mentioned in the text?

technology	a nine-to-five job	flexibility	having commitments
bosses	wasting time	working efficiently	feeling isolated

> I think technology will be mentioned because new technology, like the Internet, allows people to work from home more easily.

C Skim the text quickly and check your ideas.

Reading 3: practise applying your reading skills to an academic text

A Read this text about working from home and answer the questions that follow.

The Changing Workplace

A Nearly 3.5 million people now work from home in the United Kingdom. That is around 12% or one-in-eight of the working population, and is an increase of 600,000 since the mid-nineties. Advances in technology, the growth of home computer and laptop ownership, and the development of the Internet are key drivers of this trend. It is becoming increasingly appealing for people to do their job from the comfort of their living room, a study, or even a local coffee shop.

B There is a growing number of people for whom the traditional nine-to-five job simply no longer works. They may have family commitments and other reasons why they need to be at home during the day. Many simply prefer working from home because of the flexibility it offers. Many women find themselves in this situation, because they find it difficult to go back to an ordinary job once they have children.

C There are several obvious advantages of working at home. First of all, people can arrange their working day in the way that best suits them. If they have other commitments, or things that they need to be doing, they can arrange their schedule so that work can fit around them. If people do not get work done during the day, they can catch up in the evening or at the weekend. Many people with creative jobs, like writing, designing and illustrating, find that a short break to pick up children from school or meet friends for lunch re-energizes them, so they function more productively and for longer periods of time when they are working.

D People often find that they can get their work done more quickly and efficiently at home, as opposed to working from an office. To start with, working in an office means having to commute to and from work five days a week. In most cases, that is a lot of valuable time wasted. In the office, people usually spend a significant portion of their day doing things other than their work. Much time is spent assisting other people, dealing with unexpected problems or simply socializing with colleagues. Getting work done more quickly means that people achieve more in a day, or have the time to do things that they previously could not do. There is the added bonus that home workers do not have to spend the day with people they do not get on with, particularly a difficult boss or line manager.

E However, there are disadvantages of working from home, too. People can feel isolated and miss the company of colleagues. Some companies that have encouraged more of their staff to work from home, have found that these employees complain about a lack of creative interaction. Home workers may also find that the companies that employ them are less sympathetic if they say they are sick, and that benefits, such as pension schemes and health care packages, are no longer on offer. Once businesses accept that people can get work done from home, they might use the opportunity to employ people in countries where salaries are lower and they do not have to pay them as much.

F At present, it seems that most companies still have reservations about allowing their employees to work from home whenever they like, but many are experimenting with a range of options. Workers might work from home one day a week, or work from home on a particular one-off project. Bosses are beginning to realize that this is the way forward. If companies do not offer workers the option of staying at home occasionally, more people may well look to work freelance or become self-employed. It is estimated that 10 million people could be working away from a traditional office environment by 2010.

For questions 1–6, match the headings in the box below with the paragraphs A–F. Write the numeral as your answer. There are more headings than you need.

i.	Higher incomes for home workers
ii.	Arranging your own schedule
iii.	Inefficient use of time
iv.	Too much time to relax
v.	Working in an office is natural
vi.	Not yet ready for total change
vii.	New working trends
viii.	Working from home is not all good
ix.	Companies welcome home workers
x.	Nine-to-five no longer works

1. paragraph A ___
2. paragraph B ___
3. paragraph C ___
4. paragraph D ___
5. paragraph E ___
6. paragraph F ___

For questions 7–11, decide if the information given below agrees with the information given in the text. Write (T) true, (F) false or (NG) not given.

7. People usually choose to work from home so that they can look after children at the same time. ___
8. Many people who work from home work irregular hours. ___
9. Not having to travel to work is a big advantage for most home workers. ___
10. People get more work done when they work in a traditional office environment. ___
11. Bosses do not have a good relationship with workers who choose to work from home. ___

For questions 12–14, complete these sentences about the disadvantages of working from home with words from the text. Use <u>no more than two words</u> for each answer.

12. Sometimes people need to share ideas with _____.
13. Some companies might not _____ the same package of benefits to home workers.
14. Some companies might employ people to work from home in countries where they can pay _____.

B Check the key on page 274. How many questions did you answer correctly?

C Tick the sentences about the reading task that are true for you and think about how you can answer more questions correctly next time.

1. I didn't find the text much more difficult than those in the General Training course.
2. Making predictions about the content helped me to read more confidently.
3. I applied the reading skills I have learnt, and followed the stages of the reading process.
4. I timed each stage, and had time to complete the tasks.
5. I checked all my answers carefully.
6. I'm pleased with how many questions I answered correctly.

Key vocabulary in context

Look at these sentences and then look again at the key word in the texts. Highlight the correct option.

1. **Commitments** are things you *want to do / have to do.*
2. If something has **flexibility**, it *is always the same / can change easily.*
3. If people **function productively**, they *achieve a lot / don't do very much.*
4. If people work **efficiently**, they *do a job properly / don't do a job very well.*
5. A **bonus** is something people *want / don't want.*
6. If people feel **isolated**, they *have a lot of contact with other people / spend too much time alone.*
7. If people are **sympathetic** they *listen to you and respond to your problem / can help you recover if you are sick.*
8. If you **have reservations** about something, you *know it is the right thing to do / are not completely sure about it.*

WB For focus on reading skills, go to Workbook page 46.

1

Writing 1: interpreting and describing bar charts

A Look at the bar chart below. Identify the columns, the horizontal axis and the vertical axis.

B Answer these questions with your partner.

1. What information does the bar chart show?
2. What does the horizontal axis show?
3. What does the vertical axis show?
4. Were any of your predictions in A correct?

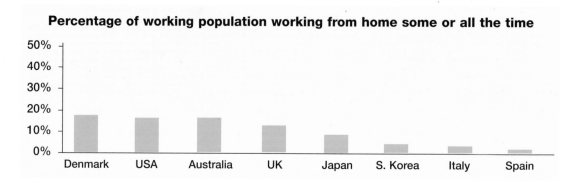

Percentage of working population working from home some or all the time

C Complete these sentences about the information in the bar chart with the words in the box.

1. _____ people work from home in the USA than in Japan.
2. A _____ percentage of people work from home in Australia than in the UK.
3. _____ people work from home in Spain than in any of the other countries.
4. A _____ percentage of people work from home in Spain and Italy.
5. The _____ percentage of people working from home is in Denmark.
6. The _____ percentage of people working from home is in Spain.

lower
more
highest
fewer
lowest
higher

Grammar check

We use *more* with both countable and uncountable nouns.
more people / more money

We use *fewer* with countable nouns and *less* with uncountable nouns.
fewer people / less money

Watch out!
typical errors

Less people work from home in Spain than in Italy. ✗

The higher percentage of people working from home is in Denmark. ✗

D Check the highlighted words in the grammar box on the next page and mark these statements (T) true or (F) false.

1. A *much / far* higher percentage of people work from home in Denmark than in Japan. ___
2. A *slightly* higher percentage of people work from home in the USA than in Italy and Spain. ___
3. *Far more* people work from home in Australia than in South Korea. ___
4. *Far fewer* people work from home in Spain than in Italy. ___

Grammar check

We use **much more** and **much less** with uncountable nouns.
much more / much less money

We use **far more** and **far fewer** with countable nouns.
far more people / far fewer people

Far can be used with both countable and uncountable phrases.
far more money / far more people

E Write some more sentences comparing the countries in the bar chart.

Writing 2: dealing with more information

 Exam tip: In the exam, you will be given more information. You will have to compare at least two sources of information.

A Look at the bar chart below. What is the key for? What information does the chart compare?

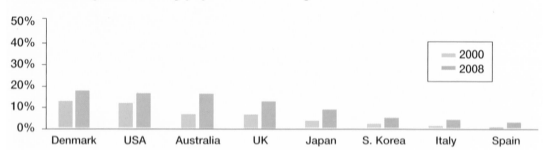

Percentage of working population working from home some or all the time

B Look at these instructions for a writing task and then mark the statements that follow (T) true or (F) false. Compare with a partner.

> The bar chart shows the percentage of the working population that worked from home some or all of the time, in eight countries in 2000 and 2008.
>
> Write a report for a university lecturer describing the information.
> You should write at least 150 words.

1. You should spend some time looking at the information before you write anything.
2. There is no time to plan with this task – just start writing.
3. You should start by showing that you understand the bar chart.
4. You must describe all the information shown in the chart.
5. You should describe information that stands out – information that will interest the reader.
6. You can make points randomly – there is no need to organize the information.
7. You must explain some of the information, for example, say why not many people work from home in Japan.
8. You should write in a formal style.
9. You must think about which tense to use – in this case, the past simple.
10. You should write a sentence that concludes your report.

 Exam tip: You cannot describe everything the chart shows in 150 words, so choose information that stands out. Don't try to explain information – just describe it. Your first sentence should show that you understand the bar graph – don't just repeat what it says in the instructions.

C Talk to a partner. Which of these opening sentences do you prefer? Explain why.

1. The bar chart shows the percentage of the working population that worked from home some or all of the time, in eight countries.
2. The bar chart shows that Denmark has the highest percentage of people working from home.
3. The bar graph shows that the percentage of people working from home increased between 2000 and 2008 in all countries, but increased more dramatically in some countries than others.
4. The bar graph shows that because of new technology, working from home increased dramatically in most countries between 2000 and 2008.

D Check the highlighted words and mark these statements (T) true or (F) false.

1. The percentage of people who worked from home increased in all countries. ___
2. The percentage of people working from home in Spain decreased. ___
3. The percentage increased most dramatically in the USA. ___
4. The number of people working from home increased slightly in Italy. ___
5. The number of people who worked from home in the UK doubled between 2000 and 2008. ___
6. The percentage of people working from home in Japan in 2008 was three times what it was in 2000. ___

WB Go to Workbook page 48 for more practice describing bar charts.

E Read these two reports. Which one do you prefer? Compare with a partner.

1.

The bar chart shows that the percentage of people working from home increased between 2000 and 2008 in all countries, but increased more dramatically in some countries than others. Denmark has the highest percentage of people working from home, with 19%. The USA and Australia both have 17% of people working from home. The percentage of people working from home has also increased in the UK. Japan does not have a very high percentage of people working from home, but the percentage increased drastically between 2004 and 2008, from 3% to 9%. The percentage of people working from home is lower in Korea than in Japan. Italy and Spain have the lowest percentage of people working from home. In 2008, Italy had only 3%, and Spain only 2%.

2.

The bar chart shows that the percentage of people working from home increased between 2000 and 2008 in all countries, but increased more dramatically in some countries than others. It also shows that in some countries, far more people work from home than in others.

Denmark and the USA have a high percentage of people working from home, but the percentage did not increase very much between 2004 and 2008. The percentage of people working from home in Australia increased more dramatically, and in the UK it doubled. Italy and Spain have the lowest percent-age of home workers and the number did not increase very much between 2004 and 2008. Japan also has fewer home workers than other countries, but that is changing. The percentage of people working from home in Japan in 2008 was three times what it was in 2004. The number of people working from home is clearly increasing everywhere, and in some countries very quickly.

WB Go to Workbook page 49 for the writing task.

Reading

A Complete each statement about the IELTS Academic Reading Module with a number.

1. I will have to read ___ passages.
2. I will have to answer ___ questions.
3. I have ___ minutes to read the passages and answer the questions.

B Complete the statement below so that it is true for you.

The biggest difference between the IELTS General Training Reading Module and the IELTS Academic Reading Module for me is ...

C Fill the gaps in these sentences with key words from the reading lesson. Letters are given to help you.

1. A lot of people who work from home feel i _ _ _ _ _ ed.
2. I can't go away on holiday at the moment. I have too many co _ _ _ _ _ _ _ _ s at home and at work.
3. I'm looking for a job with more f _ _ _ _ _ _ _ ity. The nine-to-five routine doesn't suit me.
4. Being able to work from home on Fridays is a real b _ _ _ _ for me.
5. I usually f _ _ c _ _ _ n better in the morning than I do in the afternoon after lunch.
6. The photocopier is working e _ _ _ _ _ _ ntly again now that it's had a service.

D Mark the main stress on each of the words in Exercise C above.

E Circle the correct preposition in each sentence.

1. There is an increase *in / on / of* the number of companies offering their staff the chance to work from home.
2. What are the advantages *in / of / by* working for a small company?
3. I spend a lot of my time dealing *with / to / through* other people's problems.
4. I enjoy working from the comfort *with / of / in* my living room.

Writing

A Complete the exam tip about the IELTS Academic Writing Module with words from the box.

| stands out   logically   plan   formal   explain   report   repeat   data |

Exam tip: The IELTS Academic Writing Module is different from the General Training Writing Module. For the first task, you have to write a _____, usually to a university lecturer, based on _____ that you are given. You must write 150 words. You must read the task carefully and _____ what you are going to say, as with any other composition. You cannot describe everything the figure shows in 150 words, so choose information that _____. Organize your points _____, and write in a _____ style. Don't try to _____ information – just describe it. Your first sentence should show that you understand the information – don't just _____ what it says in the instructions!

B There are errors in all of these sentences. Correct them.

1. Less people worked from home then.
2. The most high percentage is in Denmark.
3. Much more people work from an office.
4. The percentage is higher in Japan as in Korea.
5. Numbers increased dramatic during that period.
6. It is now three times that it was in 2000.

Reading

A What should you do before you read the text below? Talk with a partner.

B Look at the title. Then read the topic sentence of each paragraph and decide what the text is about.

1. how to interview people for jobs
2. how to read resumes
3. how to write a good resume

C Now read the text and answer the questions that follow. Remember to read the questions carefully first, so that you know what you are looking for.

Finding the right person for the job

Effective resume selection is an important step in the process of recruiting new staff. The employer's role in this process is to find those potential employees whose skills and experience look good on paper, and who should be contacted for an interview. But what to look for in a resume is not always clear. The main aim is to focus on the content provided, such as past experience, skills and abilities. But there are also a few subtleties that need attention, and the person recruiting will need to read between the lines.

The first thing to do is to look for gaps. Has the applicant been absent from the workforce for a long period of time? Have there been significant gaps between jobs? This does not necessarily mean the individual is not suitable, but he or she may require extra training or time to readapt to a more structured work environment. Gaps in employment history may also reveal aspects of personality and behaviour that could otherwise go unnoticed.

It is important to identify any extreme employment patterns. Employers should be wary of a resume that lists several jobs and companies within a short period of time. Jumping from job to job may suggest the individual lacks loyalty to their employer. In the same way, the applicant who has remained in the same position for a long time without gaining additional responsibilities may lack motivation and initiative.

Experience is not the only important consideration when looking for the right person. An applicant should never automatically be dismissed based only on a lack of work experience. The applicant may have spent longer in the education system and gained valuable qualifications. He or she might have travelled and learnt important skills that involve social interaction, teamwork or leadership. The ability to interact effectively with individuals of varying needs is essential to the success of any operation.

Any leisure and social activities listed on the resume should be identified and assessed, especially if the applicant is active in group-related pursuits that help promote a sense of teamwork. A list of hobbies and interests also suggests the potential employee has created a balance of personal and professional well-being.

Details are important. Has the applicant taken care to provide you with a professional resume that lists relevant skills related to the job, and does not contain errors in spelling or grammar? The best resumes are those that have been tailored to the specific requirements of the position and your business. These types of resumes send the message that the applicant really is interested in the job and has taken the extra step of demonstrating an investment of time.

It is always a good idea to read any information about past work experience very carefully, and note the detail given when describing job responsibilities or achievements. General descriptions of work experience may indicate false work experience.

It is essential to concentrate only on the requirements of the position. The employer should never determine an applicant's suitability based on personal information, such as age, gender, marital status, cultural background or religion. Personal attributes such as these have no bearing on whether the applicant is qualified for the job, and basing employment on this type of information can be illegal.

Once every resume has been carefully read, it should be filed according to its suitability, in terms of whether to proceed to the interview stage or not. During this step, it is also a good idea to make a note of any information provided on the resume that requires clarification or follow-up at the interview stage.

For questions 1–6, choose the correct answer A, B or C to complete each statement below.

1. The first paragraph implies that ...
   A the strengths and weaknesses of a resume are obvious.
   B it is not always easy to read a resume.
   C many applicants send resumes that are too long.

2. If an applicant has been out of the workforce for a long time, he or she ...
   A will probably not be right for the job.
   B probably has a history of strange behaviour.
   C might need help to get back into the habit of working.

3. The third paragraph says that ...
   A somebody who has had the same job for a long time is much better than somebody who has not.
   B having a number of different jobs on your resume looks good.
   C there are two types of applicant who might not be right for the job.

4. The fourth paragraph suggests that ...
   A the most important consideration is the applicant's education.
   B knowing how to deal with people is a very important skill.
   C travelling and meeting people is more important than work experience.

5. An employer should be most interested in a resume that ...
   A the applicant has spent time getting right.
   B has no spelling or grammar mistakes.
   C has a long list of skills and abilities.

6. If an applicant does not give details of past job experience,
   A it is not important.
   B he or she may not be telling the truth about it.
   C the employer will have to ask about it during the interview.

For questions 7–12, complete the notes in the table. Use <u>no more than two words</u> for each answer.

Notes on reading resumes

Do	Don't
check to see if there are (7) _____ in the applicant's employment history.	assume that (8) _____ is the only thing that matters.
check that the applicant has not had (9) _____ and left each one.	make decisions based on an applicant's (11) _____ – it's against the law!
check (10) _____ – note errors and look for anything specific to this business.	
file the resumes, so that you know which applicants you want to (12) _____.	

2 Technology

Reading 1: preparing to read and reading for gist

A Discuss with a partner. Do you like shopping? How do you do your shopping?

B Look at the pictures and answer these questions with a partner.

1. What different types of shopping establishment can you see in the pictures?
2. Can you put the pictures into chronological order (from earliest to latest)?

   1. __   2. __   3. __   4. __   5. __

C Skim read the text below. How quickly can you check the order of the pictures?

The Way We Shop

A The way we shop has changed drastically over time, and so have the buildings in which we do our shopping. In the Middle Ages, people shopped in markets. Market stalls were set up together in one place, and were often covered to protect shoppers from the sun or rain.

B The first shops sold one product and were typically adjoined to the producer's workshop. Bakers sold bread, tailors sold clothes and cobblers sold shoes. In the United States, retailers placed boardwalks outside their establishments so that shoppers did not have to walk in the mud.

C In the 19th century, the first arcades were constructed in Europe. These were narrow, covered streets with a number of shops, each selling a different product. In larger cities, the first department stores were opened in multi-storey buildings. The concept of a fixed price was introduced, and haggling became less common. People began to enjoy browsing, and consumerism as we know it was born.

D In the 1920s, the first supermarkets heralded the arrival of self-service and a revolution in the way people shopped. Around the same time, shopping malls combined elements of the arcade and the department store. Several retail establishments were linked by arcades within one huge building, and the retailers paid rent to the mall owner. Today, we see the fundamental elements of these concepts in the drive-in hypermarkets and retail parks of the 21st century.

Reading 2: reading for detail and dealing with unknown vocabulary

A Look at these questions. Without reading the text again, try to say in which paragraph you will find each answer. Write the paragraph letter in the space.

1. Where were the first shopping arcades built? —
2. Where did people shop in the Middle Ages? —
3. What type of shop introduced the concept of self-service? —
4. What did early retailers in the United States put outside their shops? —

B Read the text more carefully and check your answers in Exercise A. Then write the answers to the questions in the spaces below. Use <u>no more than two words</u> for each answer.

1. _____ 2. _____ 3. _____ 4. _____

 Exam tip: Remember that skimming the text gives you a general idea of what the text is about. That will help you know where to look for answers to questions when you read more carefully for detail.

C Work with a partner. Find one example of each of the following.

1. a word in the text I don't know, and I didn't need to know

   _____

2. a word in the text I don't know, but I could guess the meaning of easily

   _____

3. a word I needed to know because it stopped me understanding an important point

   _____

4. a word I don't know that I had to use as an answer to a question

   _____

Exam tip: You don't need to worry about the meaning of every word in a text. Remember:
- You won't need to understand many of the words.
- You can use the context to guess the meaning of most words you do need to understand.
- You can use a word you don't understand as an answer to a question, if you understand the words around it.

D Guess the meaning of these words in the text from the context. Compare with a partner.

stalls adjoined cobblers boardwalks multi-storey haggling browsing combined

Reading 3: practise reading for detail and dealing with unknown vocabulary

A Talk with a partner. What do the pictures tell you about how shopping has changed?

Read the text and answer the questions that follow.

A Shopping Revolution

A There is something of a revolution occurring in the retail industry. Consumers are quickly becoming more adept when it comes to using technology, and they are increasingly choosing to go online to do their shopping. Internet sales are soaring, and traditional retail outlets are transferring to the web, just like all the specialist e-retailers.

B Recent research shows that online shoppers will spend nearly £50 billion this year. That is something like ten times the amount that will be spent in London's West End shops. More than 800 million parcels will be sent out to the UK's 25 million online shoppers. Online consumers will spend an average of £1,500 each. Some online retailers are reporting rises of over 100% in their sales from last year. One company boasts that over 2 million potential shoppers visited its website in one month recently.

C It is only fourteen years ago that the first Internet shopping transaction was conducted in the US. Eight years later, in the middle of the dotcom gold rush, UK online sales had reached the £800 million mark. Since then, despite reservations about the continuing popularity of the Internet, and concerns about the safety of using credit cards online, sales have grown by a staggering 3,000%.

D Shopping has been transformed in the same way it was when the first supermarkets opened, and over-the-counter interaction was replaced by self-service 100 years ago. Traditional retail establishments only have shelf space for the products that sell best. Online, the choice is unlimited, and consumers can find exactly what they are looking for, rather than what a particular shop is offering.

E When it comes to shopping online, there are no borders, and a huge global marketplace is taking shape. Last year, more than a billion people, nearly 20% of the world population, used the Internet. Online business is worth a staggering £260 billion. Every country in the world will need to develop an e-commerce sector in order to compete in a changing economy.

F There are several factors which have influenced the popularity of online shopping. The biggest factor is probably convenience. In the modern world, most people do not have the time to go out shopping like they once did. Now they can order online and have products delivered to their home or place of work. Recent research shows that 95% of 15-year-olds have purchased something online. Their concept of shopping is shaped by their experience and not what other people have done for the last hundred and fifty years. Broadband has had a huge effect. Products can be displayed in a far more appealing way than previously, and online shopping will become more and more of a virtual visit to a shopping mall.

G Most of the major retailers now see the Internet as an opportunity, rather than as competition. The biggest supermarkets and department stores have all announced a huge growth in online sales over the last year. An ever-growing percentage of consumers prefer to shop online, and even those who still enjoy a traditional visit to the High Street retailers go online first to check out product choice and prices. The popularity of eBay* shows how keen consumers are to find the right product at the right price, and that they are prepared to invest time in getting what they want.

H Despite the online shopping explosion, there are still many who believe traditional retail establishments are here to stay. Around half of all retail businesses in the UK do not have online stores, but do have sites on which they display and promote their products. For convenience, people like to buy books and small objects online, but appear to still enjoy shopping traditionally for personal items, like furniture and clothing. The most successful retailers will probably be those who combine the various methods that consumers can use to make their purchase.

* eBay is an American company that manages an online shopping auction (customers buy and sell products online).

The passage has eight paragraphs, labelled A–H. For questions 1–6, say which paragraph contains the following information. Write the appropriate letter in the space below.

1. that this is not the first revolution in the way people shop   —
2. the type of products people like to buy in different ways   —
3. that more people know how to use a computer   —
4. that young people know a lot about online shopping   —
5. that people do not like to pay too much for a product   —
6. the first time a product was bought online   —

For questions 7–10, label the blue segments in the charts below. Choose your answers from the options in the box.

7. 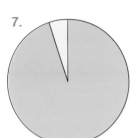 8.  9. 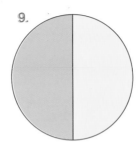 10.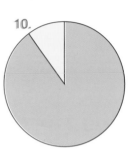

A   amount spent online this year, compared with six years ago
B   retailers that have and do not have an online store
C   15-year-olds who have and have not bought something online
D   number of people who do and do not shop online
E   amount spent in the UK online, compared with amount spent in London's West End
F   worldwide Internet users and non-users

For questions 11–14, complete this summary of why online shopping is so popular with words from the text. Use <u>no more than three words</u> for each answer.

Online shopping is very popular. The (11) _____ it offers is what most people find so appealing. Instead of going out to the shops, people can go online and wait for their order to be (12) _____ to their door. Teenagers grow up shopping online, and their (13) _____ is very different from that of their parents and grandparents. (14) _____ is making the online shopping experience even more enjoyable.

C Check the key on pages 274 and 275. How many questions did you answer correctly?

D Tick the sentences about the reading task that are true for you and think about how you can answer more questions correctly next time.

1. I found it quite easy to get the general idea of the text.
2. I found it quite easy to find details and answer questions.
3. There was a lot of vocabulary I didn't know.
4. I didn't worry about not knowing some vocabulary. I could answer questions without it.
5. I'm pleased with the number of questions I answered correctly.

E Look at these words from the text. Answer the questions with a partner.

adept   soaring   transaction   staggering   unlimited
convenience   purchase   concept

1. Which words did you know?
2. Which words could you guess from context?
3. Which words didn't matter at all?
4. Do any words relate to specific questions? Did you need to know them to answer questions?

WB For focus on reading skills and key vocabulary in context, go to Workbook page 50.

Writing 1: interpreting and describing pie charts

A Look at the pie charts 1–3. Try to match them with the opening lines a–c.

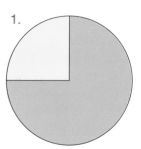

1.

a. The pie chart shows what percentage of the Chinese population used the Internet in 2006.

b. The pie chart shows the percentage of people in the US. who used the Internet in 2006.

c. The pie chart shows the number of Internet users and non-users in France in 2006.

B Match each sentence with one of the pie charts. Write the number of the pie chart in the space.

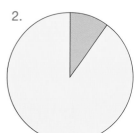

2.

1. Half the population used the Internet. chart __
2. Only 10% / per cent of people used the Internet. chart __
3. Three out of four people used the Internet. chart __
4. 50% / per cent of people used the Internet. chart __
5. Three quarters of the population used the Internet. chart __
6. Nine out of ten people were not using the Internet. chart __

C Rewrite each of the following in two other ways, as above.

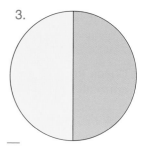

3.

1. 25% _____ _____
2. a third (approx) _____ _____
3. two out of three (approx) _____ _____

D Mark each of these sentences (T) true or (F) false.

1. Not as many people used the Internet in France as in the US. __
2. Internet use was not as common in France as it was in China. __
3. There was not as much Internet use in France as there was in the US. __
4. There were not nearly as many Internet users in China as there were in the US. __
5. The number of people who used the Internet was lower in France than it was in the US. __
6. The amount of Internet use was higher in China than it was in France. __

Grammar check

We use **not as + adjective + as** to compare things.
not as big as / not as common as

We use **not as many (as)** with countable nouns.
not as many people / not as many Internet users

We use **not as much (as)** with uncountable nouns.
not as much money / not as much Internet use

We can use **not nearly as** when the difference is extreme, in the same way that we use *much* and *far* in affirmative comparatives.

We use **the number of** with countable nouns and **the amount of** with uncountable nouns.
the number of people / the amount of Internet use

Watch out!
typical errors

There were not as much Internet users in China. ✗

Not as many people used the Internet in France than in the United States. ✗

E Look at this pie chart and complete the sentences with the words and phrases.

| most   minority   not many   majority |

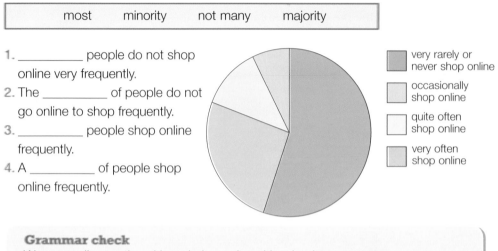

1. _____ people do not shop online very frequently.
2. The _____ of people do not go online to shop frequently.
3. _____ people shop online frequently.
4. A _____ of people shop online frequently.

- very rarely or never shop online
- occasionally shop online
- quite often shop online
- very often shop online

Grammar check
We generally use *the* with majority and *a* with minority.
the majority of the population / a (small) minority of the population

Writing 2: dealing with more information

Exam tip: Remember that in the exam, you will be given more information. You will have to compare at least two sources of information.

A Cover the pie charts on the next page. Answer these questions with a partner.

1. Do you think more men or more women shop online, or is there no difference?
2. Do men and women shop online for the same reasons?

B Look at these instructions for a writing task and answer the questions that follow with a partner.

The pie charts show what men and women give as their main reason for shopping online.

Write a report for a university lecturer describing the information.

You should write at least 150 words.

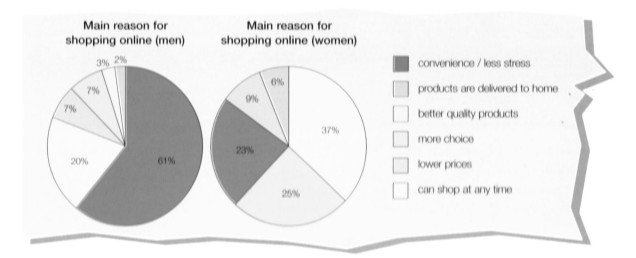

Main reason for shopping online (men)
3% 2%
7%
7%
20%
61%

Main reason for shopping online (women)
6%
9%
37%
23%
25%

- convenience / less stress
- products are delivered to home
- better quality products
- more choice
- lower prices
- can shop at any time

1. Is it easy to understand what the pie charts show?
2. What information stands out?
3. What are the biggest differences between the two pie charts?
4. What is similar about the two pie charts?

Writing 3: deciding what to say and how to say it

A A student has made comments on the pie charts. Does he notice the same data as you?

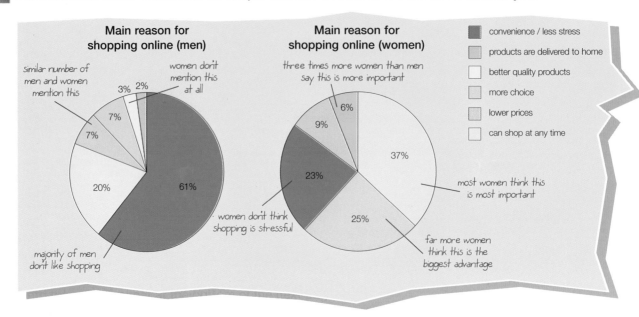

Main reason for shopping online (men)

Main reason for shopping online (women)

convenience / less stress
products are delivered to home
better quality products
more choice
lower prices
can shop at any time

Similar number of men and women mention this — 3% 2%

women don't mention this at all

7%

7%

20%

61%

majority of men don't like shopping

three times more women than men say this is more important — 6%

9%

37%

23%

25%

women don't think shopping is stressful

most women think this is most important

far more women think this is the biggest advantage

B Read the report the student wrote. Discuss what you like about it with a partner.

The pie charts show that both men and women enjoy shopping online, but that they have very different reasons for doing it.

The majority of men (61%) give convenience as the main reason for shopping online. They seem to think that going out to shop is stressful. Women, on the other hand, do not think this is so important. Only about a quarter give convenience as their main reason.

For women, the biggest advantage of online shopping is that they can shop at any time. Twice the number of women as men give this as the most important advantage.

Another big difference is giving choice as their main reason. One in four women say this is the most important advantage, while only a minority of men (7%) mention it. It is interesting that a small minority of men think the quality of products online is better, while women do not mention this at all.

A similar percentage of men and women think that lower prices is the main reason for shopping online, but it is not very important for either.

All in all, it seems that people shop online mainly because it is convenient, and they can do it at any time.

C Look at these tips on report writing. Write the number of each tip in the correct box on the report.

1. Describe two or three more important differences.
2. Say something to conclude your report.
3. Show that you understand what the pie charts show.
4. Describe a similarity.
5. Describe what you think is the most obvious difference.

Exam tip: Note that any data shown in a pie chart could also be shown in a simple bar chart. When data is compared in two pie charts, as on the previous page, it could be shown on one bar chart.

D Look at the bar chart on page 275 and compare it with the two pie charts.

E Look at the exam practice section on page 230 for the writing task.

Reading

A Answer these questions with a partner.

1. Do you find the texts in the IELTS Academic Reading Module more challenging than those in the General Training Module? Why (not)?
2. How do you deal with the amount of unknown vocabulary in the reading texts?
3. Do you feel that your reading skills continue to improve?
4. Are you reading more quickly than you did a month ago?

B Correct the spelling mistakes in these words.

1. retale   2. revolusion   3. consept   4. perchase   5. conbined

C Fill the gaps with a word made from the root words in the box.

1. Most people shop in supermarkets for _____.
2. Retail parks and hypermarkets are modern shopping _____.
3. These days, _____ have so many shopping options.
4. Most _____ these days are by debit or credit card.
5. The choice that online shoppers have seems to be _____.
6. The _____ of online shopping has surprised a lot of people.

convenient
establish
consume
transact
limit
popular

Writing

A Correct the spelling mistakes in these words. Some words are spelt correctly.

1. percentage   2. majoraty   3. minorety   4. ammount   5. harf   6. quarter   7. third

B Mark each structure (C) if it is used with countable nouns or (U) if it is used with uncountable nouns.

1. not as much __   2. not as many __   3. the number of __   4. the amount of __

C Write these fractions as percentages.

1. three quarters ____   2. two thirds (approx) ____   3. four fifths ____   4. nine tenths ___

D Write these percentages as fractions.

1. 50% _____   2. 33% (approx) _____   3. 25% _____

E Write these percentages as in the example.

1. 66% (approx) *two out of three*   2. 75% _____
3. 80% _____   4. 90% _____

F There are errors in all these sentences. Correct them.

1. Not as much people use cash these days.
2. There are not as many smokers than there used to be.
3. A majority of people drive nowadays.
4. A small minority in the population shop only online.
5. A large amount of people shop online.

2

Writing

A Answer these questions with a partner.

1. Do you think younger people or older people shop online more frequently?
2. Which age group do you think spends more money online?

B Mark each of these products (Y) if you think they are more popular with younger online shoppers or (O) more popular with older online shoppers.

C Compare with a partner. Try to give a reason for each answer.

D Look at the pie charts and instructions for the writing task below and talk to a partner. What information do the pie charts show?

The pie charts show the percentage of money spent on various online purchases made by people under 30 years old and people over 30 years old.

Write a report for a university lecturer describing the information.

You should write at least 150 words.

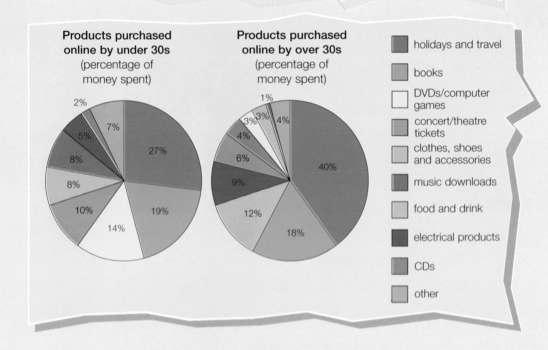

Products purchased online by under 30s (percentage of money spent)

2% 7% 5% 8% 8% 10% 14% 19% 27%

Products purchased online by over 30s (percentage of money spent)

1% 3% 3% 4% 4% 6% 9% 12% 18% 40%

- holidays and travel
- books
- DVDs/computer games
- concert/theatre tickets
- clothes, shoes and accessories
- music downloads
- food and drink
- electrical products
- CDs
- other

E Make some notes. Identify five or six points that stand out.

F Check all the exam tips in the Writing Module again and then write the report.

3 Health

Reading 1: preparing to read

A Check the highlighted words in these questions if you need to. Then answer them with a partner.

1. Do you think that the percentage of people in the world who smoke is increasing or decreasing?
2. Do you think that the consumption of cigarettes in your country is increasing or decreasing?
3. Where in the world do you think smoking is declining?
4. Are there any parts of the world where smoking is on the increase?
5. Do you think a smoking ban in public places makes people give up smoking?
6. Do you think a ban on the advertising of tobacco has an effect on the number of smokers?

B Look at the bar chart. What does it tell you? Compare with a partner.

Smoking is increasing in the developing world

Annual cigarette consumption per adult (in cigarettes)

	Developed
	Developing
	World

1970-72   1980-82   1990-92

Source: World Health Organization. 1997. Tobacco or Health: a Global Status Report. Geneva, Switzerland.

C Write four sentences using data from the bar chart. Then look at the sentences on page 275.

Reading 2: recognizing paraphrased language

A Skim the first two paragraphs from an article about tobacco use below. Does the text support the data in the bar chart?

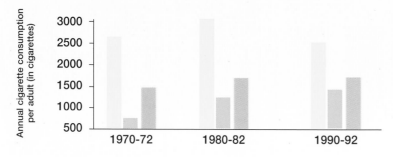

World tobacco demand is expected to increase until the year 2010 due to population and income growth, but at lower rates than in the past, according to a new study just published. The report maintains that while in developed countries tobacco smoking will continue to decline, in developing countries consumption will increase.

World tobacco production is projected to reach over seven million tonnes of tobacco leaf in the year 2010, up from just under six million tonnes in 1998. This is lower than the record tobacco production of 7.5 million tonnes in 1992.

B Decide if these statements are (T) true, (F) false or (NG) not given.

1. Tobacco use will increase because there will be more people with more money. __

2. People in developing countries will smoke far more than those in developed countries. __

3. Fewer people will want tobacco over the next six years. __

C Complete these sentences. Use <u>no more than two words</u> for each answer.

1. Over a million tonnes more _____ will be produced in 2010 than in 1998.

2. 1992 was a _____ year for tobacco production.

Exam tip: Remember that in some scanning exercises you need to look quickly for parts of the text that mean the same as the words and phrases in the question. You will not find the exact words and phrases from the question in the text.

D Talk to a partner. How is the language in each question different from the language in the text that provides the answer?

Reading 3: dealing with statistics

A Skim only paragraph 3 from the same text on the next page, and highlight all the statistics.

B Answer these questions (T) true, (F) false or (NG) not given. Then compare with a partner.

1. The number of smokers will probably increase by 0.2 billion by 2010. __

2. If the number of smokers rises to 1.3 billion, it will be an increase of 1.5% since 1998. __

3. Each adult will use on average 10% less tobacco in 2010 than now. __

4. Anti-smoking and anti-tobacco policy is reducing the number of smokers. __

Exam tip: You are more likely to read a text that has a lot of facts and statistics in the Academic exam than in the General Training exam. Sometimes you will need to answer questions about charts and graphs, as you did in Unit 2.

C Read only paragraph 6 and complete the table below with the correct figures. You will need to calculate number 7.

	developed countries		developing countries	
	1998	2010	1998	2010
tobacco demand	(1) _____m tonnes	(2) _____m tonnes	(3) _____m tonnes	(4) _____m tonnes
share of tobacco consumption	(5) _____%	(6) _____%	(7) _____%	(8) _____%

 Question-type tip: Sometimes you will need to complete statistics in a table. You will use figures provided in the text and not have to make calculations, as you did for this Course Book task.

Reading 4: practice with paraphrased language and statistics

A Read the complete text and answer the questions 1–15.

World Tobacco Use on the Increase

1 World tobacco demand is expected to increase until the year 2010 due to population and income growth, but at lower rates than in the past, according to a new study just published. The report maintains that while in developed countries tobacco smoking will continue to decline, in developing countries consumption will rise.

2 World tobacco production is projected to reach over seven million tonnes of tobacco leaf in the year 2010, up from just under six million tonnes in 1998. This is lower than the record tobacco production of 7.5 million tonnes in 1992.

3 The number of smokers is expected to grow from 1.1 billion in 1998, to around 1.3 billion in 2010. This is an increase of about 1.5% annually. Despite the overall increase of tobacco use, consumption per adult is expected to decline by around 10% by 2010, and individual consumption will probably be around 1.4 kg per year (from around 1.6 kg in 2000). If an aggressive anti-smoking and anti-tobacco policy were applied, tobacco consumption per person could even drop by 20%. Consumption per person is noticeably declining in developed countries, and is now slightly declining in developing countries, including China.

4 Cigarette smoking is the most prevalent type of tobacco consumption; manufactured and hand-rolled cigarettes account for about 85% of all tobacco consumed worldwide. With around 320 million smokers, China is the world's major cigarette consumer.

5 Around 100 countries produce tobacco. The major producers are China, India, Brazil, the US, Turkey, Zimbabwe and Malawi, which together produce over 80% of the world's tobacco. China alone accounts for over 35% of world production.

Tobacco Consumption

6 The overall pattern of tobacco consumption is influenced by two contrasting trends. Tobacco demand in developed countries is declining slowly, and will reach about 2.05 million tonnes in 2010. This is 10% lower than the 2.23 million tonnes consumed in 1998. However, more tobacco will be smoked in developing countries, where tobacco consumption is expected to grow to 5.09 million tonnes by 2010 (from 4.2 million in 1998). This shows an average annual growth rate of 1.7%. It is projected that by 2010, only 29% of world tobacco consumption will be in developed countries, down from 34% in 1998. In developing countries, the share will be 71%.

7 The decline in tobacco use in developed countries can be attributed to a slower population and income growth. In addition, in developed countries, an increasing awareness of the damaging health effects of smoking, together with the anti-smoking measures of governments, including intensified anti-smoking campaigns, the banning of advertising and increased taxation, have had a strong negative effect on the consumption of tobacco products.

8 A major part of the projected increase in demand is expected to be in the Far East, particularly in China. The share of China in total world tobacco demand is likely to remain around 37% in 2010. In India, the second most important tobacco consumer, the smoking of conventional cigarettes accounts for only 25%. Most people consume tobacco in the form of non-cigarette items, such as hand-rolled bidis* or chewing tobacco. Total demand for tobacco in India is likely to continue to increase, but more slowly than in the previous decades. In Africa, total tobacco demand increased in the 1990s, with record growth of 3.5% per year. Growth for the period to 2010 is expected to continue at a similar rate.

9 The report concludes that it is the higher demand for tobacco in the developing countries that drives the world tobacco economy, and that public policy to reduce tobacco use should focus on demand rather than supply. Reducing demand in the developing countries will not be easy, given projected population and income growth, but by adopting a combination of tax and direct restriction policies, it is achievable. Reducing demand will in turn imply a decline in global tobacco production.

* Bidi is tobacco (sometimes flavoured), wrapped in a leaf and tied with a thread.

For questions 1–5, complete these notes with words from the text. Use <u>no more than three words or a number</u> for each answer.

> Most common type of tobacco consumption (about 85%) – (1) _____.
> More tobacco smoked in (2) _____ than anywhere else –
> (3) _____ people smoke.
> 80% of all tobacco is produced in seven (4) _____.
> (5) _____ of all tobacco is produced in China.

For questions 6–8, choose <u>three</u> of the reasons why there is a decline in tobacco use in developed countries. The order is not important.

A The population is decreasing.
B Most people do not suddenly have much more money.
C People understand that smoking is not good for them.
D People are not allowed to smoke in some of those countries.
E People no longer believe what advertisements tell them.
F Cigarettes are more expensive because of higher taxes.

6. __   7. __   8. __

For questions 9–11, decide if the information given below agrees with the information given in the passage. Write (T) true, (F) false or (NG) not given.

 9. Over a third of all tobacco use is in China.   __
10. Most people in India cannot afford to buy conventional cigarettes.   __
11. The number of smokers in Africa is expected to drop.   __

For question 12, mark the graph that shows projected tobacco use in India.

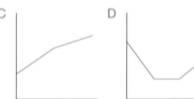

For questions 13–15, complete the summary below with words from the text. Use <u>one word</u> for each answer.

The tobacco industry relies on the fact that demand for their product is (13) _____ in developing countries. It will not be easy to make people smoke less in those parts of the world because there are more and more people with a better (14) _____. However, if smoking decreases, so too will the (15) _____ of tobacco.

B Check the key on page 275. How many questions did you answer correctly?

C Tick the sentences about the reading task that are true for you and think about how you can answer more questions correctly next time.

1. I found it quite easy to find the relevant information and answer questions.
2. I recognized when language was paraphrased.
3. I found it quite easy to work with statistics.
4. I'm pleased with how many questions I answered correctly.

WB For focus on reading skills and key vocabulary in context, go to Workbook page 52.

3

Writing 1: interpreting and describing line graphs

A Answer these questions with a partner. Try to give a reason for your answer.

1. Which of these has changed most over the last 20 years in your country?
   a. the number of smokers   b. the number of young smokers (18–24)
   c. the number of young women (18–24) who smoke
2. Are the numbers for each increasing or decreasing? When did the numbers increase or decrease most dramatically?

B Look at the line graph below. Answer these questions with a partner.

1. What information does the line graph show?
2. What does the horizontal axis show?
3. What does the vertical axis show?

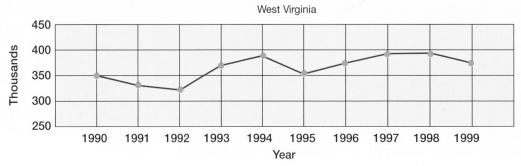

Estimated Number of Cigarette Smokers Aged 18 and Older
West Virginia

C Read these simple descriptions and circle the correct option in each.

1. Between 1990 and 1992, the number of smokers *increased / decreased*.
2. Between 1992 and 1993, the number of smokers *rose / fell*.
3. Between 1993 and 1994, the number of smokers *stayed almost the same / fluctuated*.

D Read these descriptions and circle the best option in each.

1. Between 1990 and 1992, the number of smokers fell *dramatically / steadily / slightly*.
2. Between 1993 and 1994, the number of smokers rose very *slightly / sharply*.
3. Between 1994 and 1995, the number of smokers dropped *dramatically / noticeably*.

E Read these descriptions and delete the one wrong option in each.

1. Between 1992 and 1993, the number of smokers rose *slightly / suddenly / sharply / dramatically*.
2. Between 1995 and 1998, the number of smokers rose *gradually / steadily / dramatically*.

F Complete these descriptions with a year in each space. Look carefully at the highlighted phrases.

1. Between _____ and 1992, there was a gradual fall / a steady fall in the number of smokers.
2. Between 1992 and _____, there was a dramatic rise / a sharp rise in the number of smokers.
3. Between 1993 and _____, there was a slight increase / a slight rise in the number of smokers.
4. Between _____ and 1995, there was a noticeable decrease / a noticeable drop in the number of smokers.

Grammar check
We use **adjectives** to describe nouns.
a dramatic increase / a steady fall

We use **adverbs** to modify adjectives.
rose sharply / decreased noticeably

Notice these spelling rules for adverbs.
sharp – sharply / noticeable – noticeably / dramatic – dramatically

Look at the consolidation section to practise describing graphs with adjectives and adverbs.

Watch out!
typical errors

The number of smokers rose dramatic. ✗

There was a sharply increase in the use of tobacco. ✗

Writing 2: linking a description together

A What does this line graph show? How is the data different from that in the first graph?

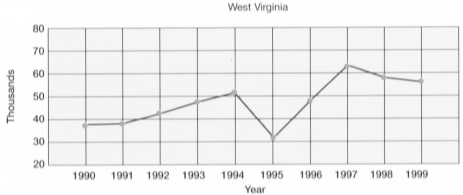

Estimated Number of Cigarette Smokers Aged 18–24
West Virginia

B Complete each of these descriptions with a year.

1. The number of young smokers rose steadily until _____, and then there was a dramatic drop.
2. The number of smokers fell to a low in _____, but then started to rise dramatically.
3. From _____, the number of smokers increased dramatically and reached a peak in _____.
4. The number of smokers reached a peak in _____, but then gradually decreased over the next two years.

 Exam tip: Remember that you should only use language that you know how to use properly. If using all the different structures is difficult, keep it simple. Don't try to use words, phrases and structures that you don't really understand.

C Look again at the two line graphs and cover all the descriptions. Practise describing the graphs with a partner.

Writing 3: dealing with more information

A Look at the line graph below. What information does it compare? Talk to a partner.

Estimated Number of Cigarette Smokers Aged 18 and Over by Gender
West Virginia

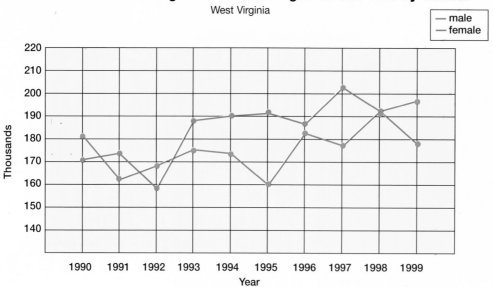

B Look at the instructions for the writing task. Choose five or six points that you want to make about the data and make notes. Then compare with a partner.

> The line graph shows the number of male and female smokers in West Virginia between 1990 and 1999.
>
> Write a report for a university lecturer describing the information.
>
> You should write at least 150 words.

C Read the report below. Did the writer include the same points that you suggested?

> The graph shows that between 1990 and 1999, the number of both male and female smokers _____. It shows that at the beginning and end of the decade, there were more _____, but that for most of the decade the number of female smokers was _____.
>
> The biggest _____ in the number of female smokers was between 1992 and 1993, when thirty thousand more women smoked. By 1993, there were more female than male smokers. For three years, the number of women smoking stayed nearly _____, but then between 1996 and 1997, there was another _____.
>
> The _____ between the two groups was in 1995, when there were thirty thousand more female smokers than male. At that time, the number of male smokers fell to _____ of only 160,000. Between 1995 and 1996, the number of male smokers _____, and by 1996, the number of male and female smokers was almost the same. Although there was a _____ between 1996 and 1997, the number of male smokers continued to rise steadily until the end of the decade.
>
> The number of female smokers reached _____ in 1997, but then started _____ dramatically. By the end of the decade, there were more male than female smokers once again.

D Complete the report with your own ideas. Use <u>one or two words</u> in each space. Then check the model on page 275.

WB Go to Workbook page 53 for the writing task.

Reading

A Answer these questions about reading with a partner.

1. What do you find difficult about reading texts with a lot of statistics?
2. What advice would you give to another student who needs to read texts with a lot of statistics?
3. Are you finding it easier to recognize paraphrased language in the questions?

B Delete the wrong option in these explanations of words and phrases from the unit.

1. If somebody **gives up** smoking, they *start / stop* smoking.
2. If something **declines**, it becomes *more / less* popular.
3. If something is **on the increase**, it *is increasing / is not increasing*.
4. If there is a **ban** on something, people *can / cannot* do it.
5. If there is a lot of **demand** for something, people *want / don't want* it.

C Correct the spelling mistakes a student has made in this exercise.

1. <u>Consumtion</u> of tobacco is very high in China.
2. 1992 was a year of record <u>groth</u>.
3. Tobacco <u>producsion</u> is increasing in developing countries.
4. Today, there is more <u>awareniss</u> of the dangers of smoking.
5. Everyone agrees that this a <u>globel</u> problem.

consume
grow
produce
aware
globe

Writing

A Rewrite these noun phrases as verb phrases. Use the simple past tense.

1. a sharp increase   *increased sharply*
2. a slight decrease
3. a dramatic rise
4. a noticeable fall
5. a steady drop

B Rewrite these verb phrases as noun phrases.

1. decreased gradually   *a gradual decrease*
2. increased steadily
3. rose sharply
4. fell dramatically
5. dropped slightly

C Delete <u>five</u> unnecessary articles and add <u>six</u> articles where they are needed in these sentences.

1. In 1994, there was drop in number of the smokers.
2. Number of the female smokers reached peak in the 1997.
3. As population in many developing countries grows and as a people have more money, consumption of the tobacco will increase.

3

Reading

A Read the title of the article below and check the three key nouns in a dictionary. Match the words and definitions below.

1. nutrition   **a.** a condition when somebody is very fat
2. transition   **b.** food and its affect on your health
3. obesity   **c.** a change from one thing to another

B Read the first paragraph of the article and then the two subheadings. What do you think the rest of the article will be about? Compare ideas with a partner.

C Skim read the whole article. Focus on topic sentences. Were your predictions correct?

D Read the article more carefully and answer questions 1–16 that follow.

The Nutrition Transition and Obesity

A Obesity in the developing world is the result of a series of changes in diet and nutrition, physical activity and general health, collectively known as the 'nutrition transition'. As poor countries become richer, they acquire some of the problems, as well as the benefits, of industrialized nations. These include obesity.

B Since urban areas are much further in this transition than rural areas, they experience higher rates of obesity. Cities offer a greater range of food choices, generally at lower prices. Urban work often demands less physical activity than rural work. Women in cities work outside the home, and they are too busy to shop for, prepare and cook healthy meals at home. The fact that more people are moving to cities makes the problem worse. In 1900, just 10% of the world population lived in cities. Today, that figure is closer to 50%.

C This does not mean that rural areas are not affected. Increased mechanization of farming leads to reduced physical activity at the same time that more food, but not necessarily better food, becomes available. Many rural farmers have given up farming multiple crops that provide a more balanced diet in favour of a single, high-yielding cash crop.

Importing Poor Eating Habits

D Another element of the nutrition transition is the increase in the amount of food imported from the industrialized world. Traditional diets, featuring grains and vegetables, are being replaced by meals high in fat and sugar.

E Some experts blame industrialized countries for producing healthier cuts of meat for their own citizens, while selling the high-fat remainders to poorer countries. Turkey tails and mutton flaps (cuts of mostly skin and fat), for example, are sold to the developing world, despite the fact that 80% of the energy in them comes from fat. As food companies watch incomes rise in the developing world, they are setting their sights on new markets. From Mexico to Morocco, the foods that endanger health in wealthy countries are now affecting poorer countries.

F Other changes in diet are occurring regardless of outside influences. In China, when per capita income grew by 400% after the economic reforms of the late 1970s, the consumption of high-fat foods increased dramatically. While incomes grew, the income needed to purchase a fatty diet decreased. In 1962, a diet containing 20% of total energy from fat correlated with a per capita GNP of US$1,475. By 1990, a GNP of just $750 correlated with the same diet.

G In a number of countries, globalization has changed the concept of obesity. In Mexico and Brazil, for example, where being overweight was once a sign of wealth, it now displays poverty. The increased availability of cheaper food means the poor have access to a richer diet. While the richest people can choose to adopt a healthy lifestyle, the poor have fewer food choices and know very little about nutrition.

The Cost of a Poor Diet

H The underweight and overweight have a shorter life expectancy and high levels of sickness and disability. Obesity increases the risk of chronic diseases, such as diabetes, heart disease and cancer. Before long, the developing world may be suffering the majority of the growing disease burden. For instance, the number of people with obesity-related diabetes is expected to double to 300 million by 2025. Three-quarters of that growth is likely to be in the developing world. For countries whose economic and social resources are already stretched to the limit, the result could be disastrous.

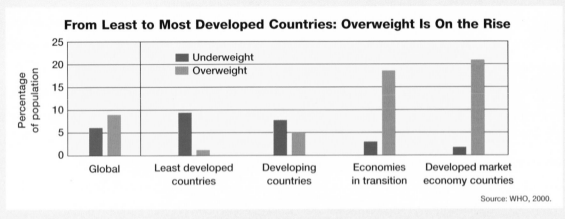

From Least to Most Developed Countries: Overweight Is On the Rise

Source: WHO, 2000.

The passage has eight paragraphs, labelled A–H. For questions 1–6, say which paragraph contains the following information.

1. healthy types of food that people are not eating anymore ___
2. unhealthy types of food that poorer countries are buying from richer countries ___
3. the global transition towards an urban lifestyle ___
4. a warning to developing countries about what the future may bring ___
5. how the exact cost of a fat-based diet has changed in one country ___
6. people using less energy because there are more machines ___

For questions 7–12, match the people A–E with the statements. Write the correct letter A–E in the spaces. Use one letter twice.

A people living in cities	B rural farmers
C the Chinese	D Mexicans and Brazilians
E Underweight and overweight people	

7. They make more money from selling just one product. ___
8. They used to think that being fat showed you were rich. ___
9. They are more likely to be ill. ___
10. They have much more money to spend nowadays. ___
11. They spend less time making food for themselves. ___
12. They don't know that what they are eating is unhealthy. ___

For questions 13–16, decide if the information given below agrees with the information given in the passage. Write (T) true, (F) false or (NG) not given.

13. Around a third of the people in the world now live in cities. ___
14. The majority of the energy content in the unhealthiest cuts of meat comes from fat. ___
15. People in China now earn on average four times what they did in 1970. ___
16. By 2025, the number of obese people in developing countries will be twice that in developed countries. ___

4 Society

Reading 1: preparing to read

A Look at this first line from a text you are going to read. Check the highlighted words in a dictionary and then answer the questions that follow with a partner.

> Disposing of all the waste we produce is a global problem.

1. What different types of waste do we produce?
2. Why is disposing of waste such a big problem?

B Look at this sentence from the same text. Check the highlighted words and then answer the questions that follow with a partner.

> One way waste is classified is by consistency; whether it is solid or liquid waste.

1. One example of solid waste is empty bottles. Can you think of a few more examples?
2. One example of liquid waste is bath or shower water. Can you think of any other examples?

C Use a dictionary. Match the words and phrases below with the pictures.

1. landfill __   2. incineration __   3. composting __
4. waste injection well __   5. recycling __

D Talk to a partner. Do you know any advantages or problems with any of the methods in Exercise C?

landfill is cheap

incineration can cause pollution

E Circle the correct option in each sentence.

1. If you **monitor** something, you *watch it and check it / say it doesn't work well*.
2. If you **dump** something, you want to *keep it / throw it away*.
3. If water is **contaminated**, it's *good to drink / dangerous*.
4. If something is **hazardous**, it *could hurt you or kill you / is very good for you*.
5. If something **leaks**, it *breaks into pieces / allows water to escape*.
6. If something is **harmful**, it is *good / not good* for you.
7. **Pollutants** are *harmful to / good for* the air that we breathe.
8. If something **decomposes**, it *breaks down / comes together*.

Reading 2: understanding references and linking

A Complete each of the sentences about waste with the reference words in the box.

1. The United States produces around 208 million tonnes of solid waste every year, and _____ is on the increase.
2. In many countries, people no longer throw away bottles and jars. _____ take _____ to bottle banks, where _____ can be recycled.
3. A long time ago, people simply took their rubbish out into the country and dumped _____ _____.
4. When rubbish was first disposed of in an organized way, _____ was dumped into large open holes. Since _____, complex systems of rubbish disposal have been developed all over the world.

| it (x 2) |
| this |
| then |
| there |
| they (x 2) |
| them |

B Complete each of these sentences about waste with the linking words in the box.

1. Most rubbish is taken to landfill sites, but it can _____ be incinerated.
2. Most people are not happy about living close to landfill sites _____ they are afraid that drinking water may become contaminated.
3. In most big cities, there are recycling systems in place. In smaller towns, _____, recycling is not such usual practice.
4. _____ the constant monitoring of waste injection wells, dangerous pollutants can sometimes escape.
5. Composting is popular with many people because it is a natural process. _____, it can be cheaper than producing chemical fertilizers.

| however |
| in addition |
| despite |
| also |
| because |

Reading 3: practice understanding references and linking

A Read the text and answer the questions 1–15 that follow.

Where Does All the Rubbish Go?

A Disposing of the all the waste we produce is a global problem. Every area of our lives involves throwing something away, whether it is household rubbish, plastic, paper, metal, commercial waste or anything else we simply do not want or need. The United States alone produces around 208 million tons of solid waste every year, and this is on the increase. Each person produces more than four pounds of waste a day. We have developed various different ways of disposing of waste, but certainly not yet a way that is absolutely safe.

B We have not always monitored the way we dispose of waste as we do today. In 18th century Europe, people with carts were paid to carry rubbish out of town and dump it. The first municipal cleaning system originated in the United States in the middle of the eighteenth century. This made the dumping of rubbish in open pits usual practice. However, since then, our waste has become more complicated, and cannot simply be placed in a hole in the ground. We have many different types of waste, and it must be disposed of properly to prevent contaminating the environment.

C There are different types of waste, and it is classified according to its physical, chemical and biological characteristics. One way it is classified is by consistency; whether it is solid or liquid waste. To classify as a solid waste, the material must contain less than 70% water. This type of waste includes materials such as household rubbish, industrial waste, mining waste and some oilfield waste. Liquid wastes must be less than 1% solid and is often from wastewater. Wastewater often contains high levels of dissolved salts and metals. Sludge is the final consistency classification, being somewhere between a liquid and a solid. Sludge contains between 3 and 25% solids, and the rest of it is made up of water-dissolved materials.

D Waste can also be classified into three categories; non-hazardous, hazardous and special waste. Non-hazardous waste does not pose any immediate danger to health or the environment. This category includes household rubbish. Hazardous waste can either be flammable or leachable. This means that it can either easily catch fire, or it can leak toxic chemicals. Examples of special waste would be radioactive and medical waste, and there are very clear rules about how this can be disposed of.

E There are a number of ways that we dispose of rubbish and waste. Landfill is the most common, and can account for more than 90% of a country's waste. It is the most cost-effective way of disposing of rubbish, as collection and transport represents 75% of the total cost involved. A landfill site is a carefully constructed site located away from heavily populated areas, and in areas where there is no flooding. Rubbish is buried in thin layers and then covered with clay, sand and fresh soil. When the landfill is full, it is covered with a layer of plastic and then more soil. Grass and other vegetation is planted, so that the site is hidden completely. Despite all this effort to minimize danger, however, it is known that landfill can contaminate drinking water. A 10-acre landfill site will leak between 0.2 and 10 gallons of liquid every day through the plastic liner.

F Waste can also be burnt in incinerators. This method is more expensive, but safer than landfill. Modern incinerators can destroy more than 99% of organic waste material. In addition, incineration recovers energy in the waste, which can be used to generate electricity. Older incinerators, however, do not separate the material that is burnt, and there are concerns that harmful pollutants are released into the air. People who live near incinerators usually object to them because of the health risk.

G Some hazardous waste can be pumped into deep wells inside the earth. This is called waste injection. The wells are constantly monitored to check that pollutants cannot escape and contaminate drinking water. Many people are strongly opposed to this method because it has caused explosions and even earthquakes in the past.

H Organic material that contains little or no heavy metals can be detoxified biologically. This is done by composting and land farming. Waste materials are spread over a large area of land so that they decompose more quickly. Hazardous waste must be detoxified because it can leak into the groundwater, causing water contamination.

I Presently, the aim of governments all over the world is to reduce the amount of waste that we need to dispose of. Firstly, to reduce the amount of waste that is created in the first place, and then to reuse and recycle waste rather than discard it. Many strategies are in place or are being considered. They might cost us more now, but will almost certainly bring benefits to future generations.

For questions 1–6, match the headings below with some of the paragraphs A–I.
Write the letter of the paragraph as your answer.

1. It used to be easy   —
2. Up in flames   —
3. Don't throw it away   —
4. How dangerous is it?   —
5. We all produce rubbish   —
6. Most rubbish goes under the ground   —

For questions 7–10, choose the correct answer a, b or c to complete each statement below.

7. The methods used to dispose of waste in the eighteenth century ...
   a. were very complicated.
   b. meant that town centres were very dirty.
   c. would not be appropriate today.

8. Sludge is ...
   a. mostly solid.
   b. mostly liquid.
   c. is about the same amount of solid and liquid.

9. All special waste ...
   a. can easily catch fire.
   b. must be disposed of carefully.
   c. cannot be destroyed.

10. Landfill is popular because ...
    a. it is not expensive to move rubbish from one place to another.
    b. it helps to prevent flooding.
    c. once rubbish is under the ground, it is not at all dangerous.

For questions 11–15, mark each of the statements below with one of the following abbreviations. Use some abbreviations more than once.

I   incineration

WI   waste injection

C   composting

11. Experts check the process very carefully.   —
12. Disposing of waste in this way can produce power.   —
13. This process is natural, but not totally without risk.   —
14. Only newer equipment is really efficient.   —
15. This process has been linked to natural disasters.   —

B Check the key on page 276. How many questions did you answer correctly?

C Tick the sentences about the reading task that are true for you and think about how you can answer more questions correctly next time.

1. I could quickly see what reference words referred to.
2. Understanding references helped me to answer some questions.
3. I understood how linking words and phrases were used.
4. I didn't need to understand every word of the text to answer the questions.
5. I'm pleased with how quickly I did the tasks and how many questions I answered correctly.

 Exam tip: Technical words in a text are often explained. Notice how *sludge*, *flammable* and *leachable* are explained in the text that you have just read. Recognizing that a word or phrase you don't know has been explained will help you to read more quickly and understand more of a text.

Key vocabulary in context

There are a lot of synonyms (words that have a very similar meaning) in the text. Delete the <u>one</u> word in each list that is different from the others.

1. waste / rubbish / layer
2. destroy / produce / generate
3. danger / method / risk
4. dispose of / throw away / dump / contaminate / discard

WB For focus on reading skills, go to Workbook page 55.

Writing 1: describing a flow chart

A What do you remember about flow charts? Complete the extract with these words.

> event   arrows   stages   effect   process

Flow charts show the _____ in a _____. They help you to understand how something happens, and sometimes why something happens. Flow charts usually show cause and _____. They demonstrate how one _____ can be the reason for another. Flow charts are usually designed with _____ that show you the direction of the sequence.

B Answer these questions with a partner.

1. Which of these materials and products are often recycled in your country?

> glass   plastic containers   newspapers and magazines
> car tyres   electrical appliances

2. Do you recycle glass bottles and jars? Where do you take bottles and jars when they are empty?

3. What happens to glass when it is collected for recycling?

C Cover the diagram below. Put these stages of glass recycling into the correct order 1–7. Check any key words in a dictionary.

___ glass crushed into small pieces called cullet / different colours of cullet made
___ molten glass moulded into new bottles and jars
___ glass transported to processing plant / metal tops and plastic sleeves removed
___ new bottles and jars shipped to companies for filling and distribution
___ mixture heated to high temperatures in furnace
___ glass collected from bottle banks / clear, green and brown glass separated
___ cullet mixed with sand, limestone and soda ash

D Now look at the diagram below and check your order of the stages.

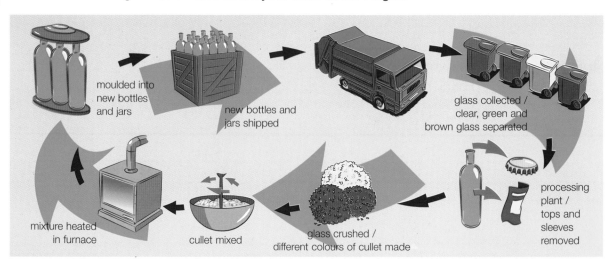

moulded into new bottles and jars

new bottles and jars shipped

glass collected / clear, green and brown glass separated

mixture heated in furnace

cullet mixed

glass crushed / different colours of cullet made

processing plant / tops and sleeves removed

E Look at the instructions for a typical writing task and answer the questions that follow with a partner.

> The diagram shows the process of glass recycling.
>
> Write a report for a university lecturer describing the information.
>
> Write at least 150 words.

1. Do you need to know a lot about glass recycling to answer the question?
2. Do you need to add your own ideas to make the description more interesting?

F Read this student's report and decide what you like and don't like.

> They collect the glass from bottle banks and separate the clear, green and brown glass. They transport the glass to a processing plant. Any metal tops and plastic sleeves removed here. They crush the glass into small pieces what is called cullet. They make three different colours of cullet. The cullet mixes with sand, limestone and soda ash. The mixture are heated to a very high temperature in a big furnace. The molten glass makes new bottles and jars. The new bottles and jars shipped to companies for filling and distribution.

G Read these teacher's comments about the report and mark each (T) true or (F) false.

1. The report is difficult to follow. I don't really understand it. __
2. The report is much too short. You need to write more. __
3. There is no sentence to introduce the report – to say what the process shows. __
4. You have used active forms when passive forms would be better. __
5. When you have used passive forms, they are not used correctly. __
6. You have spelt words wrongly when you copied from the information given. __
7. You have not used any linking words and phrases to bring the report together. __

Writing 2: using the passive to describe a process

A Work with a partner. Underline examples in the report where a passive would be more natural than an active form and circle examples where passive forms are grammatically incorrect.

> **Grammar check**
> We use the passive when we want to focus on what happens rather than who or what does the action. Passive forms are very frequently used to describe a process.
> *The glass is crushed into small pieces.*
> *Bottles and jars are collected from bottle banks.*
>
> Sometimes who or what did the action is also important, so we put it at the end of the sentence and use *by*.
> *Bottles and jars are collected by a waste disposal company.*
>
> Make these two sentences passive.
> 1. They transport the glass to a processing plant.
>
> _____
>
> 2. Somebody fills the new bottles and jars ready for distribution.
>
> _____

Watch out!
typical errors

Bottles and jars collected. ✗

Bottles and jars is collected. ✗

Bottles and jars are collect. ✗

Exam tip: If the first writing task involves describing a process, you will need to use the present simple passive. Remember that many of the most common verbs in English are irregular.

B Complete this version of the report with the correct passive form of the verb in brackets.

The glass _____ (collect) from bottle banks. Clear, green and brown glass _____ (separate). The glass _____ (transport) to a processing plant. Metal tops and plastic sleeves _____ (remove) here. The glass _____ (crush) into small pieces called cullet. The cullet _____ (make) in three different colours. The cullet _____ (mix) with sand, limestone and soda ash. The mixture _____ (heat) to a high temperature in a furnace. The molten glass _____ (make) into new bottles and jars. The new bottles and jars _____ (ship) to companies for filling and distribution.

Grammar check
Passive forms are usually reduced when they are part of a relative clause.
The glass is crushed into small pieces called cullet.
NOT *The glass is crushed into small pieces which is called cullet.*

If more than one participle follows a subject, there is no need to repeat the auxiliary verb.
The glass is collected and transported.
NOT *The glass is collected and is transported.*

Writing 3: linking a description of a process together

A Here is an improved version of the report. Delete the incorrect option in each case.

The diagram shows the different stages in the process of glass recycling. It shows what happens to glass from when it is disposed of in a bottle bank, to when it becomes a new bottle or jar, ready to be reused. (1) **At the beginning / First of all**, glass bottles and jars are collected from bottle banks all around the area. (2) **At this point / In this time**, clear, green and brown glass is separated. The glass is (3) **then / after** transported to a processing plant, (4) **where / which** it is crushed into small pieces called cullet. This cullet is made in three different colours. (5) **Next / Secondly**, the cullet is mixed with other materials (6) **such as / which is** sand, limestone and soda ash. The mixture is heated to a very high temperature in a huge furnace. (7) **When / While** it is ready, the molten glass is moulded into new bottles and jars, (8) **what / which** are ready for reuse. (9) **Finally / In the end**, these new bottles and jars are shipped to various companies for filling and distribution.

B This is a description of how tins and cans are recycled. Put the verbs in brackets into a passive form and add appropriate linking words and phrases.

(1) _____, aluminium tins and cans (2) _____ (collect) from recycling points. They are (3) _____ transported by truck, train or ship to smelting plants, (4) _____ they are unloaded and (5) _____ (test) for quality. (6) _____, they are checked to see if they contain any liquid. (7) _____, the tins and cans are shredded into small pieces and (8) _____ (place) in an oven to remove paint and labels. They (9) _____ (heat) to over 500 degrees in a furnace, (10) _____ they melt and mix together with other molten metal. Salt and other chemicals (11) _____ (add) to the mixture. (12) _____ the chemistry of the molten mixture has been checked, it (13) _____ (remove) from the furnace and (14) _____ (pour) into moulds to be made into rectangular blocks. These blocks (15) _____ (allow) to cool and are (16) _____ passed through huge rollers to become metal sheets. (17) _____, these metal sheets are transported to a can manufacturer, where they (18) _____ (make) into new tin cans.

C Look at the exam practice section on page 250 for the writing task.

Reading

A Tick the option that is true for you in each pair of statements.

1. A I know immediately what reference words refer to in a longer text.
   B I sometimes have difficulty knowing what reference words refer to and it slows me down when I read.
2. A I recognize most linking words now and they help me make predictions about what will follow.
   B I still confuse some linking words and phrases when I read more challenging texts.

B Complete each of these definitions with a word from the Reading Module. The first letter is given.

1. If something l _ _ _ _, it allows water in or water to escape.
2. If you d _ _ _ rubbish, you throw it away or leave it somewhere.
3. If something is h _ _ _ _ _ _, it isn't good for you and it could hurt you.
4. If something is a r_ _ _, it isn't safe and it could hurt you.
5. If material d _ _ _ _ _ _ _ _ _, it breaks down and goes back into the earth.
6. If you m _ _ _ _ _ _ a situation, you watch it carefully and check that there is not a problem.
7. If something c _ _ _ _ _ _ _ _ _ _ _ water, you cannot drink it.
8. If power is g _ _ _ _ _ _ _ _, it is produced from a process.
9. One way of defining consistency is to say if something is s _ _ _ _ or l _ _ _ _ _.

Writing

A These verbs are typically used to describe a process. Write the correct past participle.

1.	make	_____	2.	take	_____	3.	break	_____
4.	bring	_____	5.	build	_____	6.	give	_____
7.	leave	_____	8.	send	_____	9.	throw	_____
10.	hold	_____	11.	put	_____	12.	write	_____

B Rewrite these descriptions using a passive structure. Only mention the agent if necessary.

1. Somebody breaks the glass into small pieces.
2. Robots build cars in most factories.
3. Secretaries send the parcels out to the various offices.
4. Workers package the drinks in plastic containers.
5. Ships transport the coal to North Africa.
6. An official writes a number on each envelope that he sends.

C Below is part of the report from the Writing Module. Find **eight** words that are spelt wrongly and correct them.

First of all, glass bottles and jars are colected from bottle banks all around the area. At this point, clear, green and brown glass is seperated. The glass is then transported to a prosessing plant, where it is crushed into small peaces called cullet. This cullet is made in three diferent colours. Next, the cullet is mixed with other meterials, such as sand, limestone and soda ash. The mixcher is heated to a very high tempriture in a huge furnace.

4

Writing

A Look at the pictures and answer the questions with a partner.

1. What do the two pictures show?
2. What are the similarities and differences between the two pictures?

B Read the short text below and then answer the questions that follow with a partner.

> In most countries nowadays, people are encouraged to dispose of unwanted computers in an appropriate way. In some countries, there are strict laws about the disposing of computers and computer equipment, and people are not allowed to simply throw them away. There are a number of options when disposing of an unwanted machine:
>
> - donate it directly to a charity or an organization that helps people in need
> - send it back to the original manufacturer / exchange it in part for a new computer
> - arrange for a recycling organization to collect it and take it away

1. Are there laws in your country about the disposing of computers?
2. Have you disposed of a computer recently? What did you do with it?
3. What do you think happens to a computer if it is sent for recycling?

C Look at the flow chart on the next page and the instructions for the task below and answer these questions with a partner.

1. Is each stage of the recycling process clear?
2. Are there any key words you need to check in a dictionary or with your teacher?

> The diagram shows the process of reusing or recycling unwanted IT equipment.
>
> Write a report for a university lecturer describing the information.
>
> Write at least 150 words.

IT Equipment Reuse and Recycling

(protecting the environment and ensuring benefits to the community)

request to collect unwanted IT equipment

↓

collection booked with licensed waste carrier

↓

convenient collection time arranged with donor

↓

equipment collected and transported by waste carrier

↓

data wiped from equipment

↓

equipment tested by technicians (reuse or recycle)

working equipment refurbished   non-working equipment prepared for recycling

↓

refurbished equipment given
to charities / people in need   parts treated and recycled

D   Write the report. Think about ...

1. introducing the report without simply copying the instructions.
2. using the appropriate grammatical structures.
3. using the appropriate linking words and phrases.

5 Movement

Reading 1: timing yourself

A Answer these questions with a partner.

1. How many texts will you have to read in the IELTS Academic Reading Module?
2. In what ways are the texts in the Academic exam more difficult than those in the General Training exam?
3. Are all the texts of equal difficulty?
4. Should you spend an equal amount of time on each text?

 Exam tip: It is not easy to decide how long to spend on each part of the Reading Module. Most students plan to spend a little longer on the second text than the first, and a little longer on the third than the second. However, at your level, you may decide that you want to spend longer on the first part because you will have more chance of getting answers correct and scoring marks. Whatever you decide, it is very important that you try to improve your reading speed as much as you can.

B Read the sentence below and decide if it's true. Then answer the questions 1–6 with a partner.

Now that you have read lots of texts and know all the different types of reading task, you will know how long to spend on the various stages of the reading process for each part.

1. How long do you spend reading the heading and looking at any visual support?
2. How long do you spend skimming the text to get a general idea of what it's about?
3. How long do you spend reading the instructions and questions?
4. How long do you spend reading more carefully to complete the tasks?
5. Do you take more time to complete some types of tasks than others?
6. How long do you spend checking that your answers are spelt correctly and that you are happy with them?

Reading 2: checking answers

A Here are some possible mistakes you can make when you write your answers onto the answer sheet. Complete each with <u>one word only</u>.

1. You might _____ a word wrongly when copying it from the text.
2. You might not use a _____ letter for the name of a person, a place or a month.
3. You might use more _____ than the instructions say are allowed.
4. Your final answer might not be _____ to the examiner if you cross or rub out a previous answer.

 Exam tip: Remember that in the reading exam, you do not have extra time to transfer answers. You write answers directly onto the answer sheet as you read. Nearly half of the tasks that can occur in the Reading Module involve writing words and phrases as answers. You MUST spell your answer correctly – the words that you need to use occur in the text or the summary box, so make sure you copy them correctly. You MUST NOT use more than the stated number of words. If you change an answer, rub it out or cross it out completely. Your final answer MUST be clear.

Reading 3: preparing to read

A Answer these questions about tourism with a partner.

1. When do you think people first started travelling for pleasure?
2. When do you think tourism as we know it today really began?
3. When do you think mass tourism started to develop?

B Work in small groups. Think of examples of each of the following.

1. the benefits of tourism to tourists
2. the benefits of tourism to the people who live in the place that is visited
3. the negative impact of tourism

C Look at the pictures and answer these questions with a partner.

1. What negative effects of tourism do the pictures show?
2. Can anything be done to reduce these negative effects?

D Look at the three highlighted words in the text on the next page and the sentences in which they occur. Answer these questions.

1. Do the three words have a similar meaning, or do they all have different meanings?
2. Are the words more connected with people, or with organizations and systems?
3. What do you think the text will tell you about infrastructure, resources and facilities?

Reading 4: practise timing yourself and checking answers

A Skim the text quickly and match parts of it with some of the pictures.

B Read the text and answer the questions 1–13 that follow. Write your answers directly onto the answer sheet provided on page 255.

The Impact of Tourism

In recent years, any debate about the effect of increased travel on the environment has tended to focus mainly on issues of aviation, global warming and man-made climate change. Discussions about the negative impact of tourism in particular have centred on the issue of carbon emissions. The ever-growing number of flights that take people to more and more distant corners of the globe, and the resulting release of fossil carbon into the atmosphere is a concern, but it is certainly not the only concern.

In many parts of the world, the physical environment can be hugely affected by the passage of tourists, especially for popular destinations, where the sheer number of people visiting can simply prove too much.

As a tourist destination becomes more popular, a period of construction frequently follows the expansion of the original settlement, usually to the detriment of the local environment. Since the beauty of the local environment is what attracted visitors in the first place, this can be disastrous. More hotels and restaurants put more strain on the local infrastructure, but they also mean more light pollution, and this can have a dramatic impact on nature. In the Greek islands, it is known that the light from the many restaurants along the coast confuses young turtles. Instead of heading for the natural light of the sea, they head inland towards the artificial light of the buildings, where there is no protection from cats and seagulls.

The seasonal invasion of tourists puts a huge additional demand on local resources, especially in more remote and poorer parts of the world. Water, energy and food, for example, are often used far less wastefully in those countries than in the west. The typical tourist generally requires far more than what locals would consider necessary by the standards of the region. Even where the infrastructure exists to meet this demand, and in many places it simply does not, the end result often leads to a gradual environmental deterioration, unless considerable new investment is made. It does not take too much additional water extraction from watercourses or groundwater to begin to see changes to rivers and wetlands. At the same time, hydroelectric schemes that aim to resolve the problem can in fact have an effect on aquatic habitats.

Tourism also increases the pressure on the arrangements for managing waste and wastewater. Even in the developed world, this can be a significant issue, especially if the resort has a small year-round local population. It is unlikely that the original facilities have been made large enough to cope with the additional load placed on them during the holiday season.

The problem of over-usage is not limited to seaside resorts. Many of the most popular national parks, mountain paths and forest walks show the signs of wear and tear, too – eroded paths, excessive litter and general damage. A growing number of people look to reduce the number of flights they take and reconnect with nature. They take their holidays in the country, closer to home, but while attempting to help resolve one problem, they unknowingly contribute to another.

The impact of tourism is far worse for many developing countries, where the existing infrastructure is basic and has difficulty coping with the demand of the local population alone. Resources can be significantly stretched by any additional visitors to the area. It is almost impossible for travellers to avoid having some kind of negative environmental impact when they travel. The very act of going on holiday inevitably means causing some kind of damage and making some demands, however unintentional.

For questions 1–7, complete these sentences with words from the text. Use <u>no more than three words</u> for each answer.

1. Most discussions about the impact of tourism focus on the number of ... that tourists make as they travel around the world.
2. When destinations become popular, the ... can be badly affected by increased building work.
3. ..., caused by an increase in buildings along the coast, sometimes results in local wildlife behaving unnaturally.
4. Western tourists often use resources more ... than people local to a poor area would.
5. Areas where infrastructure is poor need ... before they are able to cope with large numbers of visitors.
6. ... do not necessarily resolve the problem of water extraction from rivers and wetlands.
7. Even a ... in a developed part of the world will have difficulty coping with large numbers of tourists if the facilities were designed for fewer people.

For questions 8–13, complete the summary below with words from the text. Use no more than three words for each answer.

Not only (8) ... are affected by an increase in the number of visitors. Many people choose to go on holiday closer to home and visit areas of natural beauty in the country, hoping (9) ... air pollution. However, although people do not mean to do harm, they drop (10) ... and cause (11) ... . Generally speaking, in (12) ..., an increase in tourism has a more dramatic impact. Travellers do not wish to damage the environment, but it is almost impossible (13) ... doing so.

1		8	
2		9	
3		10	
4		11	
5		12	
6		13	
7			

C Check the key on page 276. How many questions did you answer correctly?

D Answer these questions about the reading task with a partner and think about how you can answer more questions correctly next time.

1. Did you answer the questions in the time that you had?
2. Did you get any answers wrong because they were not spelt correctly or transferred wrongly?
3. Did you use the correct number of words for each answer?
4. Are you happy with the number of questions you answered correctly?

Key vocabulary in context

A Find the nouns of these verbs in the text and write them in the spaces.

1. expand _____
2. settle _____
3. protect _____
4. invade _____
5. extract _____

B Now find the adjectives of these nouns in the text and write them in the spaces.

1. disaster _____
2. season _____
3. addition _____
4. excess _____

WB For focus on reading skills, go to Workbook page 57.

5

Writing 1: composition content

A Answer these questions about the IELTS Writing Module with a partner.

1. How is the second writing task in the IELTS Academic exam similar to that in the General Training exam?
2. How is it different?

 Exam tip: The second writing task in the Academic exam is more challenging than that in the General Training exam. In both exams, you will need to write a discursive composition, argue a point and express an opinion. However, the topics in the Academic exam are more academic, and your arguments will need to be more sophisticated.

B Mark each of these composition instructions (GT) if you think they are typical of the General Training exam and (A) if they are more typical of the Academic exam.

1. If you could make one change to your town or city to make it more appealing to visitors, what would it be? ___

2. Many people believe that large numbers of tourists visiting an area has a negative impact on the physical environment. However, there may be beneficial effects of increased tourism, too. What are your views about this topic? ___

3. Many people believe that as ever-growing numbers of people travel, local customs and traditions are dying out, and lifestyles all over the world are becoming identical. Do you agree or disagree with this view? ___

4. Do you think people should travel independently and try to learn about the place they are visiting, or do you think that buying a package holiday in which everything is included is the better option? ___

5. The number of private vehicles on the road has increased hugely in recent years. What can governments do to improve public transport and encourage more people to use it? ___

Writing 2: a balanced composition

A Here are points you must consider when you write a composition for the second writing task. Mark each as follows. Then compare with a partner.

✓　I am good at this. I have no concerns.
?　I'm not sure about this. I think I need to work on it.
✗　I have difficulties with this. I definitely need to work on it.

1. knowing what to say and having enough ideas to write 250 words ___
2. planning and organizing before I write ___
3. organizing my points as I write ___
4. using paragraphs and topic sentences to introduce them ___
5. generally expressing my ideas in language that is easy to follow ___
6. using words and phrases that introduce ideas and link points together ___
7. giving examples that support my opinions ___
8. using appropriate grammatical structures correctly ___
9. spelling words correctly ___
10. using the appropriate register ___

B Look at these instructions for a typical writing task. Is it a question you can answer?

> As part of a class assignment, you have been asked to write about the following topic: Many people believe that large numbers of tourists visiting an area has a negative impact on the physical environment. However, there may be beneficial effects of increased tourism, too.
>
> What are your views about this topic?
>
> Give reasons for your answer and include any relevant examples from your experience. Write at least 250 words.

C The text in the Reading Module gave examples of the negative effects of tourism. What positive effects can you think of? Talk to a partner.

D Read the composition a student wrote below. Did they mention the positive effects that you mentioned?

> Of course large numbers of turists are having a negative impact on the physical invironment of a place. You can see in popular resorts all around the meditereneon sea that hundreds of big hotels, resteronts and night clubs has ruined a very beautiful part of the world. Old buildings and important monuments now are serounded by modern buildings and all looks horrible. What is more if too many tourist come to a small place the inferstructure can't cope. Sistems for dispose of waste and provide water are not big enough. When they extract too much water from the ground in one place rivers and lakes can dry out. I think maybe there are some positive affects of tourism but not so many. More hotels and resteronts provide jobs for local people and local people can use some facilities that build for tourists – like swimming pools and tennis courts for example. The negative affccts of tourism are not only in resorts. In the country too there are tourists who drop rubbish and spoil natural places. In mountains there are skiing towns that spoil the view that is so beautiful there. I think people must to think first before go to places where many other people are going for holidays.

E Make notes about what you like and what you don't like about the composition.

Writing 3: improving your compositions for the Academic exam

A Answer these questions about the composition in Writing 2D with a partner.
1. Does the composition appear to be well planned?
2. Is the composition easy to follow? Do you understand the arguments?
3. Does the writer make points in a logical order?
4. Does the writer use paragraphs and introduce paragraphs with topic sentences?
5. Does the writer open and close the composition appropriately?
6. Is the general register appropriate or does the writer make points too strongly?
7. Does the writer use words and phrases to introduce ideas and link points?
8. Is the language grammatically correct and is most of the spelling correct?

B Read this student's composition. How is it better than the first one?

> The world is getting smaller and nowadays tourists are visiting more and more remote places. Many of these places are very beautiful, and people go there because of the natural environment. Unfortunately, it is not possible for so many people to visit a place without having some impact, and a lot of that impact is negative.

Firstly, most people get to their destination by plane. This means that an airport needs to be built somewhere close, and that flights are arriving and leaving and causing air pollution. This all spoils the natural environment. In addition, when a destination becomes more popular, there is a lot of construction. Hotels, apartments, bars and restaurants are built, and sometimes built very quickly without taking into consideration the local atmosphere.

The increased number of travellers puts a lot of strain on the local infrastructure. More water is needed, and this can result in rivers and lakes drying up. I am from Spain and I can personally see how the south coast of Spain has been changed dramatically by all the new buildings and the facilities that support the tourist industry.

Impact on the environment is not just about holiday resorts, though. If people walk in the country, they erode paths and drop litter. Skiing villages turn beautiful mountain chains into noisy resorts. We all know that coral reefs are destroyed by too many people diving and snorkelling. Everywhere the effect of tourism can be felt.

Of course, there can be beneficial effects of increased tourism, too. Local people can use the facilities and resources that have been provided for tourists. They might want an airport closer to where they live, and roads and rail links might improve. There might be a swimming pool or tennis court where there was not before, and people may enjoy the fact that there are more cosmopolitan restaurants. These places also provide employment for local people, but that might be another issue.

All in all, I would say that too much tourism certainly does have a negative impact, and I think that it is a shame that wherever you go in the world, you now see the same architecture and the same chains of shops and coffee bars.

C Answer each of the questions in Writing 3A about this composition.

D Look closely at the highlighted linking words and phrases. Match each to its use below.

1. I think this is clear to everyone. _____
2. I want to add something to what I said before. _____ _____ _____
3. I want to introduce a general conclusion. _____
4. I want to make a point that is in slight contrast to something I said before. _____
5. This is something I know from my own experience. _____
6. I want to soften a negative point as I introduce it. _____

E Complete each sentence with your own ideas about the issue of increased tourism.

1. Unfortunately, _____.
2. In addition, _____.
3. Personally, _____.
4. Of course, _____.
5. All in all, I would say _____.

Grammar check

Remember, we use the passive when we want to focus on what happens, rather than who or what does the action. Look at these active and passive examples from the letter.

active: ... *tourists are visiting more and more remote places. This all spoils the natural environment.*

passive: ... *an airport needs to be built somewhere. Everywhere the effect of tourism can be felt.*

Highlight more examples of active and passive forms in the letter. Then talk to a partner and say why the form is used.

Watch out!
typical errors

Resources that have provided for tourists. ✗
The effects of tourism can been felt. ✗

F Look at the exam practice section on page 262 for the writing task.

Reading

A Mark each of these statements about your reading skills (T) true or (F) false.

1. My reading speed is improving all the time. ___
2. I feel more confident reading longer academic texts. ___
3. I know how long I want to spend on each part of the Reading Module. ___
4. I can usually complete the tasks in the time I have. ___
5. I do not make mistakes when I write my answers onto the answer sheet. ___

B Correct the spelling mistakes in these words.

1. resorses   2. fasilities   3. inferstructure   4. inviroment   5. presure   6. skeme

C Fill the gaps with a word made from the root word in the box.

1. There are arguments for and against the _____ of resorts.
2. There is only a limited _____ demand for some products.
3. _____ tourism is bound to have an impact on an area.
4. Local people might see increased numbers of tourists as an _____.
5. Travellers must try not to use local resources _____.
6. Some events have a _____ effect on a country's economy.

expand
season
excess
invade
waste
disaster

Writing

A Answer these questions with a partner.

1. Do you feel more confident about the first or second writing task in the Academic exam?
2. What concerns do you have about the second writing task?
3. What aspects of writing a discursive composition have you most improved?

B Without looking back to the Writing Module, complete each linking word or phrase.

1. I think this is clear to everyone.   of _ _ _ _ _ _
2. I want to add something to what I said before.   a _ _ _ / t _ _ / in a _ _ _ _ _ _ _
3. I want to introduce a general conclusion.   _ _ _ in _ _ _
4. I want to make a point that is in slight contrast to something I said before.   t _ _ _ _ _
5. This is something I know from my own experience.   p _ _ _ _ _ _ _ _
6. I want to soften a negative point as I introduce it.   unf _ _ _ _ _ _ _ _ _

C Rewrite these sentences using a passive structure. Only mention the agent if necessary.

1. People should not use water wastefully.
   Water _____ .
2. Tourism has changed many small towns dramatically.
   Many _____ .
3. Society can feel the effects of mass tourism across the globe.
   The effects _____ .

5

Reading

A Earlier in this unit, you talked about how tourism started. Can you remember what you said?

B Now answer these questions with a partner.

1. Why did tourism develop more quickly in Britain than anywhere else?
2. Why didn't British people travel abroad until much later?
3. Do you know the names of any famous British tour operators?

C Read the text and answer questions 1–14 that follow. Write your answer directly onto the answer sheet at the bottom of the next page.

The Origins of Mass Tourism

In 1841, a man organized what was probably the world's first package tour. He chartered a train to take a group of people from one town in the middle of Britain, to another town just twenty miles away, to take part in a local political event. The man's name was Thomas Cook. On that day, he saw the business potential of his idea, and he soon became a tour operator. Today, Thomas Cook is regarded as 'The father of mass tourism', and the company he founded is known throughout the world.

Other entrepreneurs followed Cook's lead, and the tourist industry grew rapidly in early Victorian Britain. At first, it was the growing numbers of wealthy middle-class people who supported it. They could afford the luxury of travel and they had the time on their hands to enjoy it. However, for mass tourism to really explode, two things needed to happen. Firstly, an improvement in transport that meant large numbers of people could quickly be taken to places of interest, and secondly, an increase in leisure time for ordinary working people, so that they, too, could enjoy the benefits of travel.

The invention of the railway was a significant development. Suddenly, the coast was in easy reach of Britain's largest industrial cities. At the same time, as the Industrial Revolution was having an impact and working conditions were improving, hundreds of thousands of people were given free days and short holiday breaks. As a result, the first holiday resorts developed in seaside towns all over the country. In the north, Blackpool and Scarborough were very popular, and in the south, Brighton, Eastbourne and Southend became frequent visiting spots for Londoners. Some resorts became known throughout Europe as the most fashionable destinations of the time.

In the 19th century, health tourism began to develop. Wealthier British holidaymakers would visit resorts in Southern Europe, and on finding the higher temperatures favourable, would decide to stay for the winter months, and in some cases forever. Some tourists began to visit places that were supposed to have health-preserving mineral waters, in the hope of treating a range of illnesses and conditions. King George III was known to have regularly visited the sea whenever he was feeling unwell.

For nearly a hundred years, however, the majority of tourism was domestic. Only the very wealthy or those who travelled for educational purposes ventured to foreign destinations. In Britain, holiday villages, like Butlins, became popular. Here, families could be beside the sea in cheap accommodation and enjoy a range of entertainment organized by the tour provider. These establishments only went into decline when the option of flying became accessible to ordinary people, and when people became confident that they could enjoy the same comforts abroad as they could closer to home.

Some of these early developments in tourism were seen in other parts of Europe, like France, Belgium and Holland, but it was in Britain that industrialization occurred more quickly, and that allowed tourism to grow in a way that was not possible elsewhere. It also allowed a greater number of wealthier people to experience overseas travel. This is reflected in the fact that all over Europe, hotels bear the names of British cities, and British kings and queens. In Nice, one of the most famous resorts on the French Riviera, the long walkway to the sea, is known to this day as the Promenade des Anglais.

For questions 1–3, decide if the information given below agrees with the information given in the passage. Write (T) true, (F) false or (NG) not given.

1. Thomas Cook discovered the business potential of tourism by chance.
2. There were several well-known tour operators in Victorian Britain.
3. Mass tourism grew because there were so many rich people in Britain.

For questions 4–6, answer these questions with words from the text. Use <u>no more than three words</u> for each answer.

4. Which method of transport had most impact on early tourism?
5. Which historical event allowed mass tourism to develop in Britain?
6. Which people typically visited holiday resorts in the South of England?

For questions 7–8, choose <u>two</u> of the following statements that are true according to the text. Write the letters on the answer sheet below.

A Some British holidaymakers moved permanently to warmer places.
B Some British tourists became ill when they travelled outside Britain.
C Some people believed that a certain type of water was good for their health.
D King George III was not a very healthy man.

For questions 9–14, complete this summary with some of the words and phrases from the box.

in Britain	escape	to see	alone	visit	afford	to fly
	abroad	in France	to learn			

For almost a century, most British people holidayed (9) ... Wealthy people or people who wanted (10) ... about foreign countries travelled (11) ..., but it was not common. Holiday villages near the sea that ordinary people could (12) ... were very popular until quite recently. More people began to travel overseas when it was possible (13) ... more cheaply and travel more comfortably. The fact that early tourism developed most quickly in Britain is plain (14) ... all over Europe. Hotels and tourist attractions in many places are named after British institutions.

1		8		
2		9		
3		10		
4		11		
5		12		
6		13		
7		14		

Writing

A Look at the pictures and think about the cultural effects of tourism. Do the images show a positive or negative effect?

B Look at these instructions for a typical writing task and think about how you would answer it.

As part of a class assignment, you have been asked to write about the following topic:

A lot of people feel that increased tourism has a negative effect on the traditional lifestyles and culture of people in developing countries.

Do you agree, or do you feel that tourism benefits the way of life in those places?

Give reasons for your answer and include any relevant examples from your experience.

Write at least 250 words.

C Read these extracts from a conversation between two friends. Who do you agree more with? Compare with a partner.

Tony: Tourists bring a huge amount of money into developing countries.
Lisa: Yes, but many hotels and tourist-related businesses are run by Western companies. The money doesn't always go to the local community.

Tony: Yes, but tourists buy products that are made by local people.
Lisa: Once the local people know that tourists will buy those products, they mass produce them and gradually commercialize what was traditional art and craft.

Tony: Tourism creates a lot of jobs for local people.
Lisa: Not always. Managerial jobs often go to Westerners, while local people are given jobs serving guests or cleaning. Local people can feel exploited by tourism.

Tony: The more tourists travel, the more they learn about traditional cultures and learn to respect lifestyles that are different from their own.
Lisa: Maybe, but wealthy tourists often just want to take what a country has to offer and not learn about the local way of life. The local people actually learn more about the visitors' culture and sometimes want what wealthy tourists appear to have.

Tony: Don't you think that tourism helps people to be tolerant about the way people live in other countries?
Lisa: Not necessarily. Holidaymakers don't always respect local customs. They sometimes behave in a way that is inappropriate or even offensive to local people.

D Talk in small groups. Are there any other points you want to make about this issue?

E Decide which points from the conversation and which points of your own you want to use. Then write the composition.

_____

_____

_____

_____

_____

_____

_____

_____

_____

_____

_____

_____

_____

_____

_____

_____

_____

_____

_____

_____

_____

_____

_____

_____

_____

_____

Key exam vocabulary

Academic reading and writing

The key vocabulary is a list of words and phrases that occur in this book and that you should learn to improve your performance, particularly in the Reading and Writing Modules of the IELTS Academic exam. It is a list of words and phrases that frequently occur in the type of texts that you will read in the IELTS General Training exam and which you will need to write effectively in both writing tasks. These words will also help you to understand certain topics in the Listening Module better.

Words and phrases that were included in the key vocabulary of Target 5.0 General Training are included again here whenever they occur in a unit. Notice how many words and phrases that occurred in the General Training course occur again here – you can see that many words and phrases really are typical of the IELTS exam. Some very common words and phrases are not included in the list because you will already know what they mean and how to use them.

Spend some time checking all the words and phrases in the list and check anything you are not sure about in a good dictionary.

A
account for (phrasal verb)
achievements (n)
acquire (v)
(in) addition (idiom)
additional (adj)
adept (adj)
adjoined (to) (adj)
advantage (s) (n)
affect (v)
aim (v/n)
amount (n)
applicant (n)
available (adj)
availability (n)
average (adj)
awareness (n)

B
ban (v/n)
basic (adj)
beneficial (adj)
benefit (v/n)
bonus (n)

C
category (n)
choice (n)
colleague (n)
collect (v)
collection (n)

combine (v)
comfort (n)
concept (n)
consistency (n)
consume (v)
consumer (n)
consumerism (n)
consumption (n)
contaminate (v)
convenience (n)
convenient (adj)
conventional (adj)
cope (with) (v)

D
damage (v/n)
data (n)
deal with (v phrase)
decline (v/n)
decompose (v)
decrease (v)
demand (v/n)
despite (prep)
develop (v)
(the) developed world
  (n phrase)
(the) developing world
  (n phrase)
development (n)
disadvantage(s) (n)
disaster (n)

disposal (n)
dispose (of) (phrasal verb)
distribute (v)
distribution (n)
dramatic (adj)
dramatically (adv)

E
effect (n)
efficiently (adv)
element (n)
employee (n)
employer (n)
equipment (n)
establishment (n)
event (n)
excess (n)
expand (v)
expansion (n)
experience (v/n)

F
facilities (n)
finally (adv)
first of all (adv phrase)
flexibility (n)
fluctuate (v)
function (v)

G
generate (v)

global (adj)
globalization (n)
gradual (adj)
gradually (adv)
growth (n)

H
harmful (adj)
hazardous (adj)
however (adv)

I
illegal (adj)
impact (n)
income (n)
increase (n)
increase (v)
(on the) increase (n)
inefficient (adj)
influence (v/n)
infrastructure (n)
invade (v)
invasion (n)
isolated (adj)

L
layer (n)
limit (v/n)
liquid (n/adj)
(fall to a) low (n)

M

major (adj)
majority (n)
market (n)
method (n)
minimize (v)
minority (n)
mixture (n)
monitor (v)
motivation (n)

N

noticeable (adj)
noticeably (adv)

O

(be) opposed (to)
    (v phrase)

P

past (work) experience
    (n phrase)
(reach a) peak
    (n/v phrase)
percentage (n)
(at this) point
    (prep phrase)
policy (n)
pollute (v)
pollution (n)
pollutants (n)
popularity (n)
pressure (n)
prevent (v)
prevention (n)
process (n)
produce (v)
production (n)
professional (adj)
protect (v)
protection (n)
(make a) purchase (n)

Q

quality (n)

R

rate (n)
recycle (v)
reduce (v)
reduction (n)
relevant (adj)
remote (adj)

(have) reservations (n)
resolve (v)
resources (n)
responsibility (n)
revolution (n)
rise / rose / risen (v)

S

salary (n)
separate (v)
sequence (n)
settle (v)
share (n)
sharp (adj)
sharply (adv)
slight (adj)
slightly (adv)
soar (v)
solid (adj)
stage (n)
stand out (phrasal verb)
statistics (n)
steadily (adv)
steady (adj)
strategy (n)
suitable (adj)
system (n)

T

test (v)
transaction (n)
transition (n)
transport (v)
trend (n)

U

unlimited (adj)
usage (n)

V

valuable (adj)

W

waste (v/n)
worldwide (adj)

Answer key

Answers for selected listening and reading tasks and model compositions for writing tasks.

Unit 1, Listening 2A

1.	Austin	2.	110
3.	47	4.	three children / 3 children
5.	2003	6.	Moore
7.	Cedar	8.	650396
9.	twenty-two / 22	10.	single

Unit 1, Reading 2A

1.	B	2.	D
3.	E	4.	C
5.	A	6.	F

Unit 2, Listening 2A

1.	c	2.	c
3.	September 18	4.	12 / twelve
5.	December 14	6.	96
7.	6	8.	7
9.	Merton	10.	3
11.	109	12.	28

Unit 2, Reading 2B

1. a professional
2. family and friends
3. a teaching certificate
4. goggles
5. plastic sandals
6. support

Unit 2, Writing 3A

I am writing about a business English course I recently took at your school. I studied on an intensive two-week course, but I learnt very little.

Your advertisement says that the business English classes are small. I expected to study in a group of between six and eight students, but I was in a large class of 16. It was difficult for the teacher to give time to everyone.

During my stay, there were three different teachers. Nobody explained why, and none of the teachers seemed to have experience teaching business.

Your advertisement promises that the Course Book and Workbook are provided, but this was not true. I received my Course Book on the Monday of the second week so could only use it for a week. I never got the Workbook.

You claim that your school is modern and in a central location. In fact, the building is old and the classrooms are not suitable. The technology is out of date. The building is

5km from the city centre, and I needed to catch a bus to get there from where I was staying.

Unit 2, Writing 4B

I hope you understand why I am unhappy with the service your school provided. In total I paid 1,200 euros for the course and I would like you to refund 50% of that. I look forward to hearing from you.

Unit 2, Exam Practice, Writing B

Dear Sir/Madam,

I am writing to complain about the driving lessons that I recently took with your driving school. There are a number of reasons why I am not happy.

Firstly, I had three different instructors, so it was difficult to build any kind of relationship with the person teaching me. Secondly, the lessons were supposed to be for one hour, but the instructors frequently ended lessons five minutes early.

In my opinion, the instructors were not very good either. They spent most of the time explaining what I should do, and did not give me the time I needed to practice.

Finally, I was unhappy that your cars were not very modern and sometimes not clean inside. They were not what I expected from a professional driving school.

I hope you understand why I am unhappy with the service your school provided. In total I paid 500 euros for the lessons and I would like you to refund 50% of that. I look forward to hearing from you.

Yours faithfully,
Terry Black

Unit 3, Listening 2A

1.	b	2.	c
3.	a	4.	d
5.	c	6.	b
7.	a	8.	a
9.	c	10.	b
11.	a	12.	b

Unit 3, Reading 2B

1. advert A – d
2. advert B – b
3. advert C – a
4. C (be computer literate)
5. A (working directly with the chief executive)

6. B (You will receive full training)
7. C (more than a million satisfied customers)
8. B (deal with people face-to-face regularly)
9. A (Closing date for application)

Unit 3, Writing 2D

Dear Mr Lucas,

I am writing to apply for the position of sales executive that I saw advertised in yesterday's *Daily Argus*. I hope to work in sales, and I am interested in working for your company.

I recently finished a Business Studies degree at York University. I achieved very high grades in Economics and Marketing. Part of my degree course involved designing and developing new ideas. I learn quickly and work well with other people.

My father runs an import and export company, and from the age of 16 I have helped him in his office. I have learnt many useful business skills and communicated with clients both on the telephone and face-to-face.

I am outgoing and confident and I enjoy a challenge. I think I would be the right person for a position in your company. I can attend an interview at any time and look forward to hearing from you.

Your sincerely,
Ahmed Khatani

Unit 4, Listening 3B

1. c	2. b
3. a	4. b
5. A	6. B
7. E	8. G
9. H	10. c

Unit 4, Reading 1B, C and D

1. T (the student in D is correct)
2. T (again, the student in D is correct)
3. NG (the student in D has made an assumption – the text does not give him that information)
4. F (the student in D is correct)
5. F (the student in D is wrong. The text says that some experts believe that not having a normal childhood can do long lasting damage – it does not only say what the mother and father think)
6. T (the student in D is correct)
7. NG (the student in D is wrong – yes, the text only mentions one programme but that does not tell us that Ainan doesn't watch other programmes)
8. F (the student in D is correct)

Unit 4, Reading 3B

1. d
2. e
3. b
4. a
5. T (Parents and teachers spend much of their time emphasizing the need ...)

6. NG
7. F (there are plenty of entrepreneurs and high-fliers who dropped out of school)
8. F (He dropped out of school ... and started his first successful business venture, a magazine called *Student*)
9. NG
10. NG
11. T (he left Harvard College in 1975 to set up his own computer software company)
12. F (... doesn't mean that everyone can get to the top in business without a college or university degree)

Unit 4, Exam Practice, Writing C

Some people think that having great talent is enough to succeed in life. They see actors and artists and great sportsmen and think they are successful because they were born with talent. They forget that these people also worked very hard to get where they are.

In my opinion, talent can only take you so far. To reach the top you also need the desire to be the best and the discipline to work hard to be the best. You must also get the right advice and listen to it. You need the support of the people around you – your friends and family.

I think there are many talented people who are not successful because they are lazy. Some don't succeed because their parents or their teachers don't push them to do well. Some talented people are quite unusual and their friends and family don't take them seriously. Then they don't have the confidence to succeed.

My hero is the basketball player Michael Jordan. He had incredible natural talent, but he was the first player to arrive for training every day and the last player to leave. This desire to work hard and to practise is what made him the best.

To sum up, I want to say that talent, hard work and support from others must go together if somebody is successful. There are many people in top positions who have less natural talent than another person who has not achieved very much at all.

Unit 5, Listening 2A

1. f	2. e
3. d	4. b
5. a	6. c
7. two	8. movement
9. space	10. sleep
11. messages	12. heart
13. connects	14. grow

Unit 5, Reading 3B

1. T (techniques that will help you memorize names, faces ...)
2. NG (Although probably false, the text doesn't provide an answer)
3. T (people who really make things happen don't forget)
4. F (using scientifically proven techniques)

5. F (will put you ahead of the rest)
6. NG
7. ten / 10
8. gains
9. forget
10. retrieve
11. focus on detail
12. In minutes

Unit 5, Writing 2D

First composition: Points are relevant and well balanced – arguments that support both points of view. / Points not planned or organized. It seems like the writer is making points as he or she thinks of them. / Not organized into paragraphs so not easy to follow. / No introduction – writer goes straight into argument. / Some points are made in a repetitive way. Writer explains what the reader can understand from what has already been said. / Ideas not linked with typical linking words or phrases. / Vocabulary is used properly, but quite simple.

Second composition: All points are relevant and argument is well balanced. / Very good introduction – shows he or she understands question. / Very easy to follow – organized into paragraphs. / Points are planned and organized and linked together with linking words and phrases. / Good range of vocabulary used to make points more interesting to read.

Workbook Unit 5, Writing B

I have heard many people say that it is easier to learn new things when you are young than it is when you are old. I think they say this because children learn naturally and seem to absorb things without trying. However, I think it probably depends what you are learning and how much you really want to learn.

I know that I learnt how to use a computer very quickly when I was only about six years old, while my mother still finds it difficult. I think it was easy for me because I did not really realize I was learning something, and I just wanted to play the games. My mother does not like technology, and she was nervous about learning something she did not really want to.

People say that children learn languages more quickly than adults, but I am not sure this is true. It takes a child ten years to learn to speak their language properly, but an adult can learn a foreign language if they live in another country in only two or three years. Because they have more experience of life they can apply it to translate and learn grammar rules. I think older people can learn just as quickly if they really need to.

I think young people can learn things like swimming much more quickly than older people. My father really wants to be good at golf and he practises a lot, but he does not get any better. My cousin started playing when he was ten and soon he was very good. However, some children want to learn a sport, but are not good at all. My answer to the question is, it depends what you are learning, and it is not always easier for young people.

Unit 6, Listening 3A

Note that letters in 1–4 can be in any order as long as the correct three letters are used. The answers here in alphabetical order.

1. A
2. B
3. D
4. H
5. D
6. F
7. A
8. H
9. I
10. C

Unit 6, Reading 3C

1. E
2. B
3. D
4. A
5. C
6. 700,000 (Now it is a huge modern city with a population of over 700,000)
7. adventure (Holidaymakers can enjoy a relaxing break, and people looking for adventure can ...)
8. business conferences (The excellent hotels and facilities make it a popular place for business conferences and exhibitions)
9. more relaxing (More relaxing is a cruise in a wooden dhow)
10. take photographs (... many opportunities to take photographs. The traditional architecture is amazing, and ... magnificent palaces and mosques.
11. low custom duties (Low customs duties mean that many products are less expensive ...)

Workbook Unit 6, Writing B

In most countries these days, most young people go to university when they leave school. In some countries, it is usual to apply to the university which is closest to your hometown, so that you can continue to live with your family. In other countries, young people want to move away to a more exciting place where they can begin a new life. Moving is part of the university experience.

Many young people choose to move away from home because they want an adventure. They can live in a university residence or rent an apartment with other students. They are free from their parents' rules for the first time.

Moving away from home has disadvantages, however. Students can become homesick if they do not make new friends, and they can miss their friends from school and their brothers and sisters. Some young people do not know how to cook and are not very good with money, so they need their parents' support. If students go to university near their home, they can live at home and have the support of their family. It will also be much cheaper because they do not have to pay for accommodation or to travel home at the weekend or during holidays. My brother and two of my cousins go to university in our city and are happy that they can live at home.

Some students who live at home feel that they miss the fun that some of the other students are having. They see other students living in a big house with lots of other young people and feel a bit envious.

Personally, I would prefer to live at home when I study, and I think I will do that. The university in my city has a good reputation, so there is no need to move away. I think I can concentrate on my studies better if I don't have to think about looking after myself and making friends.

Unit 7, Listening 1D

1. own car
2. the weekend
3. parking
4. £2,000 / 2,000 pounds
5. the same place

Unit 7, Listening 3C

1. short journey
2. 24 / twenty-four hours
3. allowed to
4. book
5. is using
6. in advance
7. for longer
8. open
9. membership
10. Petrol

Unit 7, Reading 2D

1. TS (... the transport secretary says that modern planes are ... less noisy ...)
2. BAAE (... believes that a third runway could be worth around £10 billion a year to the economy)
3. STS (... feels that high-speed rail links are a much better option)
4. SAG (... adds ... will mean destroying around 700 homes ...)
5. TS (believes that Heathrow will lose some of its reputation ... if it is not expanded)
6. BAAE (... says that the airport has been running at full capacity for more than 15 years)
7. T (she warns that some of the 170,000 jobs at the airport could be lost)
8. F (spokesman says that noise from planes on a new runway will affect more than fifty towns ... However, the transport secretary says that modern planes are becoming ... less noisy)
9. NG (He doesn't say 'the busiest in the world')
10. T (other methods of transport should be developed instead)

Workbook Unit 7, Writing A

Dear Sir/Madam,

I am writing to complain about a train journey that I took recently with your company. There was a serious delay, which meant that I arrived at a wedding later than I planned. I was travelling from Brighton to London, and needed to change at Croydon. However, because the train from Brighton was delayed for 20 minutes, I missed the connection. The next train to London was then cancelled, and there was not another for nearly an hour.

I knew I would be late, so had to take a taxi instead. This cost £35. I am angry that I had to spend this money when I had already paid for the train journey.

I had planned to arrive some time before the wedding, but I arrived just as it started. The journey was very stressful, and I could not enjoy the wedding as I hoped.

I hope you understand why I am unhappy with the service you provided. I would like a refund of the £35 taxi charge. I look forward to hearing from you.

Yours faithfully,
Monica Hart

Unit 8, Listening 2A

1. printing	2. to read
3. 14th / fourteenth	4. Books
5. (printed) newspaper	6. Photography
7. truth	8. moving
9. homes	10. Satellite
11. incident	12. their own

Unit 8, Reading 3B

1. b	2. e
3. d	4. a
5. different	6. first time
7. fun	8. hobby
9. voluntary work	10. retirement
11. work	12. wait

Unit 8, Exam Practice, Writing D

Dear Sir,

I am writing to request some time off from my studies from next week until the end of the month. I am studying American History, and I am enjoying the course very much. However, my father is ill in hospital and I want to spend some time with him. I also want to help my mother, who is finding it very difficult to cope alone.

I will ask my lecturer, Professor Watkins, to tell me in advance what the class will study while I am away, and I will ask one of my classmates to scan and e-mail the notes he takes during the lectures I miss. I will do everything possible to keep up with my studies.

I hope you understand the decision I have made. I would like to apologize and hope my request will not cause too much inconvenience. Thank you for your kind consideration.

Yours sincerely,
Martin Wood

Unit 9, Listening 2B

1. b
2. a
3. b (expenses, mortgage, fees)
4. c (emergencies)
5. package

6. deal (note that 'value' is uncountable and so does not fit)
7. showroom
8. treat
9. rainy day

Unit 9, Reading 2C

1. T (it also has a hugely damaging effect on the profit that companies make)
2. NG
3. NG
4. NG
5. T (it might be more convenient to put it in the bin …)
6. profit
7. to reduce
8. left on standby
9. light bulbs
10. both sides
11. in colour

Workbook Unit 9, Writing B

There are some people who are materialistic and want the good things in life. For them, having money is very important, and they think it makes them happy. There are other people who believe that the simple things in life matter more than money. For them, it is more important to have friends and family, and to be in good health.

I do not think it is really possible to say who is right and who is wrong, and I think it also depends on what people mean when they say 'happy'. Of course, if people are so poor that they have no home and nothing to eat, it is impossible to be happy, but there are plenty of people who do not have much money and really enjoy life.

There are also a lot of very rich people who are not happy at all. You always hear about rich movie stars who take drugs because money does not bring them everything they want. I think some rich people are happy because they have more than other people. They see money as proof that they are successful. Perhaps if everyone else was also rich, they would not be so happy.

Personally, I do not think that having more money than other people will make me happy. I want to be successful and I want to have nice things, but having a job I like and being with a man I love are the most important things. I have an uncle who is very rich, but does not have a wife and does not have any children. He does not seem happy to me.

Unit 10, Listening 3B

1. B (… worry when the spring turns to summer …)
2. A (… avoid being at the top of tall buildings …)
3. A (… may panic and want to escape the situation – the quickest way to escape is to jump)
4. B (… especially common in children …)
5. A (… people confuse it with vertigo, which is a normal feeling …)
6. C (… will avoid watching a programme or movie …)

Unit 10, Reading 3C

1. B (They want to see … an end result.)
2. F (Most people … don't feel they are doing this if they are repeating a routine day after day.)
3. A (… are less likely to leave the company.)
4. E (The whole paragraph explains the point.)
5. D (… they want to have a conversation and share a joke.)
6. C (The whole paragraph explains the point.)
7. benefit
8. better
9. achieve
10. appreciate
11. colleagues
12. control
13. improve
14. same

Workbook Unit 10, Writing C

Dear Mr Hardwick,

I am writing about some problems I have been having with students who are renting one of your houses. They are at 47, Colwell Gardens, which is the house next door to mine. I am at 45.

Your tenants are very inconsiderate, and seem to have no respect for neighbours living around them. Firstly, they play loud music all day and until late at night. What's more, there is frequently a lot of shouting and arguing. If they go out for the evening, they come home in the middle of the night and make a lot of noise.

I tried to speak to them about their behaviour, but they were very rude. When I complained about the noise, they seemed to find it funny, and nothing has changed. I am really very angry about the situation now.

Please could you speak to your tenants about their behaviour, and warn them that other people in the street have had enough. If nothing changes, I will report the problem to the local council and I do not want to have to do that.

Yours sincerely,
Greg Warren

Unit 11, Listening 2A

1. (the) flu
2. medicine
3. neck
4. your eyes
5. brain
6. hospital
7. your head
8. blood

Unit 11, Reading 3C

1. E (The first meeting is free for all!)
2. I (The whole ad provides this answer.)
3. F (… individual advice that will ensure you achieve your goals …)
4. A (… provide new products that you can try out and purchase if you are satisfied.)
5. B (… simply eating less doesn't necessarily equal weight loss.)
6. C (… people who we have already helped and show

you videos that tell the story of their progress.)

7. J (There are no penalties for missed classes!)
8. G (... a whole month of free meetings if you introduce a friend to FEELGOOD!)

Unit 11, Exam Practice, Writing F

People are living longer. In some parts of the world, the number of young people is staying the same, while the number of old people is growing all the time. In the future, most people might live to be a hundred or more. Of course, this is good if people can remain healthy, but most old people need more health care, and governments are finding it difficult to provide the money that is needed.

It would be nice to say that everyone should have free health care, but I do not think that is realistic. Younger people would have to pay more and more tax, and there are other things the government needs to spend the money on. Perhaps private insurance is the answer.

The problem with people paying privately for health care is that not everyone can afford it. Richer people would have better health care in their old age than poor people, and that is not really fair. Of course, there are a lot of rich people now who have private health insurance, but poorer people can still get treatment in hospitals if they are ill. These poorer people might not get this treatment in the future if they cannot afford the insurance.

Unit 12, Listening 4B

1. Sahara Desert / desert
2. strong wind
3. wave
4. C
5. B
6. A
7. eye
8. eyewall
9. rain bands
10. dramatic
11. ice
12. crops

Unit 12, Reading 3A, B and C

1. C
2. D
3. F
4. floor
5. outside
6. people
7. calm
8. leave
9. place
10. T (my little boy was in the bath. I knew that he was in a place that was very unsafe – under a window with a huge piece of glass right above his head)
11. T (there were no safe places inside the house and we had to try to get out to the garage)
12. T (I grabbed Daniel in my arms)
13. NG

Unit 12, Writing 3D

There are zoos in most big cities all round the world, and thousands of people visit them. Nearly everybody goes to a zoo as a child, and it is probably the only time that they see real wild animals. Although most people like going to zoos, they understand that the animals are not in their natural environment and may not be happy. Some people even think that zoos are cruel and should be closed.

In a lot of zoos, animals are in small cages and they are miserable. Big animals cannot run around or hunt as they do in the wild. In some zoos the animals are not treated well, and children shout and throw things at them. Some people think that because nowadays we can see wild animals on TV whenever we like, it is no longer necessary to keep them caged up in zoos.

However, I think the conditions in most zoos are improving. There are more wildlife parks where big animals can run around. Near my city, there is a big park where you can drive your car and take photos of animals. Some people argue that we need zoos because some rare animals would die out and become extinct if they were left in the wild. Zoos help animals like pandas to multiply and survive.

In my opinion, there is a need for zoos so that children can see real animals and not just read about them in books. However, the zoos should be modern and the animals well cared for. Their cages should be big enough that they can run around. The best solution would be to have more big wildlife parks where animals are in an environment like their natural one.

Workbook Unit 12, Writing C

In most countries pets are important, but I think that they are more important to people in some countries than in others. Pets are important to people at different times in their life, too. I think pets are more important to children and to old people than to people who are busy and out of the house a lot. I suppose it is true that pets are even more important to some people than other people are.

If people are very old and they spend a lot of time alone, a dog or a cat can be very important. A dog can be an old person's best friend, and taking the dog for a walk can be an opportunity to get out of the house and take a walk. A cat can provide a lot of comfort if somebody is unable to get out of the house so easily.

Some children do not have brothers and sisters. Others are shy and not good at making friends. For them, a pet can be a best friend. I can imagine that if something happens to a child's pet dog, it seems worse than something happening to another person. When I was little I had a rabbit, and I came home from school every day to see him. However, I cannot say that he was more important than my sister or my friends.

Personally, I find it difficult to understand how a pet can be more important than other people. In my country, old people live close to other people in their family and they see people every day. When I stayed in Scotland I saw that old people seem to spend more time alone, and I can imagine why their pet becomes so important. I think it depends on the country how important pets are to people.

Unit 13, Listening 3B

1. office
2. celebrate
3. a billion
4. famous
5. library
6. worse
7. ambitious
8. entertainment

Unit 13, Reading 3B

1. d (Around 95% of the population of Egypt lives within ...)
2. g (There is a long history of ...)
3. i (The whole paragraph provides the answer.)
4. j (The statistics in the paragraph provide the answer.)
5. e (... has brought many benefits.)
6. a (... there have been problems, too.)
7. c (... how similar problems can be overcome in other countries)
8. 500km / kilometres
9. 35 km / kilometres
10. 90 metres
11. 1,000 metres
12. 111 metres

Answers for questions 13–17 here are in alphabetical order but any order is fine as long as the three correct letters are given.

13. A
14. B
15. C
16. E
17. G

Unit 13, Writing 3A, B and C

Dear Sir/Madam

I am writing to complain about an apartment that I am renting through your letting agency. It is Flat 3 at 74 Belle View Gardens. I moved in a week ago and paid a deposit of £600 and a month's rent in advance, which was £750. I now realize that the apartment is not in a good condition and I am not at all happy.

Firstly, the air conditioning is not working properly so the apartment is very hot all the time. I have found it very difficult to sleep until late at night in this hot weather.

Secondly, most of the furniture is very old and some of it is broken. The leg of the coffee table in the living room is broken and some cupboard doors do not close properly. Finally, you told me that the apartment would be cleaned before I moved in. However, when I arrived it was very dirty and I spent all day cleaning it myself.

I am very disappointed and would like you to resolve the problem as soon as possible. Please arrange for the air conditioning to be repaired immediately, then please contact the landlord about

replacing the broken furniture. Finally, please refund a percentage of the advance I have paid for not cleaning the apartment properly. I think £100 would be fair.

I look forward to hearing from you.

Yours faithfully,
Marco Bendetti

Unit 14, Listening 2A

1. B
2. C
3. D
4. E
5. G
   (The answers above are in alphabetical order but they can be in any order as long as the five correct letters are given.)
6. public
7. London
8. (a) screen
9. reporters
10. projected image
11. colour
12. nearly 20 / twenty years
13. on the Moon
14. 1981
15. 5 and 7 / five and seven
16. atmosphere
17. bake bread
18. shared
19. each house
20. 3 is the correct diagram

Unit 14, Reading 3A and B

A
1. B
2. D
3. A
4. C
5. the cable / (the) supply cable / electricity supply cable
6. detergents
7. (a) qualified engineer
8. (your) local council

B
1. T (e-mail is now the most common form of communication)
2. NG
3. NG
4. F (most of fourth paragraph)
5. T (all of sixth paragraph)
6. F (all of seventh paragraph)
7. NG

Unit 14, Writing 2C

Recently, the use of computers has increased dramatically. These days, most families have a computer at home and there are usually computers in a typical classroom at school. Most schools also have a computer lab where children learn IT skills. Clearly, children are using computers far more than they did in the past.

Personally, I think this is a good thing and that there are more advantages than disadvantages. Everyone needs to know how to use a computer, so learning when you are young is good. It is easier to learn how to use new technology when you are young than it is when you are older. The Internet has made it possible to find information about any subject and to learn about every part of the world. When I was at school, I really enjoyed doing projects that involved looking for information online.

However, I can understand why some people are concerned about children using computers too much. Some of the sites on the Internet are not appropriate for children, and they can visit chat rooms that might put them in danger. It is not always easy for parents to check what children are looking at. Some people think that if children work on computers, they will not read books or learn to write, but I disagree. I used computers at school, but it didn't stop me wanting to read books, too.

To sum up, I would say that computers are beneficial for children, but that an adult should regulate how much time they use one. Parents must make sure that children do not spend all their time e-mailing instead of going out with friends and that they are safe when they are online.

Unit 14, Exam Practice, Writing F

Nowadays, almost every family in the world has a television, and in the developed world there might be a television in every room in the house. Many children have their own television in their bedroom. All this probably means that children are watching a lot of television. The question is, though, are they watching more television than is good for them, and are they watching television when they should be doing other things?

There are some people who think that children spend all day, every day sitting in front of the television. They think that children never leave the house, never meet their friends and never play any sports. What's more, these people probably think that children only watch cartoons and action movies. In my experience, this is just not true. Most parents limit how much television their children watch and encourage them to watch programmes that are educational. There are a lot of programmes now that encourage children to go out and do things, or make things at home. I know that my nephew started playing tennis because he loved watching tennis on television so much.

I think it is important to say that children can learn a lot from watching television. There are all sorts of documentaries about different parts of the world and the history of the world. When I was young I couldn't watch the programmes that children can watch now.

To sum up, I would say that I disagree with the statement. There are some children who watch too much television, but most children watch the same amount as children did twenty years ago.

Unit 15, Listening 3A

1. option
2. afford
3. a job
4. drugs
5. mental health
6. prison
7. violent
8. property

Answers 9–10 are given in alphabetical order but the order is not important.

9. A
10. C

Unit 15, Reading 3A

1. F
2. C
3. H
4. B
5. E
6. A
7. common
8. isolated
9. authority / power
10. conversations
11. to resign
12. the atmosphere

Unit 15, Writing 3B

Dear Samuel,

Leon asked me to write to you and tell you all about Bradlow, where I stayed last year. I understand you're thinking of staying there soon. Personally, I would consider going somewhere else. I was happy with my host family, and the school where I studied was excellent. However, Bradlow itself is not such a nice place to stay, in my opinion.

It is quite a poor town and there is a lot of unemployment. Teenagers get together in the shopping centre because there is nowhere else for them to go. There are a lot of closed-down shops and there is graffiti on buildings. There are quite a lot of homeless people, and sometimes they beg for money in the street. In the town centre, there are a lot of bars and discos and young people can be quite loud. I didn't feel very safe walking around in the evening.

It depends what you want, but I think there are nicer places to stay. I went to see some friends in Harkeley and it is very nice there. Anyway, I hope you have a really good time, wherever you decide to stay.

Best wishes,
Vicente

Unit 15, Exam Practice, Writing D

There are a number of reasons why people think that offenders should be sent to prison. Firstly, they think that other people are safer if criminals are locked up and unable to commit more crime. Secondly, people think that somebody who does something wrong should be punished, and prison is the obvious solution. Finally, people think that the fear of going to prison stops people committing crime.

However, I think it too simplistic to say that prison is the only way of dealing with offenders, and it is certainly not the best way to deal with all offenders. There are all sorts of reasons why people commit crime, and some crimes are not very serious. There are other punishments.

Of course, if somebody commits a terrible crime they should be punished, and if there is no death penalty then prison is the only option. If a criminal is likely to hurt or even kill, he or she should be locked up so people feel safe. Society has always had prisons, so people would be very concerned if they did not exist.

On the other hand, I think there are arguments against sending people to prison. If the crime is not serious, it is better to fine the criminal or make him or her do community service. It costs a lot to keep somebody in prison so the other options make more sense financially. Also, when criminals go to prison they often learn more about crime, and when they come out they go straight back to a criminal lifestyle. There should be a way of helping offenders to learn and to not want to commit more crime.

Personally, I think prison should be for serious offenders who are a danger to society and not for everyone who commits a crime. If we lock up everyone who does wrong, prisons will be full in no time.

Review 3, Writing E

Hi Henri I'm Sorry that I didn't can come at your brothers weding last week I am very bisy resently. I'm taking an examination in english It called IELTS. I need it for go university next year. I just finish a course that help me prepare for this examination It dificult but I enjoy it too much. My speaking english is much better than before but I don't can write so good like can you see. Ha ha! The examination it is next friday and I am too nervos about it. There is a speaking part a lisening part a reading part and a writing part. The reading and writing parts is which I am nervos about. I think you should to take this IELTS examination too. Your good in english and so you can get high score I think it is good have this examination for find a work. ok goodby now William.

Hi Henri,

I'm sorry that I couldn't come to your brother's wedding last week. I have been very busy recently. I'm taking an examination in English called IELTS. I need it to go university next year. I have just finished a course that has helped me prepare for this examination. It is difficult but I enjoyed it very much. My spoken English is much better than before but I can't write very well, as you can see – ha ha! The examination is next Friday and I am very nervous about it. There is a speaking part, a listening part, a reading part and a writing part. The reading and writing parts are what I am nervous about.

I think you should take this IELTS examination, too. You're good at English and so you can get a high score. I think it is good to do this examination to find work.

OK, I must get on now. Hope to see you soon.

Best wishes,
William

Academic section

Unit 1, Reading 3A

1. vii
2. x
3. ii
4. iii
5. viii
6. vi
7. NG
8. T (... they can arrange their schedule so that work can fit around them. If people do not get work done during the day, they can catch up in the evening or at the weekend)
9. T (... working in an office means having to commute to and from work five days a week)
10. F (People often find that they can get their work done more quickly and efficiently at home as opposed to working from an office – the rest of the paragraph provides more evidence)
11. NG
12. colleagues
13. offer
14. lower salaries

Workbook Unit 1, Writing task E

First sentence: The bar chart shows that the way people travelled to work changed very much between 1960 and 2000.

The bar chart shows that the way people travelled to work changed very much between 1960 and 2000. The percentage of people who used their car to get to work increased dramatically from only 22% in 1960 to 55% in 2000. At the same time, the percentage of people using public transport decreased. Nearly four times the number of people used the bus to get to work in 1960 than in 2000. The number of people who get to work by train fell by 50% too.

A small percentage of people use a motorbike to get to work, but the percentage of people who used a motorbike decreased by more than 50% between 1960 and 2000. Using a bicycle to get to work became slightly more popular.

The percentage of people who walked to work also fell dramatically. In 1960, 18% of the working population walked to work, but in 2000 half that number walked to work.

Unit 2, Reading 3B

1. D (Shopping has been transformed in the same way it was when ...)
2. H (people like to buy books and small objects online, but appear to still enjoy shopping traditionally for personal items ...)
3. A (Consumers are quickly becoming more adept when it comes to using technology)
4. F (... 95% of 15-year-olds have purchased something online.)
5. G (... how keen consumers are to find the right product at the right place ...)
6. C (It is only fourteen years ago that the first Internet shopping transaction was conducted in the US.)

7. C
8. F
9. B
10. E
11. convenience
12. delivered
13. concept of shopping
14. Broadband

Unit 2, Writing 3D

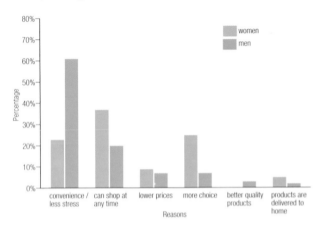

Unit 2, Exam Practice, Writing F

The pie charts show that there are some differences between the products that under 30s and over 30s spend money on when they shop online. However, there are similarities between their shopping habits too.

Both groups spend the highest percentage on holidays and travel, though over 30s spend more than under 30s. Almost a third of the money that under 30s spend is on holidays and travel and an even higher percentage (40%) of the money that over 30s spend. Books are also a popular purchase for both age groups. Almost a fifth of the money spent online is on books.

A noticeable difference is with DVDs and computer games. Younger people spend five times as much as people over 30. Under 30s pay to download music far more than the over 30s while the over 30s spend twice as much on CDs. It is interesting that over 30s shop online for food and drink while under 30s seem not to.

All in all, whether people are under or over 30, they are buying quite a range of online products.

Unit 3, Reading 1C

Between 1970 and 1980, smoking in both the developed and developing world increased noticeably.
Between 1980 and 1990, smoking declined dramatically in the developed world.
At the same time, tobacco consumption continued to rise in the developing world.
Between 1980 and 1990, world tobacco consumption stayed at the same level, which means that all of the increase was in the developing world.

Unit 3, Reading 4A

1. cigarette smoking / cigarettes
2. China
3. 320 million
4. countries
5. 35% / 35 per cent
   (Answers here are given in alphabetical order but any order is fine)
6. B (... can be attributed to a slower ... income growth)
7. C (... an increasing awareness of the damaging health effects)
8. F (... and increased taxation)
9. T (The share of China in total world tobacco demand is likely to remain around 37%)
10. NG (the text doesn't say why they smoke alternatives to conventional cigarettes)
11. F (In Africa ... demand increased in the 1990s with record growth of 3.5%. Growth for the period to 2010 is expected to continue at a similar rate.
12. C (demand for tobacco in India is likely to continue to increase, but more slowly than in the previous decades)
13. higher
14. income
15. production

Unit 3, Writing 3D

The graph shows that between 1990 and 1999, the number of both male and female smokers fluctuated. It shows that at the beginning and end of the decade, there were more male smokers, but for most of the decade the number of female smokers was higher.

The biggest increase in the number of female smokers was between 1992 and 1993, when thirty thousand more women smoked. By 1993, there were more female than male smokers. For three years, the number of women smoking stayed nearly the same, but then between 1996 and 1997, there was another sharp rise.

The biggest difference between the two groups was in 1995, when there were thirty thousand more female smokers than male. At that time the number of male smokers fell to a low of only 160,000. Between 1995 and 1996, the number of male smokers rose dramatically, and by 1996, the number of male and female smokers was almost the same. Although there was a slight drop between 1996 and 1997, the number of male smokers continued to rise steadily until the end of the decade.

The number of female smokers reached a peak in 1997, but then started to fall dramatically. By the end of the decade, there were more male than female smokers once again.

Workbook Unit 3, Writing task D

The line graph shows that the percentage of the population that smoke decreased dramatically between 1948, when records began, and 2005. The percentage of male smokers decreased more rapidly than the number of female smokers.

In 1948, around 65% of men smoked compared with around 41% of women. By 2005, the number of male and female smokers was almost the same.

Between 1955 and 1957, there was a rise in the number of both male and female smokers, though the rise in the umber of female smokers was sharper. Over the next few years, the numbers of both male and female smokers fluctuated.

Between about 1961 and 1963, there was a noticeable fall in the number of men smoking, and the difference between the number of men and women smoking became smaller.

Between 1970 and 2000, the number of both male and female smokers fell steadily. By around 1990, less than 30% of both men and women were smoking. Despite a couple of slight rises in the percentage of male smokers, the numbers of both men and women smoking continued to fall until 2005.

Unit 4, Reading 3A

1. B
2. F
3. I
4. D
5. A
6. E
7. C (However, since then, our waste has become more complicated, and cannot simply be placed in a hole in the ground)
8. B (Sludge contains between 3 and 25% solids, and the rest of it is made up of water ...)
9. B (Examples of special waste would be radioactive and medical waste, and there are very clear rules about how this can be disposed of.)
10. A (It is the most cost-effective way of disposing of rubbish, as collection and transport represents 75% of the total cost involved)
11. WI (The wells are constantly monitored ...)
12. I (... incineration recovers energy in the waste, which can be used to generate electricity)
13. C (Organic material ... detoxified biologically ... Hazardous waste must be detoxified because it can leak ... causing water contamination)
14. I (Older incinerators ... do not separate the material that is burnt ...)
15. WI (... it has caused ... earthquakes in the past)

Unit 4, Exam Practice, Writing D

The flow chart shows what happens to unwanted IT equipment. It shows the various stages of how the equipment is collected and then prepared for either reuse or recycling. First of all, there is a request from a company or individual to collect some unwanted IT equipment. A collection is booked with a licensed waste carrier and a convenient time to collect the equipment is arranged with the donor. The equipment is then collected by the waste carrier and transported to a place where it can be prepared for reuse or recycling.

Next, any data is wiped from the equipment and it is tested by technicians. If the equipment is working properly, it can be refurbished and reused. If it is not working properly, the various parts are treated so that they are ready for recycling.

Finally, working equipment is distributed to charities or to individual people who are in need, while equipment that cannot be used is recycled.

Unit 5, Reading 4B

1. flights
2. local environment
3. light pollution / artificial light
4. wastefully
5. (new) investment
6. hydroelectric schemes
7. resort
8. seaside resorts
9. to reduce
10. litter
11. damage
12. developing countries
13. to avoid

Unit 5, Exam Practice, Writing E

The world is getting smaller, and more and more tourists are visiting developing parts of the world, as well as the more typical holiday resorts. Travellers usually visit these countries because they want to see a traditional way of life and a culture that is very different from their own. However, it could be that by visiting these places, they have more of a negative impact than a positive one.

Of course, tourists bring a lot of money into countries that are often very poor, but the hotels that they stay in are often run by Western companies and not much of the money goes to the local community. Although local people are employed in hotels, restaurants and other tourist-related businesses, managerial jobs go to Westerners. Travellers buy traditional products and souvenirs, but quickly these are mass-produced. This commercialization destroys traditional art and craft.

Many people believe that tourists try to learn something about local customs and lifestyles, but it might be that local people actually end up learning more about Western culture. They see wealthy visitors who seem to have every material possession and they want the same. We have all seen pictures of children in poor African villages wearing Manchester United shirts and holding mobile phones. Tourists do not always respect local customs, and they sometimes behave in a way that is inappropriate or even offensive to local people. When I was on holiday in Greece, I was shocked to see how some young travellers behaved at night.

All in all, I would like to believe that tourism is of cultural benefit to both people travelling and the people in the country that is being visited. However, I am not sure that that is really the case, and I am worried that traditional lifestyles are being changed by the increased number of visitors.

Tapescript

Note that in some listening extracts where the speakers are foreign students, there are occasional grammatical errors or words used wrongly. These errors are reproduced in the tapescripts.

Track 1
Unit 1 Speaking 2

B   Listen and check your answers.

1
Examiner: Where are you from?
Student: From Riyadh. It's the capital city.
2
Examiner: What's your city like?
Student: It's very big and very busy.
3
Examiner: How old are you?
Student: I'm twenty-four.
4
Examiner: What do you do for a living?
Student: I'm an accountant.
5
Examiner: Do you have a big family?
Student: Yes, I have five brothers and two sisters.
6
Examiner: Are you married?
Student: No, I'm single.
7
Examiner: Do you have any children?
Student: Yes, one son. His name's Sam.
8
Examiner: What are your hobbies and interests?
Student: I read a lot and sometimes play chess.

Track 2
Unit 1 Speaking 2

Pronunciation check
Listen to these questions again. Notice the contraction of *is* and the pronunciation of *are* and *do*.
1   What's your city like?
2   Where are you from?
3   Do you have a big family?
Practise asking the questions using the weak forms.

Track 3
Unit 1 Vocabulary 1

A   Listen and write the words. Focus on your spelling.
1   father   2   mother
3   brother   4   sister
5   grandfather   6   son
7   daughter   8   aunt
9   uncle   10 cousin

Track 4
Unit 1 Vocabulary 1

Pronunciation check
Listen again and notice that in *mother*, *brother* and *son* the letter 'o' is pronounced /ʌ/. The sound /ʌ/ is very common in family words.
Practise saying the words.

Track 5
Unit 1 Listening 1

C   Now listen and check your ideas.
1   Hi, is that Martin? Hi, I'm here in New York. I'm staying at the Ocean Inn on Tenth Avenue.
2   (*fade in*) … and she died in 1984, a year after her husband.
3   (*fade in*) … and, of course, you can contact us on 0207 389 152, twenty-four hours a day.
4   I'm not really sure. I think the best person to talk to is Tom Henderson.
5   (*fade in*) … and the whole package costs $320.
6   (*fade in*) … Yes, that's Bournemouth, and the host family address is 56 Green Lane.
7   (*fade in*) … and incredibly, he started playing the violin at just four years old.
8   Simon and Rebecca have known each other for twenty years.
9   (*fade in*) … and the tour ends in Manchester on the fifteenth of July.
10 (*fade in*) … so, I think that's everything. The next meeting will be on April the seventeenth.

Track 6
Unit 1 Listening 1

D   Listen again and fill in the missing information.
   [Play track 5 again]

Track 7
Unit 1 Listening 2

A   Listen and complete the notes about two people who work at Esco Engineering. Write no more than three words or a number for each answer.
Greg: Oh, hi Maggie. It's Greg.
Maggie: Hi, Greg.
Greg: I'm phoning to check some information about some of the staff. I'm putting all the staff data into new files, and I notice that I don't have files for two people. I think you might have them.

Maggie: Oh, really? What are their names?

Greg: Peter Austin and Jane Moore.

Maggie: Let me have a look. Yes, I've got them here. Shall I send them to you?

Greg: No, you don't need to. Just give me the information now. I can write it on some new files. I don't really need the photos if you've got photos there.

Maggie: OK. Well, Peter Austin first.

Greg: Now, is that Austin with an 'i' or Austen with an 'e'?

Maggie: It's A-U-S-T-I-N, and his address is a hundred and ten Argyle Street, Tunbridge Wells, Kent TN3 5RQ.

Greg: A hundred and ten?

Maggie: Uh-huh.

Greg: And his phone number?

Maggie: It's 07984 645792.

Greg: OK – and how old is he?

Maggie: He's forty-seven.

Greg: Forty-seven. And what about his marital status?

Maggie: He's married. There's a note here that he has three children – two boys and a girl.

Greg: OK, and finally – when did he join the company?

Maggie: He started with Esco in August two thousand and three.

Greg: Thanks, Maggie. Now, what about Jane?

Maggie: Her name's Jane Moore. That's M-O-O-R-E, and her address is 72 Cedar Road, Crowborough, Kent CR3 5RQ.

Greg: CR3 and what, sorry?

Maggie: CR3 5RQ.

Greg: And how do you spell Cedar?

Maggie: C-E-D-A-R. Her phone number is 07984 650396.

Greg: 07984 650396.

Maggie: Yes. Now, she's twenty-two and she's single.

Greg: OK.

Maggie: And she started with Esco in 2005 – February 2005.

Greg: Right, thanks, Maggie. That's very helpful. Goodbye now.

Maggie: Goodbye.

Track 8

Unit 1 Consolidation – Vocabulary

C Mark the main stress on these key words from the unit. Then listen and check. Practise saying the words.

1 interests
2 family
3 relatives
4 teenager
5 retirement
6 adolescence
7 improve

Track 9

Unit 1 Exam practice – Listening

A For questions 1–4, listen and complete the notes. Write no more than three words or a number for each answer.

Guest: Good evening.

Receptionist: Good evening. How can I help?

Guest: I have a reservation in the name of Hunt – a reservation for two nights. That's Charles Hunt.

Receptionist: Yes, Mr Hunt, let me see. Ah, here it is. Yes, two nights. I'll just need to photocopy your passport – do you have it?

Guest: Um, yes, of course – there you are.

Receptionist: Thank you. Could you just write your home address on the form here, while I copy the passport?

Guest: Yes, of course.

Receptionist: Thank you. Oh, you're from Manchester. I was there two years ago for a football match. Manchester has a very good team.

Guest: Yes, that's true. I'm actually more interested in rugby myself.

Receptionist: Here's your key. You're in room one-oh-four – that's on the first floor. It's an interior room, so it should be very quiet. I think you asked for that.

Guest: Oh yes, thank you. It's very important to sleep well when you have work to do. Can you tell me if the bill is already paid? I'm here for a conference and my company is paying the bill. Usually they pay it before I travel, but sometimes I have to pay and then claim expenses.

Receptionist: Let me check. Don't worry, sir, the bill has been paid in full.

Guest: Oh, good, that's one thing I don't need to worry about. Is the restaurant still open? I know it's late, but the meal on the plane was tiny – and not very tasty either.

Receptionist: I'm sorry, sir – the restaurant closes at nine-thirty, but there are two or three very nice places near the hotel. They will be open for a while.

Guest: Oh, good. I'll have a quick shower and then get something. Which restaurant do you recommend?

Receptionist: Mamma Mia's is probably best. It's very close to the hotel, and it isn't at all expensive – the food is delicious. When you come out of the hotel, you go right and then take the first left. You'll come into a big square and you'll see Mamma Mia's on the right.

Guest: That sounds great. Oh, and one more thing – sorry – is there a cash machine nearby? I didn't have time to get any euros at the airport.

Receptionist: Yes, the nearest bank is very close, too. Turn left out of the hotel and go down to the harbour. Turn left and you'll see the bank. There are two cash machines outside.

Guest: Thank you very much.

Receptionist: Not at all. I hope you enjoy your meal and your stay with us. Goodnight.

For questions 5–7, listen and choose the correct answer.
[Play track 9 again]

For questions 8 and 9, label the map. Write the correct letter A–F next to the places below.
[Play track 9 again]

Track 12
Unit 2 Speaking 1

Pronunciation check
Listen to the pronunciation of these subjects. Practise saying the ending /ɪ k s/, as in 'Physics', 'Mathematics', 'Economics'.

Track 13
Unit 2 Speaking 1

Pronunciation check
Listen to the pronunciation of the regular verbs in the sentences. Note the difference between /t/ and /d/ and /id/ at the end of verbs.
1   I finished my homework late last night.
2   I played football after school.
3   I hated Physics at school.

Track 14
Unit 2 Speaking 2

A   Look at these questions about being at school. Then listen to some students answering them. Tick the speaker who gives a better answer.
1
Examiner: Did you enjoy being at school?
Speaker 1: No, I didn't.
Examiner: Did you enjoy being at school?
Speaker 2: Well, I enjoyed school when we studied the subjects I was good at, but I didn't really enjoy it when we studied Maths and Physics. I found those lessons very difficult.
2
Examiner: What was your favourite subject at school?
Speaker 1: History. I was very good at remembering dates, and I loved learning about kings and queens.
Examiner: What was your favourite subject at school?
Speaker 2: Maths. I like my teacher of Maths.
3
Examiner: Who was your favourite teacher at school?
Speaker 1: Mr Adams. But I also liked Mr Brown.
Examiner: Who was your favourite teacher at school?
Speaker 2: I think it was Mr Lindsey. He was our English teacher. He made the lessons really interesting and wasn't strict like some of the other teachers.

Track 15
Unit 2 Listening 1

B   Listen and check. Then practise saying the numbers again.
16
60
100
160
166
600
606

616
660
666

Track 16
Unit 2 Listening 1

C   Listen and write the numbers that you hear.
1   18   2   80
3   96   4   120
5   243   6   531
7   852   8   984

Track 17
Unit 2 Listening 1

D   Listen and practise saying these bigger numbers.
1,000
10,000
100,000
1,100
1,500
1,550
1,555

Track 18
Unit 2 Listening 1

G   Listen to the pronunciation of the months. Then practise saying them.
January
February
March
April
May
June
July
August
September
October
November
December

Track 19
Unit 2 Listening 1

I   Listen to the pronunciation of the ordinal numbers. Then practise saying them.
1   first   2   second
3   third   4   fourth
5   fifth   6   sixth
7   seventh   8   eighth
9   ninth   10 tenth
11 twelfth   12 fifteenth
13 twentieth   14 twenty-fifth
15 thirtieth

Track 20
Unit 2 Listening 1

J Listen to someone saying the date below in two different ways.
1. The fifteenth of December
2. December the fifteenth

Track 21
Unit 2 Listening 1

L Listen and write the dates that you hear.
1. the second of June
2. November the twenty-first
3. the seventeenth of July
4. August the thirty-first

Track 22
Unit 2 Listening 2

A A man is telephoning his local college about a course. For questions 1 and 2, listen and choose the correct answer.

Receptionist: Good morning, City College.

Graham: Oh, good morning. I'm phoning about the photography course that you run.

Receptionist: Well, actually, there are three courses. It depends on your level. One course is for beginners, the second is for people with a little experience – we call that the intermediate course – and the third is an advanced course, for people who already know quite a lot about the subject.

Graham: Oh, I see. Well, I'm quite a keen photographer, but at the moment it's just a hobby. I want to learn more so that I might be able to do some work professionally at some time. I think the intermediate course would be a bit easy for me. Perhaps the advanced course would be best. When does it start?

Receptionist: The advanced course starts on September the eighteenth.

Graham: OK, just let me note that down – the eighteenth of September. And how long does the course run for?

Receptionist: It's a twelve-week course, but there's a week off in the middle for half-term. So, you do twelve lessons over thirteen weeks.

Graham: So, what's the date that the course finishes?

Receptionist: It finishes on the fourteenth of December.

Graham: The fourteenth – OK – that's quite near Christmas, isn't it? Can you tell me how much the course costs?

Receptionist: Yes, it's ninety-six pounds.

Graham: Ninety-six, that's not too bad.

Receptionist: That's paid in advance. And I'm afraid there's no refund if for any reason you can't complete the course.

Graham: Yes, of course. That's fair. How many people are there usually in the class? I've heard the groups are quite small.

Receptionist: Well, we can't say for sure, but there are usually between six and ten people in a group. On the last advanced course, there were seven participants.

Graham: Oh, good. That sounds perfect. Can I enrol for the course now – on the phone?

Receptionist: Yes, of course. I'll take your details now, and you can pay by card now or send us a cheque if you prefer. So, first of all, what's your name?

Graham: It's Graham Merton – that's M-E-R-T-O-N.

Receptionist: And your address?

Graham: Flat three, a hundred and nine Chelsea Court. That's in Oxford.

Receptionist: OK, and how old are you? We like to know more or less the age of each group.

Graham: I'm twenty-eight.

Receptionist: OK, Graham. We'll send confirmation and some course information in the post. Now, how would you like to pay?

Graham: I'll pay with my card now.

Receptionist: OK, if you can … (fade out)

For questions 3–8, complete the man's notes. Write <u>no more than three words or a number</u> for each answer.
[Play track 22 again]

For questions 9–12, complete the booking form that the receptionist fills in.
[Play track 22 again]

Track 23
Unit 2 Consolidation – Speaking

B Listen and check.

1
Examiner: What was your favourite subject at school?
Student: I loved History because I was really good at it.

2
Examiner: Who was your best friend at primary school?
Student: His name was Marcus. He lived next door and we walked to school together.

3
Examiner: How did you get to school in the morning – did you walk or take a bus?
Student: Actually, my dad used to drive me to school.

4
Examiner: Why did you go to college instead of staying at school?
Student: Because the college had more subjects to choose from. I wanted to study Philosophy.

5
Examiner: Do you remember any school trips? Where did you go?
Student: I remember once we went to a museum in London. I think it was the Natural History Museum.

6
Examiner: In some countries, children learn languages from an early age. When did you start learning English?

Student: When I was eleven. We didn't do English at primary school.

Track 24
Unit 2 Consolidation – Speaking

C   Listen again and notice how the second speaker answers each question.
[Play track 23 again]

Track 25
Unit 2 Consolidation – Vocabulary

C   Mark the main stress on these words. Then listen and check. Practise saying the words.
1   favourite
2   advantage
3   professional
4   safety
5   licence
6   certificate
7   support

Track 28
Unit 3 Vocabulary 1

A   Listen and write the job names. Be careful with your spelling.
1   accountant
2   engineer
3   architect
4   lawyer
5   mechanic
6   electrician
7   manager
8   assistant

Track 29
Unit 3 Vocabulary 1

B   Listen again and mark the main stress on each word.
[Play track 28 again]

Track 30
Unit 3 Speaking 2

Pronunciation check
Listen and notice the pronunciation of *would you* and *could you*. Practise saying the sentences.
1   What job would you most like?
2   Do you think you could do his job?

Track 31
Unit 3 Listening 1

B   Listen to the four extracts and match them with the pictures. Write the number of the extract in the box.
1
Female voice: So, why do you want to leave the job you're doing now?
Male voice: Well, I don't really want to leave, but I need a new challenge. I need to try something I haven't done before. I've been at the same place for longer than I planned.

Female voice: So, would you say that you're ambitious?
2
Male voice: Take a look at this.
Female voice: What is it?
Male voice: It's the design for the new web page. Tony has just sent it through. What do you think?
Female voice: Well, it looks good, but I'd need to ...
3
Female voice: Steve – have you seen this job? It looks like what you're looking for.
Male voice: Let me see. Oh, that's the one in Croydon, isn't it? The job looks quite interesting, but it's not very well paid, and travelling to Croydon every day would be so expensive.
Female voice: What about this one? It's more local.
Male voice: Yeah, I saw that one, too. I'm thinking about it, but the money's not great, is it?
4
Male voice 1: Mike – hey, Mike!
Male voice 2: Oh, hi Peter. I didn't know you worked in London. I haven't seen ...
Male voice 1: No, I'm just going up for the day. I've got to see some people about a new project. So, do you do the journey every day? It must be a bit repetitive.
Male voice 2: Oh, it's not too bad. It gives me thinking time, and I usually get some work done on the laptop ... (*fade out*)

Track 32
Unit 3 Listening 1

F   Listen to the four extracts and match them with the images in Exercise E.
Extract 1
Young male 1: Have you applied for that job you saw in the paper last week? You said you were interested.
Young male 2: Yeah, but I haven't heard anything yet. I really hope they give me an interview.
Extract 2
Receptionist: Do you know where to find us? OK – well, when you come out of the station, take a left. Walk for about five minutes and then take a right into Wallingham Road. You'll see us there. It's a big red-brick building.
Extract 3
US male voice: So, what sort of day have you got today?
US female voice: Oh, don't ask! Really, really busy. I've gotta be at a meeting with Doug by nine, and then at eleven I'm supposed to be seeing Tim at ABC. I hope I get there in time. I'll be working on the Chicago project all afternoon ... I've no idea what time I'll finish this evening. How about you?
Extract 4
Male voice: I'm pleased to say that the first half of this year is looking better than for the same period last year. March was an especially good month – sales hit ten thousand for the first time in nearly three years, and ... (*fade out*)

Track 33
Unit 3 Listening 2

A **Listen to the four extracts. For questions 1–4, match the extracts with the pictures. Write the number of the extract in the box.**

Extract 1

Assistant manager: Oh, good morning. It's Toby, isn't it? Let me just finish this e-mail and I'll be with you. Sit down for a minute.

New staff member: Thanks.

Assistant manager: OK, that's done. Hello again, I met you when you came for the interview last month – I'm Julie. I'm Keith's assistant manager.

New staff member: Yes, I remember.

Assistant manager: I'm afraid Keith isn't here this morning, so I'm going to show you round. You're starting with us on Monday, aren't you?

New staff member: Yes, that's right.

Assistant manager: Well, thanks for coming in today. We always think it's good for people to have a good look round and meet some of the other staff before they start the job properly. Would you like a tea or coffee before we start?

New staff member: Um, no, thank you – I had a coffee on the train.

Assistant manager: OK, well, where shall we begin? First of all, this is the office I share with Keith. It can be very busy in here – people just come in and out when they like ... (*fade out*)

Extract 2

Male speaker: OK, now I'm going to show you the plans for the new city-centre offices. Let me just turn this on ... here we are. This is the ground-floor plan and, as you can see, the area surrounding the offices – the car park and gardens, and so on.

Male speaker: The entrance is here on West Street, and there's quite a large area here outside the front entrance. We'll probably have some bays here, where you can lock up bicycles. The car park is at the back, here – there are spaces for thirty cars. Now, I know that thirty spaces isn't nearly enough ... (*fade out*)

Extract 3

Female voice: Oh, hi Justin. Can I speak to Robert, please? Thanks. Hello, Robert, it's Debbie – listen, I'm afraid I'm going to be a bit late. There's trouble with signals or something. We haven't moved for ten minutes and I don't know when it'll be clear again. I'm still seven stops from the office – I'm sorry, I should have left home earlier. Can you start the meeting, and then I'll ... (*fade out*)

Extract 4

Salesman: Good afternoon, madam.

Customer: Oh, hello.

Salesman: Did you see the catalogue I put through the door last week – Kleenhouse Products?

Customer: Oh, yes, I did have a quick look, but ...

Salesman: Well, today I'm here to show you some of the products. Have you got ten minutes?

Customer: Well, actually, I'm rather busy – I was in the middle of ...

Salesman: Five minutes, then. You won't find any of these kitchen and bathroom products at such low prices anywhere else.

Customer: No, I'm sorry, I said I was busy. I don't really need anything like this at the moment ... (*fade out*)

Read through the questions. Then listen to the extracts again. For questions 5–12, choose the correct answer a, b or c.

[Play track 33 again]

Track 34
Unit 3 Consolidation – Speaking

C **Listen to a student doing the exam. Which words does he check? Highlight them on the card.**

Student: Can I check a few words on the card before I start to make my notes?

Examiner: Yes, please do.

Student: This word 'ideal' – does it mean something like 'perfect'?

Examiner: Yes, it means more or less the same thing.

Student: OK, and what about 'personal qualities'? I'm not sure I understand exactly what that means.

Examiner: Your personal qualities are the things about you that make you good for the job – the right person for the job.

Student: You mean, like if I'm hard-working or lazy?

Examiner: Yes, those are good examples.

Student: Thank you. Finally, I want to check 'appealing'. Does it mean 'what makes me want to do the job'? Is it a bit like 'attractive'?

Examiner: Yes, that's right. Now, are you ready? You have a minute to plan what you want to say and make notes.

Track 35
Unit 3 Consolidation – Speaking

D **Look at the tapescript and listen again. Notice how the student asked questions and how the examiner answered.**

[Play track 34 again]

Track 36
Unit 3 Consolidation – Vocabulary

B **Listen and write these words from the unit in your notebook. Check your spelling. Then mark the main stress on each word.**

1 experience
2 successful
3 career
4 challenging
5 promotion
6 professional
7 financial
8 qualified
9 advertisement
10 applicant

Track 37
Unit 3 Exam practice – Listening

B Look through the questions carefully. Then listen and answer the questions. For questions 1 and 2, choose the correct answer a, b or c.

Female voice: So, Simon, I hear you're working from home, too, these days.

Male voice 1: Yeah, that's right. Well, I go into the office once a week, but I'm at home most of the time.

Female voice: Are you enjoying it?

Male voice 1: Well, there's good and bad, you know how it is. I didn't really choose to start working from home, and the rest of the family are not very happy about it – I'm always telling them to be quiet. The company decided that they had to close one of the offices. About twenty people had no office, and there wasn't enough space in the main office for twenty more people. So, they decided some of us would work at home.

Male voice 2: So, do you find that you get more work done?

Male voice 1: Well, yes and no. Sometimes, I really get a lot done in a very short time. In the office, there's always someone coming and asking a question, or starting a conversation about something. At home, you don't have that, of course. On the other hand, it's easy to get distracted by jobs around the house. You start cleaning or tidying up or mending something. When you're in the house all day, it's difficult to leave things alone. Sometimes it's midday before I really start work.

Female voice: Yeah, and I find that I often get distracted by the TV or surfing the net. When everyone's out of the house, I like to make a cup of coffee and watch the TV for ten minutes. I must admit, it's often more like an hour.

Male voice 2: My wife and the children don't really understand that I'm really working when I'm at home. You know – they think I have time to do jobs around the house as well. 'Jerry – could you fix the tap in the bathroom today?' 'Dad – can you drive me to football club this afternoon?' It makes me crazy.

Female voice: You just have to tell them you're at work. I have a friend who works from home and he puts his suit on in the morning. He says that it makes him feel like he's really at work.

Male voice 1: I must say that one thing I *do* like is not having to get ready for work in the morning. I can just put on a pair of jeans or shorts – and I don't need to shave for three days.

Female voice: So, has your company set you up with a new computer or given you a new laptop?

Male voice 1: That's a bit of a problem, actually. They've set me up with a new computer – it's really modern, and the Internet is really fast, but they say that I should only use it for work – you know – they don't want me using it for personal business. They want me to use my own computer for anything that's not connected with the job.

Male voice 2: So, you have two computers?

Male voice 1: Yeah, I don't really understand. So, do you two get a bit lonely working from home? I mean, don't you miss having other people around – discussing things and solving problems together?

Female voice: Yeah, I would like to spend more time with people. I had some good friends at work and I don't really see them much now.

Male voice 2: I'm always really pleased when somebody phones or e-mails me. You know – sometimes you go all day without speaking to anyone. My wife says that in the evening, I never stop talking.

Female voice: Well, I think more and more people will have to do it. Now that everyone has a computer at home and e-mailing is so fast, there's just no need for everyone to travel to work.

Male voice 1: Yes, I think you're right. In the future, it'll be … (*fade out*)

For questions 3–8, choose <u>six</u> answers from A–J. Which of these points do the speakers mention when they talk about working from home?

[Play track 37 again]

Track 39
Unit 4 Speaking 1

C Listen to some people talking. Match each extract with one of the photos in Exercise A.

Extract 1

I want to talk about [BLEEP]. I don't like everything about her, but to become the Prime Minister of Britain at that time was incredible. Not only was she the first woman to become the Prime Minister, but she was from a normal background – you know, she didn't come from a rich family or anything like that. She had a very big influence on the twenty-first century – certainly in Britain.

Extract 2

Real achievement means creating something – leaving something for people to see in the future. Writers, artists and film-makers are important, but I think architects are special. They leave something real – something that everyone can look at and use. [BLEEP] is probably the most important architect in the world at the moment. More people should know about him.

Extract 3

[BLEEP] is the ruler of Abu Dhabi. He's one of the most powerful men in the Middle East and one of the richest in the world. He uses his wealth to help his country. He pays the best designers and architects to turn Abu Dhabi into a very important country.

Extract 4

Well, here's someone who has really overcome difficulties to succeed. Her name's [BLEEP]. It's difficult for fully able people to succeed in sport – to do it when you have a physical disability like hers is just amazing. She's a superwoman.

Extract 5

I'd like to say something about [BLEEP]. He's the only one who's no longer alive. I think he died in the nineteen-twenties. I think what he achieved shows true courage. He had the mental strength to achieve his dream and the physical strength to succeed in terrible conditions.

Extract 6

This is a picture of the child prodigy, [BLEEP], from Singapore. I think he's only about six years old, but he's already passed exams. Now, he's studying Chemistry at a college. Achieving something like this at such a young age is just fantastic. What will he achieve by the time he's forty or fifty?

Track 40
Unit 4 Vocabulary 2

Pronunciation check

Listen to the contractions in these sentences.
1   I've achieved a lot this year.
2   He's overcome many difficulties.
Now listen to how the negative forms *haven't* and *hasn't* are pronounced in natural speech.
3   I haven't achieved what I wanted to.
4   She hasn't done everything yet.
Now listen to how *have you*, *has he* and *has she* are pronounced in these questions.
5   Have you achieved all that you hoped?
6   Has he done what he wanted to do?
7   Has she been successful?
Practise saying all the sentences.

Track 41
Unit 4 Listening 2

B   Listen to this extract that provides an answer to the question in Listening 1D. Choose a, b or c.

Male voice: (*fade in*) ... so, once you've got that, you then have to do your homework. Look through local directories or take a tour of the town. If other companies are providing a similar service, you should try to offer something a bit different. Of course, you must expect competition, but starting up a business in an area where everyone is trying to sell the same thing is dangerous. And don't just put your prices down. Customers are not always attracted to the provider who charges less than everyone else.

Track 42
Unit 4 Listening 2

C   Listen again and identify the words and phrases that provide the answer and tell you that the other options are wrong. Then check the tapescript on page 284.
[Play track 41 again]

Track 43
Unit 4 Listening 3

B   Listen to somebody giving a talk about how setting goals can help you achieve more. For questions 1–4, choose the correct letter a, b or c.

Good evening, everyone. It's good to see that so many people managed to make it – an achievement in itself when I'm sure you're all so busy. This evening, I'm going to talk with you about setting goals, and how setting goals can help you understand what you really want to achieve. First, though, I'd like to start by saying what I think achievement actually means. I think some people think it's simply about being successful in a job or making money, but it certainly doesn't have to mean that. Achievement is simply accomplishing goals that you set for yourself – doing what you planned to do – and people might plan to do all sorts of different things.

Achievement is about realizing your dreams. I would also like to say that to achieve, you must have belief – belief that you can do whatever it is you want to do. There is more to achievement than simply wanting to do something. Anyone can say that they want something, but actually getting it is not so easy. To get it, you must believe that it is yours. Not having belief is the main reason that so many people do not achieve. If you really want something, you must talk and act like you already have it – then you have belief, and then you will achieve.

So, goal setting. Goal setting is about imagining the future, and then turning the dream into a reality. Setting goals helps you to be clear about what you really want, and helps you concentrate on getting what you want. Setting goals will help you see what is stopping you from knowing what's important. And because achieving goals makes you feel good, you will be more confident and succeed more easily. Goal setting is something that all achievers do, whether they are high-flyers in business or successful athletes.

It is important that you set both long-term and short-term goals. First, you need to have an idea of what you want from life – I call this the 'big picture' – then, you break this down into a number of smaller goals that you need to achieve in order to achieve the overall goal. As I say, the first step is to see the big picture. Think about what you want in the next fifteen or twenty years – doing this will influence all the smaller goals that you set yourself. You need to think carefully about different areas of your life and how they influence each other. You should identify the important areas of your life, and try to set goals in each of those areas.

Here are the areas that most people want to focus on, but remember that everyone is different. First, think about your career – how important is your career to you? Do you want to be a manager or run your own business, or are you happy working for other people? Connected to this is the financial side of your life – what sort of income do you want to have? Is wealth important to you?

You need to think about long-term relationships – at what age do you hope to be married? Do you want to have children? How much time do you want to spend with the people you love?

You need to think about your health and how that could change what you can achieve. How will you stay healthy as you get older? Do you do anything that is not good for your health, and how will you try to do those things less or stop doing them completely?

Finally, you need to think about your free time – your hobbies and interests. How much time do you want to have to do what you really enjoy? It is difficult to achieve goals in one area if you feel that you don't have the time to do the things that really make you happy.

Now, when you have this overall picture, try to set yourself one goal for each area. Make sure the goals are what you really want, and not what you think other people want from you. Of course, in life, it is important to make the people around you happy, but you must focus on what you want.

Now, I will go on to talk about how to break your lifetime plan down into short-term goals. But first, does anyone have any questions about what I've said so far?

For questions 5–9, choose <u>five</u> answers from A–H. When the speaker talks about different areas of life, which of these does he mention?
[Play track 43 again]

For question 10, choose the correct letter a, b or c.
[Play track 43 again]

Track 44
Unit 4 Writing 2

C   **Two British students are brainstorming ideas before they do this writing task. Listen and note down the points they make.**
   Male voice: So, first of all, do you agree with the statement?
   Female voice: Yes, I do. Too many people think that if you make a lot of money, you are successful. I don't think making money means that you are happy, and for me, being happy is the most important thing. Being happy is an achievement.
   Male voice: Yes, I suppose so, but I don't think that you must be happy to say that you have achieved something. People like artists and scientists achieve great things, but that doesn't mean they are happy. Sometimes people like that are quite unhappy.
   Female voice: Yes, that's true, but the important thing is that the people you mention – artists and scientists – achieve great things, but not only for the money. People should see that.
   Male voice: Don't you think that people do recognize the achievements of people like that?
   Female voice: No, not really. If you ask people to name a modern-day scientist, they will know one or two, but if you ask them to name actors or footballers, they will know hundreds. I think they know those people because they are rich and famous.
   Male voice: Yes, I guess some people are even famous just because they are rich – like Paris Hilton.

   Female voice: And I'm sure most people know Bill Gates because he was the richest man in the world – not because he was so brilliant.
   Male voice: You mentioned footballers before. Don't you think that people in sport are considered successful because they win medals and prizes? They don't all make lots of money. Everyone likes Olympic athletes because they do something special.
   Female voice: Yes, I agree, but most sportsmen are very rich – especially footballers, and they are the most famous. It seems that more and more of them are doing it for the money.
   Male voice: OK, but what about ordinary people? Do you think that people who do important jobs, like nurses and teachers, think that they have achieved something?
   Female voice: Maybe – but I'm not sure that most people think that nurses and teachers are real achievers. Images on TV and in magazines make people think that they should make big money and live in beautiful houses and drive expensive cars. That's what they understand by success.
   Male voice: Yes, people who work in advertising, for example, are considered successful, even though other people do more useful jobs. Perhaps we should think that real achievement is helping people and doing good for people – even saving somebody's life. If somebody goes to Africa to save children, people respect them – but I'm not sure that they really think that that person is successful.
   Female voice: Yes, that's a very good point. Doing good for other people is an achievement, but I still think that being happy is the real aim of life. If you are happy and your family is happy, then you have really achieved something.

Track 45
Unit 4 Writing 2

E   **Listen to the students in Exercise C again. Highlight the points in the composition as you hear them.**
   [Play track 44 again]

Track 46
Unit 4 Consolidation – Speaking

C   **Listen to some students answering the question. Mark each speaker (G) good answer or (NG) not a good answer.**
   Examiner: … and do you think people are born to achieve or do they learn to achieve?
   Speaker 1: Yes, I think so.
   Examiner: … and do you think people are born to achieve or do they learn to achieve?
   Speaker 2: I don't know – maybe are born with this ability.
   Examiner: … and do you think people are born to achieve or do they learn to achieve?
   Speaker 3: Mm, I didn't think about it before. Some people is born very clever so maybe can achieve a lot. Other people is not so clever, but try and try and

try – maybe that is learn to achieve.

Examiner: ... and do you think people are born to achieve or do they learn to achieve?

Speaker 4: Mm, it's a good question. I guess some people are born to achieve. You know, like a genius or someone with an incredible talent, but some people learn to achieve. Maybe their parents teach them good things or they learn by mistakes.

Track 48
Unit 5 Vocabulary 1

B Listen and check your answers.

1 This is very difficult to calculate.
2 I predict a fall in the price of oil.
3 Can you be quiet? I can't concentrate.
4 Can you imagine living somewhere like that?
5 Mm, I can't decide which one I want.
6 I'll consider your offer and call you in a few days.

Track 49
Unit 5 Vocabulary 1

Pronunciation check

Listen and notice how /t/ at the end of *don't* and *can't* is not pronounced clearly in fast natural speech, especially when the following verb begins with a consonant sound.

1 I don't think so.   2 I can't concentrate.
3 I don't know.   4 I can't decide.

Practise saying all the sentences.

Track 50
Unit 5 Speaking 2

B Listen to some students answering the questions. For each question, tick the speaker who gives the better answer.

1 Speaker A
Examiner: So, are you going to university next year?
Speaker A: Yes, I am.
1 Speaker B
Examiner: So, are you going to university next year?
Speaker B: Yes, I'm really looking forward to it.
2 Speaker A
Examiner: Tell me something about your job.
Speaker A: I'm a lawyer.
2 Speaker B
Examiner: Tell me something about your job.
Speaker B: I'm a lawyer. It's quite challenging, but I really enjoy it.
3 Speaker A
Examiner: Do you work hard?
Speaker A: Yes, but I don't mind. It's always interesting.
3 Speaker B
Examiner: Do you work hard?
Speaker B: Yes, very hard.

4 Speaker A
Examiner: Tell me about your hometown.
Speaker A: It's a very big town.
4 Speaker B
Examiner: Tell me about your hometown.
Speaker B: Well, it's very big, but not too big. I really enjoy living there.
5 Speaker A
Examiner:. What do you do in your free time?
Speaker A: I'm very keen on basketball. I think it's the most exciting sport.
5 Speaker B
Examiner: What do you do in your free time?
Speaker B: I play basketball on Fridays.

Track 51
Unit 5 Speaking 2

C Listen again and complete the phrases below.
[Play track 50 again]

Track 52
Unit 5 Listening 1

B Listen to these extracts from five listening tasks. Match each with one of the diagrams in Exercise A.
1
Estate agent: OK, here we are. This one is a little bigger than the last one we saw, as I guess you can see. The owners are out for the day, so I'll need the key. Here we are. Right, as we go in, you'll see we're in a fairly large entrance hall – plenty of room for bicycles and wet umbrellas. Now, through here is the hall itself – very large and ... (*fade out*)
2
Voice: Now, remember we said that the human brain is not a single mechanism. It is, in fact, made up of a number of different parts. Each part controls a different function. Think of your brain as an orchestra, with many musicians playing an important part. First, we will look at this top view of the brain. As you can see, the frontal lobes are located just behind the forehead. It is the frontal lobes that are responsible for complex thinking, like imagining and planning. Behind the frontal lobes are the parietal lobes, and they ... (*fade out*)
3
Voice: Now, as most of you will already know, from the fifteenth century until 1956, the house was owned by the Clifton family – then, of course, it was bought by the Trust. I'd like to stop in the hallway here to take a look at the Clifton family tree. Right at the top here, you can see Charles Clifton, the original owner, and his wife, Margaret. They bought the property ... (*fade out*)
4
Voice: And down here, of course, we have the pedals. Most pianos have two or three pedals. They sustain or soften the sound as the instrument is played. They

are connected to the action by levers. Like all other parts ... (*fade out*)

5

Voice: With an old-style cathode-ray tube, the TV set takes the incoming signal and breaks it into its separate audio (sound) and video (picture) components. The aerial on the roof of the house picks up waves from the transmitter. The audio part feeds into an audio ... (*fade out*)

Track 53
Unit 5 Listening 1

C Listen again and fill in the missing information on each diagram. Use <u>no more than two words</u> for each.

[Play track 52 again]

Track 54
Unit 5 Listening 2

A Listen to the continuation of the lecture about the human brain. Look at the diagram before you listen. For questions 1–6, match the parts of the brain 1–6 with the parts a–f in the diagram. Write the letters in the space after each number.

Voice: OK, we have looked at the top view of the brain and seen how it is divided into lobes. Now, we are going to look at a more complex diagram of the centre of the brain. I will briefly go through some of the important parts that make up the brain, and then talk more about what each does. First of all, you can see that by far the largest part of the brain is the cerebrum, and it is made up of the three lobes we have already talked about. The lobe below, coloured yellow on the diagram here, is the cerebellum. Right in the centre of the brain, here, is the thalamus. The hypothalamus is part of it, but it has a slightly different function. Now, here, running down from the centre of the brain, is the brain stem. It is made up of the midbrain, the pons and the medulla oblongata, and is connected to the spinal cord, which you can see here at the bottom of the diagram. Now, finally, this little gland just to the left of the midbrain – it looks like a little tail – is the pituitary gland.

OK, let's go back and say something about the function of the various parts of the brain. The cerebrum – the largest part, as we have said – has two halves or hemispheres. I will talk more about the difference between the two hemispheres later. The cerebrum is the part of the brain that is really our intelligence. It controls voluntary movement – that is, movement that we are in control of – speaking, for example – but it is also responsible for our emotional thinking and memory. The cerebellum is responsible for fine movement and coordination. It helps us with balance, for example, and to understand where we are ... in relation to space around us. The thalamus, here in the centre, processes what we feel with our

body – touch and temperature, for example – and controls how we react to those senses. The hypothalamus has a similar function, but regulates bodily needs such as hunger and thirst, and tells us when we need sleep. Now, at the top of the brainstem is the midbrain. This is a sort of switchboard – a very complex switchboard. It sends messages which help the brain communicate with other parts of the nervous system. The pons, in the middle of the brain stem, here, sends messages from the cerebrum to the cerebellum and spinal cord. The medulla oblongata is here, just above the spinal cord. It regulates essential bodily functions, like breathing and the rate of our heartbeat. The spinal cord is part of the central nervous system and runs down inside the spinal column. It connects the brain to nerves that go to the rest of the body. Now, the pituitary gland – this little gland – has a hugely important function. It releases hormones to the body that regulate all sorts of things – how quickly we grow and the size we grow to, the rate at which we age ... It also regulates whether we have a slow or fast metabolism and how we relate to stress. Now, I am going to show you a model of the human brain and I want you to identify ... (*fade out*)

For questions 7–14, complete the descriptions. Use <u>one word only</u> for each answer.

[Play track 54 again]

Track 55
Unit 5 Consolidation – Vocabulary

B Listen and mark the main stress on the words in Exercise A above.

1 consider	2 prediction
3 imagination	4 concentrate
5 decision	6 memory

Track 56
Unit 5 Exam practice – Listening

A You will hear someone giving a talk about how mind-mapping can help you think more clearly. For questions 1–6, listen and complete the notes. Write <u>no more than three words or a number</u> for each answer.

Female voice: Good morning. I'm really pleased that so many of you are here. I know you are all busy. In some ways, that is what I'm going to talk about today – managing time, so that you feel more is getting done, that you are achieving more. I'm sure you have all heard something about mind-mapping, but most people I meet don't really know much about it. Mind-mapping is really a technique that helps you to think more clearly. It improves the way you solve problems and encourages you to solve problems creatively. Mind maps help you to understand the various parts of a topic or subject, and to then see how those parts fit together. The way you write down your ideas on a mind map means that information is easy to retrieve and to review.

So, how is mind-mapping different from conventional note-taking? By conventional note-taking, I mean simply listing points on a page, as you probably do now. Well, mind maps are more two-dimensional – they allow you to see the shape of a topic, and make it easier to see what's important. Mind maps generally fit on a single side of paper – they are more compact – and that also helps you to go back and review.

So, now I'm going to show an example of a mind map, and I hope it will make clear what I've been saying. Let me just switch on the projector. OK, here we are. Now, this is a mind map for time management – a mind map designed to help you manage your time better, and see where you are wasting time and where you could save time. Remember – this is only a very simple example. Your mind maps can be bigger.

Now, first, you need to write the topic in large letters in the middle of your page – in this case, 'time management'. Put a circle or a box around it, if you like. Then, draw lines out to the main subheadings – the main points that you want to consider as parts of the topic. In this case, the major subheadings are red. Put general ideas on the left. In this case, there are three general points that the author wants to keep in mind: assessing time – how much time he has. Personal performance – by personal performance, he means how well he thinks he uses his time. And wasting time – how much of his time he thinks he uses badly, how much of his time is wasted. Above the main heading, the author thinks about having more time and how perhaps he could have more time. His mind map has branched out, and he puts examples of having more time in another colour – in this case, blue. He thinks about two ways that he could have more time. Firstly, delegating, and secondly, getting up earlier. Of course, if you get up earlier, the day is longer and you have more time! Above delegating, he gives an example of how he could delegate. He makes this another subheading and uses another colour – this time green. When he looks back at his mind map, he will see that one way that he could delegate is to get other people to do more around the office – perhaps he does too much himself at the moment.

Now, on the right, the author thinks about how he can use time more effectively – note again that this is one of his main subheadings, so it is written in red. As subheadings of that, he gives examples of how he could use time more effectively.

At the bottom, he thinks about prioritizing, and then he gives two examples of how he wants to prioritize – firstly, he explains what he means by prioritize – he must decide what is most important. Then, he notes how he can prioritize – by setting goals. The mind map will help him to remember that

he must always have a clear idea of what is important, and that by setting goals, he can achieve more.

Finally, he decides that planning is important, and that is another subheading. He notes that keeping a diary is a good way to plan ahead, and so use time more effectively. Perhaps he doesn't keep one at the moment, but he will start keeping one now he has his mind map.

Now, as I say, the author will probably add more ideas – each time you review a mind map, you can add points or delete them. Of course, time management is only one area in which mind-mapping can be a help. Now, I'm going to talk about other areas of your life where mind-mapping can ... (fade out)

For questions 7–14, label the time management mind map below. Write no more than three words or a number for each answer.
[Play track 56 again]

Track 59
Unit 6 Vocabulary 1

C   Listen and tick the words and phrases as you hear them.

Voice: Hello, I'm Ubaid. I come from Cairo, which, as you probably know, is the capital of my country – Egypt. It's a huge city – one of the biggest and busiest in the world. I have lived here all my life and I love it. Some of the most famous attractions in the world are in Cairo, and it is a very popular tourist destination.

Voice: Hi. My name's Gulay, and I come from a small town on the south coast of Turkey called Fethiye. Not long ago, Fethiye was a little fishing village, but now it is a popular seaside resort. During the summer months, hundreds of thousands of tourists visit and it is very lively.

Voice: Hello. My name is Cinzia. I live in a tiny village called Savoca. It is in Sicily, which is an island off the south coast of Italy. Savoca is in the mountains and it's very rural – most people are farmers. It is quiet, but very beautiful.

Voice: Hello there. I'm Mohammed, and I'm from Libya. I live in Benghazi, which is a large port on the north coast. Benghazi is Libya's second city, and it is an important economic centre. It is growing bigger all the time, but it is a very exciting place to live.

Track 60
Unit 6 Vocabulary 2

Pronunciation check

The ~est at the end of superlatives is pronounced /ɪst/. The /t/ is not pronounced clearly in fast natural speech, especially when the following noun begins with a consonant. Listen and practise these phrases.

1 the biggest city
2 the tallest building
3 the busiest street
The /t/ at the end of *most* is not pronounced clearly in fast natural speech, especially when the following adjective begins with a consonant.
Listen and practise these phrases.
1 most beautiful
2 most congested

Track 61
Unit 6 Listening 1

A   **Listen and match the extracts with the maps.**

1

Voice: The south of England is a very popular part of the world for students to come to learn English. London is, of course, the most popular destination. Hundreds of thousands of students study at one of the capital's many language schools every year. Brighton is a busy city on the south coast. It, too, has a large number of schools, and many attractions that young visitors can enjoy. Brighton is about an hour away from London by train. Eastbourne and Hastings are smaller seaside towns to the east of Brighton. Hastings is the larger of the two, and has a few more study options. Another seaside resort – this time further west, in Hampshire – is Bournemouth. Bournemouth is a large town with several popular schools, and a busy student scene. For a quieter stay, students come to the Isle of Wight, an island just off the south coast. A ferry service connects the island with the mainland. Inland, the best option is Tunbridge Wells, a small but historic town between the coast and London. Students like to stay in Tunbridge Wells because it is quieter than London, but close enough to London to visit easily.

2

Voice: Andalusia is the largest region in Spain, stretching from the border with Portugal in the west, to the south-east coast of Almeria. Most tourists come to Andalusia for the sandy beaches and nightlife, and know very little about the fantastic sights that the region offers. Seville and Cordoba are both historic cities with much to see, but Granada is perhaps the most impressive of the bigger cities. It is only an hour from the coast, and is the home of the Alhambra Palace, one of the most famous buildings in Europe. The palace was built over 800 years ago, but remains largely in one piece. Ronda is a smaller town, but the Roman Aqueduct brings visitors from all over the world. Ronda is a pretty town, and the viaduct is one of the most important examples of Roman architecture in Spain. Andalusia also offers other forms of relaxation and adventure. South of Granada is the Sierra Nevada, a mountain range that offers some of the best skiing in western Europe. Many skiers stay in Granada and drive up into the

mountains each day, but the mountain range now has a number of resorts with excellent accommodation. Much of the north of Andalusia is forest, and much of that is national park. The area also has some of the largest lakes in the country. Cazorla is probably the most popular village from which you can explore the forest and lakes by car or on foot.

3

Voice: Hi, Leo speaking. Hi, Tony. Didn't you bring a map with you? Oh, well, never mind – it's very easy. Come out of the station and walk straight down Queen's Road. Yeah, straight down – don't turn left or right. Walk past the cinema on the right, and then after three or four minutes, you'll come to a crossroads with a small clock tower in the middle of it. Turn right at the clock tower and walk up the hill. Take the third on the left – there's a taxi rank on the corner. No, on the left – the third turning. My apartment is on the right, about a hundred metres up the road.

Track 62
Unit 6 Listening 1

B   **Listen to the first extract and match the letters on the map with the places below.**
[Play track 61 again]

Track 63
Unit 6 Listening 1

C   **Listen to the second extract and complete each space with one word.**
[Play track 61 again]

Track 64
Unit 6 Listening 1

D   **Listen to the third extract and circle Leo's apartment on the map.**
[Play track 61 again]

Track 65
Unit 6 Listening 2

A   **Listen again. Notice examples of a speaker repeating information.**
[Play track 61 again]

Track 66
Unit 6 Listening 3

A   **Listen to a man talking to a group of people at a weekend work conference in a hotel. For questions 1–4, choose four correct statements from A–H.**

Voice: OK, can everyone listen again now, please? Now you know how much of the weekend will be work, and what some of the meetings and sessions are about, I'd like to tell you something about how you can spend some of the free time you have over the weekend – both inside the hotel, and outside in the town centre. As I've said, you'll be free from around five today and on Saturday, and from lunchtime on Sunday, and there's plenty to do. This is the first time we've had the conference at the Royal Spa Hotel, and I'm sure you'll agree it's a very nice place – really, there's no need to leave the hotel at all if you don't want to, but I'm sure some of you will want to get out for a change of environment.

OK – first, restaurants and bars. I'm sure you all saw that there was a bar near the entrance as you came into the hotel, but there are actually two more bars. One is also on the ground floor behind the main restaurant, and the other is on the top floor. That one has a very nice terrace where you can sit outside and enjoy the view. That bar is for hotel guests only, and is usually a bit quieter. As I say, the main restaurant is on the ground floor – we will have breakfast and lunch there, so you will get to know it well. There is also a smaller restaurant for coffee, sandwiches and snacks on the third floor, and that is also only for hotel guests. There is a gym and health club in the basement – the gym has a good range of equipment, and is open from seven a.m. I know some of you were talking about a swimming pool, but unfortunately there is no swimming pool. I will tell you where there is a pool close to the hotel in a moment. The health club has a sauna, which is open from ten a.m., but is not open on Sunday. There is a charge of four dollars for the sauna.

Now, I hope to see some of you around the hotel over the weekend, but I'm sure you will want to get out and see the town at some point. If you'd like to look at the map on the screen, I'll show the area around the hotel. There is a map of the town centre in your welcome pack, too. OK, you can see the hotel, here, in the middle of the map, and the main entrance, here, at the top in Carlisle Street. OK, that swimming pool I promised to tell you about is here in Cromwell Road. If you turn right out of the hotel, it's about ten minutes up the road, in the third street on the left. It's open until seven p.m., and until five on Sunday. There's a very nice park here to the north – again, about ten minutes away. In the middle of the park is a boating lake, so if the weather's good on Sunday, it might be a nice way to relax. If you want to see a movie this evening or on Saturday night, the cinema is here in the High Street.

Come out of the hotel and turn left. The High Street is only three minutes away. The cinema is here at the top of the street, next to a fairly large car park. Now, restaurants. There is a good Chinese restaurant in the middle of the High Street, here, on the right. It's directly opposite the Town Hall. It's called the White Orchid. Another very nice restaurant is Leonardo's. It does Spanish and Mexican food. It's here at the

bottom of the High Street. So, turn left at the end of Carlisle Street, walk down for five minutes, and you'll see it on the other side of the road. I went to Leonardo's last time I was here, so I can recommend it. Now, if anyone wants to see some live music, there is always a jazz band playing at the Pink Coconut. Yeah, that's right – the Pink Coconut. That's here in a little street behind the hotel. The street name is not on the map, but it's easy to find. Turn right out of the main entrance, and then take the first right to go back round to the back of the hotel. So, I think that's everything – please ask me if ... (fade out)

For questions 5–10, match the places with the letters on the map. You do not need to use all the letters on the map.
[Play track 66 again]

Track 67
Unit 6 Consolidation – Speaking

C Listen to some students giving good answers to the questions.

1
Examiner: Which city in the world would you most like to visit?
Student: I'd really like to go to Beijing and see the Forbidden City. I can imagine China is a very exciting place to visit.

2
Examiner: So, why do so many people live in cities?
Student: I think they have to live in cities because of their job. In Thailand, people leave the country and come to Bangkok because it is the best place to find work.

3
Examiner: Are some cities becoming too big?
Student: Yes, I think so. I don't know the biggest city, but Mexico City and Shanghai are huge. There are a lot of poor people and pollution is a problem. The capital of my country is Istanbul. It is very crowded, and it is very expensive to buy or rent an apartment.

4
Examiner: Do you enjoy city life or would you like to live somewhere quieter?
Student: I really enjoy living in Tehran. The university is the best in Iran, and I meet people from all over the country. There is much more to do in Tehran than there is in my hometown.

Track 68
Unit 6 Consolidation – Speaking

D Read the answers below. Then listen again and fill in the missing words.
[Play track 67 again]

Track 69
Unit 6 Exam practice – Listening

A You will hear an estate agent (a person who sells houses) showing a man and woman a house.
For questions 1–5, listen and complete the notes in the estate agent's diary.

Estate agent: Good morning. You must be Mr and Mrs Clarke.

Man: Yes, that's right. Good morning.

Woman: Good morning.

Estate agent: So, is it Clarke with an E, or Clarke without an E? I wrote it in my diary, but I wasn't sure if I spelt it correctly.

Man: It's with an E. C-L-A-R-K-E.

Estate agent: Yes, that's what I thought.

Man: Anyway, please call me Andy.

Woman: And I'm Laura.

Estate agent: And I'm Ian. Thanks for coming over to the office. I hope this time is convenient for you. Nine o'clock is a bit early for some people, but I like to make an early start if I can. I've got three houses that I want you to see today.

Man: Nine o'clock is fine. I have to go into work when we've seen all the properties.

Estate agent: OK, well let me show you on the map where the three houses are. They're all quite close together near Blaker's Park. Do you know Blaker's Park?

Woman: Yes, we know it really well. It's a nice area.

Estate agent: Well, the first one I'll show you is the closest to the park. It's actually on the road that runs around the park, Park Avenue, just here on the right – number 14, I think. Yes, number 14.

Man: So, you get a view of the park from the front windows?

Estate agent: Oh, yes, the view of the park is fantastic. The second house is here – on the left side – that's the west side of the park – in Havelock Road. That's number 35. It's right next door to St Anne's School. Do you have school-age children?

Woman: Well, we have a boy of three, so near the school would be very nice in a couple of years.

Estate agent: Well, all three houses are pretty near the school, as you can see. Now, the third property – that's actually the furthest from the park, up here on the north side – that's Whitely Road, number 62. It's still only a few minutes' walk to the park, though.

Man: Number 62 – that's the number we live at now.

Estate agent: Oh, really? So, shall we go and have a look? I'll drive and you can collect your car when we come back.

Man: OK, that sounds fine.

Estate agent: OK, here we are. As you can see, the front of the house is very nice. It's been painted recently. The front garden is small, but very pretty.

Woman: Oh, yes, it's a lovely little garden.

Estate agent: Shall we go in?

Man: Yes, I'm looking forward to seeing inside.

Estate agent: So, this is the hall. It's quite a good size –

room for a buggy. The first room, here on the right, is the living room.

Woman: Oh, this is very nice.

Man: Yes, it's big, isn't it?

Estate agent: Yes, it is a big room. Do you like the natural fireplace?

Man: Yes, very much. In fact, I like the whole room. I can imagine it's very relaxing.

Woman: Mm, well, let's see some more.

Estate agent: OK, next door here is a downstairs bathroom. There's a bigger family bathroom upstairs. This one is sandwiched between the living room and dining room.

Man: Oh, this is quite big for a second bathroom.

Woman: Yes, it'll be good to have two bathrooms. We only have one where we are now.

Estate agent: OK, next door here is the dining room.

Man: Oh, I like a separate dining room – it's quite big, too.

Estate agent: Yes, a bit smaller than the living room, but still a good size. There are doors here out to the patio.

Woman: Oh, how lovely – it's a nice patio – and the garden looks nice from what I can see from here.

Estate agent: Yes, I'll show you the garden, but first let's see the kitchen. That's out of the dining room and to the left. You can see that the kitchen is to the right of the back of the house. There's a window here on the left looking over the patio, and another one here looking out onto the garden.

Man: It's not the biggest kitchen, is it? I like a kitchen to be a bit bigger than this.

Estate agent: Well, it's not a bad size. Don't forget, you'll be able to eat in the dining room, so the kitchen is only for cooking.

Man: Yes, I suppose so.

Estate agent: So, shall we go out and see the garden or would you like to see upstairs first?

Man: I think we should … (fade out)

For questions 6–8, write the letter of the three houses the estate agent shows the couple. The first house is number 6, the second one is number 7 and the third one is number 8.
[Play track 69 again]

For questions 9–12, write the rooms into the spaces below.
[Play track 69 again]

Track 70
Unit 6 Exam practice – Listening

B Listen to a lecturer talking to a group of students about what makes a good city. For questions 13–20, choose the correct answer a, b or c.

Speaker: (fade in) … now, in the future, some of you will probably be working as architects, some of you as interior designers, and some of you in town planning. For all of you, what I'm going to talk about is very important, and you should certainly know what it is about a city that attracts somebody or drives somebody away. Now, environment. What is environment, and what makes people like an environment? When people arrive in a city for the first time, the thing that they notice is the environment. People notice the buildings and the space between the buildings. They appreciate the way a city works with the natural features around it – the hills and mountains, the trees and the rivers. People quickly have a sense of what is beautiful or ugly about a city. People notice that the air is clean or unclean, they notice noise and smells. People know whether they can travel easily around the city – if interesting places are within walking distance, if it is possible to drive, and if the public transport system is good. All of these first impressions can make people want to stay in a city or go somewhere else.

Another important aspect of a city's character is its economy. For many people, the choice of where to live is influenced by economy. During their working lives, people go where there is work. If that work is well paid and satisfying, people feel good about where they live. Homes are often a person's biggest investment – the value of a person's home increases, and affects his or her wealth. People like living in towns and cities where the value of their home is growing. Remember that people choose to live where they can afford to live – and they are unhappy if what they can afford is unpleasant. People hope that wherever they live, they will enjoy the same services and quality of life as everyone else.

Now, people often decide that they like or don't like a city because of its society. By society, I mean the people in the city, and how these people relate to one another. If people feel safe, they will like a place – if they feel unsafe, they won't. People are not happy if they think that where they live is dangerous – where they are afraid to leave their home. Some people want to feel that they are part of a community – they want to know the people around them. They want to talk to the neighbours – whether that is at the local shop or waiting at the school gates. Other people don't want that at all. They like the fact that in a big city they can get lost in the crowd. They enjoy the excitement, and want to meet new people all the time.

So, does the perfect city exist? Well, of course, the answer is no. As we go into the 21st century, cities are getting bigger and bigger, and people seem to be less happy with the cities they live in. You may be interested to know that for the last two years, Zurich, in Switzerland, has been identified as the best city in the world to live in. However, Switzerland is a rich country and the population is small. Is it possible to take what has worked in Zurich and try to make that work in Asia or South America or Africa, in cities with twenty or thirty million people? As planners and designers, this is a problem you must think about. You can help to shape the future. Now, I wonder if anyone would ... (*fade out*)

Track 73
Unit 7 Speaking 1

Pronunciation check

Notice that *usually* has three syllables. It is pronounced /ˈjuːʒʊəlɪ/. *Occasionally* has four syllables. It is pronounced /əˈkeɪʒnəlɪ/.
1 usually
2 occasionally
Listen and practise.

Track 74
Unit 7 Speaking 2

B **Listen to some students answering the questions. Match each speaker with a question.**
   A No, not really. I get quite nervous – especially when the plane is taking off and landing. I hate waiting for my bags at the airport, too.
   B Yes, especially young people. It's very economical. I think older people are cycling more, too – petrol is becoming so expensive, and cycling keeps you fit.
   C Well, I have a Lamborghini, so of course, the answer is yes. I love to get onto the motorway and really put my foot down.
   D Yes, when I was in Greece I travelled from Athens to an island near Turkey. It was an eight-hour journey. I got really seasick. I don't really like being at sea at all.
   E Yes, I take a bus to and from college every day. In the morning, I always have to wait in a queue. When the buses come, they are sometimes full, and I have to wait for the next one.

Track 75
Unit 7 Speaking 3

B **Listen to some students answering the questions. In the second column, match each speaker with a question.**
   A Yes, I think so. There are lots of companies that offer cheap flights these days. Planes use a lot of petrol, and it is not good for the environment.
   B Yes, I think so. The trains are modern and comfortable, and very fast. We have small buses that are clean and comfortable. You only have to wait ten minutes.
   C That's a good question. Perhaps wealthy people will travel more in small planes, or even have their own little flying machines.
   D Yes, people should use buses and trains or the underground in very big cities. More streets can be used only for people walking, and the air will be cleaner.
   E We can make public transport cheaper and nicer to use – you know, more modern trains and buses. We can also ban cars in city centres, or make people pay to take their car into the city centre.

Track 76
Unit 7 Listening 1

C Listen to the first part of a talk about belonging to a
  car club. Answer the questions in Exercise B.
  Voice: More and more people in cities are joining car
    clubs. They are doing this because belonging to a car
    club, and using a car club car, is much more
    economical than running a car of their own. People in
    cities use public transport to get to work. They walk
    their children to school and they walk to the
    supermarket. They may only use their car once or
    twice a week – perhaps only at the weekend. Why pay
    so much to keep a car on the road when you so rarely
    use it? If you add up the cost of keeping a car on the
    road, it is frightening. There is insurance and road tax,
    which goes up every year. Then, there is the cost of a
    yearly service – expensive, even if your car is new. If
    you drive an older car, of course, you will have to pay
    for repairs and new parts, too. For many people, there
    is the additional cost of parking. Finally, there is the fall
    in the value of your car – the average car falls in value
    by £2,000 a year. People who belong to a car club
    don't need to worry about any of this. They can use a
    car club car twenty-four hours a day, seven days a
    week. They can pick up a car from close to their home
    and leave it in the same place when they end their
    journey. Anyone can belong to a car club and save
    thousands of pounds every year ... (fade out)

Track 77
Unit 7 Listening 1

D Listen again and complete the summary of the talk
  below. Use no more than three words or a number in
  each space.
  [Play track 76 again]

Track 78
Unit 7 Listening 3

A With a partner, write three questions about belonging
  to a car club. Then listen to the rest of the speech
  and check if your questions are answered.
  Voice: Using a car club car is easier and more convenient
    than hiring a car from a large car hire company. Firstly,
    you can use a car club car for as long as you like. You
    can take it for an hour, or you can take it for a month.
    Being able to use a car for very short journeys is a huge
    advantage of a car club – a car hire company will always
    have a minimum twenty-four hour rental time. Most car
    club members use the cars for day trips and have the
    car back by the evening. They don't need to have it for
    twenty-four hours. Secondly, there are cars all around
    the city, so you will never have to walk more than ten
    minutes to pick up a car. The cars are parked in private
    car club parking spaces, which no other driver is
    allowed to use. When you bring the car back, the space
    will be waiting for you. Parking is never a problem.

Booking the car is very simple. You can book
online, or you can book by telephone. Booking online
couldn't be easier. You simply go onto the car club
site and follow the instructions to make your booking.
If the car you want is free, you can pick it up five
minutes later. If another member is using the car you
want, there will be another car nearby that you can
use instead. If you want to book a car a month or
two in advance, that is also possible. When you are
in the car, you can extend your booking time if you
need the car for longer. When you get to the car, you
open it with your car club membership card, key in
your identification number and then use the car keys,
which you will find in the glove compartment.

So, how much does it all cost? Car club
membership costs £60 a year. You then pay an
hourly rate of between £2.50 and £3 to use the car –
the cars with a bigger engine are a little more
expensive than the smaller cars. You then have to
pay fifteen pence a mile for petrol. Each month, your
bill shows exactly what you have been charged for. If
you need to fill the car with petrol at any time, you
use the car club debit card, which you will find in the
car. As I said before, it is all very reasonable. You
would have to use a car club car very often for it to
cost anything like it costs to keep your own car on
the road. Now, with me I have ... (fade out)

Track 79
Unit 7 Listening 3

C Listen again and complete the summary. Remember,
  you may not hear the exact words that appear in the
  summary. Use no more than three words for each
  answer.
  [Play track 78 again]

Track 81
Unit 8 Vocabulary 2

Pronunciation check
When one word ends in a sound that is similar to the sound
at the beginning of the following word, the two sounds
merge together. Listen to these examples from the unit.
1 waste time
2 spend time
Now listen to these new examples.
1 take care
2 big gun
3 time machine
Practise saying all the phrases.

Track 82
Unit 8 Speaking 3

B Listen to some students answering the questions in
  Exercise A. Mark each sentence (Y) if the student
  answers the question and (N) if the student doesn't.

1

Examiner: Does modern technology really save us time, or is it just one more thing to worry about?

Student: Mm, I think both. Of course, washing machines and microwaves save people a huge amount of time. The trouble is, we then spend a lot of that time worrying about why our computer isn't working!

2

Examiner: Does modern technology mean that some people have *too much* free time?

Student: Of course, modern technology makes us too much free time. People can listen the music, watch some DVDs and play on computer games. Lot of free time activities is done with technology.

3

Examiner: Do people spend too long thinking about the future instead of enjoying now?

Student: The most important is think about your future. If you want have good job and have family, you need think about future and make plans about it.

4

Examiner: What is more important – time or money?

Student: I think time is more important, and too many people spend all time trying to make money, and then have no time for enjoy it. However, if you have a lot of time, it is difficult to enjoy it properly if you haven't money.

Track 83
Unit 8 Speaking 3

C Listen again as you read the tapescript. Notice that answers do not have to be grammatically perfect to be good answers.

[Play track 82 again]

Track 84
Unit 8 Listening 1

C Listen to the first part of the talk and complete the table. Write <u>no more than two words or a number</u> for each answer.

Voice: Good morning, again. I realize a few of you aren't here yet, but I'll make a start anyway. I'm going to talk this morning about an important aspect of history, and that is how history is recorded and how the way we record history has changed over the centuries. I'll talk about how the storytelling of primitive man has developed into the modern methods of communication that we have today. I've got some images that I'll show you as I talk, so just let me turn on the power point.

OK, now – man has been on Earth for something like two hundred thousand years, and we don't really know when man first used language to communicate. But we do know that as soon as man did have language, he used it to tell stories. Now, these stories were the first example of man recording his history. The stories were passed on from one generation to

the next, and children would have known something about the people that came before them. One problem, of course, with a spoken history is that it's unreliable. The storyteller forgets facts and adds elements to the story that might not have been true.

The earliest attempts to record day-to-day life in anything other than spoken language were around 32 thousand years ago. That is when we believe the first cave paintings were made. Now, it might be that cave paintings were not an attempt to record history at all – the most common images in cave paintings are large wild animals, so perhaps man made them to bring him luck when he was hunting. They might have simply decorated his living space. Whatever they were for, they certainly are a record, and they tell us a great deal about how people so long ago lived their lives.

Many people believe that history really began when man learnt to write down information, and for that reason we say that what came before man could write is 'prehistoric'. However, you should remember that we have learnt a great deal from people in many parts of the world who could not write. The first people to record experience in written form were the Egyptians. Around 5,000 years ago – that's 3,000 BC – the Egyptians used hieroglyphics, a system of symbols and sounds, to record beliefs and events on the walls of their temples and on their monuments. Who knows if this was an attempt to leave something for future generations to understand?

The word 'history' comes from Greek, and it is the people of ancient Greece who, in around 500 BC, really began the long tradition of writing down everything that happened for future generations to read. In ancient Greece lived the first historians – the first people whose job was to record history.

Track 85
Unit 8 Listening 2

A Listen to the second part of the talk and answer the questions. For questions 1–12, complete the table. Write <u>no more than two words or a number</u> for each answer.

Voice: The next important development in how history is recorded came with print. In the eighth century, the Chinese invented paper and woodblock printing. Remember that up to this time very few people could read and write, and so only a very small number of people could understand written history. Suddenly, many books appeared, and many more people learnt to read.

In the fourteenth century, the first printing press was invented in Germany. This reduced how long it took to produce books. The new printing technique quickly spread to other parts of the world, more books appeared and even more people learnt to read. The first printed newspaper appeared in 1605 and the first daily newspaper in 1702. Now, people could read news stories soon after the event happened and every event was recorded and stored.

The problem with newspaper history is that newspaper reporters could tell the stories they wanted to tell and not necessarily the truth.

Photography was the next important development. We generally agree that photography was born in 1839. Some of the earliest photographs that the public saw were images of the American Civil War. People were shocked by the photographs of dead soldiers, and for the first time saw the reality of war. By 1850, photographs appeared regularly in newspapers, and people now expected the truth. At the end of the nineteenth century came the first motion-picture camera. Soon, history was being recorded as moving images. In the 1930s, television brought moving images into people's homes. More and more people saw history as it happened, and more and more history was recorded.

Today, of course, we expect that every event in the world is recorded. Satellite TV and the Internet allow people to watch any event, anywhere in the world as it happens. It doesn't matter if the TV cameras are not there – people carry around mobile phones and can record any incident, and then share it online. Families have their own video cameras and record their own history. Children now grow up watching their parents and grandparents on film.

I'm sure you'll agree that the transition from storytelling to what we have today has been dramatic, and I hope that ... (*fade out*)

Track 86
Unit 8 Listening 2

Pronunciation check
Century is pronounced /ˈs e n tʃ ə r ɪ/. Listen to these phrases and then practise saying them.
1   eighteenth century   2   nineteenth century
3   twentieth century

Track 87
Unit 8 Consolidation – Speaking

C   Listen to some students answering the questions. How do they give themselves time to think?
1
Examiner: Does modern technology really save us time, or is it just one more thing to worry about?
Student: Mm, that's a very good question. I think it's a bit of both. Of course, ... (*fade out*)
2
Examiner: Does modern technology mean that some people have *too much* free time?
Student: Too much free time? Of course, modern technology ... (*fade out*)
3
Examiner: Do people spend too long thinking about the future instead of enjoying now?

Student: Mm, I haven't really thought about it before. I guess the most important is ... (*fade out*)
4
Examiner: What is more important – time or money?
Student: Oh, I don't know if I can answer that in only a minute. It's a very big question. It depends ... (*fade out*)

Track 88
Unit 8 Consolidation – Speaking

D   Listen again and fill the gaps below.
[Play track 87 again]

Track 90
Unit 9 Speaking 2

Pronunciation check
Listen to how *of* and *for* are pronounced weakly in these phrases.
1   plenty of money   2   short of time
3   pay for the meal   4   save for the future
Practise saying the phrases.

Track 91
Unit 9 Vocabulary 2

B   Listen and check your answers.
1   Personally, I think designer clothes and accessories are much too <u>expensive</u>. A pair of sunglasses just can't be worth $500. People I know buy <u>cheap</u> clothes at the market.
2   I think it's wrong that a small number of people have huge <u>wealth</u> while people all over the developing world live in <u>poverty</u>. Many people can't afford food and clothes for their children.
3   The banks <u>lend</u> people too much money. People <u>borrow</u> more than they should and get into debt. They end up losing everything.
4   I think film stars and footballers are <u>overpaid</u>. They earn crazy amounts of money while other people earn very little. Nurses and schoolteachers are <u>underpaid</u>, in my opinion.

Track 92
Unit 9 Listening 1

B   Listen to four short extracts. Match each with a picture from Exercise A.
Extract 1
Young adult 1: ... and look at these. Aren't they great?
Young adult 2: Oh, they're really lovely. They must have been really expensive.
Young adult 1: No, not at all. They were only £35 in Topshop – down from £70. I think I got a bargain, don't you?
Young adult 2: Definitely!

Extract 2

Man 1: Good afternoon.

Man 2: Oh, good afternoon. I'm going to Moscow tomorrow, and I want to change some money – say, about £200. To tell you the truth, I don't know what the currency in Russia is.

Man 1: In Russia the currency is roubles, sir.

Man 2: Roubles? OK, well, can I have £200 worth of roubles then, please?

Extract 3

Old man: Hello, there. What are you collecting for?

Young man: We're trying to raise money to buy computers for our school. St Mary's, do you know it?

Old man: Yes, of course. Here you are.

Young man: Thank you very much.

Old man: I think it's great that you're trying to raise the money yourselves. Is it going well?

Young man: Well, a lot of people are giving money, but we need to raise two thousand pounds.

Old man: Well, good luck.

Extract 4

Woman: Excuse me, officer.

Policeman: Yes, madam, are you all right?

Woman: No, not really. Somebody's just taken my purse. I was taking it out of my handbag to pay for something, and a young man just grabbed it and ran away. I don't know what ...

Policeman: Try to calm down, madam. Now, how long ago was this?

Woman: Just a couple of minutes. I was ... (fade out)

Track 93
Unit 9 Listening 1

C Listen again and mark these statements (T) true or (F) false.

[Play track 92 again]

Track 94
Unit 9 Listening 1

E Listen again and write the words you hear into the spaces. You will need to guess the spelling.

[Play track 92 again]

Track 95
Unit 9 Listening 2

A Some students are conducting a survey about people's spending habits. Look at the questions on the survey. Listen and match each extract to a question on the survey. Write the question number in the space. You will not hear all the questions on the survey answered.

Extract 1

Male: I use my debit card for most things these days. I have two credit cards, but I don't like using them. I prefer to pay for things immediately, otherwise I feel I'm getting into debt. I pay my bills online or over the telephone. I usually have between ten and twenty pounds in cash with me to pay for emergencies – taxi fares and that kind of thing.

Extract 2

Male: Yes. I collect radios – old radios. I have nine now, and they're quite expensive. I paid £350 for a 1950s radio last month – I didn't have much money for the rest of the month after that! My wife thinks I'm crazy, but it's important to treat yourself occasionally – don't you think? My wife buys nice perfume and lots of clothes, and I have my radios.

Extract 3

Male: Personally, I don't understand why anyone buys a new car. They are so expensive, and as soon as you drive them out of the showroom, they're worth three thousand pounds less. Perhaps I'm just saying it because I can't afford a new car myself, but to me it seems so much more sensible to buy a good second-hand car for half the money.

Extract 4

Male: Well, most of it goes on monthly expenses. I've got a big mortgage on my house, and my children's school fees are very high. After I've paid for gas and electricity and water, and all the insurance on the house and my car, I don't have much left. I like taking my wife out to a nice restaurant once a month, but I don't very often buy clothes. Oh – and I collect radios – old radios.

Track 96
Unit 9 Listening 2

B Listen to the whole survey in the correct order and answer the questions. For questions 1–4, choose the correct letter a, b or c.

Female student: Excuse me – good morning – we're students from St Anne's School, and we're doing a class survey. Have you got five minutes to answer a few questions?

Man: Um, I suppose so. What are the questions about?

Female student: About spending habits – people's attitudes to money and what they spend money on.

Man: Well, yes, OK. But only five minutes.

Female student: Thank you. OK, first of all – if you don't mind answering – what income band are you in?

Male student: You just need to say low, average or high.

Man: Oh, that's difficult to say – I don't know how much everyone else makes. I'm certainly not poor, but I'm not rich either – certainly not after I've paid all my bills.

Male student: Shall we say in the middle then?

Man: Yes, I think so.

Female student: And how much money do you feel you have to spend? You said that you have to pay a lot of bills.

Man: Yes, I feel that I don't have very much. I earn quite good money, but it doesn't feel like that most of the time. I guess everyone would like to have a bit more money, though.

Male student: OK, so what do you spend most of your money on?

Man: Well, most of it goes on monthly expenses. I've got a big mortgage on my house, and my children's school fees are very high. After I've paid for gas and electricity and water, and all the insurance on the house and my car, I don't have much left. I like taking my wife out to a nice restaurant once a month, but I don't very often buy clothes. Oh – and I collect radios – old radios – that's my hobby.

Female student: And how do you usually pay for the things you buy?

Man: I use my debit card for most things these days. I have two credit cards, but I don't like using them. I prefer to pay for things immediately, otherwise I feel I'm getting into debt. I pay my bills online or over the telephone. I usually have between ten and twenty pounds in cash with me to pay for emergencies – taxi fares and that kind of thing.

Male student: What do you think is good value for money?

Man: Mm, not very much, to tell you the truth. Everything seems to cost more than it should these days. I think my telephone and Internet broadband package is good value for money, though. That's my telephone line, any number of national calls and unlimited Internet use for only £22 a month. I think at least one member of my family is online for an hour or more every day. I think £22 is a very good deal.

Female student: And what do you think is a waste of money?

Man: Personally, I don't understand why anyone buys a new car. They are so expensive, and as soon as you drive them out of the showroom, they're worth three thousand pounds less. Perhaps I'm just saying it because I can't afford a new car myself, but to me it seems so much more sensible to buy a good second-hand car for half the money.

Male student: Do you ever buy anything you can't afford?

Man: Yes. I collect radios – old radios. I have nine now, and they're quite expensive. I paid £350 for a 1950s radio last month – I didn't have much money for the rest of the month after that! My wife thinks I'm crazy, but it's important to treat yourself occasionally – don't you think? My wife buys nice perfume and lots of clothes, and I have my radios.

Female student: OK – so, finally – would you say that you're a spender or a saver?

Man: Well, as I said, I don't really have much to save, but I guess I'm a saver rather than a spender. It's good to enjoy money if you have it, but you must save for a rainy day. You never know what will happen in the future.

Female student/Male student: Thank you very much for talking to us – have nice day, now.

For questions 5–9, complete the notes. Use no more than two words for each answer.

[Play track 96 again]

Track 97
Unit 9 Consolidation – Speaking

B Listen and check your answers.

1

Man: I don't mind shopping in supermarkets. It's not much fun, but everyone has to do it.

2

Woman: I prefer shopping in small local shops. The shopkeepers are so much more friendly.

3

Man 2: I don't really like shopping for clothes. I always want a pair of shoes or a jacket that I can't afford.

4

Woman 2: I really enjoy shopping for DVDs. I usually find something I want to see.

5

Man 3: I don't enjoy shopping in markets. They're too busy, and a lot of what they sell there isn't very good.

Track 98
Unit 9 Exam practice – Listening

A You will hear a man giving a talk to some Economics students about managing money. For questions 1–6, choose the correct letter a, b or c.

Voice: Good morning, everyone. I think you all know me now. For anyone who doesn't, my name's Brian Sinclair, and I work for an independent financial advice service. Coming in and talking to students makes a nice change.

Now, you might think that because you're young, you don't really need to start worrying about money yet. You might feel that now is the time to enjoy life, and that you have plenty of time before you really need to start managing your money. Some of you probably think that you haven't got any money to manage anyway. I hope that by the end of my talk, you'll see that it's never too early to start planning ahead, and never too early to start making your money work for you.

Now, first of all, the key to good money management is time. The more time you are prepared to spend managing your finances, the better your money will work for you. So, the earlier you start managing your money, the more effective the process becomes. Too many people start that process too late in life. Rather than managing their money, they end up trying to manage on the money they have.

Basically, there are four questions that any money management programme should answer: What are your financial goals? When do you want to achieve them? What money is available to you now? And what risks are you happy to take in order to reach your goals?

Now, the first question is really the key question, and the first thing I want to talk about is houses. You might say that a house is a necessity rather than a financial choice – everyone needs a house – but buying one, or more than one, is the biggest financial transaction that most of you will make in your life. How much money you invest in a house or apartment, and how much that property costs each month, will affect all other aspects of your financial programme. You will also need to think about the kind of lifestyle you want to enjoy. If travelling round the world or taking holidays in exotic places is very important to you, you will have less money to save and less to invest. Now, I'm certainly not saying that good money managing means not having a holiday. I'm saying that managing your money well means that you have to consider each choice you make. It puts a cost on the choices you make, if you like.

Now, when you have set yourself financial goals, you have to think about timing. The most obvious consideration is retirement. When do you want to stop having to work? It may seem a long way off to most of you, but if you want to retire when you're fifty, you will need to start planning very soon. To achieve your goal in terms of timing, a lot will depend on how much surplus money you have. By surplus money, I mean money that you have left after you have paid all your expenses.

Now, it is important that you don't simply accept that what you have left after you pay all your expenses is the only money you have. Far too many see finance in this very simple way. You must think about your assets – what you have that is worth money, and whether your expenses can be reorganized so that you have more surplus cash. Let me give you some examples. One asset might be your house. You might decide to sell it, and buy another one in an area where property is cheaper – you might decide to rent one of the rooms to a student for a while. One expense might be keeping a car on the road – you might realize that it makes more financial sense to sell the car and use the train or take taxis.

Now, this is where investment and risk-taking come in. When you have decided how much surplus money you have, you should think about how you can best invest it. The more risk you are prepared to take, the more money you can make. Remember, though, you can also lose money – so, unless you know a lot about the area in which you invest money, it is best to get advice from people who know what they are doing.

Now, like all programmes, you need to revise your financial management programme from time to time. You might suddenly earn more money, or you may find a way of freeing money that was previously unavailable. Perhaps some of the goals that you set … (*fade out*)

For questions 7–13, complete this summary of the final part of the talk. Use <u>no more than two words</u> in each space.
[Play track 98 again]

Track 99
Unit 9 Exam practice – Listening

B You will hear the owner of a taxi firm talking to his accountant. For questions 14–19, complete the information in the table. Use <u>no more than two words or a number</u> for each answer.

Accountant: Hello, Mehmet. How are you?

Businessman: Oh, good morning, James. I'm not too bad. I'm glad you could come and see me.

Accountant: Yes, when you spoke to me on the phone I got the impression that things are not going so well. Is there a problem?

Businessman: Please sit down. Would you like a coffee?

Accountant: No, I'm OK – I had a coffee on the train. So, Mehmet, tell me.

Businessman: I'm very worried. I just don't understand what's been happening recently – business is down, and the money is just not coming in like it was.

Accountant: Mm, well, have you made any changes to the way you operate the business – changes that could affect profit?

Businessman: Well, yes. I've cut the number of drivers operating at the airport.

Accountant: By how many?

Businessman: Down from ten to eight.

Accountant: Why?

Businessman: Because I expected a fall in the number of people using the airport. The number of flights coming in has reduced by fifteen per cent. There are fewer evening arrivals – during the day, more people take a bus into the city centre – it saves them a lot of money, and it doesn't take that long. The drivers were waiting longer for customers.

Accountant: OK. Have you made any other changes?

Businessman: No. Well, I transferred the two airport drivers to the city centre.

Accountant: Why did you do that?

Businessman: Well, I didn't want to just dismiss them. It wouldn't be fair. Anyway, I predicted a rise in business in the central business district – everyone is talking about expansion there – more jobs and so on. I expected more people to use pre-booked taxis.

Accountant: So, you've reduced the number of drivers operating at the airport, and increased the number of drivers operating in the city centre?

Businessman: Yes, James. I've explained that.

Accountant: So, how many drivers do you now have operating in the city centre?

Businessman: Sixteen.

Accountant: Did you look carefully at the profitability of airport taxis and city-centre taxis when you made your decision?

Businessman: You mean, separately? No, not really. I just looked at the overall figures, and then made predictions.

Accountant: Mm, it might have been better to lay off two or three of the airport drivers – at least for a month or two – and then re-employ them if business improved.

Businessman: No, all the drivers have worked for the company for a long time – they have families to support. I couldn't do that. Anyway, who says they would be available when I wanted to re-employ them? They might find a job somewhere else. Good drivers are difficult to find.

Accountant: Mehmet – I think you're trying to keep everyone happy. You must think more like a businessman. It seems clear to me that the problem here is that ... (*fade out*)

For questions 20–23, complete the notes. Use <u>no more than two words or a number</u> for each answer.
[Play track 99 again]

Track 101
Unit 10 Vocabulary 1

B **Listen to some students and check the pronunciation. Then practise saying the words.**

1
Student 1: They're very happy with their new baby.
Student 2: Yes, and probably very proud, too.
2
Student 1: He looks very relaxed. He doesn't have to worry about anything.
3
Student 1: She's disappointed. She expected to get the job.
4
Student 1: The little boy's sad.
Student 2: Yes, he looks very upset. His toy's broken.
5
Student 1: He looks bored.
Student 2: Yes, it must be a very boring lesson.
6
Student 1: They're confused. They don't know which way to go.
7
Student 1: I think he's feeling quite nervous.
Student 2: Yes, he's worried that he's going to fail his test.
8
Student 1: They're really excited about going on the ride.
Student 2: They might be feeling a bit nervous, too.
9
Student 1: They're scared. They don't want to go up to the castle.
Student 2: Yes, they're really frightened.
10
Student 1: She's surprised. She wasn't expecting a present.
11
Student 1: Oh dear, he's very annoyed. They've broken his window.
Student 2: I think he's really angry.

Track 102
Unit 10 Vocabulary 1

Pronunciation check
Words like *frightened* and *frightening* are difficult for students to say. Most native speakers produce a sound that you cannot find on the phonetic chart. The sound is made in the top of the nose. Listen to these words that have the sound. Then practise saying them.

1 frightened
2 frightening
3 certainly
4 curtains
5 important

Track 103
Unit 10 Speaking 2

B **Listen to some students answering the questions. Make notes.**

1
Examiner: What makes you happy?
Student: Being with my family at the weekend makes me happy – and sunny weather.
2
Examiner: When were you last excited about something?
Student: I went to see Germany play during the World Cup. I was very excited, and a bit nervous, too – I didn't think we would win that game.
3
Examiner: What makes you really angry?
Student: I get angry when people drop rubbish in the street or write things on the walls. I just don't understand why people want to make the place they live in look horrible.
4
Examiner: What do you worry about?
Student: I worry quite a lot about money. I always feel that I should have more.
5
Examiner: When did you last get nervous about something?
Student: I got very nervous when I took all my exams last year. It was OK, though – I passed them. I sometimes get nervous before I fly, too.
6
Examiner: What do you do to relax?
Student: I listen to music with my headphones on, or go for a swim.

Track 104
Unit 10 Vocabulary 2

B **Listen to some students using extreme adjectives to answer questions.**

1
Examiner: So, what sort of thing makes you really angry?
Student: I get absolutely furious when people are cruel to animals. People think animals are less important than people.

2

Examiner: Parachute jumping sounds very exciting. How many jumps have you made?

Student: I've made five now. I made my first jump last year. I was absolutely terrified before I jumped, but then when I was in the air, it was absolutely fantastic.

3

Examiner: And so how did you feel when you got your exam results?

Student: Well, I was in Italy with some friends. My mother phoned to tell me I had passed them all. When I heard the news, I was absolutely delighted.

Track 105
Unit 10 Vocabulary 2

C Listen again and complete these sentences.
[Play track 104 again]

Track 106
Unit 10 Listening 1

B Listen to the introduction to a radio programme about phobias. Answer the questions in Exercise A.

Voice: Good afternoon. On today's programme, we're going to hear about phobias, and learn what some of the most common phobias are. Now, a phobia is really a fear or an anxiety, but it's a very strong fear or anxiety. In fact, phobias are often called anxiety disorders – a disorder is something that is wrong. People don't understand why they have a phobia – they can't explain why they are so afraid of what it is they have a fear of. It is difficult to know exactly how many people are affected, but some doctors think around fifteen per cent of us have a phobia of one kind or another. Some phobias can make it very difficult for people to live a normal life – a fear of water or of open spaces, for example. Nobody knows exactly why people have phobias, but it is probably a mix of brain chemistry – something that is just there inside us – and past experience – fears caused by what has happened to us some time earlier in our life. Today, I have in the studio Doctor Alan Carling. He is an expert on phobias, and he is going to tell us about the five most common phobias. Later, he will talk about how people can overcome a phobia, or at least learn to live with one.

Track 107
Unit 10 Listening 1

D Listen to the rest of the programme. In what order does the speaker mention the phobias in Exercise C?

Female voice: Doctor Carling, welcome to World Wise.

Dr Carling: Good afternoon. Now, Anne has described what a phobia is, so I won't go back over that. I'll go straight on to talk about the most common phobias, and how some phobias have similar qualities and cause similar difficulties to the people who suffer from them.

The most common phobia is arachnophobia. Now, that might not be surprising – most people don't like spiders – but a phobia about spiders is more than just a fear. People who suffer from arachnophobia may panic if they see a spider – however big or small it is. They don't want to go to places where there could be spiders, so they will feel uncomfortable if they go down to the cellar, up to the attic or find themselves in any room that hasn't been cleaned. They may not want to go out into their garden.

Female voice: Mm, I don't like spiders, but I don't think my fear is quite that bad.

Dr Carling: No, probably not. The second most common phobia is social phobia. Now, this is complex, and the person who suffers will be afraid of a range of situations. The real fear is of being with other people, especially large groups of people. People who have social phobia have very little confidence, and feel that other people are judging what they do and say all the time. They feel that what they say is stupid and that people are laughing at them. A person with social phobia could not speak in front of a group of other people, for example. Some sufferers do not like eating with other people – even members of their family. The phobia can make it very difficult for those who have it to live a normal life.

Female voice: That's very interesting. I have friends who are uncomfortable in large groups. They don't like parties, and so on.

Dr Carling: Yes, it's a common fear, but not necessarily a phobia. Now, another phobia that will probably not surprise people is aerophobia – the fear of flying. A lot of people don't really like flying, but a small number of people simply cannot fly. They know it is safer than driving a car, but they panic as soon as they are near a plane. It is usually a result of seeing a plane crash on TV or reading about one in the news. Aerophobia is unusual because it seems that the person who suffers from it can do something about it. It seems that if the person makes one successful flight, they may not be frightened again in the future, and will fly quite happily.

Female voice: That's amazing. I really didn't know that.

Dr Carling: Now, the fourth phobia is agoraphobia. This is similar in some ways to social phobia, and certainly means that the person who suffers doesn't like to be around a lot of other people. Agoraphobia is a fear of not being able to escape from a crowded place. The person who suffers will panic in a crowd, and will often feel physically sick. The condition is made worse because the person who suffers is then afraid of having a panic attack in front of so many other people. In some cases, those who suffer will not want to leave their house.

Female voice: That sounds terrible.

Dr Carling: Yes – a very serious condition. So, the fifth and final phobia I'm going to talk about is claustrophobia – a fear of being trapped in a very small space. People with claustrophobia will not want to be in a lift, or 'elevator', as the Americans say. They will often avoid travelling by train or bus, as they are afraid that an accident could mean being trapped somewhere. They do not like a room with all the doors closed. It seems that people who suffer from claustrophobia can become very anxious simply by imagining being in a small space, and not being able to escape.

Female voice: That sounds terrible. Even if they are not in a small space, they can experience fear and anxiety?

Dr Carling: Absolutely.

Female voice: OK, now, thank you for that summary. I think what we really want to know now is ... (fade out)

Track 108
Unit 10 Listening 2

A Read the questions carefully. Then listen again and answer them. What does the speaker say about each of the phobias 1–5?

[Play track 107 again]

Track 109
Unit 10 Listening 3

A Listen to the same speaker talking about three more phobias. Match the pictures with the extracts. There are two pictures that you do not need.

Extract 1

Voice: Acrophobia is a fear of heights. A lot of people confuse it with vertigo, which is a normal feeling that people get in a very high place. Acrophobia is a phobia and can be very dangerous. The person who suffers may panic and want to escape the situation – the quickest way to escape is to jump. People who suffer from acrophobia will avoid being at the top of tall buildings, and will not like going up long staircases. It may be a phobia that is a result of past experience. Children see things fall and break, and so become very frightened of the same thing happening to them.

Extract 2

Voice: Now, this phobia has a number of different names – brontophobia, astraphobia and keraunophobia. It is a phobia of storms – especially storms with thunder and lightning. It is especially common in children, but can continue into adult life. People who have a serious phobia worry when the spring turns to summer – they expect there to be more storms during that time. When a storm is approaching, they feel very uncomfortable and even physically sick. Many of those who suffer – especially children – hide when there is a storm, perhaps in a cupboard or under the bed. Adults with the condition may watch weather forecasts on television every thirty minutes to check that the weather is good.

Extract 3

Voice: Now most people are, to some degree, afraid of dying, but necrophobia is a fear of anything connected with death. It is more than a fear of dying.

People who have necrophobia are terrified of seeing dead things. They will stay away from museums where there are mummies or skeletons, and avoid any images of dead people. They will panic if they see a dead animal in the street or in a forest, and will avoid watching a programme or movie that shows people dying or near to death. This phobia may be something that is natural in all of us to some degree, but is probably made worse by seeing a dead person or a favourite pet dying at some time in the past.

Track 110
Unit 10 Listening 3

B Listen again and answer the questions.

For questions 1–6, write:
    A If the statement refers to the first extract.
    B If the statement refers to the second extract.
    C If the statement refers to the third extract.

[Play track 109 again]

Track 111
Unit 10 Consolidation – Speaking

A Look at these exchanges between an examiner and some students. Then listen. What do you think about the students' answers?

1

Examiner: So, were you disappointed when you didn't get into university?

Student: No, I didn't care.

2

Examiner: So, working in advertising must be very exciting.

Student: No, it's very boring most of the time.

3

Examiner: Are you nervous about the exams that you're taking next month?

Student: No, I'm not nervous. I like exams.

4

Examiner: What did you think of London? Did you get confused travelling around on the tube?

Student: No, it was easy.

Track 112
Unit 10 Consolidation – Speaking

B Listen to these students answering the same questions. How are their answers better?

1

Examiner: So, were you disappointed when you didn't get into university?

Student: Actually, I didn't mind too much. I wasn't sure that I really wanted to go to university anyway.

2

Examiner: So, working in advertising must be very exciting.

Student: Mm, yes and no. It can be quite boring, actually. You do the same thing a lot of the time.

3

Examiner: Are you nervous about the exams that you're taking next month?

Student: I'm quite looking forward to them, actually. I quite like doing exams.

4

Examiner: What did you think of London? Did you get confused travelling around on the tube?

Student: It wasn't too bad, actually. I've been to a few big cities before.

Track 113
Unit 10 Consolidation – Speaking

C Look at the tapescript and listen again. Highlight expressions you want to use.

[Play track 112 again]

Track 114
Unit 10 Consolidation – Vocabulary

B Listen and mark the main stress on the words in Exercise A above. Then practise saying them.

1	emotional	2	disappointed
3	annoying	4	frightened
5	furious	6	anxious
7	anxiety	8	pressure
9	sociable	10	appreciate

Track 115
Unit 10 Review 2 – Writing

A Look at the interviewer's first question and then listen to the first part of the interview. Mark these statements (T) true, (F) false or (NG) not given.

Examiner: Well, the first composition is completely different. I think it's fair to say that the General Training writing exam is easier. In the Academic exam, students need to look at a graph or chart and then explain what they see. They need to learn how to use a very specific type of academic language. In the General Training exam, they write a letter. It is usually formal, but it can be informal. Of course, they must learn how to write various types of letter, but generally it is an easier task. The second composition is similar in both versions of the exam. It involves discussing a topic or agreeing or disagreeing with a statement. In the General exam, the topic may be a little more general – about a social issue, for example. In the Academic exam, the topic can be more academic – discussing technology or space travel, for example. Students taking the General Training Module often find the second composition much more difficult than the first.

Track 116
Unit 10 Review 2 – Writing

B Look at the interviewer's second question and then listen to the second part of the interview. Put the points into the order in which you hear them.

Examiner: Well, there are quite a lot of different things to look for and, of course, it depends on the level of the student who's writing. I can quickly see if the composition is written by a student with a lower level of English, or if it's been written by a very advanced learner. I need to look for different things then, so I can decide what grade to give. However, there are certain aspects of a composition that are very important – in fact, essential – and that is the same for any student who takes the exam. Firstly, what the student writes must be relevant to the question – it doesn't matter how well written a composition is, if it doesn't answer the question, it won't pass. Then there's the word count – the letter must be at least a hundred and fifty words, and the second composition two hundred and fifty. Sometimes a student writes very well but just doesn't say enough, and I'm afraid I can't pass the composition. All examiners say that a composition must be easy to read. That means they can understand what the student is trying to say. It doesn't have to be perfect English, but it must be easy to follow – sometimes that means that the student should keep it simple. A simple composition that is easy to follow is better than a very complex composition that is difficult to follow. Now, organization: all compositions should be organized – of course, that's what makes them easier to read. The student must make his or her points in a logical order, and they should introduce and conclude their ideas. Any type of composition should be divided into paragraphs, and each paragraph should have a purpose. Even lower-level students should understand that a topic sentence introduces a paragraph, and helps the reader to follow what the writer is saying. Students should be able to use reference words – at lower levels, these can be simple references, like 'this' and 'that', but at higher levels I expect to see more advanced reference and linking words. Finally, the student needs to use language that is appropriately formal or informal. If the composition is a letter to a college principal, it's not good to have lots of contractions and very informal vocabulary.

Track 117
Unit 10 Review 2 – Writing

C Look at the interviewer's third question and then listen to the third part of the interview. Complete the summary below. Use no more than two words for each answer.

Examiner: Well, these are all important, but not quite as important as what I mentioned before. In order to score a very high mark, students need to use an advanced range of vocabulary – which is all spelt correctly, of course. To score a lower grade, but to get the grade they want, students should keep it simple. Of course, if they know the right word or phrase they should use it, but it is more important to make their point simply and clearly. Too many students try to use words and phrases that they have only heard once or twice and don't really understand properly. As for grammar, the same applies. Advanced students will show that they can use all sorts of grammatical structures and score a high mark, but it's just not necessary if you are aiming for a lower score. Lower-level learners should make sure they use basic structures accurately. Then, if they feel confident with more challenging structures, they can try to use them. Students shouldn't try to say what they don't know how to say – they can usually make their point without having to use very complicated grammar.

Track 120
Unit 11 Vocabulary 2

Pronunciation check

The *ough* at the end of words is sometimes pronounced in different ways. Sometimes it is pronounced /ɒ/, sometimes /ʌ/ and sometimes /əʊ/. It is difficult to know which way is correct if you see a new word.
Decide how these words are pronounced.

1 cough   2 enough
3 though   4 rough

Listen and check your answers.

Track 121
Unit 11 Listening 1

B Look at the next part of the flow chart. Listen and complete the notes using <u>no more than two words</u> for each answer.

Voice: If you are not showing those symptoms, you may have another problem. You should ask yourself – do I have a bad cough, and is it difficult to breathe? If it is difficult to breathe or you feel out of breath, you may have bronchitis. Bronchitis is really a bad cold with a cough, but it can last longer than a typical cold and be more difficult to treat. If you have bronchitis you should get plenty of rest and drink lots of water. If you smoke, you will make things much worse by smoking while you are ill. You should try to stop completely while you have the symptoms. You can buy medicine at a chemist that will relieve the pain of the coughing, but you really should contact a doctor immediately if the symptoms don't clear up or get worse.

Now, if you don't have a bad cough, but you do have a runny nose and sore eyes, it could be an allergy. Perhaps you are allergic to something common, like cat hair, or perhaps it's something unusual that you don't know about yet. Explain the symptoms to somebody at a chemist, and they may be able to give you medicine that will help. It might be better to see

your doctor and get some advice, though.

Track 122
Unit 11 Listening 2

A Look at the first part of a flow chart that shows you what to do if you have a headache. Listen and complete the notes using <u>no more than two words</u> for each answer.

Voice: There are various different reasons why you may have a headache. Some of them are not serious and can be treated easily – perhaps by simply taking a painkilling tablet, like an aspirin. Some headaches, however, may be a symptom of something far more serious, and you should get immediate advice.

First of all, ask yourself if you think you have other symptoms that suggest you have a cold. Do you have a fever, a runny nose, a cough or a sore throat? Have you been sick at all? If you have, then you probably have a bad cold or the flu, and the headache is just one of the symptoms. Get plenty of rest and drink plenty of water. There are many types of medicine that you can buy at a chemist, and these will relieve some of the symptoms. Remember, though, medicine will not actually cure the condition, and you might prefer to just drink hot water with some lemon and honey and take a couple of aspirin.

Now, if you don't think you have a cold, you must ask yourself how bad the headache is. If the headache is really bad and you have a stiff neck, there may be a bigger problem. If you feel that normal light is hurting your eyes, it may also be cause for concern. Meningitis is a serious condition. It is caused by an infection of blood around your brain and spinal cord. The condition can seriously affect your brain if not treated immediately. You must see your doctor or go immediately to the nearest hospital.

If you do not show these symptoms, you may still have something that needs treatment quickly. You may have an injury of some kind, and you must try to remember if you have hit your head at all in the last few days. If you have, you may be suffering from concussion. Concussion occurs after an injury to the head, when blood pushes against the brain. It is very serious and you must make sure that you get treatment immediately.

Now, if you don't remember any recent injury, you must ask yourself if you feel ... (*fade out*)

Track 123
Unit 11 Consolidation – Speaking

B Listen to a student talking and answer the questions.
Examiner: OK, so are you ready?
Student: Yes, I think. OK, I was on my bicycle. I was riding quite fast, but there was not much traffic. ... um ... um ... there were a lot of cars parked along the side of the road. One man – he opened the door of the car and, bang, I didn't have time to stop ... um ... I hit the door and came off the bicycle.

Examiner: And?

Student: Err ... oh, yes ... let me see the card again. What did I do? Um ... I was in the road ... and I could see a car was coming towards me. Um ... I jumped up and the first thing I wanted to know was 'is my bicycle OK?' ... I thought I was OK, but I was worried about my bicycle. Um, my bicycle was OK, and I took it to the side of the road. I realized that my chest hurt quite badly. I sat down, and the driver of the car called an ambulance. I discovered that one of my ribs was broken.

Track 124
Unit 11 Consolidation – Speaking

D **Listen to the same student trying again. What does he do better the second time?**

Examiner: OK, so are you ready?

Student: Yes. Well, this was about a year ago. I was on my bicycle, and I was riding quite fast on a main road. It was a new bicycle, and I was really happy with it – maybe I was riding too fast. There wasn't much traffic, but there were a lot of cars parked along the side of the road. Suddenly, the driver of one car opened the door of his car. I'm sure he checked to see if any cars were coming, but he didn't see me on my bicycle. I tried to brake, but I didn't have time to stop and, bang, I hit the door and came off the bicycle. Then, I remember that I was lying in the road, and I could see a car was coming towards me. I jumped up and the first thing I wanted to know was 'is my bicycle OK?' I thought I was OK, but I was worried about my bicycle. My bicycle was OK, and I took it to the side of the road – the pavement, I think. That is when I realized that my chest hurt quite badly. I sat down, and the driver of the car called an ambulance. I soon discovered that one of my ribs was broken.

Track 126
Unit 12 – Speaking 2

A **Think about how you could answer these questions from the first part of the speaking exam. Then listen to some students and tick the speaker who gives a better answer.**

Question 1 – Speaker 1

Examiner: What sort of climate does the area you live in have?

Student 1: Sometimes it's hot, and sometimes it's cold.

Question 1 – Speaker 2

Examiner: What sort of climate does the area you live in have?

Student 2: Well, it's quite an extreme climate. Summers are usually very hot and sunny, but winters are very cold. There's usually snow in January and February.

Question 2 – Speaker 1

Examiner: Tell me about the weather in your country.

Student 1: It's always very hot.

Question 2 – Speaker 2

Examiner: Tell me about the weather in your country.

Student 2: Well, it depends on the time of year. In summer, it's always very hot and dry. The temperature can reach forty-five degrees. It doesn't rain for months. In the winter, it is quite cold, especially at night. It rains a lot in spring.

Question 3 – Speaker 1

Examiner: Is there one season that you especially like?

Student 1: Yes, I like spring. I always feel happy because winter is over and it's like a new start. The weather is nice, but it's not too hot.

Question 3 – Speaker 2

Examiner: Is there one season that you especially like?

Student 2: Yes.

Examiner: Err ... which season do you like?

Student 2: I like summer.

Question 4 – Speaker 1

Examiner: Do you do the same things in summer as in winter?

Student 1: No.

Examiner: Oh, err ... so you different things in the winter?

Student 1: Yes, different things in the summer and the winter.

Question 4 – Speaker 2

Examiner: Do you do the same things in summer as in winter?

Student 2: Um, well, a lot of things are the same. I go to work the same, and spend free time with my family, but some things are different. During the summer, I take my little girl to the park a lot and have days out with her. In the winter, we stay at home more. During the winter, I go skiing at least once a month.

Track 127
Unit 12 – Speaking 3

Pronunciation check

Notice how the ~ture at the end of *temperature* is pronounced. Here are some more words that have the same ending. Listen and then practise saying them.

1 picture
2 nature
3 adventure
4 culture

Track 128
Unit 12 – Listening 1

B **Listen to the weather forecast and check your predictions.**

Voice: Tomorrow will be another wet day across most of the country. The south-east can expect the worst of the weather, with heavy rain early in the day. Towns along the south-east coast may experience severe storms with thunder and lightning. Later in the day conditions should improve, but showers are still likely in most places during the afternoon. It will also be cold for the time of year, with the temperature remaining at around six degrees.

Track 129

Unit 12 – Listening 1

C Listen again and complete the notes. Use <u>no more than two words</u> for each answer.

[Play track 128 again]

Track 130

Unit 12 – Listening 2

B Listen to the conversation and check your predictions.

Male 1: Oh, no – is it raining out there?

Male 2: Raining? It's absolutely pouring down. They said on the weather forecast that it would rain, but I didn't think it would be like this. How come you're not wet?

Male 1: Ah, well, I heard the forecast, too, so I took a taxi from the station.

Male 2: Mm, you're lucky. I'm absolutely soaked. It's really chilly out there, too. I hope I don't get pneumonia!

Male 1: Well, never mind. They say it's going to get better later on.

Male 2: Yes, but that doesn't help me. I'm going to be in these wet clothes all day!

Track 131

Unit 12 – Listening 2

C Listen again and complete the lines. Use <u>no more than two words</u> for each answer.

[Play track 130 again]

Track 132

Unit 12 – Listening 4

A Listen to the four extracts and match them with the descriptions below.

Extract 1

Voice: Hi, everyone – I'm a bit nervous about doing this, so ... err ... Anyway, as you all know, I come from Libya, and I'm going to talk about sandstorms. Sandstorms are very common in the Sahara desert, and so people in Libya, which is near the Sahara desert, know all about them. Now, we say 'sandstorm', but it's not really a storm – there's no rain or thunder and lightning. There are sandstorms when a strong wind picks up sand and carries it. As the wind blows, the sand in the wind causes more sand to move around, and that is also picked up. A very strong wind can pick up a huge amount of sand – look at my first image on the board, here. As you can see, a severe sandstorm looks like a huge wall or wave of sand. Can you imagine that coming towards you? Now, I will tell you what you should do if you know a sandstorm is coming, or even if you get caught in a sandstorm ...

Extract 2

Female 1: So, have you decided where you're going on holiday yet? You were talking about Spain.

Female 2: No, we've changed our minds. We're going to Egypt for two weeks.

Female 1: Wow, really? When are you going?

Female 2: The second week in August.

Female 1: Egypt in August – you're brave. It'll be absolutely boiling then, won't it?

Female 2: Yeah – that's what I want! We'll go and see the sights early in the morning when it's still quite cool, and then lie around by the swimming pool in the midday heat.

Female 1: Mm, I went to Morocco in the summer a few years ago. I couldn't sleep until about two in the morning. I always said that if I went anywhere like that again, I'd go in the spring or autumn.

Female 2: Well, I can't wait. You just see my tan when I get back!

Extract 3

Female: Good evening, Professor Drake, and welcome to the programme.

Prof: Good evening.

Female: Now, as we have heard, it appears that there are a greater number of hurricanes now, particularly in the Atlantic, and that hurricanes are becoming more violent and causing more damage. First of all, could you explain what causes a hurricane?

Prof: Yes, certainly. Hurricanes – or tropical cyclones, as they are also known – are really huge storms, or a number of storms that occur together within a small area. They are caused by low pressure and moist air rising from the Earth's surface – usually the surface of the sea. As the moist air rises it becomes warmer, and this is what forms the hurricane. If the hurricane is strong enough, it will develop an eye. The eye, which is circular, is at the centre of the hurricane and can be huge – three hundred kilometres in diameter, perhaps. The eye is usually calm – it is the area around the eye – the eyewall – where the storms occur. The eyewall surrounds the eye like the wall of a huge vertical passage, and is made up of the strong winds that cause the damage when the hurricane passes over land. Spreading out from the eyewall is the vast area of clouds and rain that we call the rain bands. These rain bands can spread for hundreds of kilometres.

Female: Thank you for that, professor. Now, why is it that the world is experiencing a greater ... (fade out)

Extract 4

Voice: Floods occur when the water level rises in an area where there was previously little or no water. Floods can be dramatic – they occur suddenly, and the water level rises quickly – or creeping – the water level rises over a longer period of time. They occur either because there is a larger amount of rainfall in an area than is usual, or because ice melts. Floods generally cause damage and negatively affect the economy of an area, but they can also be beneficial. The River Nile floods annually, and the water brings nutrients to the soil in surrounding fields. This, of course, means better crops. Most floods occur naturally, but they can be ... (fade out)

Track 133
Unit 12 – Listening 4

B Listen again to each extract and complete the tasks below.

[Play track 132 again]

Track 134
Unit 12 – Writing 2

C Listen to the discussion and circle the option you hear.

Teacher: So, personally, I have quite strong views about this issue, but I want to hear what you have to say. I don't need to practise my English. I'll tell you what I think at the end. Now, I'm not going to ask individual people what they think, but I'd like to hear from everyone, if possible – OK? So ...

Student 1: Well, I have mixed feelings. I think zoos are quite cruel, but I enjoy going to them. I like to see animals that I know I will probably never see in the wild – like tigers and elephants.

Student 2: But if you really want to see them, you can go on a safari or a jungle trek.

Student 3: No, that's not true for everyone – safaris are really expensive and you don't see all the animals you want to see anyway.

Student 2: I think in this day and age, people can see wild animals on TV all the time. There are really realistic DVDs and Internet pages.

Student 1: But that's not the same as seeing the real animal.

Student 2: I think it's better to see an animal on TV in its natural environment – hunting or playing with its babies – than see it in a little cage at the zoo looking miserable. Big animals that hunt, like lions, tigers and bears, always look very unhappy in a zoo. I heard that they don't live as long in a zoo as they do in the wild.

Student 4: Yes, in my country, zoos are not very well-kept. The children shout at the animals and sometimes even throw things at them. The animals suffer from stress.

Student 1: Well, somebody should stop them doing that. In most countries, zoos are better these days. Animals are in big cages and they can climb and run around.

Student 2: Um, I'm not so sure. When did you last see a lion chasing a zebra in a zoo?

Student 1: Well, there are some big wildlife parks in most countries. Lions might not hunt zebras, but they are free to walk around. People drive their car through the park and take photos.

Student 2: Yes, maybe they are better than small zoos, but they can't keep every type of animal. People go to a zoo to see as many animals as possible.

Student 3: Yes, and these days there are lots of interactive activities, too – like in a museum.

Student 1: People say that zoos are cruel, but I think some species of animal would become extinct if there were not zoos. Zoos help them to survive and keep them safe.

Student 3: Yes, that's true – animals like pandas in China find it very difficult in the wild because their homes are destroyed. They are safer in zoos, and people can help them to produce more pandas. I know it's not perfect to have animals in zoos, but one day it may be the only place that many types of animal exist.

Student 4: I really hope not. People should be doing more to protect the environments of animals in the wild.

Teacher: Um, that's true, but I think it's a whole new question. So – do you want to hear what I think?

Track 135
Unit 12 – Consolidation – Speaking

C Listen to some students and match the answers they give to the questions in Exercise B.

Speaker 1: Yes, I think so. We are cutting down forests to build towns and cities, and using the wood from the forests for industry. We are polluting the air and the seas and rivers.

Speaker 2: Yes, I think everyone can see that it is. The ice is melting in the Arctic and Antarctic, and some countries are getting hotter. There are natural disasters, like hurricanes, in more places now.

Speaker 3: Yes, especially big animals like pandas and rhinos that people love. They must have special places where humans are not allowed to build and animals are safe from hunters.

Speaker 4: Mm, I'm not sure. It seems to rain much more than it did when I was little, but maybe I just remember the sunny days.

Speaker 5: Yes, if any more ice melts, some parts of the world will be under water. Some islands will disappear. I heard that some diseases from Africa and Asia will be common in Europe if it gets any warmer.

Track 136
Unit 12 – Exam practice – Listening

A You will hear someone talking to some students about how to stay safe when there is lightning. Look at the notes below carefully before you listen. For questions 1–10, complete this student's notes. Use no more than three words or a number for each answer.

Voice: Now, a big storm can be quite exciting, and you may want to go outside or stand by a window to get a better view, especially if it's not something you have seen much of before. However, it's not really a good idea. Thunder and lightning can be very frightening, and lightning can be very dangerous, too. You will all know that recently there have been a lot of storms, and that's why I want to warn you of the dangers.

Now, first of all, if you can hear thunder that means the storm is close, and it's close enough for you to be struck by lightning. Lightning can strike as far as fifteen kilometres away from the centre of the storm. Have you tried counting how many seconds there are between the thunder you hear and the flash of lightning that you see? The less you can count, the closer the centre of the storm. If there's less than thirty seconds between the thunder and the lightning, there is a danger.

If they say on a weather forecast that there will be a thunderstorm you should cancel any outdoor activities that you have planned, especially if they are in areas where it will be difficult to get to safe cover. Don't go camping and don't play golf. Avoid any activities near still water, like fishing – water conducts electricity.

If you are outside when a thunderstorm starts, take cover inside a building as quickly as possible. If there are no buildings and you have a car, shelter in that. Make sure all the windows are closed. Sheltering under a tree or in a bus stop is not really safe – you do not have as much protection as you should. If you are in an open space, don't put up an umbrella and, whatever you do, don't use a mobile phone. The metal directs electricity into the body and can make any injury much worse. Anyone who is swimming or rowing a boat must get to dry land as quickly as possible.

Inside your home there are dangers, too. Don't take a bath or a shower when there is a thunderstorm – if lightning strikes a house, it can send surges of electricity through metal pipes. If a storm appears to be serious, unplug electrical appliances, like TVs and music systems. If the light goes out during a storm, try to use a torch – lighting matches or holding cigarette lighters inside the house is very dangerous.

Finally, don't go out or leave your shelter too soon after the storm has passed. Many lightning strikes occur after the storm has passed. Stay indoors for at least half an hour. Now, I hope I haven't frightened you too much, and I hope you enjoy the rest of ... (fade out)

Track 137
Unit 12 – Exam practice – Listening

B You will hear an English family talking about their holiday options. Read the statements carefully before you listen. For questions 11–16, mark each of the statements on the following page with one of the following abbreviations.

Mother: OK, since we're all together for a change, let's talk about holidays. It's the summer holiday soon, and Dad and I have been discussing some places that everyone might like. Now, I don't want arguments, so let's hear what everyone has to say. Justin, have you thought about a summer holiday yet?

Justin: Can we go skiing again?

Ellie: I don't want to go skiing – not in the summer. It was freezing last time we went skiing – I had the flu for most of the holiday.

Mother: OK, Ellie – let's calm down. We can all make suggestions. We don't have to decide on anything today.

Father: Mum and I were talking about Turkey. Lots of people go to Turkey in the summer. It's very popular at the moment. There's lots to see and some lovely beaches to relax on, too.

Justin: Yeah, but it'll be absolutely boiling – probably about fifty degrees.

Father: I think you're exaggerating a bit, Justin.

Justin: Maybe. But anyway, you know I get bored just lying on the beach all day.

Mother: Yes, but like Dad said, there's lots to see as well. We can go for day trips to sights and museums.

Ellie: Boring!

Father: I was thinking we could spend some time by the beach, and then go up to Istanbul for a few nights.

Mother: Mm, I don't know about that. I don't really want to go anywhere that's too crowded. I want to get away from stress – not go looking for it.

Father: Well, OK – perhaps just a day trip, then. I'd like to see it. They say it's one of the most exciting cities in the world.

Justin: A day trip from the coast to Istanbul – no way. We'd be on the bus for five hours there and five hours back. That's not my idea of fun.

Mother: OK, it's just one of the options. I said we don't have to decide anything today. I wouldn't mind staying in this country. We could drive to Cornwall or the Lake District. We could go up to Scotland – we've never been there.

Ellie: Mm ... except ... it'll be wet every day – probably pouring down most days. That's the trouble with holidays in Britain.

Father: Look ... we're not getting very far here, are we? Everyone is saying where they don't want to go and nobody is being very positive.

Justin: I said I want to go skiing.

Track 138
Unit 12 – Exam practice – Listening

C You will hear a lecturer talking about avalanches. Look carefully at the questions and at the diagram and box of words. For questions 17–19, complete the notes. Use no more than two words for each answer.

Voice: Most of you have probably never experienced an avalanche – they only occur in mountainous areas and not very often – but you've probably seen one on TV.

The most dangerous type of avalanche occurs when snow is loose and wet. Wet snow is very heavy – it moves slowly, but it causes a huge amount of damage. Most avalanches are started by the victim – that means the person who starts the avalanche is usually killed or injured in it. Not many avalanches destroy towns or villages, like you see in movies. People think that the wind can cause an avalanche, but that's not true. The wind can make snow loose and dangerous, but it doesn't actually make the avalanche start.

Now, look at this diagram on the board. Right at the top here, you see the trigger. That means the cause – what makes the avalanche start. It's usually a person walking on loose, unstable snow. Below that is the start zone – the area where the avalanche builds up, and the snow starts moving. As the snow starts to move with more force, it creates a track. This is the path down which the snow slides. As the snow moves, it creates its own track. As more snow becomes loose, it follows the track down the mountain. On each side of the track are the flanks. The snow here is pulled into the track by moving snow. Finally, down here at the bottom, is the debris toe. This is where the avalanche ends. It will either be on the mountain, where there is not a steep enough slope for the snow to continue moving downwards, or it will be at the bottom of the mountain. Obviously, if it's the bottom of the mountain, a huge amount of damage could be caused. As I said before, however, this is not common, and ... (*fade out*)

For questions 20–24, match some of the words A–H in the box with the numbers on the diagram. Write the letters in the spaces.
[Play track 138 again]

Track 140
Unit 13 Speaking 2

A **Listen to some students describing their homes. Which statement below is true?**

Speaker 1: Mm, my apartment is very small, but very expensive. On the other hand, it's very close to where I work, so I save money on bus fares.

Speaker 2: I rent a house with some friends. It's not in very good condition, and my room is small, but I guess it's cheap, and it's better than being at home with my parents.

Speaker 3: I moved to a new house with my husband last year. It's very comfortable, and in a part of the city that we like. However, our neighbours are not very friendly, and they make a lot of noise.

Speaker 4: My apartment is right next to a busy main road – it's really noisy, and the windows are always black! On the plus side, it's very central, and I can walk everywhere.

Track 141
Unit 13 Speaking 2

B **Listen again and fill each space with one word. Notice the incomplete highlighted phrases.**
[Play track 140 again]

Track 142
Unit 13 Speaking 2

Pronunciation check
Listen again to sentences 1, 3 and 4 in Exercise B. Notice how the speaker pauses when a linking device introduces a contrast.
Practise saying the sentences.

Track 143
Unit 13 Listening 2

B **Listen and complete the notes that one of the tourists made. Use one word only for each answer.**

Voice: OK, is everybody still with me? Good. Now, before we walk up to the building, I would like to tell you a few things. You will enjoy looking around the building more if you have some background.

As I'm sure you know, many people think the Taj Mahal is the most beautiful building in the world, and I hope you now understand why. Look at the gardens and how they have been designed. They are the same on both sides of the building, so there is a sense of symmetry. The fountains and pools create a sense of calm. You will see as we approach the building that it is reflected in a large pool. This is where most tourists stop to take their first photos, and I'm sure you will, too.

We will see the building up close, of course, but from here what you notice is the dome on top of the building and the four towers, or 'minarets' as they are properly called, in each corner. Most people are surprised by the size of the dome and wonder at how its weight is supported. When you are closer you will see how the light at this time of the day makes the dome appear a blue-white.

Now, I expect most of you will know something about the story behind the Taj Mahal, but I will quickly summarize for those who do not. It is a truly romantic story – perhaps the most romantic story ever told. Shah Jahan was one of the most important men in India. He had built wonderful constructions all over the north of India. Suddenly, in 1629, his favourite wife died and the Shah was terribly sad. They say his beard turned white in one night. He wanted to create something to remember her by, and he decided to build the most beautiful monument he could imagine. The work started in 1632. It was finished thirty years later. 20,000 men worked on the construction.

Unfortunately, Shah Jahan did not have very long to enjoy his project. His son ... (*fade out*)

Track 144
Unit 13 Listening 3

B Listen to part of a lecture that an architect is giving about the Millennium Dome. Read the summary below before you listen. For questions 1–8, complete the summary with words that you hear. Use <u>no more than two words</u> for each answer.

Voice: Now, you might ask why the Millennium Dome is so unpopular – why people are so upset by it. After all, there are ugly buildings all over the world. Blocks of flats and office blocks in every city in the world are truly unpleasant to look at. I'm sure you have plenty of ugly buildings in your city.

However, the important difference is that the Millennium Dome was not constructed quickly and cheaply like some 1950s block of flats. It was built to celebrate a special occasion. It took years of planning and years of construction – and it cost an enormous amount of money – not far off a billion pounds.

The Millennium Dome is supposed to be beautiful. It is, however, quite horrible. It was built to bring one of the world's great cities into the twenty-first century. Now, less than ten years later, nobody wants to look at it. I am afraid that it will always be famous for its ugliness.

In the United States we have our ugly buildings, too. The Chicago Public Library is a good example and the Experience Project Museum in Seattle is awful. But there is something about the Millennium Dome that makes it worse – in my opinion, at least.

I admit that the design of the building is ambitious and, of course, is a great achievement of engineering. However, I'm afraid that for me that is not enough. To my mind, the Millennium Dome was, and is, a huge disappointment.

So, what will become of the building now? I understand that it has been bought by a company that hope to turn it into a venue for entertainment events, like shows and concerts. I suppose that considering how much it cost, it is good that it will be used for something. Personally, however, I would prefer to see it pulled down.

Track 145
Unit 13 Writing 1

D Listen to some people talking about problems they had when they rented an apartment. Did you mention any of the same things?

Speaker 1: I moved in and the apartment was really dirty. The agency hadn't arranged for anyone to clean it properly.

Speaker 2: The landlord kept coming round to the house without telling us first. He just walked in – right in the middle of a meal or a movie.

Speaker 3: The shower didn't work, so I had to have a bath all the time. It took a long time for the water to get hot.

Speaker 4: The heating didn't work, and it took the landlord a month to repair it.

Speaker 5: The furniture was old, and some of it was broken. There were only two cooking pans and we didn't have enough plates or glasses.

Track 147
Unit 14 Speaking 1

Pronunciation check

When the form of a word changes, the stress usually falls on a different part of the word. The noun is *technology*. The adjective is *technological*. Listen and mark where the stress falls in these related words.

1 photograph   2 photography
3 photographic

Track 148
Unit 14 Speaking 2

B Listen to some students. Match each answer with a question above.

Speaker 1: Oh, it has changed every aspect of people's working lives. In factories, for example, machines have replaced people completely, and now do the most repetitive jobs. In offices, people spend much more time looking at a computer screen than they ever did before.

Speaker 2: Well, I think the way we travel around will change. Everyone has a car now, so it's actually sometimes a slow way to get around. I think people who have money will want something faster, like a small helicopter or some kind of flying car.

Speaker 3: Well, I suppose they do. Personally, I love to go camping because I like to get back to nature. I find it a bit strange when I see other campers with lots of machines and gadgets, such as computer games and portable TVs.

Speaker 4: I suppose life at work has changed the most, especially the way I communicate with people. I e-mail people all the time – even people on the same floor! I don't use the phone nearly as much as I once did.

Track 149
Unit 14 Speaking 2

C Listen again and complete the sentences. Use <u>one or two words</u> in each space.
[Play track 148 again]

Track 150
Unit 14 Listening 1

D Listen to four people talking about the inventions and check your ideas.

Speaker 1: Most people probably don't realize what a clever thing a boomerang is. People think they're toys or used for sport. In fact, they were the very first objects made by human beings that were heavier than air and could fly. They were used for weapons and for hunting. The oldest Aboriginal boomerangs date back to 10,000 years ago. At that time, they would have been very advanced in terms of technology.

Speaker 2: Of course, it's not really clear who exactly invented the television – a number of different scientists and inventors were working on similar projects at the same time. But a man from my country, John Logie Baird, is the man who created the first working television system. He first demonstrated his invention to the public in 1925.

Speaker 3: Everyone knows that we have achieved a huge amount in terms of space exploration. The space race between ourselves and Russia went on for nearly twenty years, but we were the first to land a man on the Moon. At that time, the space race was very close, and the Russians very nearly got to the Moon before us. For me, the most exciting invention, and the invention that really showed we were ahead in the space race, was the reusable space shuttle. It was first successful in 1981 and has since been used on many missions.

Speaker 4: Although the remains of very early ovens have been found in many parts of the world, it was here that they were first used frequently in people's homes.

In ancient Greece and in other parts of Europe and Turkey, it seems that people used ovens to bake bread. But it seems there was only one large oven that everyone shared. Here, the remains of villages from 5,000 years ago show that each mud-brick house was constructed with an oven, and that baking bread and perhaps cooking meat was common.

Track 151
Unit 14 Listening 1

E Listen again. Can you hear different accents? Who do you think has the strongest accent?
[Play track 150 again]

Track 152
Unit 14 Listening 2

A Listen to each speaker say more about each invention and complete the tasks. For questions 1–5, choose five answers from A–H. Which of these statements about boomerangs does the speaker make?

Speaker 1: Most people probably don't realize what a clever thing a boomerang is. People think they're just toys or something used for sport. In fact, they were the very first objects made by human beings that were heavier than air and could fly. They were used for weapons and for hunting. The oldest Aboriginal boomerangs date back to 10,000 years ago. At that time, they would have been very advanced in terms of

technology. The remains of boomerangs have been found in North Africa, India and parts of America, but it's the Aboriginal boomerang that everyone knows about. When it's thrown correctly it follows a curved path and comes back to where it was thrown from. Some boomerangs are only about ten centimetres long, but the biggest can be over two metres. Not all boomerangs are designed to come back to the thrower. Hunting boomerangs, some of which are still used by Aborigines in Australia, are designed as flat throwing sticks and are used for hunting. These boomerangs that followed a straight path and flew very fast were actually more difficult to make, and it could be that the famous returning boomerang was actually invented by accident as attempts were made to develop a faster hunting weapon. Nowadays, boomerangs are made mainly for tourists. It can be quite difficult to learn to throw one so that it comes back to you, and you may need a few lessons before you can do it properly.

For questions 6–11, listen and complete the flow chart. Use one word only for each answer.

Speaker 2: Of course, it's not really clear who exactly invented the television – a number of different scientists and inventors were working on similar projects at the same time. But a man from my country, John Logie Baird, is the man who created the first working television system. He first demonstrated his invention to the public in 1925. At one of London's most famous department stores, Logie Baird demonstrated how silhouette images could be seen to move on a screen. In 1926, he demonstrated his invention again – this time at his laboratory, to the Royal Institute and to reporters from the *Times* newspaper. The quality of the projected image had improved greatly and the event is considered to be the first real demonstration of a television system. In 1928, Logie Baird developed his invention and demonstrated the first transmission in colour.

For questions 12–16, complete the notes. Use no more than three words or a number for each answer.

Speaker 3: Everyone knows that we have achieved a huge amount in terms of space exploration. The space race between ourselves and Russia went on for nearly twenty years, but we were the first to land a man on the Moon. At that time, the space race was very close, and the Russians very nearly got to the Moon before us. For me, the most exciting invention, and the invention that really showed we were ahead in the space race, was the reusable space shuttle. It was first successful in 1981 and has since been used on many missions. The reusable shuttle can carry astronauts on space missions and can serve as a laboratory in which to conduct experiments. It can be used to transport equipment to space stations, or to collect or repair satellites. The shuttle carries between five and seven crew members. When a mission is complete, the shuttle fires thrusters, which propel it back into the earth's atmosphere. It then glides down to make its landing.

For questions 17–19, complete the short summary. Use <u>no more than two words</u> for each answer.

Speaker 4: Although the remains of very early ovens have been found in many parts of the world, it was here that they were first used frequently in people's homes. In ancient Greece and in other parts of Europe and Turkey, people used ovens to bake bread. But it seems there was only one large oven that everyone shared. Here, the remains of villages from 5,000 years ago show that each mud-brick house was constructed with an oven, and that baking bread and perhaps cooking meat was very common. The ovens were made of clay and shaped like a beehive. Inside they had shelves, so that a number of loaves could be cooked together, and an opening at the bottom from which ash could be removed.

Track 155
Unit 15 Vocabulary 2

Pronunciation check
When one word ends in a consonant and the next begins with a vowel, you hear the consonant sound at the beginning of the second word rather than at the end of the first. Listen to these examples from the unit.

1   social issues
2   drug abuse
3   serious offences
4   have been arrested

Practise saying the phrases.

Track 156
Unit 15 Speaking 3

B   Listen and answer these questions.

1
Examiner: Are there any crimes that are particularly common in your country?
Student: Mm, I think we have the same as other countries. But one crime that is a big problem is, erm ... you know, when somebody takes a child and asks for money ...
Examiner: You mean kidnapping?
Student: Yes, kidnapping. It is a big problem in my part of the world.

2
Examiner: Do you feel that London is a safe city to stay in? Is it as safe as Switzerland?
Student: No, not really. I think people are a little more aggressive. Sometimes, I think there will be a fight. The first flat I stayed in was on the ground floor, and there was a ... erm ... when someone comes in the flat and he steals things, erm ... anyway, that happened in my first flat. I wanted to move to another one after that.

Examiner: Oh, I'm sorry to hear about that.

Track 157
Unit 15 Listening 1

B   Listen to somebody giving a talk about homelessness and check your ideas.
Part 1
Voice: Good evening. I'm so pleased that so many people have attended my talk. I know many of you are concerned about the number of homeless people that there are in the town centre. I know a lot of you will feel that the situation is becoming worse and that nobody is doing anything about it. However, I think that coming along this evening shows that you want to know more about homelessness and understand the issue, and not simply see it as a problem that affects you as individuals.

Now, I'll start by explaining what 'homeless' means – and it means a little more than simply sleeping out in the street. The people you see in parks and gardens, or bus stops and shop doorways, are a small percentage of the people that we class as homeless. People are homeless if they are sleeping on the floor or on the sofa at a friend's house. They are homeless if they are sleeping in a hostel or shelter for homeless people. They are homeless if they are sleeping in a car or any other vehicle. We also class people as homeless if they are separated from family or other people that they would normally live with. People are homeless if they live in conditions that are so bad that their health is affected, and they are homeless if they are in danger of violence or physical abuse. That means, as I said before, that homelessness is a much bigger issue than a few people sleeping in bus stops or shop doorways. This is just what you see.

Part 2
So, why do people become homeless? People do not choose to be homeless. They are not sleeping rough because they have chosen to leave a safe home or families who love them. They are homeless because there is no other option. People become homeless because they are poor – because they cannot afford to pay rent, or sometimes because they cannot afford to pay the mortgage on a house or apartment that they have bought. People become homeless because they lose their job or have never had a job. There are related problems that often result in a person becoming homeless. Many homeless people have a drug addiction – they are either homeless because they spend their money on drugs, or they have become addicted to drugs because they are homeless. A high percentage of homeless people have mental health problems and find it difficult to make the decisions about their lives that most people can make. A number of homeless people are ex-prisoners – when they are released

from prison, it is very difficult to find a job and a place to live. Many people become homeless because the owner of their home – a landlord or landlady – evicts them. If people have lived in the same place for a long time and then suddenly lose it, they can find it impossible to afford the increased rent for a new home. Many people have to move out of the place they live because it is dangerous – a young person may have a violent father, or a wife a violent husband. These people are too afraid to stay in their home, and they risk making themselves homeless. Finally, in many parts of the country there is just not enough housing – certainly not enough housing that poor people can afford. The increase in the value of property has made life difficult for many people – not just homeless people. I'm sure many of you will understand that.

So, how do we deal with a problem as big as this? It isn't easy. In this country, people with very poorly paid jobs or no jobs at all receive some kind of financial support. In some cases, all or part of their rent is paid by the government. This helps to stop people becoming homeless, but if you are already homeless, it doesn't help. Most towns, like this one, have shelters for people who are temporarily homeless, but they cannot stay at them permanently. They have to move on after a certain period of time. Some towns have food kitchens where homeless people can get a meal two or three times a week. The problem is that shelters and food kitchens don't really deal with the cause of the problem – they deal only with the effect. People can stay in a shelter for a while, but it will not help them to find a home of their own – and that is what they need, of course. Now, I'm going to go on in a moment to talk about some of the suggestions that have been made in terms of dealing with homelessness – ideas for dealing with the problem in a more permanent way. I'll also talk about some of the programmes that are in place and are, in some cases, very successful in other parts the world. Before that, does anyone have any questions about what I have said so far?

Track 158
Unit 15 Listening 2

B Listen to the first part of the talk about homelessness again and answer these questions. For questions 1 and 2, choose the correct answer a, b or c.
[Play part 1 of track 157 again]

For questions 3–7, complete the notes. Use <u>no more than three words</u> for each answer.
[Play part 1 of track 157 again]

Track 159
Unit 15 Listening 3

A Listen to the rest of the talk about homelessness again. Answer the questions. For questions 1–8, complete the summary below with words from the text. Use <u>no more than two words</u> for each answer.
[Play part 2 of track 157 again]

For questions 9 and 10, choose <u>two</u> answers from A–D.
[Play part 2 of track 157 again]

Track 160
Unit 15 – Exam practice – Listening

A You will hear two people telephoning their local council to complain. Answer the questions.
For questions 1–5, choose the correct answer a, b or c.

Telephonist: Good morning, you're through to Hereford Council. How can I help you?

Woman: Oh, good morning. I'm telephoning about graffiti. Not for the first time, I might add.

Telephonist: Oh, yes? Where is this graffiti? Which part of the city do you live in?

Woman: I'm in the Port Hall area. It's a quiet residential area – as you probably know. These days I expect to see graffiti all over the city centre, but not round here. I looked out my window this morning and some ... well, someone has sprayed names and football teams all over the wall opposite. There's more on the house on the corner of the street. Can't somebody stop it happening?

Telephonist: I'm sorry. I know graffiti is a problem. Did you phone the police about it?

Woman: What's the point? I didn't actually see anyone spraying. What can the police do the next morning? There should be cameras in the streets. Then you'd know who did it. Oh, it makes me so angry.

Telephonist: Um, I'm not sure about having cameras in residential areas. A lot of people already think there are too many cameras in the street as it is.

Woman: Well, do you think you could tell me who's going to clean it off? You can't expect the people who own the houses to keep cleaning it off every time it happens.

Telephonist: Well, I'm afraid it is the responsibility of the owner to clean up graffiti. I know it's not really fair, but we just don't have people to come out and clean up all over the city. Walls usually need to be repainted.

Woman: And what about graffiti on telephone boxes and lamp posts – whose job is it to clean that off?

Telephonist: Well, that is the council's responsibility, but we can't promise that it will be done straightaway.

Woman: No, I didn't think you could. You know who I blame? The parents ... If only they ... (fade out)

For questions 6–10, choose <u>five</u> answers from A–H.
Which of the following is the man unhappy about?

Telephonist: Good morning, you're through to Hereford Council. How can I help you?

Man: Oh, hello there. I'm phoning about the rubbish collections. Why the rubbish hasn't been collected again this week, to be more specific.

Telephonist: Oh, I see. Which part of the city do you live in?

Man: I live in Chester Road. That's in the West Cliff area.

Telephonist: And which day is your rubbish normally collected?

Man: Well, who knows? I thought it was supposed to be Friday, but it seems to be a different day every week at the moment. Some weeks there isn't even a collection. I'm really fed up with it.

Telephonist: Mm, the collection in West Cliff is supposed to be Tuesday, but the council has had a few problems recently. A new company has taken over the collection. It's taking a while to get the operation running smoothly. They had an issue with their drivers last month – I think that meant that collections were affected.

Man: Well, it's not good enough. If the rubbish isn't collected the streets look terrible. Seagulls fly down and peck at the bags for food. They pull the rubbish all over the street. For the last three or four weeks I've had to go outside and sweep up the rubbish and put it in a new bag. I'm too busy to keep doing that every week.

Telephonist: Yes, I understand.

Man: You know, things are bad enough even when the collection is regular. Some neighbours put their rubbish outside the house whenever they like, anyway. They are supposed to put it out on the Tuesday morning – they know that, but they don't care. By the time the lorry comes round, the rubbish is all over the street.

Telephonist: Well, people know they shouldn't put their bags outside until Tuesday morning. If you know who's doing it you can tell us what number they live at and we'll call them.

Man: Mm, I don't see why the men who do the collection can't pick up some of the rubbish that's in the street. They just throw the bags in the lorry and leave the loose rubbish where it is in the street.

Telephonist: I'm afraid it's not their job to clean the streets. They are paid to collect the bags from outside the houses – no more than that. The street cleaner comes to West Cliff on a Wednesday.

Man: Ah, yes – well, that's another thing ... (fade out)

Track 162
IELTS Target 5.0. Three mock tests.

TEST 1

You will hear a number of different recordings and you will have to answer questions on what you hear. There will be time for you to read the instructions and questions and you will have a chance to check your work.

All the recordings will be played once only. The test is in four sections.

SECTION 1

Now turn to section one.
(four-second pause)

Section one. You will hear a conversation about a language course. First, you have some time to look at questions 1–5.
(fifteen-second pause)

You will see that there is an example that has been done for you. On this occasion only, the conversation relating to this will be played first.

Receptionist: Good morning, Borgheimer Language Courses. How may I help you?

Customer: Oh, yes. I contacted you some time ago about following a German course in Germany, and you advised me to take your placement test before we go any further. Well, I've done that now, so I'd like to go ahead with booking the course for this summer, if that's possible.

Receptionist: Certainly, sir. You said you took the placement test. What was the result?

Customer: I was placed at the 03 level.

Receptionist: 03. Right, that's Lower Intermediate. Fine, Mr ...?

The answer is 'Level Three or Lower Intermediate', so the course level has been filled in for you. Now we shall begin. You should answer the questions as you listen because you will not hear the recording a second time. Listen carefully and answer questions 1–5.
(four-second pause)

Customer: Pettersson. John Pettersson.

Receptionist: Could you spell that for me please, Mr Pettersson?

Customer: P, E, double T, E, R, double S, O, N.

Receptionist: That's a double T and a double S, am I right?

Customer: That's right. Now, could I ask you where the course takes place?

Receptionist: Well, we offer courses in Hamburg and Berlin. For your level, there's never a problem. There are always plenty of people for the intermediate classes.

Customer: Oh, dear. Does that mean that there might be a lot of students in my class? I wouldn't be very happy about that.

Receptionist: No, don't worry, Mr Pettersson. The maximum class size is 12, but I've never known there to be more than nine or ten in a class. It could even be five or six.

Customer: Good. Actually, I'd prefer to study in Berlin. And how long is the course?

Receptionist: Three weeks, five hours a day. Two hours only on Saturday. Sundays free.

Customer: I see, and what about accommodation?

Receptionist: There you have a choice, Mr Pettersson. You can either stay with a German family, who are used to having such guests, or you can stay on the university campus, or we can book you into a nearby bed and breakfast.

Customer: Is there a big difference in price?

Receptionist: Not really. Staying with the family works out the cheapest, and the bed and breakfast is a bit more money. Staying on the university campus comes somewhere between the two, price wise. But Berlin is not too expensive anyway.

Customer: Which do you recommend?

Receptionist: Well, if you want to practise your German and be part of a German family, I would recommend staying with a family. Our families are all hand-picked, and we've never had any sort of complaint.

Customer: Yes, I'll probably do that then. What are the dates of the course?

Receptionist: The first summer course starts on the first of June in Hamburg, and a week later in Berlin, which is what would concern you as you have chosen the Berlin course. That's the 8th of June. The next course would begin on the 2nd of July, and then ...

Customer: The second of July course would be perfect for me. Can you put me down for it now?

Receptionist: Certainly, Mr Pettersson. Can I have your address, please?

Customer: 26, Mayfield Drive, Orpington, Kent. I'm afraid I can't remember the postal code.

Receptionist: Don't worry, Mr Pettersson. I'll check on it.

(four-second pause)

Before you hear the rest of the conversation, you have some time to look at questions 6–10.
(fifteen-second pause)

Now listen and answer questions 6–10.

Customer: There are a couple of other things I'd like to ask.

Receptionist: Certainly.

Customer: What do I need to bring on the course?

Receptionist: Well, apart from the obvious, you'll need our textbooks. I'll e-mail you the name and publisher. You should be able to find it in your local bookstore. If you do have problems, call me or e-mail me and I'll see what I can do. We provide the computers, computer disks, translation exercises and all that sort of thing, but you will need a good dictionary. We recommend Langenscheidt, which is more than adequate for your level. You don't have to go and spend a lot of money on an expensive dictionary – not yet, anyway! Maybe you will when your German reaches a very high standard.

Customer: That would be very nice. Now, finally, what about the cost of the course, and how do I pay?

Receptionist: Would you like to pay that in pounds or in euros?

Customer: Euros would be fine.

Receptionist: In that case, it's 550 euros. You can pay by credit card, if you like.

Customer: Oh, dear. I'm afraid I haven't got a credit card. How else can I pay?

Receptionist: That's not a problem, Mr Pettersson. You can pay by bank transfer.

Customer: Fine. By the way, I forgot to mention I am a full-time student.

Receptionist: Have you got a student card?

Customer: Oh, yes.

Receptionist: Then that does make a difference, you'll be pleased to hear. You are entitled to 35% off the full price. And if you can persuade a few people to join you, it would work out even cheaper.

Customer: How do you mean, exactly?

Receptionist: Well, for every five people you find, one goes free. In other words, if there are six of you, you get one free course. Of course, in reality, you would divide up the savings amongst you, presumably.

Customer: Right, well, I'll see what I can do. Thank you.

Receptionist: Not at all, Mr Pettersson, and I'm sure you'll enjoy the course. There are, of course, sightseeing possibilities. Would you like me to send you our brochure describing them?

Customer: Yes, thank you. I'd appreciate that. Anyway, thanks for your help. If I want to call back, who do I ask for?

Receptionist: Susanna. I'm here most of the time.

That is the end of section one. You now have half a minute to check your answers.
(thirty-second pause)

Now turn to section two.
(four-second pause)

Track 163

SECTION 2

You will now hear a radio talk on agricultural regulations. First, you have some time to look at questions 11–15.
(fifteen-second pause)

Now listen carefully and answer questions 11–15.

Could there be clearer proof of the arrogance and indifference of those who are supposed to keep our food safe, than the muzzling of John Verrall? Agriculture is a business, true, and businesses have to make money, but this shows how ministers and officials put the profits of the agriculture business before the well-being of the British people.

Mr Verrall, a pharmaceutical chemist, was appointed to represent consumers on one of the many committees that advise the government on food safety. When he tried to do his job, though, and wanted to warn ministers of a danger to children's health, he was refused permission to do so.

The danger comes from hormones given to cattle in the USA, and some other countries, to make them grow faster. They speed up the animals' development to maturity, thus making meat production more profitable.

There have, however, long been fears that the hormones have horrendous effects on the people who eat them, causing diseases as serious as cancer. Once, these hormones were used on British cattle, too, but over twenty years ago they were banned in Europe for being too dangerous.

Indeed, so concerned is the European Union that it banned imports of hormone-fed beef years ago, much to the fury of the US government, which wants to sell it all over the world.

Several years ago, the USA and Canada asked the World Trade Organization to declare the ban illegal and to punish Europe for failing to lift it. The WTO, with its long record of refusing to let environmental or safety concerns interfere with trade, agreed, imposing fines of more than $120 million a year on the EU for its refusal to back down. The British government now backs the Americans, claiming that there is no proof that hormone-fed beef does any harm.

This is where Mr Verrall comes in. He is very angry with the government, especially as their claim comes out just after a Danish study shows that growth hormones are 200 times more dangerous than was previously thought. Worried by these findings, Mr Verrall spoke to government representatives, who did nothing.

(four-second pause)

Before you hear the rest of the talk, you have some time to look at questions 16–20.

(fifteen-second pause)

Now listen and answer questions 16–20.

Not only that, but they have not been testing beef which is imported, which by law they are required to do. This directly affects the British public as about 40% of the beef British people eat comes from abroad, supposedly from countries like Brazil, which does not allow the use of growth hormones. Brazilian beef is stocked by some British supermarkets and widely used in catering. Yet when a Brazilian farm was recently visited by EU inspectors, a large stockpile of this banned substance was found.

This is not the first food scandal we have had in our country. Take the present concern over a well-known chocolate company. Several months ago, the company found out that its sweets were contaminated with a rare form of salmonella, but they did nothing about it, leaving their sweets in the shops to be bought by the unsuspecting public. It was not until five months later, when several children had suffered food poisoning, that the chocolate bars were removed from the shelves. It makes you wonder how many other dangerous foods have been allowed onto our plates.

That is the end of section two. You now have half a minute to check your answers.

(thirty-second pause)

Now turn to section three.

(four-second pause)

Track 164

SECTION 3

You will hear a conversation between a tutor and two students, Amanda and Jake.
First, you have some time to look at questions 21–25.

(fifteen-second pause)

Now listen carefully and answer questions 21–25.

Tutor: So, Jake and Amanda, how did the project go?

Amanda: Very well, I think, Dr Hinton. I certainly learnt a lot and enjoyed myself at the same time.

Jake: Me too.

Tutor: So, remind me. What was your project about?

Jake: Basically, what makes successful people – let's call them 'top achievers' – successful.

Amanda: Yes, how are they different from us? What do they do that other, less successful people, don't do?

Tutor: Interesting, and did you come to any conclusions?

Amanda: Quite a few, actually.

Tutor: Good. Share some with me, then.

Jake: Well, I'd always thought that a top achiever would be the sort of person who would bring work home every night and slave over it, but it appears not. Those types tend to peak early and then go into decline. They become addicted to work itself, with much less concern for results. We found that high achievers were certainly ready to work hard, but within strict limits. They knew how to relax, could leave their work at the office, prized close friends and family life, and spent a healthy amount of time with their children and friends.

Tutor: There's a lesson for us all there. Anyway, go on.

Amanda: It's also very important to choose a career which you enjoy, not just one that pays well or which assures you of a pension many years down the line.

Tutor: Surely that's important though, Amanda?

Amanda: Yes, I agree, but being happy in your work is far more important than anything else. Top achievers spend over two-thirds of their working hours on doing work they truly prefer, and only one-third on disliked chores. They want internal satisfaction, not just external rewards, such as pay rises and promotions.

(four-second pause)

Before you hear the rest of the conversation, you have some time to look at questions 26–30.

(fifteen-second pause)

Now listen and answer questions 26–30.

Jake: Actually, in the end they often have both because they enjoy what they are doing, so their work is better and their rewards higher.

Tutor: Yes, Jake, that certainly makes sense. Now, can I ask you something? Do high achievers, as you call them, take many risks?

Jake: Yes and no. I interviewed one business executive who told me he was able to take risks because he carefully considered how he could salvage the situation if it all went wrong. He imagined the worst that could happen, and if he could live with that, he went ahead. If not, he didn't take the chance. Other people prefer to stay in what I heard described as the 'comfort zone'-setting for security, even if it means settling for mediocrity and boredom, too.

Tutor: Would you call top achievers 'perfectionists'?

Amanda: Contrary to what I expected, no, I wouldn't. We came to the conclusion that a lot of ambitious and hard-working people are so obsessed with perfection that they actually turn out very little work.

I happen to know a university teacher, a friend of my mother's, who has spent over ten years preparing a study about a playwright. She is so worried that she has missed something, she still hasn't sent the manuscript to a publisher. Meanwhile, the playwright, who was at the height of his fame when the project began, has faded from public view. The woman's study, even if finally published, will interest few people.

Tutor: So, what has this got to do with top achievers?

Amanda: Well, top achievers are almost always free of the compulsion to be perfect. They don't think of their mistakes as failures. Instead, they learn from them, so they can do better next time.

Tutor: Hmm ... well, would you call them competitive?

Jake: High performers focus more on bettering their own previous efforts than on beating competitors. In fact, I, or we, came to the conclusion that worrying too much about a competitor's abilities – and possible superiority – can be self-defeating.

Amanda: Yes, and we found that top achievers tend to be team players, rather than loners. They recognize that groups can solve certain complicated problems better than individuals and are eager to let other people do part of the work.

Jake: Yes. Loners, who are often over-concerned about rivals, can't delegate important work or decision-making. Their performance is limited because they must do everything themselves.

Tutor: Well, it looks as if you two have done a thorough job, and learnt something into the bargain, too. Now, there are just a couple of points I'd like to clarify with you ...

That is the end of section three. You now have half a minute to check your answers.
(*thirty-second pause*)

Now turn to section four.
(*four-second pause*)

Track 165

SECTION 4

You will hear a talk on Seasonal Affective Disorder. First, you have some time to look at questions 31–40.
(*fifteen-second pause*)

Now listen carefully and answer questions 31–40.

In the past few years a new condition has been identified and given a name – SAD, short for Seasonal Affective Disorder. This is now recognized as a distinct kind of clinical depression, where people become depressed at the onset of winter, accompanied by a craving for sweet things, causing weight gain. Each spring and summer would then bring on almost maniacal highs, and feelings of boundless energy and happiness.

Experiments to combat this depression showed that increased exposure to bright light in humans could suppress their production of a darkness-related hormone called melatonin. The light needed to induce this change was about 2,000 lux, or about four times brighter than ordinary household lighting.

It was then calculated that if bright light could suppress melatonin secretion, then it might have other effects on the brain, including the reversal of symptoms of depression. While melatonin's precise role in SAD has not been pinned down, the theory led to effective treatment.

Not surprisingly, SAD affects more people where winter nights are longer and days shorter. In the UK, an estimated half a million adults develop full-blown SAD in winter, and twice this number suffer the milder condition called sub-syndromal SAD. About 80% of sufferers improve when given light therapy, and improvement usually comes within two to four days. Scientists are still unsure why winter depression happens, but more than a decade of research has turned up some surprising findings.

Nearly 80% of SAD victims are women. Researchers are uncertain why this is so. SAD can affect people at any age, but typically it begins around the age of twenty and becomes less common between 40 and 50. SAD is comparatively rare in children and adolescents, but so far researchers have been unable to come up with a logical reason for this. As many as half of SAD sufferers have at least one family member with depressive illness, suggesting that the depression has a genetic component.

Some patients experience shifts in their body clocks when they're depressed in winter. They are 'morning people' at one time of the year, and become 'evening people' at another. What is the underlying difference between SAD sufferers and others? A clue can be found in carbohydrate craving, a common symptom. People often become obsessed with chocolate, for example. Carbohydrates alter brain chemistry by increasing the level of a soothing chemical called serotonin, a neurotransmitter that carries signals between brain cells. SAD sufferers crave carbohydrates because they may need serotonin to lift their mood. This craving can be intense – in fact, an addiction.

It may be that the serotonin system of the brain has problems regulating itself during the winter. Some SAD sufferers respond well to the drug Prozac, thought to influence the brain's serotonin-using system.

Other brain chemicals and hormones probably play a role in winter depression. Another neurotransmitter, dopamine, for example, may be inadequate in certain cases. Researchers hope to uncover clues to SAD's secret by probing similarities between SAD and hibernation. Though no valid link between the two has been established, some SAD patients say they feel like hibernating animals. SAD sufferers tend to put on fat in autumn and early winter, roughly the time when such hibernators as bears and squirrels do.

That is the end of section four. You now have half a minute to check your answers.
(*thirty-second pause*)

That is the end of the listening test. In the IELTS test, you would now have ten minutes to transfer your answers to the listening answer sheet.

Track 166

TEST 2

You will hear a number of different recordings and you will have to answer questions on what you hear. There will be time for you to read the instructions and questions and you will have a chance to check your work.

All the recordings will be played once only. The test is in four sections.

SECTION 1

Now turn to section one.
(*four-second pause*)

Section one. You will hear a conversation between a university counsellor and two students, Joseph and Kara. First, you have some time to look at questions 1–5.
(*fifteen-second pause*)

Now we shall begin. You should answer the questions as you listen because you will not hear the recording a second time. Listen carefully and answer questions 1–5.
(*four-second pause*)

Counsellor: Hi, Joseph, how are you today?

Joseph: Fine, thanks.

Counsellor: And Kara, how are you?

Kara: Good.

Counsellor: As we discussed on the phone earlier, I wanted to speak with both of you about the subjects you have chosen to study, and how you are managing your time. OK?

Joseph: Yes.

Kara: I think so.

Counsellor: OK, so I'll start with Kara. You've been here for how many months now?

Kara: I've been here for six months.

Counsellor: How are you finding it?

Kara: It's good. I'm enjoying the course.

Counsellor: And what about life outside? Are you making friends and socializing?

Kara: Not really. People here are quite closed. They don't talk to you.

Counsellor: I see. So, what do you do after classes?

Kara: I usually go home and study, and I might go out for a walk, but never really with anyone. Sometimes my roommate, Louisa, comes with me, but she always seems to be busy.

Counsellor: How is this affecting your schoolwork?

Kara: I don't think it is, but I miss home.

Counsellor: Kara, what I suggest for now is that you look into joining one of the social clubs on campus. There are a variety of them. You can go camping, skiing, snorkelling, painting, dancing, reading, horse riding, rowing. There's a list on the school website. Have a look and work out which one you're interested in, and which suits your timetable. You'll meet friends that way, and people who have the same career interests as you. As for the subjects you've chosen for a career in microbiology, I think you should look into dropping one of your subjects and picking it up again next year as a minor. You have a lot on your plate and this will just cause great pressure. It doesn't mean that you aren't coping, but you're doing about ten hours more than the average student a week. Think about it and we can make another appointment to discuss it. When are you free?

Kara: I have an hour free usually on Wednesdays at 11.30.

Counsellor: OK. Good. Come to my office at 11.45 and wait in reception. OK?

Kara: OK. I'll see you then.
(*four-second pause*)

Before you hear the rest of the conversation, you have some time to look at questions 6–10.
(*fifteen-second pause*)

Now listen and answer questions 6–10.

Counsellor: Joseph, how are you finding the university?

Joseph: I love it. It's very different from home. Life here is very much focused on study and also socializing through sport. People have been very friendly and curious about my culture.

Counsellor: So, you've managed to integrate well?

Joseph: I think so. I've joined the rugby team – something I'd never thought I'd be interested in.

Counsellor: And how are your studies going?

Joseph: I think I'm doing well. I have a few assignments that need some work, but overall I'm coping.

Counsellor: That's good. I'm happy that you're enjoying the university, but remember, don't let your schoolwork get too far behind, because it will pile up, and before you know it you will be late handing in work. You know that there's a penalty for handing in work late?

Joseph: No, I didn't.

Counsellor: You would have been told at the start of the course, during orientation.

Joseph: I don't remember.

Counsellor: You need to remember these things. They are very important. You might be an excellent student, but if you consistently hand in work late you'll be penalized and you might end up losing your degree over it. That's a lot of years of work, OK?

Joseph: Yes, I'll remember that.

Counsellor: And also remember that you have to attend 90% of your classes. So far, you have missed five tutorials. Be careful here. These could also cost you your degree. Is there any particular reason you missed these classes?

Joseph: I'd been training for our rugby match the night before and well, we went out afterwards, and I slept past my alarm clock.

Counsellor: Joseph. I know this culture must be very different from where you come from, but please try and be a little more conservative with your time. I think maybe you should spend more time on your studies and less time on socializing. The subjects you've chosen are intensive. I want you to spend three hours a night studying before you decide to do anything else. I'll make an appointment to see you in a month, and we can assess your progress. I'll give you my business card. All my contact details are there. Call me in three weeks to organize another meeting. Do you have any questions for me?

Joseph: No, none.

Counsellor: OK, I'll see you in a month.

That is the end of section one. You now have half a minute to check your answers.
(*thirty-second pause*)

Now turn to section two.
(*four-second pause*)

Track 167

SECTION 2

You will now listen to a talk on bicycles.
First, you have some time to look at questions 11–20.
(*fifteen-second pause*)

Now listen carefully and answer questions 11–20.

Today, we're going to talk about the latest bikes for professionals and novices. There's something to suit everyone from price to function.

The Atlantis is a touring frame. It's also perfect for commuting and trail riding, and anything short of super-fast road riding. The tubes are stout, to take touring loads and trail abuses. The tyre clearances are majestic, so you can fit tires up to 2.35 inches. It's designed for cantilevers or V-brakes. If you have to limit yourself to just one bike, and you want to be able to ride just about anywhere, this is the bike to be on. It is our most popular model for just that reason, and there isn't an unhappy Atlantis owner in the land.

The Rambouillet, our all-around road bike, is available either as a frame with fork and headset for $1,400, or as a complete bike, for $2,300. Compared to the Atlantis it is a lighter frame, not intended for loaded touring or rough trail riding. As a road bike, it has sidepull brakes.

The Quickbeam is our version of the single-speed bike. We've done it a little better, though. The crankset has a 42/34 combination, running an 18-toothed freewheel cog in the rear. And the rear hub is threaded opposite the driveside, so you can install a fixed cog of your own choice. In essence, you can have four speeds on the Quickbeam, if you choose. The Quickbeam is available as a frame with fork and headset, for $900, or as a complete bike, for $1,300. This is a rugged, versatile bike that you can ride on the road, as well as on rough trail.

The Saluki is our roadish, light-touring/randonneuring frame. It's designed for 650B wheels. If '650B' means anything to you, you'll either love it or think it's marketing suicide. If you're new to 650B and a follower, you won't want it. If you're new and a rebel, you will.

Now, I'll just talk a little about saddle comfort. The road bike, for the most part, has turned into a high-tech, uncomfortable machine, and the proof is all around us. Look through any bike magazine or catalogue and you'll see the saddle up to six inches higher than the handlebars. It is impossible to be comfortable on such a bike. It forces you to lean forward, putting more weight on your groin, hands and arms. People ride these bikes with straight, locked-out arms, and wake up with aching backs. They endure it, get used to it or buy recumbents.

When we custom-design a bike for you, you'll be able to get a comfortable position. Your back will be between 45 and 50 degrees and there will be a noticeable bend in the arms, and most importantly, your arms won't be supporting your body weight. You won't have to look up to look ahead, because you won't be hunched over and low. That means our bikes are more accessible for riding on the flats, or even for short climbs. We consider this when we design and build your custom frame.

That is the end of section two. You now have half a minute to check your answers.
(*thirty-second pause*)

Now turn to section three.
(*four-second pause*)

Track 168

SECTION 3

You will hear a conversation between two students, David and Claire.
First, you have some time to look at questions 21–24.
(*fifteen-second pause*)

Now listen carefully and answer questions 21–24.

Claire: Hi, David. How are you going with your History studies?

David: Very well. I've actually finished it.

Claire: That's great. What era did you write on?

David: I researched Roman London, something I never thought I'd be interested in.

Claire: That sounds interesting.

David: I wanted to tie it in to the work I've been doing on engineering, and I found it fascinating, and learnt many things along the way.

Claire: Such as?

David: Well, although there were prehistoric settlements throughout the vast area now called London, strangely enough no evidence has yet been found for any such community at the northern end of London Bridge, where the present city grew up.

Claire: The origins of London lie in Roman times, right?

David: Right. When the Romans invaded Britain in 43 AD, they moved north from the Kentish coast and traversed the Thames in the London region, clashing with the local tribesmen just to the north. It has been suggested that the soldiers crossed the river at Lambeth, but it was further downstream that they built a permanent wooden bridge, just east of the present London Bridge, in more settled times some seven years later. As a focal point of the Roman road system, it was the bridge which attracted settlers and led to London's inevitable growth.

Claire: So, London Bridge has been there for hundreds of years?

David: Yes, and though the regularity of London's original street grid may indicate that the initial inhabitants were the military, trade and commerce soon followed. The London Thames was deep and still within the tidal zone – an ideal place for the berthing of ships.

Claire: What other industry did they have?

David: Well, as the area was also well-drained and low-lying, it was geologically suitable for brickmaking. There was soon a flourishing city called Londinium in the area where the Monument now stands.

Claire: Londinium? That's Latin.

David: That's what I thought, too, but the name itself is Celtic, not Latin, and may originally have referred merely to a previous farmstead on the site.

(four-second pause)

Before you hear the rest of the conversation, you have some time to look at questions 25–32.
(fifteen-second pause)

Now listen and answer questions 25–32.

Claire: Wasn't London burnt to the ground at some stage?

David: It happened in AD 60, by the forces of Queen Boudicca of the Iceni tribe, from modern Norfolk, when she led a major revolt against Roman rule. The governor, Suetonius Paulinus, who was busy exterminating the Druids in north Wales, marched his troops south in an attempt to save London but, seeing the size of Boudicca's approaching army, decided he could not mount an adequate defence and evacuated the city instead. Not everyone managed to escape though, and many were massacred.

Claire: What about the beautiful old architecture? Did you research that, too?

David: I sure did. The major symbol of Roman rule was the Temple of the Imperial Cult. Emperor worship was administered by the Provincial Council, whose headquarters appear to have been in London by AD 100. A member of its staff, named Anencletus, buried his wife on Ludgate Hill around this time. Pagan worship flourished within the cosmopolitan city. A temple to the mysterious Eastern god, Mithras, was found at Bucklersbury House and is displayed nearby.

Claire: I quite like St Paul's.

David: Traditionally, St Paul's cathedral stands on the site of a Temple of Diana. Other significant buildings also began to appear in the late 1st century, at a time when the city was expanding rapidly. The forum, a marketplace and basilica, which housed the law-courts complex at Leadenhall Market, was erected, and then quickly replanned as the largest such complex north of the Alps. The forum was much

bigger than today's Trafalgar Square.

Claire: Who was in charge of all the town planning at the time?

David: Procurator Agricola. He encouraged the use of bath houses and had a grand public suite made, which has now been excavated in Upper Thames Street. They were as much a social venue as a place to bathe. There was a smaller version at Cheapside and, in later centuries, private bath houses were also built. Another popular attraction was the wooden amphitheatre erected on the north-western outskirts of the city. It's possible that gladiatorial shows were put on here, though lesser public sports, like bear-baiting, may have been more regular.

Claire: I thought that happened mainly in the Colisseum in Rome, but I guess London being settled by the Romans explains their lust for blood.

David: By about AD 200, the administration of Britain was divided in two. York became the capital of Britannia Inferior and London of Britannia Superior. Around the same time, the city also acquired its famous walls, probably about 20ft high.

Claire: Why did they build such high walls?

David: It was a protective measure which may have been due to civil war, initiated when Governor Clodius Albinus tried to claim the Imperial Crown in Rome.

Claire: Was Paganism still predominant then?

David: Yes, but Christianity appears to have reached the province at an early date and, only a year after the religion became officially tolerated in the Empire, London had its own bishop, Restitutus, who is known to have attended the Imperial Council of Arles.

Claire: You really delved deep. I think you'll do well on your tutorial paper. Good luck, David.

David: Thanks.

That is the end of section three. You now have half a minute to check your answers.
(thirty-second pause)

Now turn to section four.
(four-second pause)

Track 169

SECTION 4

You will hear a lecture about staying healthy in university. First, you have some time to look at questions 33–40.
(fifteen-second pause)

Now listen carefully and answer questions 33–40.

Peter: Good morning, all. Welcome to our regular lecture on health issues. This series of lectures is organized by the Students' Union, and is part of an attempt to help you stay healthy while coping with study and social life at the same time. It's a great pleasure to welcome back Ms Mary Kirk, who is a professional health advisor and physical education officer.

Mary Kirk: Thank you, Peter, for the introduction. It's a pleasure to be back. Today we're going to discuss the benefits of exercise. University life is hectic and stressful. It also involves a lot of sedentary work, that is, sitting for many hours at a time. What I'd like to focus on is how to approach exercise, not only from the aspect of health benefits, but also as a form of stress relief. I know it's hard to organize your time around studies and socializing, but you can socialize while exercising. If you have an hour free in the morning, afternoon or evening, it would be a good idea to get together with your friends and create a sports team. The grounds of the university are ample enough to support every student's need to become active. There are also readily available facilities at your disposal, such as a football field, tennis and badminton courts. There's also a swimming centre, and within that building is a gymnasium with a variety of programmes, such as aerobics and weight training. If the idea of attending one of these facilities seems daunting, then you can walk along the river. Oh, and that reminds me, the university also offers rowing. If there is a sport that you're interested in that's not on offer, you can approach either your Student Union representative or speak with Sports Administration Manager, Mr Lawrence Cavendish. Now, I want to talk about why exercise is beneficial physically and emotionally. The obvious results are physical. You can keep fit by using muscles that ordinarily don't get used in the classroom. The health benefits are astronomical. You'll live longer, be happier and look good. By building muscle, you strengthen your bones – a definite advantage for women in their later stages of life, as women are prone to osteoporosis. It also strengthens your heart. Yes, don't forget your heart is a muscle, and the more exercise you do and the harder you work, the more blood is pumped from your heart to your brain. Now, this brings me to the psychological advantages of exercise. When we are active, endorphins are released into our brain. An endorphin is a chemical that is released when your heart rate is pumping beyond its normal capacity. It's the same as adrenaline. You can actually feel when endorphins kick in. You feel a rush, almost a high. The benefits of this are numerous. Your brain works at peak capacity for a longer period of time, your awareness is maximized and the fatigue you usually feel at four o'clock in the afternoon will be non-existent. In one word, exercise makes you 'sharp'. Now, I'm not saying you should overdo exercise, because too much of anything can be dangerous, but if you think about your daily routine, you spend about six hours a day in lectures and another two or more hours studying. That's a long time to be sitting. And that is a long time for your body not to be moving around, so try and find at least one hour a day to get some exercise. If you can't fit in one hour a day, try one

hour every second day or half an hour a day. You will see rewards instantly. You'll feel great and look great. This I can promise you.

That is the end of section four. You now have half a minute to check your answers.
(*thirty-second pause*)

That is the end of the listening test. In the IELTS test, you would now have ten minutes to transfer your answers to the listening answer sheet.

Track 170

TEST 3

You will hear a number of different recordings and you will have to answer questions on what you hear. There will be time for you to read the instructions and questions and you will have a chance to check your work.

All the recordings will be played once only. The test is in four sections.

SECTION 1

Now turn to section one.
(*four-second pause*)

Section one. You will hear three conversations – the first and the third between two students, and the second between a student and a clerk.
First, you have some time to look at questions 1–5.
(*fifteen-second pause*)

Now we shall begin. You should answer the questions as you listen because you will not hear the recording a second time. Listen carefully and answer questions 1–5.
(*four-second pause*)

Phoebe: Hi. It's Mike, isn't it?

Mike: Yes, and you're …?

Phoebe: Phoebe.

Mike: Phoebe. Right. Where are you headed?

Phoebe: I'm looking for the Main Hall.

Mike: So am I. Are you going there to register for next year?

Phoebe: Yes. I was told to go to Administrations and fill in an application form.

Mike: That's what I'm about to do. I went to Information and they told me it was at the end of this corridor. Then we have to turn left, and immediately right. That should lead us to the exit, where opposite we should find the entrance to ground level, Main Hall. It's a big old red building. From there, we need to go to the first level, and then follow the signs. Apparently, it's the second office opposite the foyer. It would be pretty hard to miss.

Phoebe: That sounds easy. It shouldn't be too hard to find. Well, since we're both heading in that direction, let's go together.

Mike: Hopefully it won't take too long. I haven't had anything to eat and I'm starving.

Phoebe: Me too.

Mike: Well, how about I go to the canteen and get us

something while you make your way to the Main Hall? I'm sure there's going to be quite a wait. There always is. I can meet you there.

Phoebe: Sounds like a good plan.

Mike: What do you want me to get you?

Phoebe: Um, how about a chicken and salad roll and a drink?

Mike: OK. What if they don't have a chicken and salad roll?

Phoebe: Anything similar, like ham and salad, or just plain salad and cheese. Oh, and don't forget the drink. I feel so dehydrated.

Mike: No problem. What type of drink?

Phoebe: I don't know. Um ...

Mike: How about a Coke?

Phoebe: No, nothing like that. Something healthier.

Mike: An orange juice.

Phoebe: They're usually full of sugar, unless you get it freshly squeezed.

Mike: Water?

Phoebe: Yes. That's perfect. Here, take two pounds. That should cover it. If it's more, I'll give it to you when you get back. I only have a twenty, and you know that they get cranky if you give them large notes.

Mike: OK. See you in five minutes.

(four-second pause)

Before you hear the second conversation, you have some time to look at questions 6–10.
(fifteen-second pause)

Now listen and answer questions 6–10.

Phoebe: Hi, I'm here to register for first-year Economics.

Clerk: I'll just have to fill out this form for our records. What's your name?

Phoebe: Phoebe Payne.

Clerk: Can you spell that for me?

Phoebe: Sure. P-H-O-E-B-E P-A-Y-N-E.

Clerk: Your address?

Phoebe: 6 Wainright Avenue, that's W-A-I-N-R-I-G-H-T, Nottingham.

Clerk: Nottingham. And your phone number?

Phoebe: It's not connected yet. I've just moved in.

Clerk: OK, when you get your phone connected, contact us. I'll just make a note that your phone number is to be advised.

Phoebe: I'll do that.

Clerk: What course were you doing? Law?

Phoebe: No, Economics. First-year.

Clerk: First-year Economics.

Phoebe: Yes, that's right.

Clerk: OK. Take this card across to the Economics Department and get it stamped, and then you need to come back here to pay your fees.

Phoebe: I've made an arrangement to pay in instalments.

Clerk: Do you have any documentation verifying that?

Phoebe: Yes, I have a statement from Administration.

Clerk: OK, when you return we'll have a look at it.

Phoebe: Thank you very much.

(four-second pause)

Before you hear the next conversation, you have some time to look at questions 11 and 12.
(fifteen-second pause)

Now listen and answer questions 11 and 12.

Mike: Here you are.

Phoebe: It was quicker than I thought, but I have to get this card stamped and return here to organize my fees.

Mike: That's good. It means that I won't have to wait long, either.

Phoebe: How did you get on?

Mike: What with? Oh, the food. Well, there wasn't much left so I got you a cheese and tomato sandwich and water.

Phoebe: That's fine. Do I owe you any more?

Mike: No, I need to give you back three pounds.

Phoebe: But I only gave you two.

Mike: Oh, yeah. I thought you gave me a fiver. OK, so we're square. So, what do I have to do?

Phoebe: Go to the desk and give your personal details. Then, they'll give you a card that you need to take to your faculty. What's your major?

Mike: Environmental Science.

Phoebe: OK, so you'll have to take the card to the Environmental Science Faculty and get the card stamped, return to Administration in the Main Hall and organize your fees.

Mike: And that's it?

Phoebe: Yes, that means you're registered. Then we receive a letter with the details of our course, where we'll be informed to go to the notice board, or online to find out when and where our lectures are.

Mike: OK. Let's have this bite to eat first.

That is the end of section one. You now have half a minute to check your answers.
(thirty-second pause)

Now turn to section two.
(four-second pause)

Track 171

SECTION 2

You will now hear a speaker talking about student loans. First, you have some time to look at questions 13–21.
(fifteen-second pause)

Now listen carefully and answer questions 13–21.

Thanks for turning up today, and welcome to this short talk on student loans. What you'll hear from me today are a few starting points, which should guide you in the right direction for what is suited for you. I'm assuming that most of you have an account at a bank or building society that you can draw funds from. These funds will either be your own or through a loan you may have with the bank. You may even have a credit card you can use. If you don't have a bank account, I suggest you open one with one of the major banks. It's the best option, as you will find major banks have more outlets. Within the city and in close proximity to the university are HSBC in City Plaza, Barclays in Ragdale Square, National Westminster in Preston Park and Halifax in Hope Street. At this stage, I just want to inform international students that not all the services available for resident students will be available to you. As international students, you need to provide documentation stating that you have funds available to see you through the duration of your study. Different banks have different policies, so search out the one that will benefit you the most. You will also need to provide a photocopy of your passport and certification of your enrolment in the university.

The most common way of taking out a student loan is either through the university or through a banking institution. If you decide to go with the university, again, you need to supply certification of enrolment and passport if you're an international student, or if you're a resident, you will only need the enrolment details. One word of warning is that you need to be clear on the interest you will be paying on your loan. The interest level through some universities is almost as much as the loan itself, so if you borrow ten thousand pounds you might have to pay back close to twenty. Also, with student loans through the university, you have a limited time to pay them back and this time is not flexible. You might have only one year, you might have five. As I said, different universities have different policies. This university, for example, has an interest rate of 23.5%. It's quite high, but not as high as many of the other larger universities. The other option is to take out a loan through your bank. You will find that most banks will have lower interest rates than the university. They average roughly between 14.5–18.5%. Banks also give you an option of over how many years you want to make repayments. You can basically choose to pay it back in a year or in ten – even more if you are finding it difficult. Make sure you have an account with the bank you decide to go with. Either a current account or a savings account is enough. With either of these accounts, you can use your card to make withdrawals and deposits from automatic teller machines at any time, and make payments over the Internet if you choose. You can also use Maestro, one of the systems which automatically take the money from your account at a time that you have specifically stated, and deposits it into a nominated account of your choice. You might decide to have 150 pounds taken out each month, and each month this is what will happen. Also, check what fees apply with what services. Some services are free of charge, but they are few and far between. OK, so that's all from me. If there are any questions related to what I've covered today, please raise your hand.

That is the end of section two. You now have half a minute to check your answers.
(*thirty-second pause*)

Now turn to section three.
(*four-second pause*)

Track 172

SECTION 3

You will hear a dialogue between two students, David and Jim.
First, you have some time to look at questions 22–25.
(*fifteen-second pause*)

Now listen carefully and answer questions 22–25.

David: Hi, Jim.

Jim: Hi, David! I'm glad I found you. I've got a topic for our presentation next month.

David: What is it?

Jim: I thought it would be a good idea to talk about glass and how it's recycled.

David: That doesn't sound very interesting.

Jim: That's what I thought, but it is. Did you know that glass has been around since as early as 4000 BC, when glass was used in the Middle East as a glaze to decorate beads?

David: Is it really that old?

Jim: Yes, and by 1550 BC, coloured glass vessels were widespread and used for cooking and drinking. The earliest-known clear glass is a vase found in Nineveh in Assyria, dating from around 800 BC, which is now in the British Museum here in London.

David: You know, I think I've seen that. I was at the British Museum a couple of months ago with Lisa.

Jim: We don't realize how valuable glass was. It wasn't used widely back then. Until the 18th and 19th centuries, glass was very expensive and was used for limited applications, such as stained glass windows for churches. Large-scale glass manufacturing began with the Industrial Revolution, with the mass production of glass containers beginning at the onset of the 20th century, and glass light bulb production automated in 1926.

David: How expensive?

Jim: I don't know, but nowadays glass is much less expensive, and is taken for granted as a packaging material, in addition to its use in windows and other applications.

David: Do you know what glass is made from?

Jim: New glass is made from a mixture of four main ingredients: sand, soda ash, limestone and other additives. These additives include iron for colour (brown or green), chromium and cobalt for colour (green and blue respectively), lead to alter the refractive index, alumina for durability and boron to improve the thermal options. Annually, total glass use in the UK is estimated at around 3.6 million tonnes.

(*four-second pause*)

Before you hear the rest of the conversation, you have some time to look at questions 26–31.
(*fifteen-second pause*)

Now listen and answer questions 26–31.

David: You're kidding. That's phenomenal. What do we do with all that glass? Where does it go?

Jim: Using present technology, the UK glass industry has the capacity to recycle over one million tonnes of glass each year and this, coupled with the material's unique ability to be infinitely recycled without compromising its quality, creates a compelling case for the recycling of glass. Despite this, glass makes up around 7% of the average household dustbin and last year, over 2.5 million tonnes of this material was landfill.

David: How can glass be recycled?

Jim: It can be recycled indefinitely as part of a simple but hugely beneficial process, as its structure does not deteriorate when reprocessed. In the case of bottles and jars, up to 80% of the total mixture can be made from reclaimed scrap glass, called 'cullet'.

David: What's it called?

Jim: Cullet. C-U-L-L-E-T. Cullet from a factory has a known composition and is recognized as 'domestic cullet'. From bottle banks it is known as 'foreign' and its actual properties will not be known. Recycling two bottles saves enough energy to boil water for five cups of tea.

David: You know, I wouldn't mind a cuppa now.

Jim: Did you know that recycling reduces the demand for raw materials? There is no shortage of the materials used, but they do have to be quarried from our landscape, so from this point of view there are environmental advantages to recovering and recycling glass. For every tonne of recycled glass used, 1.2 tonnes of raw materials are preserved. Recycling also reduces the amount of waste glass which needs to be used as landfill.

David: I know. It's a social conscience we all need to have.

Jim: Taking part in recycling the waste we produce makes us think about the effect we are having on our environment and enables us to contribute towards a greater level of sustainability. It's not all about economics, you know.

David: I'm sure you're right, Jim.

That is the end of section three. You now have half a minute to check your answers.
(*thirty-second pause*)

Now turn to section four.
(*four-second pause*)

Track 173

SECTION 4

You will hear an orientation lecture on sports therapy. First, you have some time to look at questions 32–40.
(*fifteen-second pause*)

Now listen carefully and answer questions 32–40.

Good morning, and welcome to the university's Open Day and to our lecture on Sports Therapy. There are two good reasons to be here. Firstly, you will experience what a university lecture is like – so take out your notebook and pen – and secondly, you will find out about the Sports Therapy programme. OK, so what does a Sports Therapy programme involve? Everybody in today's society knows the impact sport, health and fitness makes on the population's physical and mental health. Studying at Kent will develop your understanding of the ideas and issues within the sports therapy, health and fitness industries. Sports therapy is one of the fastest-growing careers within the sports sector. The programme teaches you all the specialist knowledge you need in order to work within these industries. This includes scientific aspects, such as anatomy and physiology and sports psychology. You learn how to design training programmes and lifestyle profiles for a range of clients, and to understand the role of sports promotion and event management. The degree also covers the treatment and prevention of sporting injuries and the importance of referral programmes. There will be a full description of these subjects for you available at the door when you leave this lecture. Now, just to talk a little about teaching and assessment. The programme involves taking part in and designing practical sports sessions, lectures, small-group seminars and private study. On average you have six lectures, three practical sessions and a one hour-long seminar per week, and you also spend additional time developing your coaching and theoretical knowledge in real-life situations. At Stage 1, the first half of the year is assessed by 100% coursework and observed assessments. A majority of the modules also have written exams within the final half of the year, with the rest practically assessed. Stage 2 and 3 assessment varies, from 100% coursework to a combination of examination and coursework, usually in the ratio 50:50, 60:40 or 80:20. You're probably wondering what career paths you can take once you've completed this degree. Well, careers can vary from employment in health and fitness clubs, sports injury clinics, sports development within local authorities, or with national governing bodies of sport, working in community leisure or sports attractions, self-employed personal trainer or sports therapist. There are some requirements you need to fulfil to enter this course. International students can qualify with the following: School Certificates and Higher School Certificates awarded by a body approved by the university; matriculation from an approved university, with a pass in English Language at GCSE O level, or an equivalent level in an approved English language test, passing one of Kent's foundation programmes, provided that you meet the subject requirements for the degree course you intend to study; or an examination pass accepted as equivalent to any of the above. In order to enter directly onto a degree course, you also need to prove your proficiency in English, and we ask for one of the following: average 6.5 in IELTS test, minimum 6.0 in Reading and Writing; grade B in Cambridge Certificate of Proficiency in English; grade A in Cambridge Advanced Certificate in English; a pass overall in the JMB/NEAB Test in English for Overseas Students, with at least B in Writing, Reading and Speaking Modules; a TOEFL score of at least 580 (written test) or 237 (computer test). If you haven't yet reached those standards, Kent runs a foundation course for international students which gives you a year's academic

and language training before you begin on your degree.
Right, that's about it. Any questions?

**That is the end of section four. You now have half a
minute to check your answers.**
(*thirty-second pause*)

**That is the end of the listening test. In the IELTS test,
you would now have ten minutes to transfer your
answers to the listening answer sheet.**